Civano: From Experiment to Model of Resilient Urbanism

Civano: From Experiment to Model of Resilient Urbanism

Stefanos Polyzoides & L.R. Rayburn

INTRODUCTION BY ELIZABETH MOULE

ORO EDITIONS

ORO Editions
Publishers of Architecture, Art, and Design
Gordon Goff: Publisher

www.oroeditions.com
info@oroeditions.com

Published by ORO Editions

Author: Stefanos Polyzoides and L. R. Rayburn
Book Design: Mary Cay Walp
Editor: Holly Limon
Project Manager: Jake Anderson

10 9 8 7 6 5 4 3 2 1 First Edition

ISBN: 978-1-954081-92-5

Color Separations and Printing: ORO Group Ltd.
Printed in China.

AR+D Publishing makes a continuous effort to minimize the overall carbon footprint of its publications. As part of this goal, AR+D, in association with Global ReLeaf, arranges to plant trees to replace those used in the manufacturing of the paper produced for its books. Global ReLeaf is an international campaign run by American Forests, one of the world's oldest nonprofit conservation organizations. Global ReLeaf is American Forests' education and action program that helps individuals, organizations, agencies, and corporations improve the local and global environment by planting and caring for trees.

TABLE OF CONTENTS

INTRODUCTION

It may be that when we no longer know what to do
we have come to our real work, and that when we no
longer know which way to go we have come to our
real journey. The mind that is not baffled is not employed.
The impeded stream is the one that sings.

Wendell Berry[1]

1 Berry, Wendell. *Standing By Words*. Counterpoint, 2011.

This story is one of the past directly talking to the future. Dear Reader, you picked up a book on how to settle in a desert. It is also a compelling guide, a template, for making a highly livable home and settlement, adapting and mitigating climate change wherever you happen to live. As you read through this book, I urge you to see your own life in it and start to imagine how you might make change wherever you make your home. It is you who must generate the kind of social, environmental, and architectural changes our world dearly needs.

Civano is a cross breed between two previously different approaches to land planning, a unique marriage between New Urbanism and environmental sustainability. There are many good New Urbanist projects. There are far fewer projects attempting environmental resilience. Civano stands alone combining them both. Civano's creators, myself included, were unaware that the project would stand as such a remarkable transformative model.

To say that the creation of Civano was an idea before its time is to wildly underestimate the urgent action needed to address climate change. Civano was conceived in ways to make a sustainable place in an inhospitable environment, the Sonoran Desert. Acknowledging Arizona's abundant solar capital, Civano was originally conceived by a group of citizens as a "solar village" with its principle objective being to reduce water and energy consumption. As the project evolved, with public input being a critical part of its evolution, further objectives were developed to reduce air pollution and "tread lighter on the land." On-site employment goals were added, and special zoning created. All this in an effort to create a more resilient community of enduring value. A number of its accomplishments stand out:

Both Adaptation and Mitigation | Civano demonstrates that one can mitigate climate change as one adapts to it; they are not two opposing projects competing for resources, or as a colleague recently put it, Sophie's Choice. Civano's design reduces energy consumption through the passive cooling of the architecture and urbanism at the scale of building (rapidly renewable materials, low embodied energy construction, high insulation, etc.) and at the scale of the town (narrowing the street right-of-ways, planting a tree canopy for consistent coverage, designing the building morphology and massing to shade the public realm, etc.). Aimed at human thermal comfort, the goal is to increase walking over driving, to further diminish greenhouse gas emissions, and improve quality of life.

Regional Specificity | Civano deploys techniques, methods, and materials specifically developed for the Sonoran Desert. First and foremost is the generation of passive cooling. This is done by strategically deploying shade, created through extensive an tree canopy on streets, in patios, gardens, and walks.

While taking a regional approach, many of these techniques can be easily deployed to reduce the effect of excessive heat across many biomes. Creating high albedo surfaces, dramatically increasing tree coverage and vegetative density along with taking advantage of the morphological and spatial characteristics of urbanism can be done anywhere. All of it plays a role in reducing the mean radiant temperature (MRT). This is the temperature that humans actually feel in outdoor public space—an important metric for the human experience and thermal comfort.

Further to adaptation goals in ever longer drought conditions, Civano reduces overall water usage. A particular characteristic of its biome is the amount and the bi-seasonality of its rainfall. One period in the winter sees light rainfall while the summer sees a monsoon season of bursts of heavy rainfall. Great attention was paid in how to direct the rainwater runoff so that it was recognized as the precious resource it is, and not as "waste product" to be collected and discarded. Rainwater is captured, slowed to allow it to absorb into the ground, and directed to adjacent arroyo areas. All this creates a verdant community, with a tree canopy coverage that makes walking and outdoor living so pleasant.

Reconsidering Market Housing | The home building industry over the years has produced very uniform homes, promoting the idea that market and consumer preferences demand this. Little variety is delivered whether it be in size, amenity, or style. The only variety that exists is typically by market segment, which is to say low-, middle-, or high-end houses. Civano challenged the conventional notion that people do not care about individualization. People do want a unique home that they can call their own and that looks and feels like it belongs to a specific place.

Making Architecture in the Era of Production Home Building | The home builders in Civano were local mainstream and custom builders. Through a highly directed effort, they were encouraged to produce more than their usual fare: patio homes and compounds chief among them.

Of all the building types that are most under-realized today, the compound stands out as one that is highly adaptable to wide range of densities, fitting nicely into lower density settings—even areas of single-family homes. While not used expansively at Civano, the compound has an ingenious blend of public and private space—with large, shared courts, combined with small private gardens for individual units. It is an easily scalable land use pattern making it suitable for small communities at the scale of the large parcel or block, a profoundly useful template in many settings.

Time-Honored Low Tech | What ought to be commonplace, but is sadly rare, is the usage of simple building technologies and forms developed regionally over centuries. Conventional home building is ubiquitously delivered in wood construction, almost no wood being forest certified. At Civano, there is conventional technology and some experimental technology like SIPS panels. While very limited, the project makes a real effort to cleanse the palate of common materials used for construction, and considers traditional and regional materials like straw bale, rammed earth, and adobe.

An Imperfect Experiment | In its completed form, Civano isn't perfect, and the authors do not shy away from examining the shortfalls and near misses. In strict New Urbanist terms, Civano remains an isolated, largely residential neighborhood, minimally connected to commercial and retail uses. There are few jobs within walking distance, though this is offset by a robust presence of businesses in homes and ancillary units. Access to public transit—a condition for creating a true jobs/housing balance—is minimal, but that is a Tucson-wide problem.

At the time of its planning, and in the context of the region, Civano's layout was shockingly compact. That perceived compactness was a source of much struggle for the developers in the entitlement process. Having said that, Civano could be much more compact, about 25% tighter—using that much less land, asphalt, utilities, and other services. More compact, it would be more walkable, more energy conserving, more conserving of habitat, and even more enchanting.

Regrettably, Civano's subsequent phases were built very conventionally. So, the story being told here is not only one of a strong vision but also how the powerful forces of conventional thinking remain deeply baked into our building and financing systems. Yet as time passes and Civano's performance is measured and its market desirability is recognized, it stands as a powerful example and template I hope you will follow.

While slow and imperfect, citizen action does bring about change. There is no greater lesson at Civano. Indeed, when we no longer know what to do, we have come to our real work.

—Elizabeth Moule

PREFACE

THE VICE PRESIDENT
WASHINGTON

April 16, 1999

Dear Community of Civano Partners:

Once in a great while each of us is lucky enough to have an opportunity to clearly see the future. Today, the grand opening of Civano is one of those unique times.

Since Henry David Thoreau spent his years at Walden Pond, America has had a vision that, to be truly free, one must live in harmony with nature. Civano demonstrates that through creativity and imagination — and some risk — we as a nation can build stronger communities whose development does not conflict with the environment, but actually can support and enhance a sustainable society.

I want to congratulate the staff of the Community of Civano partners, Mayor Miller, and the City of Tucson, for showing us that a 19th Century dream can become a 21st Century reality.

Sincerely,

Al Gore

Letter written by Vice President Al Gore to celebrate the Grand Opening of Neighborhood One of Civano, April 16, 1999

REVEALING HISTORY

We offer this study as the most complete to date on the history, evolution, implementation, and lessons learned from Civano: a mixed-use neighborhood of some 600 homes located in Tucson, Arizona. Although modest in scale, this is a notable project. It was the first attempt in the United States to counter suburban sprawl by integrating architectural and urban design based on aggressive resource, environmental, and social goals considered in unison. Its final built form illustrates a quality of place significantly higher than equivalent middle-income housing subdivisions designed and constructed under typical, mass-production methods.

The Civano Initiative started as an experiment. Like all experiments, its first steps as a project were difficult, its financial and management record mixed. Yet, just as it was finding market approval and success, it was truncated by its then owner, Fannie Mae. In the years following, the versions of Civano's history that have been advanced by various authors are incomplete. Virtually everything written about the project to date has been from a partial or academic perspective, and with a tendency to focus on how it did not fully achieve the goals envisioned by its original framers. Under the impression that these goals were diluted by Civano's multiple developer teams and by the demands and expectations of the buying public, the project is generally assessed as a "noble failure": with Fannie Mae gallantly supporting it through the development of the first neighborhood, before turning over the remaining two neighborhoods to a more "pragmatic builder."

Under this perspective, previous studies tend to focus on the compromises and failings of this complex undertaking while obscuring its many accomplishments. The original project vision is detached from its subsequent constant friction with the demands of the development process and is enshrined as immutable, with little understanding of the complexities of a business undertaking of Civano's size. Partial attainment is seen as diminution of original intentions, without any understanding of the context in which market performance metrics force a project to evolve and change. There are exceptions, of course. We will review studies done at Arizona State University and UCLA of the post-build out environmental performance of all three sections of Civano: Neighborhood One, developed under New Urbanist protocols; and what would have been Neighborhoods Two and Three, developed under slightly modified standard production housing protocols.

We believe that much of what has been assumed about Civano has tended to obscure its factual history. This book will provide a detailed investigation into its development from an entirely different perspective; one that is based on the benefit of having free access to the archives of the architects and developers that created it, including Civano's principal planners, Moule & Polyzoides, Architects and Urbanists; Wayne Moody, a key figure in the original visioning of the project; and Lee Rayburn, the director of the last development entity before Civano's liquidation. With the entire written and drawn record of the project at their disposal, the authors will fully explore the origins and evolution of Civano's planning, design, and development process in all its contradictions and complexities.

The focus of the book on the complete project record from its inception to its partial completion invites us to examine Civano for what it was truly intended to be: a living endeavor to create new affordable and resilient greenfield neighborhoods and towns on the outskirts of Tucson. And in the process, produce a more balanced and sustainable model for urban growth in the American Southwest.

TWENTY YEARS ON, A VINDICATION OF THE NEW URBANISM

In September 1996, a week-long planning and visioning charrette was held in Tucson for this new community. Out of that charrette would come a set of documents that would be the first attempt to wed the concepts of the New Urbanism with an aggressive set of resource management and environment goals; and to do so in the context of production housing aimed at a middle-income market. This was also the first New Urbanist charrette in the Southwest and one of the very first to be held west of the Mississippi. Two firms, including four of the six founders of the New Urbanist movement, Moule & Polyzoides and Duany Plater-Zyberk, organized this charrette.

There is a body of work by others that implies, and sometimes outright states, that the New Urbanist planning and design protocols adopted in Civano's development contributed to its difficulties: specifically in compromising the full implementation of its environmental goals, especially those related to the use of solar energy. We emphatically reject this view.

Our key thesis is this: After over a decade of attempts to implement a sustainable residential development in the Sonoran Desert of Arizona, it was the overlaying of a New Urbanist planning and design process that finally created a project that addressed and met the original goals of that long advocacy while also finding enthusiastic acceptance in the marketplace. We believe that this mix of New Urbanism and environmentally conscious design and planning offered then, and still offers, the possibility of convincing a broad segment of the marketplace to change its buying habits and its assumptions about what a "good place to live" should be. This is especially important in the aftermath of the economic crisis of 2008, which brought into sharp and bright focus the financial follies and the enduring physical negative impact of "sprawl development" and all that has come to be associated with it.

On April 16, 1999, Civano's grand opening was held, model homes were presented to the public, and home sales started. Although invited, Vice President Al Gore could not attend, but did send a congratulatory letter which noted Civano's potential impact on future community building in America. Almost twenty years after its completion, it stands as a testament to the vision, ambitions, perseverance, and hard work of its promoters, developers, designers, and builders. Civano may not be the final destination on the path to a more humane and resilient urbanism, but it is and can continue to be a signpost and way station on that critical journey.

AN AMERICAN IDEAL

A view of Savannah, Georgia as it stood in 1734, founded by John Oglethorpe (1696–1785)

In 1630, aboard the ship *Arbella* on its passage to the founding of the Massachusetts Bay Colony, John Winthrop gave what surely must be considered one of the most impactful sermons in American history. Speaking to his fellow Pilgrims—no doubt suffering from all the ills, doubt, and worry that a transatlantic passage offered at that time—Winthrop reminded them of their mission and purpose in creating the community to come. For those who know the sermon, it is often and commonly remembered as the earliest statement of American exceptionalism, envisioning the American experience and community to come "...as a city upon a hill—the eyes of all people are upon us."

A deeper read of the sermon provides a more nuanced and complete view of the nature of community that was envisioned in this statement. Winthrop's sermon was a call to find in the new physical community that they would build both a symbol of and a contract for a new vision of living, one that called on the colonists to create a community of shared interest: *"...we must be knit together in this work as one man, we must entertain each other in brotherly Affection, we must be willing to abridge ourselves of our superfluities, for the supply of others necessities, we must uphold a familiar Commerce together in all meekness, gentleness patience and liberality, we must delight in each other, make others Conditions our own; rejoice together; mourn together; labor, and suffer together."*

In the centuries following that voyage, American history would be frequently marked by the intentional founding of new communities that arose from a desire for a new vision of living in this "New World." These communities were sometimes created for economic benefit, but often for some greater non-economic good. A quick (and very incomplete!) list, with their non-economic rationale for being founded noted would include: Providence (to create a refuge for religious tolerance); Philadelphia and other Quaker communities (to bring about a just—if very pragmatic—new world); Salt Lake City (religious tolerance and safety); Amish and Mennonite Communities that dot our landscape (to be apart from the corrupting world, while engaging it warily); Greely (to create a new image of western expansion and American renewal); and on the list can go. Community founders often sought to find renewal by separating themselves and their adherents from the failings of the world around them and with the hope that those physical places would grow to exhibit a new attitude in how its members would relate to one another and to the vast American continent.

It would be perhaps simplistic, but not entirely incorrect, to say that many of the small towns and communities where most Americans lived up through the first half of the 20th century saw themselves as heirs and reflections of that sense of ideal community. It can be said that the vision of "familiar commerce" and "delight in each other" of Winthrop's sermon was more often found than not, if only imperfectly.

A MID-20TH CENTURY DIVERSION

In the aftermath of World War II, the United States stood triumphant as few—if any—societies in history have. The war years had touched every American life. Some 16.5 million citizens, about 11% of the entire population, had served during the war for an average of 33 months; and 73% of those citizen soldiers had served overseas for an average of 16 months. Multiply the number serving by the families they represented, and the dimension of this seminal event begins to become clear. Other countries were impacted far more. Americans tend to forget that the United States alone exited those traumatic years with the wealth and power to do all manner of things.

One was to fulfill a tacit bargain that had been assumed by its citizenry: that after the tumult of the war, peacetime would be tranquil, prosperous, predictable, and focused on "the good life," however that might be defined. For many, that would mean leaving the crowded city with its aging housing stock for a new life somewhere else.

Two images speak to this period. The first is N.C. Wyeth's *The Homecoming,* painted in 1945. (See image on following page.) In it, one can see all the classic and potent American rural imagery on display (including "amber waves of grain"). But the soldier is pausing at the fence. Even though he may be longing to return to this ideal image and place, he is paused by the realization that he is not the boy who left, can never be again, and will not linger long at this place. There is a certain sadness just beneath the surface. And then there is just this plain practicality: how many returning vets and their families could obtain to this bucolic ideal?

Two years after that evocative painting, we have the boisterous image from *Better Homes and Gardens* (see image on following page), the magazine which would become the guide and bible of what could be achieved: GI loan-financed small homes built in the form of a subdivision on a track of open land near a crowded city. There is no undertone of sadness here! Activities of all kinds are everywhere to be seen.

This was the near-utopian vision proposed to resolve the implied conflict of *The Homecoming:* everyone gets their scaled-down bucolic house (with "purple mountains majesty" off in the distance, no less), but with all the conveniences at hand. No slums, no decay, no factories, no "others," and no worries about connecting those elements in a cheap car with a vast supply of cheap fuel. Importantly, everyone is there in a community of people who had shared the experience of war and is on the same path as everyone else.

As the post-WWII years rolled on into decades, another model of urban growth would become the norm to the point of a new cultural orthodoxy. It was, in fact, a novel experiment in community building and growth accommodation: one based on assumptions of continuing wealth-generation, endless mobility, and an undeniable diminution of the social bonds expected of community life in established cities and towns. Eventually, this orthodoxy became nothing less than a purposeful cultural intent, whose key programmatic ingredients were (and remain dominant to this day): a supply of cheap suburban and eventually exurban land, vast tracts of supportive single-use zoning; the availability of cheap energy; and a continuing dependency on both direct and hidden government subsidies to defray the costs of infrastructure, transportation, and financing that supported and still support this pattern of urban expansion.

From a vision of interconnection and mutual obligation among all citizens of the city on a hill, we devolved to a physical world notable for its disconnection, fragmentation, and isolation; one navigated by an ever-increasing network of congested roads. From a vision of individual and community resourcefulness, we became dependent on unceasing supplies of cheap

The Homecoming, N.C. Wyeth, 1945

Better Homes and Gardens cover, 1947

foreign energy. From a vision of living in balance and stewardship with the land, we descended into a reality lacking any measure of resilience and sustainability, especially notable for our individual and community disconnect from nature. This was—and by and large remains to this day—a model that came to be recognized as industrial scale home building in vast affordable single-family housing subdivisions. It is most commonly referred to today as production home building. It has done exceptionally well as a business enterprise and to an extent has provided over the years entry-level housing options to a significant number of middle-income Americans.

However, as the model became an institutionalized norm and began to falter, it was given a new name: Sprawl Development. By whatever name, it was marked by its demand for social conformity and separation, uniformity of home design, a deadening form and site repetition, and almost always a use of the lowest common denominator of construction technologies. (See images on page 7.) The rise of this new paradigm first overshadowed and then all but obliterated learning from and updating living local building traditions and vernacular design.

That bucolic suburban landscape popular in post-war images slowly morphed into the picture of a relentless suburban expansion dominated by the needs of the car to the detriment of just about everything else. The house, and the land it would sit on, were scaled down and regularized for the convenience of builders, banks, and buyers. Predictability—such an understandable desire in the aftermath of a global war—had become a stifling sense of conformity and regularity.

It is easy to mock the optimistic images and the reality behind them in hindsight, but for millions, even the pared-down versions of those mid-1940s visions represented a dream: one that seemed possible and attainable then, but now far less so. It is critical in our day—some eighty years after that experiment began in earnest—to acknowledge that for many it appeared to be a dream made manifest. But understanding that this appearance of a dream has become a litany of deficiencies is one of the challenges in combating the sprawl paradigm.

GROWING AWARENESS OF THE FAILURE OF THE SPRAWL MODEL

The 1973 oil embargo was an awakening to the tenuousness of access to the energy sources that supported and literally fueled the post-WWII model for growth accommodation. The shocking realization of American dependence on offshore energy, the availability and price of which was not controllable, cast a profound doubt on the viability of the post-WWII fundamental assumptions of American suburban life. Could growth always be met indefinitely by expanding out towards cheap land?

By the latter part of the 20th century, the unintended consequences of this great experiment with low-density suburban sprawl development so dependent on ever-expanding roadways and dependency on cars were becoming clear. The impact wrought by this system on families both in financial burden and social life was increasingly clear. The cost of operating cars; the time

The Race to Conformity. A price of embracing industrial-scale housing production was that regional realities and building traditions were ignored. Levittown-like houses can be seen in almost identical form throughout the United States. The National Homes ad takes this to the extreme: the same house, the same colors, the same décor shown in "hundreds of cities..."

Levittown, Pennsylvania

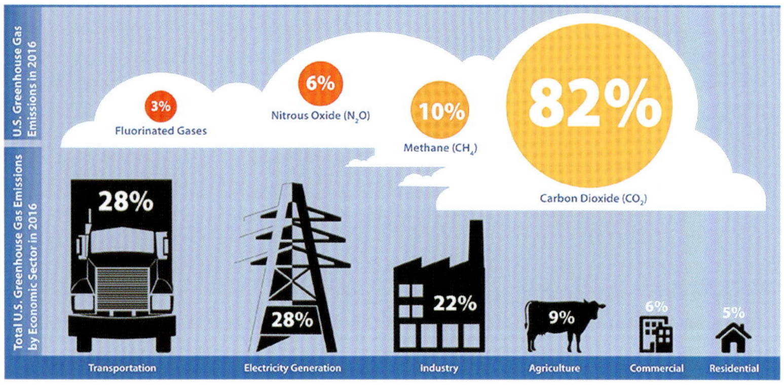

Global Greenhouse Gas Emissions by Economic Sector

Residential energy use and overall transportation contribute significantly to the generation of greenhouse gas (GHG) emissions in the United States. Green house gases are recognized as the primary cause of global climate change. Residential traffic accounts for 42% of all transportation; thus residential uses of all kinds account for 17% of all green house gas emissions in the US.

needed to drive around knitting together the necessary places of an average family's life—their homes, places of work, school, shopping, and worship—increased, and with that a growing sense of life being out of balance.

At the most pragmatic level, the asymmetrical growth between population and the infrastructure that this system of growth accommodation required was reaching utterly non-sustainable levels. In the first half of the 1990s, Tucson's population grew by 10%, while vehicular miles traveled grew by 40%. It did not take much to understand that this imbalance was a road to disaster. In the post-2008 world, we began to see more clearly how this model of growth came to produce an increasingly irrational, interlocking relationship with the unmonitored financial drivers that created an artificial boom, and then a crushing bust, not only in home building, but the entire global economy. The housing boom that occurred pre-2008 can be seen as the unfettered apogee of an industrialized housing and growth accommodation system taken to the max until disassociated from any sense of reality. Its collapse begs that we examine the non-sustainable artificiality of it all.

The degree to which the mode of sprawl development has contributed to and accelerated the challenges of global warming and climate change over the last eighty years may be debated but cannot be denied anymore. The impact of its negative externalities is now ever more apparent and dire: a chaotic pattern of urban growth, separation by class and income, overdependence on the automobile, extravagant investments on public infrastructure, little appreciation of real estate values, loss of agricultural land, increased pollution, weakening of the tax base of cities, a limited construction horizon, and lack of resilience of its building fabric. Further, the continuing dominance of the sprawl model may be leading us towards an irreversibly negative climate tipping point. The interlocking system of policy making, regulatory code support, easy access to financing and homogenized industrial scale production complicates—if not outright prevents—efforts to mitigate against or adapt to the growing impacts of the climate crisis.

In the mid-1970s, in the aftermath of the oil embargo, various environmental advocates in Tucson banded together to explore an alternative to suburban sprawl and environmental degradation. They focused on using solar energy and began to advocate for the creation of a "Tucson Solar Village." This vision of a conceptual neighborhood would become a challenge to sprawl in Southern Arizona by creating a more culture-, place-, and climate-specific response to growth, one that would focus on the social, environmental, and climate realities of the region. Though not at the forefront of their original advocacy, it can be seen—simply stated—as an effort to move away from that post-WWII suburban sprawl norm, at least in part. In its first iterations, as the name implied, Civano sought to create a foundation for community building based on renewable energy sources, reduced car use, and the reclaiming of the bonds of neighborhood and community.

Though their main focus may have been on "alternative energy," specifically solar, the early advocates for the Tucson Solar Village were mindful of a larger set of forces increasing the strain and degradation that the Sonoran Desert was suffering as standard development patterns to accommodate growth were expanded.

It is important to remember that the 1970s saw the beginnings of many strands of environmental advocacy. All were connected to emerging signs that the common assumptions of endless economic growth, population growth, and the exponential increase in fossil fuel use and its related release of greenhouse gases were all putting dangerous strains on both local and global environments. The Environmental Protection Agency was created in this period, under a Republican administration, no less. Back-to-the-land movements, the "Whole Earth Catalogue" ethos and movement, and the early strains of environmental advocacy all became part of the public discourse in the 1970s. The Club of Rome's impactful study, *The Limits of Growth,* was published in 1972. Though focused on population growth concerns, it linked those with an assessment of global resources to *sustain* that growth and introduced the concept of *systemic sustainability.* As the 1970s moved into the 1980s, all these components began to be seen as parts of a larger, interlocking system of concerns that would include social, economic, and even land planning ones. Bill McKibben's seminal book, *The End of Nature,* published in 1989, further knit together these topics, bringing them under an umbrella of a new set of terms: the recognition and consequences of global warming and climate change.

The Tucson Solar Village's evolution both drew on and reflected all of this. It evolved—through a process of over sixty public hearings throughout the late 1980s and early 1990s—into *Civano, A Sustainable Community.* While solar energy continued to be a central—and very public—theme, goals on job creation, community building, water conservation, housing diversity and affordability, and the reduction of dependence on the car were added. There was a desire to create a community in which one could work and live in place. In the final iteration of the project goals prior to starting the first neighborhood, two of the five requirements addressed ways to decrease green house gas emissions, and thus their direct contribution to global warming, as it was then called.

THE SEARCH FOR A NEW PARADIGM FOR GROWTH ACCOMMODATION, ONE THAT LEARNED FROM THE PAST

Another movement that grew out of this confluence of movements related to land use and the accommodation of growth was the concept of New Urbanism.

First Congress of the New Urbanism, October 8, 1993, Alexandria, Virginia; (bottom row, from right) Lizz Plater-Zyberk, Liz Moule, Joe Kohl, Geoff Farrell, Jaime Correa, Barbara Littenberg, Mark Schimmenti; (top row, from right) Peter Calthorpe, Andres Duany, Dan Solomon, Stefanos Polyzoides, Victor Dover, Steve Patterson, Erick Valle

The Congress for the New Urbanism was founded in 1993. (See photo above.) Its overarching purpose was to eradicate suburban sprawl by redefining planning as both policy and design. Its practitioners promoted and implemented projects in both center cities and suburban edges that integrated building, public space and landscape, mobility, and infrastructure ingredients. This resulted in new, diverse development patterns across the entire metropolitan spectrum from suburban to urban.

By 1996, its principles and influence had spread nationwide, with many projects underway in various stages of design and construction. The earliest operating principles of the Congress for the New Urbanism were focused on neighborhood design. They emphasized the re-introduction of street, block, and lot/building patterns as the basis for all urban design. It emphasized streets being interconnected, being of many types, and being multimodal and of reduced dimensions. Blocks were to be built out in a harmonious building fabric that defined a well-shaped and well-planted public realm. Buildings were to be of many types, uses, densities, sizes, and styles that provided high livability and broad market choice for a significant demographic range.

New Urbanist planning and design protocols would come into the history of TSV/Civano as both Tucson City officials and the private developers who would undertake the actual building of the idea came to understand that the form of the built environment could help or hinder achieving the environmental and social goals of the project. As a consequence, Duany & Plater-Zyberk of Miami and Moule & Polyzoides of Pasadena, California, were hired as co-leaders for the future planning charrette.

In this study, we will further examine how the New Urbanism came into the project and its impact; and we will explore why it was abandoned in the later stages of the project, and the consequences of that abandonment.

FROM ADVOCACY TO A STRUCTURED SET OF DEVELOPMENT OBJECTIVES

The initial idea for what would become the Community of Civano—The Tucson Solar Village—began in line with the heritage of building new communities to signal and achieve a new beginning, and then to become an example to the larger world. In its first advocacy-driven version, it was to be a self-sufficient community. Those first efforts, like so many American "cities on a hill," would, over a period of nearly 15 years, face pragmatic considerations and add new components before it could become anything like a buildable reality. It would finally evolve into a marriage of environmental goals and new urbanist community building protocols, each a departure from standard sprawl development practices. With the involvement of the public sector, this experiment was set in motion to test whether that marriage of goals could find success.

Understanding the development of the idea of Civano in its many phases—from a vaguely defined concept of "a solar village"; to something called a "sustainable community"; to a master plan with clearly defined goals; to a complex development project which added New Urbanist strategies to bring it from the realm of advocacy and intention into reality—reveals much about the challenges of creating any revolutionary development paradigm.

Studying the outcomes of that experiment is the most beneficial way to place Civano and its development in a context that is useful today. We summarize these experiments as follows:

1. Could a complex public/private partnership between a private developer and the City of Tucson and the State of Arizona succeed? What public resources would be needed to support the implementation of a resource-conscious project, priced affordably, in the local and regional marketplace?
2. Could the institutional entities that controlled entitlement and financing—the gateways to building a project—accept the innovative nature of Civano? Would—could—they become partners in the evolving experiment; or would they stand firm in established protocols that had led to exactly the problem everyone wanted to solve?
3. Could such a project be delivered to the marketplace at an affordable home price? Given the sustainability requirements, could the homes be built to meet the home-pricing realities of Tucson's middle market and still have the project be financially sustainable?
4. Would combining New Urban planning and design protocols with—for its time—aggressive energy efficiency and sustainability goals help achieve those goals? What other long-range consequences would it have?
5. As far as the City of Tucson was concerned, Civano would be a new model for growth accommodation to challenge the predominant sprawl model, with all its negative consequences. Would it work, and what would be needed to support it?

Civano did have a problematic and challenging development history, and we will not shy away from it. Like many of the "cities on hill," a history of compromises was required to move the origin of Civano from an idea to buildable reality. These were often seen by its original pioneers as fatal compromises, or choices made that were pragmatic to a fault.

It is our view that, once the problematic aspects are seen in a wider perspective, what is left is a story that offers many examples of success that are as relevant today as they were nearly twenty years ago. (See the image of Civano today on the following spread.)

Civano 2020, looking north towards the Catalina Mountains

Photograph courtesy of James Nicholas Polyzoides

PLACE

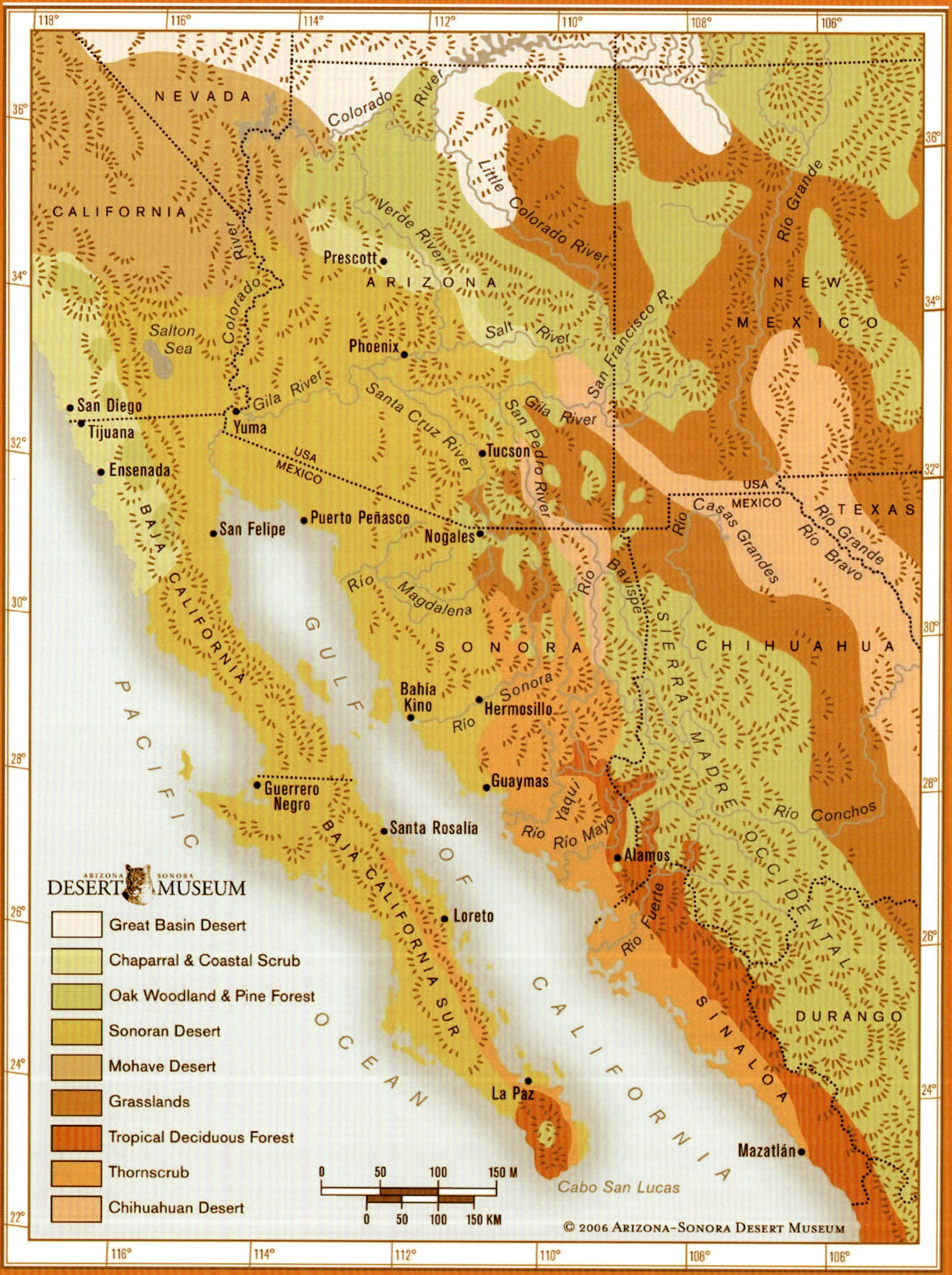

Map showing extent of the Sonoran Desert

THE SONORAN DESERT

The origins of Civano are best understood as a specific response to a set of challenges, all set in a very specific ecosystem: the Sonoran Desert. Among the world's arid habitats, the Sonoran Desert is unique. There is a great diversity of topography. The desert rises from sea level in northern Mexico to elevations of 9,200 feet at its northeastern extent, which is defined by the Catalina Mountains surrounding the northern side of the Tucson basin. In Tucson, it is possible to traverse from the baking desert floor to a mild Alpine-like environment all in a 30-minute drive up Mt. Lemmon, the highest peak in the Catalinas. The elevation changes in the desert create a variety of micro-ecologies and along with them an extraordinary abundance and diversity of flora and fauna. Many may be surprised to learn that Arizona is the third most bio-diverse state in the nation. Just short of 3,000 distinct native plant species can be found with a 50-mile radius of downtown Tucson[1]. This diversity in the midst of what most people imagine as a monotone desert gives just a hint of what can be a fundamental truth about desert living: though conditions are harsh, they do not preclude the possibility of living in abundance. If one can find the right balance with the resources and climate of the desert, its harshness can be mitigated and life can and will flourish. (See photo on following page.)

As one would expect in any desert, there is an abundance of solar energy to be harnessed. An often-quoted fact about Tucson is that it gets 360 days a year that have some sunshine. This creates an enviable solar energy potential. This abundance also creates a heat presence that needs to be addressed in order to make the desert habitable.

Water is, of course, the preoccupation of all living things in any desert environment, and the Sonoran Desert is no exception. Sitting at the base of three mountain ranges, Tucson was historically blessed with an abundant and accessible water table, and a free-flowing river. The combination of sun, year-round warmth, and water availability made the Tucson Valley habitable, if not dramatically so. The aboriginal Tohono O'odham, and the related Hohokam and Akimel O'odham groups to the north, were longtime inhabitants of the area. Current research indicates that they form one of the oldest continuous chains of habitation in the American Southwest. What is considered the classic era of this aboriginal culture reached its zenith in the mid-15th century. This period has been given the name by scholars as the "Civano" period. Most agree that it was in this period that the growth of the indigenous communities was best in balance with the natural resources available to them, especially water.

While the historical presence of water allowed for some level of cultivation, no one should mistake that presence for abundance. The Tucson region receives an average of a mere 12 inches of rainfall each year. Historically, virtually all that falls in two rainy seasons: the three-month summer "monsoon" and a month-long period in the winter.[2]

Heat is a constant presence in the Tucson region, with a five-month hot season during which it is not now unusual to see 100 straight days with the temperature well above 100 degrees. During the summer monsoon, this heat is made more difficult to bear by what passes for high humidity in this environment: 30–40%.

1 Desert Survivors Nursery.
2 Data from the University of Arizona and National Weather Bureau.

THE TRADITIONAL BUILT RESPONSE

A strong vernacular building typology developed to moderate, if not entirely offset, these harsh extremes. The aboriginal peoples employed a variety of classic heat-mitigating building strategies. They partially dug their larger common buildings underground, used adobe-like construction, and severely limited the number and size of door and window openings in their structures. They placed an emphasis on creating outdoor shaded areas using light, open, easily assembled structures. Shade and air movement go a long way towards diminishing the impact of the desert heat given the constant low humidity. (See image on page 15.)

The early 1600s saw the arrival of the Spaniards, with Tucson being one of the northernmost mission outposts of the Spanish Empire, and after Mexican independence, of the Mexican state. The Spanish and Mexicans adapted the aboriginal building technologies, adding their own cultural elements, developing what we know as classic adobe mass-wall construction. They added courtyards, patios, and arcades, all designed to create mediated exterior living areas. This type of construction would remain the unchallenged norm in the region until the late 1800s, a time of great change in the region. (See images on page 15.)

The Mexican-American War, ending in 1848, resulted in the West coming into the United States. In the post-Civil War period, expansion into the West increased rapidly, especially after it was connected to the rest of the country by railroad. The discovery of ample mineral and metal deposits, especially copper, created Tucson's first population "boom." With the railroad, industrial fired brick made an appearance as a building material. Later, different types of cured and fired block construction appeared, and classic adobe construction receded. However, all these technologies utilized the same mitigation approach to heat as did adobe: using the wall mass to slow the passage of heat into or out of the living space, depending on the season. This mitigation approach would dominate until the mid-20th century. With the arrival of the railroad in Tucson, an Anglo variation on adobe construction became common: light wood framing for roofs, porches, and other elements would cap or be added to the adobe body. (See images on page 15.)

Tucson's growth could be characterized as "slow and steady" through the first half of the 20th century. It became a destination for health treatment (especially tuberculosis) because of its mild winters, dryness, and low humidity. The University of Arizona was established in 1885 and became another and enduring growth generator to Tucson, supplementing the mining operations in Arizona.

EXPANSION DURING WORLD WAR II

World War II brought a second, larger boom in population and building activity to Tucson. Tucson's abundant clear weather made it an ideal locale for training airmen for the war effort. This period of growth continued into the '50s and '60s as Tucson became a technology center, as well as an affordable retirement destination. From 1950 to 1960, Tucson's recorded population

A view of the Saguaro National Park just east of Tucson shows the richness and diversity of the flora in the Sonoran Desert.

The 30th Parallel Global Desert Zone

While the Sonoran Desert is unique in the abundance of flora and fauna it supports, there is no mistaking Tucson's desert reality. It lies along the 30th degree of latitude global "desert zone," along with the cities shown above.

grew from 45,000 to about 220,000, according to US Census figures. (See chart on page 17.)

Building—especially residential building—during this period still held on to the tried and true "thick wall" mitigation system, though now those walls become dominantly made of double brick. Typical 1950s ranchers with evaporative cooling systems were the norm, and often included solar hot water generators. In neighborhoods closer into the center of the city, and especially around the University, a variety of regional styles cemented the reality that these homes were of a certain place. (See images on page 16.)

LEAVING BEHIND TRADITIONAL BUILDING METHODOLOGIES

The 1960s saw the general adopting of air conditioning in the Tucson region, and the arrival in force of what was then, and continues to be, the almost universal (at least in the United States) residential production-scale building system: wood framing, with insulation, clad on the exterior with stucco products. This system abandoned the time-tested concept of mass wall mitigation of heat and replaced it with the ability to run air conditioning almost continuously—a strategy that was made possible by abundant cheap energy. This system had many advantages for home builders. It was much cheaper to build than masonry, to say nothing of adobe. That it was the national building standard for middle-income home building made procurement of materials dependable and cheap.

One could make a reasonable argument that one outcome of this shift in building technology was that the cost of heat mitigation was shifted from the builder—who previously bore the expense and complexity of creating heavy mass walls—to the home owner, who would now pay for the cheap energy that ran the mechanical systems that dealt with the heat. A corollary to this argument would be to point out that this construction and operating strategy did

HOUSING IN TUCSON: A BRIEF AND SIMPLIFIED HISTORICAL SUMMARY

Original Settlers
A rendering of a Hohokam community. Like many aboriginal cultures in the Southwest, the Hohokam utilized thick adobe walls to mitigate heat gain during the hot months and loss during the winter. Minimal openings in the dwelling units helped moderate interior spaces. Top openings allowed the strong desert sun to provide adequate illumination inside. The community units were characterized by numerous public spaces.

The building traditions that came with Spanish and Mexican settlement in Tucson mixed aspects of traditional Spanish architecture with mitigating thick masonry walls found in the Hohokam settlements. Adobe continued to be the prime building material. Interior rooms tended to be organized around patios which modulated the strong desert light.

With the arrival of the railroad in 1880, there was a gradual but sure transition to a more Anglo housing look. A new material became available: fired brick, along with cheaper and more available glass. Thick masonry walls—now brick rather than adobe—remained the standard way of mitigating the heat. Porches started to move the old interior gathering space to the outside, as well as helping mitigate the sunlight's penetration.

HOUSING IN TUCSON: A BRIEF AND SIMPLIFIED HISTORICAL SUMMARY

Through most of the 20th century, thick masonry walled houses remained the constant, with porches, cross-ventilation, and whole house fans being used to mitigate the desert heat. A variety of styles were used, but the basic components remained pretty much the same. The two images above at the left are classic "bungalow" homes found near the University and built in the 1920s to 1930s. The right two houses are found in the Sam Hughes neighborhood, and date from the late 1930s through the 1940s. All are thick-walled masonry.

In the post-World War II boom in Tucson, things started to change. New homes began to reflect a more national look, leaving further behind any allusion to the historic housing of Tucson. The "rancher" look began to become dominant. Accommodation of the car became an increasingly important consideration. Well into the 1960s, the predominant cooling method was the "swamp cooler": an evaporative cooler set on the roof which used air cooled by passing it through water-saturated filters and then down through ductwork into the house as a cooling system. As air conditioning became more affordable and available, the rooftop evaporative unit was often replaced with an air conditioning unit. This new system decreased water usage, a good thing, but with a trade-off of locking the homeowner into higher energy use.

The Arrival of the National Builders in the Late 1970s/1980s
National builders began to arrive in force in Tucson in the early 1970s, and they brought their standardized building practices with them. The upper left house is from the mid-1970s and is built of wood framing with exterior cladding; in this case cementatious cladding. The other two houses are from the early 1980s. They are wood framing with stucco exterior skins. All three houses depend on insulation and air conditioning—powered by cheap energy—to mitigate the desert heat. The role of the car has gone from a consideration in the post-WWII houses noted above, to a dominate home design driver. Lots are smaller and the streetscape is dominated by garage fronts and driveways. This was the dominate housing reality in Tucson, and indeed the nation, when a search for an alternative began.

Tucson Population Growth, 1850–2020

The 1960s mark the inflection point when ex-urban low-density growth began to far outpace the organic growth of Tucson proper.

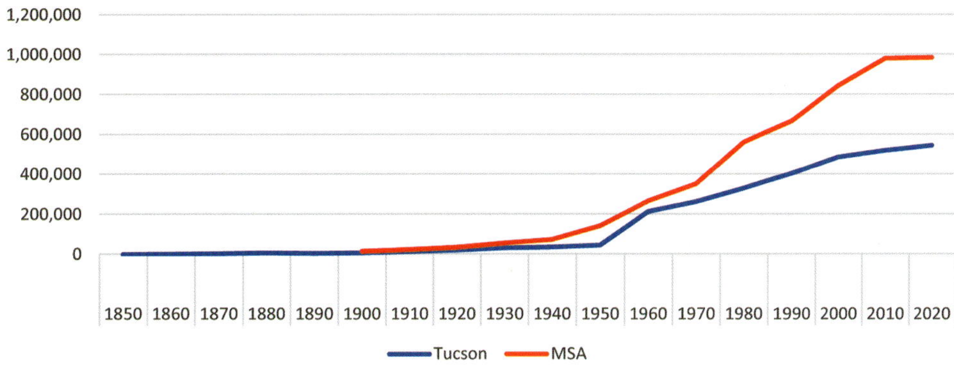

Median Incomes for Cities in the American Southwest

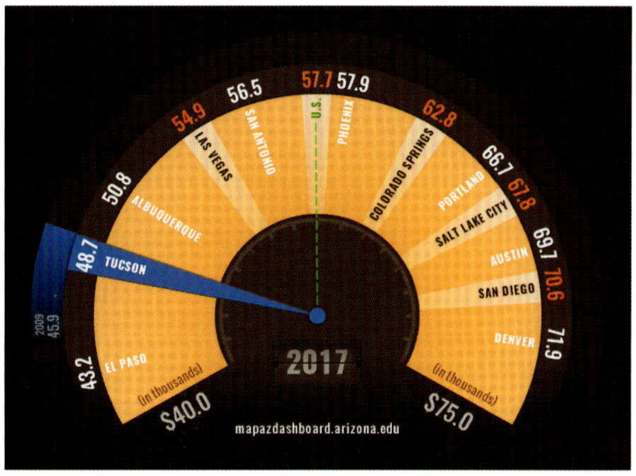

allow a substantially lower first cost of house production, an attractive proposition to the buying public and the mortgage industry that grew to facilitate their buying. As the cost of operating energy rose, so too would the financial burden on the American family. And "low first cost" came to be exposed for the partial truth it is. (See images on page 16.)

LOW FIRST COST AND ITS PLACE IN TUCSON'S HOUSING MARKET

To understand the housing market in Tucson, we need to consider its demographics. Tucson is not blessed with high demographic and economic characteristics. Median income figures have been, and continue to be, noticeably lower than the rest of Arizona and much lower than the average for the United States. The chart above on the right shows that in 2017, Tucson had the second lowest median income of all the major Southwest cities, and its median household income was about 18.5% lower than the national average. This has been a consistent ranking for a long time.

In 1999, when home sales started in earnest in Civano, Tucson's median income was about $37,500, 10% lower than the rest of Arizona and about 17% below the national average. What does this mean for our study? It can suggest what a realistic home sales price range should be in the market. Referring to the Case-Shiller Index of home prices to income, the standard reference, we note that in 2000 that ratio was about 2.5. Thus, simple math would indicate that a home aimed at the median income family of the Tucson market should be priced around $93,500. A record of one of the earliest meetings between advocates for the idea of Tucson Solar Village, a 1982 memorandum of a meeting of the Arizona Solar Energy commission, stresses the critical importance of ensuring that whatever other goals the Tucson Solar Village might aim for, affordability for the "average citizen" was at the top of the list. We will review how this goal, the economics of Tucson, and the additional cost of meeting the other goals of the project became a challenging proposition unique in the national experience of the new urbanist developments.

ANNEXATION AND SPRAWL BECOME DOMINANT

Tucson's strong post-war growth would continue through the end of the 20th century, with census figures showing that each decade from the 1960s on through the 1980s added 20–25% to the metropolitan area's population. Several factors supported this acceleration. Tucson continued to be a highly desirable—and highly affordable—retirement community. The University of Arizona shifted from being a regional institution to a more national one, drawing its students from across the nation. Raytheon and other defense-related contractors grew in size, along with the Air Force's Davis-Monthan base.

Two trends emerged as part of this rapidly expanding population. First, Tucson's city government began to pursue annexation as a way of expanding its tax base to meet its ever-increasing infrastructure costs. Critically, each "annexed tax base" dollar would add to the City's allotment of state funds. Annexation might have brought new water sources under the City's control, but this was more often accomplished by buying up area water companies, a strategy that never met increasing demand.

Secondly, it was during this period that Tucson saw the entry into its market of national builders and their standardized building practices. This model emphasized highly standardized housing design, so that a building plan could be—with slight market variations—used in almost any location throughout the country. One needed only to consider adding a few changeable components to adjust for individual regions. Tile roofs might be used instead of asphalt shingles, for instance, in a desert or hurricane-prone climate. Homes were almost always built on ¼-acre lots, which demanded an ever-expanding network of roads and lots of cheap land to accommodate growth. Lower land cost typically drove builders to the edge of town. The type of home construction was, and remains, dependent on the low-cost energy model described above. This was the golden age of sprawl development in Tucson, as it was in the rest of the nation. (See map on the following page.)

UNINTENDED CONSEQUENCES BECOME MORE VISIBLE

From the early 1980s on, some of the implications of this low energy cost/low density model of growth accommodation began to become unavoidably obvious. As the population increased, so did the demand for the infrastructure needed to support it. The transportation requirement was especially sensitive to growth, given the near universal American post-war zoning emphasis on the separation of living, institutional, and working zones. As affordable new housing tended to be built in areas where builders could find cheaper land, that housing also migrated further and further away from established work, commercial, and industrial zones. Simply put, more roads were needed to accommodate the traffic required to meet an average family's daily needs. This created an asymmetrical relationship between population growth and transportation infrastructure needs. During the period of 1990–'97, the population of the Tucson Standard Metropolitan Statistical Area (SMSA) grew by

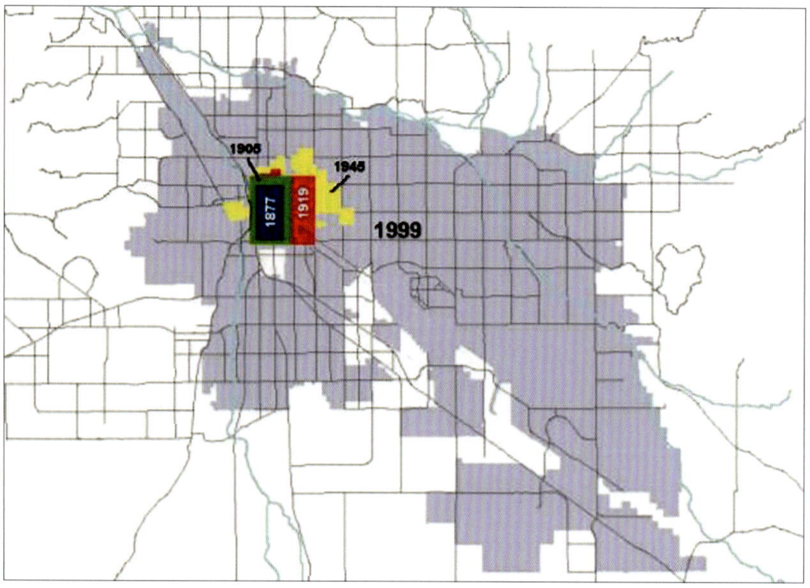

Map of Tucson Boundaries. Growth and Annexation.

Note especially the expansion from 1945 (yellow) to 1999 (purple).

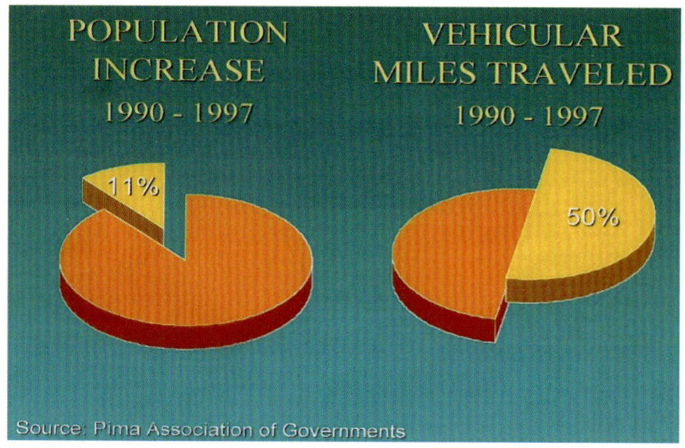

A Relationship With Dire Consequences

The low-density expansion Tucson embraced post-World War II created an asymmetrical relationship between population growth and the infrastructure needed to support it. Beyond the inevitable and increasing impact of pollution on the environment, this relationship creates a growing tax burden required to build and maintain that expanding infrastructure.

11%. During this same period, the total vehicular miles traveled in the SMSA grew by 50%.

This relationship has obvious and troubling implications. Local governments saw the need for ever-increasing infrastructure expansion funding, with the implied need to increase local taxes to support that funding. This, in turn, presented the danger of undermining Tucson's reputation for affordability—a critical component of its attraction for retirees and an educated work force for its growing technology sectors. Furthermore, this asymmetrical growth pattern, with its ever-expanding system of roads and utility grids, only led to increased traffic. That, in turn, led to increases in hydrocarbon pollution enough to present a threat to the very state of the Sonoran Desert landscape, a key part of Tucson's attraction.

Tucson's continuing growth by annexation at its edges only aggravated this asymmetry. Between 1960 and 2020, the land mass within the city boundaries of Tucson increased from 70.8 square miles to 226 square miles, an increase of 220%. As large as this increase was, it is dwarfed by the growth of the land mass of the city between 1940 and 1960. The city grew from 7.9 square miles to 70.8 square miles, an astounding 796% growth in size. This fact must be understood within the context of what is a stunning reality in Arizona: less than 20%[1] of its land mass is available for typical private—sector land development. The rest is restricted or off limits because it is on Native American reservations, in national parks or other federally controlled and protected land, or just is too mountainous or inhospitable for habitation. In Pima County, where Tucson is located, available open, unregulated, and undeveloped land drops to about 18%. Clearly, land availability is precious, and growth accommodation by constant annexation as a strategy to support low-density development faces severe constraints.

One obvious public policy that could have countered, to a degree, this asymmetry would have been to focus on denser development models and encourage development and renewal within the existing core city boundaries. However, these policies and the political will to create them just were nonexistent. This was not surprising in that it reflected fifty years of post-war growth policies in the United States: policies driven by cheap subsidized energy costs, a complete dependence on the car, and mono-use zoning. All this in service of creating home ownership at the lowest possible first cost. Lost in all of this was a knowledge of how to design, build, and promote denser urban building types and neighborhoods.

GROWTH CHALLENGED BY WATER LIMITATIONS

This accelerating post-war growth also put great pressure on the regional water resources. By the 1970s, Tucson had established a pattern of using *twice* the groundwater that was being naturally recharged. The once plentiful and easily accessible groundwater supply was receding dramatically and becoming increasingly costly to reach. The issue was made more dramatic by the increasing water demands for Southern Arizona agriculture, an agriculture that both in type and magnitude could not exist on the available and decreasing volume of groundwater. (See page 19, far right.)

The major response to the stressed sourcing of groundwater was the Central Arizona Project. The CAP sought to efficiently bring Colorado River water into the area to accommodate both urban and agricultural needs. The Colorado River is the most controlled and stressed river in the United States, if not the world. This system was, and remains, highly energy dependent. A system of pumps and canals brings water from the distant Colorado River and its reservoirs hundreds of miles away for use in Arizona. Most of the power to run this system comes from the Navajo Generating Station, originally powered by coal mined on Navajo lands. That mining and coal-fired generation had enormous health impacts on the communities that serve this system. Though now powered by natural gas, the system remains, nonetheless, highly dependent on cheap energy that contributes to green house gas emissions. Each of the components in this system presented environmentally problematic

1 Information from Arizona State Land Department and US Bureau of Land management.

An aerial view of the Central Arizona Project canal running through the desert north of Tucson—an open canal suffering about a 25% loss of water through evaporation.

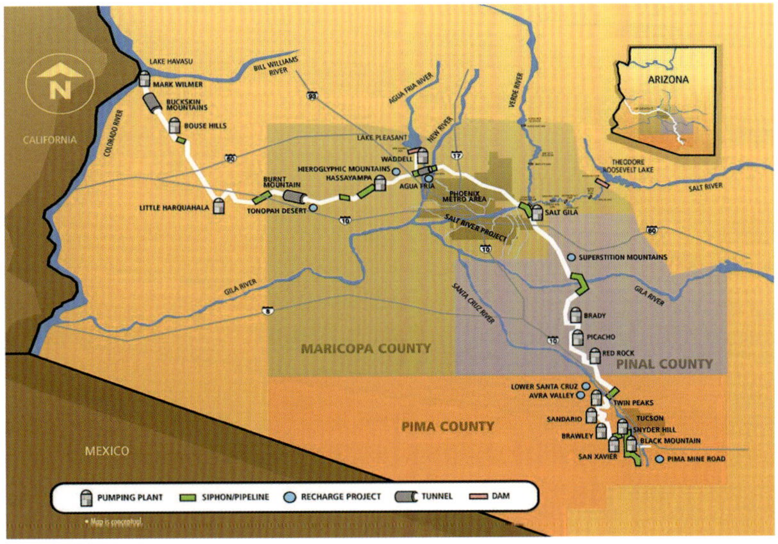

Map of the Central Arizona Project. Note the 15 pumping stations required to move the water through the system—a system dependent on cheap and available energy to ensure water availability.

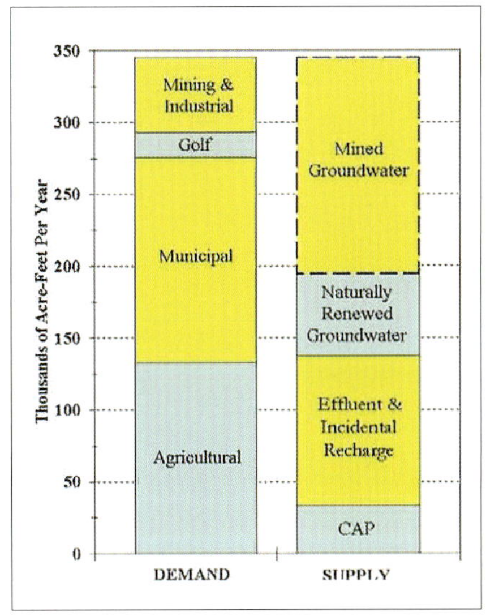

Uses of and sources for Tucson's water circa 1997. "Mined Groundwater" refers to the need to drill ever deeper into retreating groundwater tables, rather than depending on those tables being naturally renewed. About one fifth of Tucson's water was coming from naturally renewing groundwater.

outcomes. The evaporation that occurred in the open canals of the system sent about a quarter of the expensively routed water back into the atmosphere. (See photo and map above.)

By the 1980s, rising energy costs began to have an increasingly apparent impact on the true cost of offsetting the region's water supply problems with this strategy. Forward-looking studies demonstrated that any hope of a balanced use of ground water, even with implementation of some water conservation policies, would disappear by 2035, unless water use itself was substantially reduced.

Other programs were attempted, including one that recharged Tucson's aquifers with treated wastewater. It was not a success. The quality of water was not acceptable and it damaged water piping, requiring the City to reimburse a number of home owners for damage to their water systems. The recharge idea was all but abandoned. A second compensating strategy tried, to a much greater success, was the creation of a second city-wide water system that used partially treated wastewater solely for landscape irrigation purposes. This system was initially created to provide a more sustainable source of irrigation for Tucson's many golf courses. With a daily need of about six million gallons per course, anything that could divert using potable water had a positive impact. Having said that, the cost of creating two city-wide water systems is obviously not insubstantial.

A POINT OF INFLECTION ARRIVES

By the 1980s, a tipping point was becoming obvious to some in Tucson's city government policy and planning agencies. The ever-expanding cost of infrastructure to meet the ever-expanding physical boundaries of the city, disappearing water supplies, and the appearance of smog from increased traffic all were becoming evermore obvious realities. Tucson had become a classic "Sunbelt" sprawl city. It was utterly dependent on the car and cheap energy. Tucson continued expanding rapidly through low-density development and annexation, with mounting challenges to local resources and the environment becoming ever more apparent. It had embraced mono-zoning and it had become wedded to a very standardized system of home building, one that had little to do with a long tradition of vernacular building traditions that had responded to its complex and challenging desert environment.

As the environmental impact and cost of growth using these existing patterns of development became more onerous, there was a desire to find a new model for growth accommodation that could protect the very nature of the Sonoran Desert environment that attracted people to the region, while creating a more symmetrical balance between growth accommodation, infrastructure building and maintenance, and the present and future availability of critical resources like water.

Tucson had the great advantage of being home to the University of Arizona and being a place where advocates for all manner of "alternative building" had found a home. A number of academics and advocates who understood the nature of the challenges facing the region had carried on investigations of alternatives to the by now standard energy-dependent sprawl growth model. Key members of the City government returned to an idea that had begun about a decade earlier, one that had grown out of the aftershock of the mid-'70s oil embargo. An idea had sprung from the interest in alternatives to oil-derived energy and had focused on creating a model village powered by solar energy. There had been some early support from the State, but that had waned. The City revitalized that support, and through its involvement that original idea would grow to encompass much more. It would become an experiment in finding an alternative for accommodating growth, one that would stand in contrast to standard assumptions and practices. The following chapters will trace the history and evolution of that initial idea, on through the challenges it faced in its implementation.

HISTORY

RESPECT FOR PLACE

COMMUNITY

SECURITY

DIVERSITY

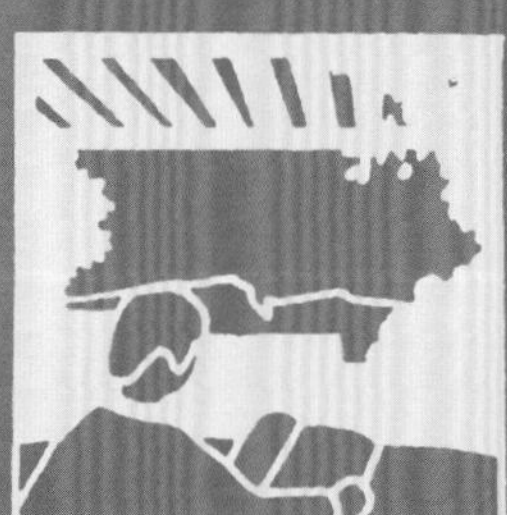

PRIVACY

IDENTITY

Ideograms introducing chapter headings from the 1991–1992 Solar Village Design Guidelines by Wayne Moody

Beginnings, Visioning & Advocacy Mid-1970s to Mid-1980s

The 1973–1974 OPEC oil embargo precipitated the first national focus on the precariousness of American dependency on oil, especially its ever-increasing dependence on imported oil. Coming as it did during the later days of the Vietnam War and all the turmoil of social change in the 1960s, and concurrent with the growing loss of components of the industrial base of the United States, it was a body blow to a key underpinning of our post-WWII culture: the assumption that cheap and abundant energy would always be available. The embargo created serious discussions about alternative energy sources, especially those that could be "home grown." Solar energy certainly fell into this category, especially in those areas of the country with abundant sunlight and milder average temperatures. Arizona would be at the top of that list.

A number of federal initiatives and funding programs were begun in the hopes of creating an expansive "solar industry" with a special emphasis on residential uses. The passage of the Public Utilities Regulation Policies Act (PURPA) in 1978 gave federal support to utilities and individuals who wanted to incorporate energy-saving technologies and promote energy generation by alternative sources to fossil fuels, especially "renewable" sources like solar. PURPA also opened the energy market to renewable energy by requiring utilities—at an extremely small scale—to purchase energy generated by non-traditional means.

These responses, though focused on energy generation and distribution, built on the growing emergence of many of the strands that would eventually be woven together into our present-day understanding of what constitutes "sustainability." Concepts like "environmental design" entered common usage, especially among planners and growth policy makers. The Environmental Protection Agency was created in 1970, reflecting a growing popular realization that unchecked growth had and would continue to damage communities. In 1972, *Limits to Growth* was published, and brought prominence to discussions about the capacity of both global and regional natural environments to sustain population growth.

In the United States there was a "back to the land" movement, facilitated by the publishing of the *Whole Earth Catalogue.* This influential publication became the go-to resource for people exploring all aspects of self-sufficiency. It contained resources and products to help people incorporate both passive and active solar energy into their homes and to investigate the use of alternative building materials. In fact, one can identify an entire design movement that sprung from all of this: the passive solar movement. Realizing that active solar devices (photovoltaic panels) were, at that time, just too inefficient to have any chance of economic sensibility, designers looked to all manner of passive ways to capture solar, wind, and geothermal energy. (See diagram of passive techniques on page 23.)

In Tucson, the University of Arizona had created an ad-hoc incubator of sorts for thinking about appropriate responses to this energy crisis. The College of Architecture and Landscape had a strong tradition of exploring the use of both traditional and high-tech building materials. The University had created the Energy Research Lab to focus on solar power generation and alternative building materials. There were several faculty members who had begun to create sophisticated ways to measure the energy use of residential buildings. A cadre of architects and builders had come together to explore how to accommodate urban growth with a lighter impact on the environment.

It was into this mix that the actions of a few homebuilders interested in incorporating solar hot water and other passive energy features to their homes acted as a catalyst for all that follows in our story, a story that would take some fifteen years to arrive at an actionable state.

The evolution of that story is perhaps best seen as advancing in discreet horizons. Each horizon builds on the previous one, with each one marking a shift in who is taking the lead in promoting or evolving the concept. Each horizon is marked by a process of distillation and codification of goals and the means of measuring those goals. It is a classic story of a vaguely defined and aspirational vision promoted by a small group of dedicated advocates growing into a more articulated and codified idea that gains the support and championing of public policy makers before being taken over by the private sector for implementation.

We shall see how this idea of adding solar and passive features to a few homes in Tucson grew into an experiment joining environmental and social concerns in search of a more appropriate way to accommodate urban growth in the Southern Arizona desert, while treading more lightly and responsibly on the land. It would, in fact, become an experiment about how to directly challenge the established model of high-environmental-impact sprawl development.

With Arizona's abundant solar energy capital, the post-embargo solar boom was seen as a potential economic development tool by forward-thinking Arizona politicians. In 1975, Democratic Governor Raul Castro created the Arizona Solar Energy Commission. Its purpose was to promote the solar industry in Arizona and funnel federal funding to solar companies in the state. Governor Castro was followed in 1978 by Democrat Bruce Babbitt. Babbitt had a long-standing and notable history of environmental sensitivity, rooted in a deep family presence in the region's history. He continued support for the Solar Energy Commission and exhibited an openness to exploring energy conservation in multiple ways. (See photos on page 22.)

John Wesley Miller
Visionary Tucson Developer

Raul Castro
14th Governor of Arizona, 1975–1977

Bruce Babbitt
16th Governor of Arizona, 1978–1987
US Secretary of the Interior, 1993–2001

SEVEN HOUSES IN THE DESERT

This openness was engaged in 1981 when Babbitt visited the "Solar Energy Parade of Homes" in Tucson. The showcase—which consisted of seven homes with solar and passive features—had been initiated by several local Tucson builders, chief among them John Wesley Miller with the backing of the Southern Arizona Homebuilders Association (SAHBA), the local homebuilding industries trade association. (See images on the following page.)

It is important to note that this showcase consisted of standard subdivision homes, set in a standard, if up-market and semi-custom home subdivision. The special features of the houses consisted of passive solar hot water, more attention to energy performance, and other passive features. This was very much in line with the "Whole Earth Catalogue aesthetic" noted in the prologue.

The positive reception for the showcase encouraged Tucson advocates to start promoting the idea of an expanded "solar village." John Wesley Miller took the lead in proposing the creation of a "square mile solar village," the basic major street grid in Tucson being a square mile. Babbitt was struck by the impact the features of the homes, especially the use of solar energy, could have on the energy use profile of an average home. He began to encourage Miller and other solar advocates to organize their ideas into a coherent vision that could, in turn, be developed into a quantifiable development proposal.

Critically, Babbitt went far beyond encouragement. He sought funding for "vision initiatives" whose purpose would be to create a more documented and research-oriented version of the Solar Village idea. He was successful in getting $1.06 million allocated to the Solar Energy Commission from federal rebate funds generated from oil overcharges and mining penalties. Over the next fifteen years, these funds would support many planning, design, and even building initiatives associated with the Tucson Solar Village and its successor, Civano.

Concurrent with these events, in 1980 the Tucson City and Pima County governments created the Metropolitan Energy Commission, a group of appointed volunteers whose purpose it was to advise local officials on energy issues, but not to directly manage any governmental effort in these areas.[1] The important function that MEC came to fill in the evolution of Civano was to be the recognized conduit for channeling the State Solar Energy Commission funding to the project and to organize the initial "vision initiatives."

THE FIRST VISION

The earliest and most complete document that we have been able to locate that can be considered an official description of the "Solar Village" idea and its components is a memorandum recording a meeting that took place in August 1982 under the auspices of the Arizona Solar Energy Commission. Many of those with the longest association with the Tucson Solar Village and its eventual transition into Civano consider this memo to be *the* founding document for all that followed.

In attendance were two members of the Arizona Solar Energy Commission Land Committee, Helen Kessler and John Wesley Miller, meeting with several staff members of the Arizona State Land Department. The State Land Department was, and is, the agency that manages all State-owned land in Arizona and its disposition through auctions. Kessler and Miller were proposing that the State Land Department identify and set aside state land in Tucson for the proposed "Solar Village."

Below we summarize the key points in the memorandum. It includes the general goals of the community, and what the solar village proponents wanted to see the future developer and builders in this community be required and be encouraged to do.

Affordability There is a repeated emphasis on *affordability.* Whatever the developer and builder of the proposed community would be required to do in terms of energy generation and environmental goals "should not increase the cost of the community's housing." In the builder options section, consideration of prefabricated and manufactured homes was encouraged. At that time, these two housing types were thought to be potential pathways to creating very affordable housing alternatives.

Self-Sufficiency and Energy The focus on affordability was a significant caveat in a document that otherwise was not too bound by considerations for practicality. For instance, the memo calls for consideration of community-based agriculture, sewer, and energy systems, all "in an effort to approach self-sufficiency." Even at that time, the idea of creating self-sufficient utility districts for small communities was understood to be utopian. The inclusion of this in the memo is a reflection of the "back to the earth" movement noted above. It is true that the Public Utility Regulatory Act, the beginning of an ongoing restructuring of utilities that continues today, had opened the door to entities other than regulated utilities to generate energy; but even that federal initiative continued to assume that independently generated power would be distributed through existing utilities' grids whenever possible. The idea of self-sufficient, community-based power generation and distribution was

1 MEC White Paper, cited in Nichols, page 41; Bauer, page 295.

The Solar Parade of Homes

To the left, renderings of the two of the homes. Below, an aerial of the homes included in the "parade." Both in home design and site plan, they are typical of up-market homes from the period in a typical suburban subdivision layout. Much more attention was paid to energy efficiency with a special emphasis on passive energy saving features. Note that some, but not all homes have solar photoelectric panels. All had solar hot water generation.

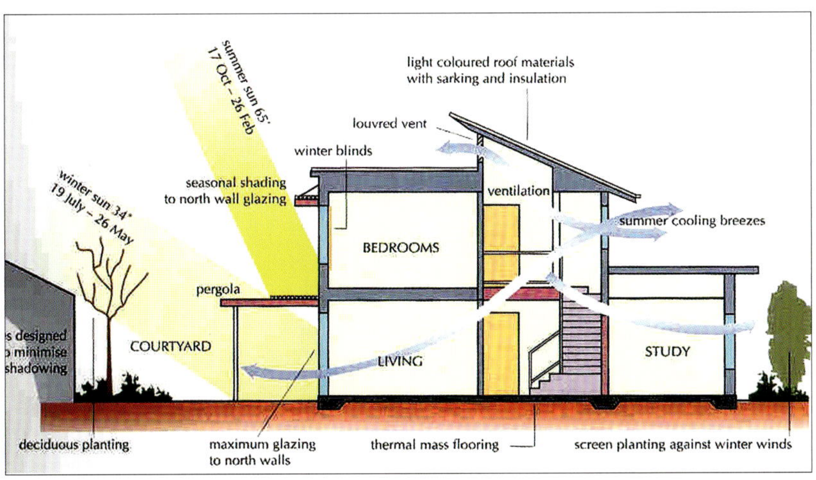

A simple diagram showing the many passive design techniques and components that were common in houses designed under this paradigm.

Map of Tucson showing the location of the State-granted Tucson Solar Village site: 818 acres located 12.5 miles from the historic center of Tucson.

a major departure from the intent of PURPA and other government energy generation initiatives. It should be said that this memo stressed the importance of energy conservation as much as it did to promote the idea of energy generation.

Solar energy was at the center of this first vision: both passive and active solar. Proper passive orientation was mandated. Community-wide solar powered energy generation coops were encouraged.

The Physical Nature of the Community Kessler's memo does offer ideas about how this proposed community would be different from a standard subdivision in its planning and form. The emphasis on housing diversity, the mix of uses, and lowering car use are all understood to require modification and changes to standard zoning and development codes. Looking to vernacular precedents was noted. However, there is no coherent approach to land planning proposed. One can speculate that given Miller's background in standard subdivision development, what was envisioned was a heavy modification of those practices with added environmental elements. An emphasis on orientation to support passive and active solar generation is noted as a key goal.

A Potential Site Set Aside The economics of this proposed community are not delved into. There was no request for public support, other than asking that public land be made available for auction at a future date. In the waning days of Babbitt's administration, some 818 worn-out grazing acres on Tucson's far east side were identified and set aside as a future site. This area was slightly bigger than Miller's initially proposed "solar mile." In return for its provisional commitment for this set-aside, the State Land Department required a number of feasibility studies be done and a master plan for development be created. These would flesh out, clarify, and test the reality of the goals enumerated in the August 1982 memo.

MOMENTUM PAUSED AND THEN STOPPED

Before any feasibility studies, much less a master plan could be developed, this initial burst of activity came to a halt. National and local factors contributed to this pause.

Energy realities had changed; the high oil prices of the immediate post-embargo period had collapsed. By the mid-'80s, the mini-boom in solar industries was long gone. In the rush to get products to market, overall product quality and dependability suffered, as perhaps was predictable in the forced hot-house environment created by the federal push to create a solar industry. More importantly, with energy prices down dramatically from where they had been in the early '70s, there simply was not a rational, much less compelling, economic argument for active solar devices. Adding to this disincentive was the fact that the federal solar installation tax credit that had been enacted in 1978 would expire in 1984.

The political landscape had also changed, both nationally and in Arizona, in the aftermath of the 1982 elections. Reaganism was in place, and with it a sea of change in the concept of what government ought to be doing. The proactive involvement of the Arizona State government came to an end with the election of Republican Governor Evan Mecham and his successors. Mecham fundamentally did not believe that government had a role in promoting policies having anything to do with supporting alternative energy sources. He felt that there was no role to be played for a Solar Energy Commission and sought to shut down the office in the name of budget reducing. Once again, John Wesley Miller played a critical role in our story. He traveled to Phoenix and, as a fellow Republican, was able to convince Mecham to keep the Commission alive and operating. It goes without saying that if the Commission had been closed, the funding that Babbitt had endowed it with for the development of the Solar Village would have disappeared into other departments and agencies. As we shall see, this critical funding covered the costs of the Solar Village's evolution over the next decade, and aided in Civano's as well.

In Tucson, the mid-'80s also saw a serious real estate crash. IBM came to Tucson to build a major manufacturing facility.[1] A boom in housing occurred that was mainly filled by local and regional builders. Unfortunately, just a few years later, IBM announced that it would close the manufacturing facility and move out of town. This precipitated a collapse in housing construction, and housing values quickly followed. The collapse hurt most local builders badly and ingrained in many of them a focus on being very conservative in tracking market demand. Builders who had been more adventuresome in creating new housing types and in promoting innovation were especially hurt. "Innovation in housing" became a concept deeply mistrusted in the Tucson home building community. The old focus on creating houses on the absolute lowest first cost basis regained dominance.

The idea of the Tucson Solar Village might well have died during this period. It did not for two reasons. First was Miller's intervention to retain the state funding. Secondly, the Metropolitan Energy Council kept the idea alive by continuing to promote it. This bought time until it dawned on some members of the Tucson City government that ideas embedded in the Solar Village initiative might offer interesting responses to the asymmetrical relationship of growth accommodation and infrastructure cost that we noted previously.

1 This facility would later become the University of Arizona Technology Park, an important regional incubator.

The City Steps In, Advocacy to Structured Concept Mid-1980s to Early 1990s

Rather than fading into the background, the idea of the Tucson Solar Village was repurposed and given new life and expanded through the intervention of the City of Tucson. City management and senior planning officials saw in the Solar Village concept the potential base on which to add additional components to explore a new model for accommodating growth, one with a lighter impact on infrastructure requirements and the environment. In essence, the City stepped forward to take over the previous State agency support for exploring the Solar Village idea. The government-sponsored Metropolitan Energy Council would continue to serve as a mechanism to organize public involvement and to channel state funding to the effort, but the City officials would now be more overtly involved in the management of future exploration of the idea. It was during this period that the old, advocacy-driven vision of the Solar Village evolved into a more structured outline for what would become "Civano, A Sustainable Community."

THE APPOINTMENT OF WILL ORR

In late 1987, the City was able to obtain the release of an additional $210,000[1] of the funding Babbitt had set aside for exploring the Tucson Solar Village concept. In November 1989, the Tucson City Council approved the use of this funding to hire a project manager to focus on evolving the idea of the Solar Village and coordinating the growing City involvement in its development.

In December, the City hired Wilson W. Orr to manage the evolution of the Solar Village. Orr taught sustainability courses at Prescott College, a well-regarded liberal arts institution in Prescott, Arizona, but he also had a business background and degree. His Prescott College credentials gave him credibility with the old Solar Village advocates. His business experience gave a sense of confidence among City policy makers that a greater degree of pragmatism would prevail as the project became better defined. Orr would be attached directly to the city manager's office. This allowed the project management process to remain outside of the established planning, review, and entitlement hierarchy of the City, while giving Orr the official backing of City Manager Tom Wilson and Mayor Tom Volgy. Given the goal of taking a very idea-driven concept and evolving it, this separation was to be a critical one. It was a tacit recognition that wherever the evolving Solar Village concept would go, offering an alternative to standard sprawl development would inevitably challenge existing zoning and building code standards. At the same time, reporting directly to the city manager gave the project manager some political clout within City agencies.[2] With a City-designated manager in place, the State Solar Energy Office began to release an additional $500,000 to fund the development of the Master Plan and Feasibility Studies the State Land Department had mandated as a requirement for setting aside the aforementioned 818 acres.

A Request for Proposal for planning services was sent out, and the proposal of Wayne Moody (acting in concert with and as the local representative of P&D Planning) was selected for the work. Moody was a former director of planning for the City of Tucson and had been deeply involved in the earlier "visioning planning" for the Tucson Solar Village. Moody advocated, and Orr agreed to use, a planning process built on a concept of "continuous consensus." This was described as "a method to assure that all stakeholders have the opportunity, ability, and encouragement to both shape and participate in achieving the objectives of the Solar Village design."[3]

FINDING AN IDENTITY THROUGH PUBLIC REVIEW

Orr considered the following as the key "official" participants in the new planning process:

- Metropolitan Energy Commission; specifically, the Solar Village Steering Committee of MEC
- Southern Arizona Homebuilders Association members
- City of Tucson Staff
- Pima County Staff
- Arizona State Solar Energy Office
- Arizona State Land Department

In addition to these "official" participants, Moody and Orr brought in experts from various disciplines. An economist was included to begin to give some financial shape to the vision. Sim Van der Ryn, who at the time enjoyed an international reputation in architectural design and its relationship to natural systems and was teaching at the University of Arizona, was included in the team of participants as a consultant.

A key part of the "continuous consensus" endorsed by Orr and Moody was going beyond "experts" to bring the general public into the discussion of what the Solar Village should and could become. Quoting Orr from a January 1990 interview in the main local paper, *Tucson Citizen:*

> "Workshops, review meetings and surveys will allow the public to offer opinions on transportation, density, jobs, energy costs, water use, solid waste management, open spaces, wildlife, recreation and affordability... Basically, our drawing board is blank right now. In the coming months, we'll be relying on the public to help us define this community and the performance standards for the community."

The first of these public workshops took place in March 1990. There would eventually be about sixty held, continuing into 1991.[4]

This emphasis on creating a broad and continuing public participation was a critical change in the sense of "ownership" of the project. Previously, a small and dedicated group had been its advocates, initially aided mightily by the office of a very sympathetic governor. Now, as increasing public funding was being used, it was important to create a demonstrable sense of public interest in and support for the concepts embedded in the Tucson Solar Village.

A great benefit of this lengthy public participatory review process was that it made the Tucson community aware of the ideas being promoted. The public process did not focus on figuring out the financing for all the proposed ideas. This made it much easier to develop a "shopping list" of laudable goals which could attract broad support. Public officials, academics, members of the general public, and focused advocates all found something to like.

A critical demonstration of this general support was the City Council agreeing to rezone the designated project land. The *Tucson Citizen* predicted, as

1 Nichols, page 48.
2 Nichols, pages 71, 44, 40–41, and 113.
3 Orr 1991 Report, pages 12 and 14.
4 Bauer, page 296.

A series of concept and planning maps developed in 1992 under Wayne Moody's direction. The first three are from the original design guidelines and show general concepts. The last three were part of the submission to the Arizona State Land Office and refine the general concepts into the first true master plans.

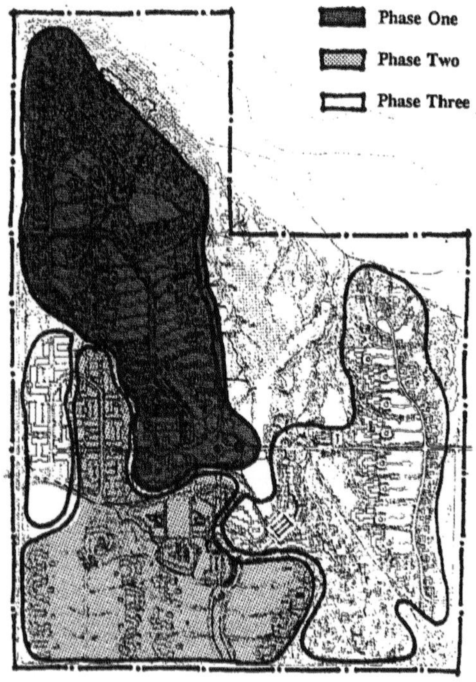

The three phases or neighborhoods plus a village center.

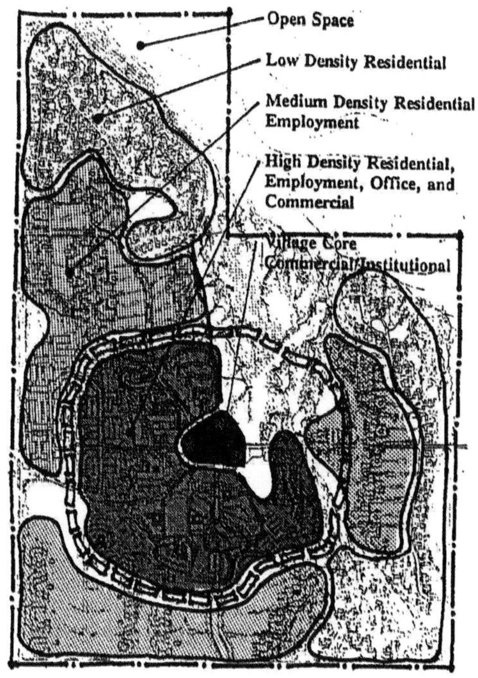

Varying densities, with the highest density around a single "village center" which has migrated to the center of the project.

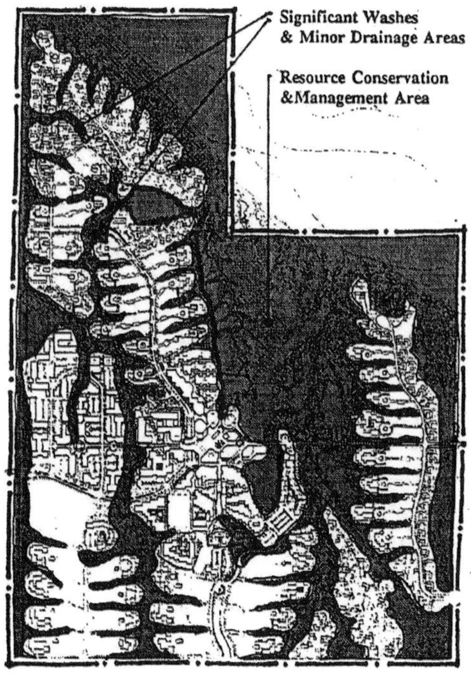

Land to be set aside.

the City Council vote approached, that "unlike private developments, this government-sponsored project is expected to sail through the rezoning process." (*Tucson Citizen*, 8/8/91) And the other local paper, the *Arizona Daily Star* noted: "Developers of the Solar Village were given cheers seldom afforded private developers who go before the City Council..." (*Arizona Daily Star*, 8/8/91) In October 1991, the City Council approved rezoning of the land along the lines recommended by Orr and Moody. Clearly, there was popular support for exploring some alternative to standard sprawl development.

A NEW NAME AND AN EXPANDED PURPOSE

Responding to the overwhelming sentiment expressed in the public planning sessions, a new name was chosen for the project: "Civano, A Sustainable Community." This critical shift in focus and in name reflected a broad desire for a true exploration of what sustainability could mean in the context of an anti-sprawl development program. This shift opened the project up to truly address the asymmetrical development challenges facing the City, as discussed previously. The shift also reflected the concurrent evolution of thinking about how to address the energy use and growth accommodation challenges facing America. One specific focus could not be the answer, but rather a more complex, holistic view was needed, one that looked at social, economic, and even political factors. Only then could a sustainable model of development for suburban growth be generated.

A FIRST PUBLIC REPORT

The input from these meetings, along with associated research paid for by City and State funds, was collected and published in the following reports:

- Market Analysis Report (P&D Tech; 1990)
- Environmental Resource Report (Wayne Moody; Planning Center; 1991)
- Services Impact Study (Wayne Moody/PC; 1991)
- Marketability Report (P&D; 1991)
- Energy Resource Analysis (Wayne Moody; 1992)
- Master Development Plan (Wayne Moody/PC; 1992)

For the first time, a more structured shape and form was given to the Solar Village, along with some consideration of how it might fit into the local housing market. The Services Impact Study began to craft an *economic* argument for pursuing the idea by quantifying the reduced infrastructure impact of a more environmentally friendly growth accommodation model.

In November 1991, Orr authored a report on the Tucson Solar Village work for presentation to PTI, a national policy advocacy institute funded by a consortium of City and County governments. This organization had supplied grant money to help defray some of the management costs for the "visioning process." This report can be considered the first full public summation of the planning and analysis work done by Orr and Moody.

THE FIRST PUBLIC DEFINITION OF GOALS AND PERFORMANCE TARGETS

In the report, Orr lists his understanding of the resource conservation and energy saving performance targets that came out of the visioning process:

- Reduce energy consumption by 75%. This reduction would be measured against the average energy use of a house designed to meet the 1991 standard energy code then being used by the City. Further, balance the community carbon budget by offsetting CO2 emissions with the installation of an architecturally integrated, utility-owned photovoltaic system.[1]
- Reduce potable water consumption by 65%, in part by using reclaimed water for outdoor irrigation uses and indoor toilet flushing.

1 A reason for the inclusion of this requirement was the State's recommendation that the four regulated utilities operating on Arizona produce 19 megawatts from renewable sources by 2000. This was later changed to a mandate that these utilities generate 1.1% of their electricity from renewable sources—with half of that coming from solar—by 2007.

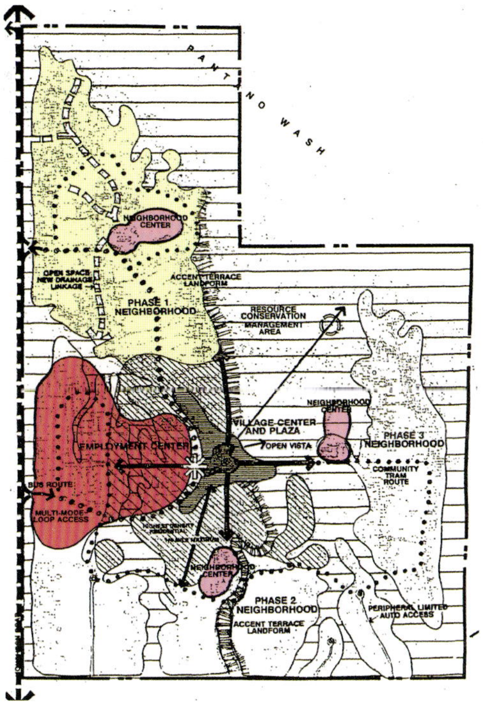

The evolved concept map, showing a town center, three neighborhood centers, and a more detailed residential and open space layout.

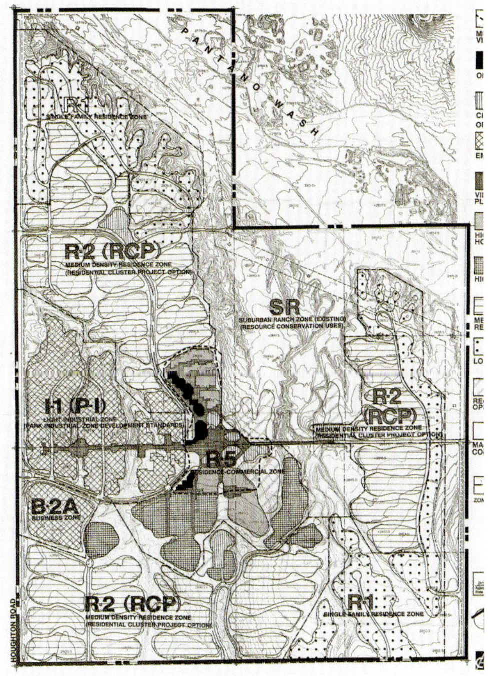

Attempting to overlay existing zoning onto the plan. Moody realized that this would be a problematic process and stated the need for a special zoning district.

A first attempt at thinking about lot and road layout.

- Reduce solid waste by 90% through aggressive reduction, reuse, recycling, and composting programs.
- Reduce air pollution by 40%, primarily by reducing vehicle pollutant sources.
- Create one new job for every two housing units built. Develop a business center within the central community with pedestrian/biking accessibility.

Curiously, an affordability goal was not included. Except for that one exception, this list can be and should be seen as the first emergence of what would become the Civano environmental and development protocols.

Orr argued that these were "standards that *no one* (emphasis ours) could object to." While one could readily agree with Orr that the standards are laudable, many of them at the time of the report were virtually impossible to achieve because of regulatory and even political opposition (decreasing potable water use by using gray water strategies, for instance); or financially infeasible at the time (the use of PV to generate residential power); or had a visionary zeal quality (developing an employment center based on the "build it and they will come" philosophy of financing).

Orr's report contained as an appendix Wayne Moody's final report on the "visioning process." It is Moody's report that was attached to the approved 1992 site plan rather than Orr's version. An examination of Moody's report, entitled "Civano Final Development Plan," reveals in its details subtle but critical differences with Orr's presentation. Here are the performance targets as identified on Page 22 of Moody's report:

- Energy: *Passive solar design, conservation, and efficiency* will reduce internal energy needs by 75%. Solar energy systems (grid connected) *shall* supply the internal energy required by this community on a net annual basis.
- Water: Residential consumption *shall not* exceed 40 gallons per capita per day. (The average for Tucson was 112 gallons per capita per day.)
- Solid Waste: Landfill-destined residential solid waste *shall* be 75% lower than the Tucson 1989 average at project startup and 90% lower at 50% occupancy.
- Transportation: Internal circulation *shall be* pedestrian, bicycle, or *(with a permit!)* electric golf cart. For external transportation, the following apply:
  - A. Air Quality
    1. Employment vehicle trip miles per capita *shall* be 40% lower than the 1989 Tucson average.
    2. Electricity *shall* be used as the motive energy for 40% of the local trip mileage.
  - B. Energy-Electrical motive energy *shall be:*
    1. Solar sourced, or
    2. Grid supplied, off-peak
- Employment: One job within the community *shall* be generated for every two residential units built. The average wage *shall* match [by which the authors believe Moody meant *shall* be able to support the financing on] the average cost of housing.

Orr's report emphasized *"working to achieve"* the performance goals envisioned for the project. Moody's articulation puts an emphasis on declarative limits: that often-used word *shall* with its connotations of demand. At the most general level, this distinction represents an important philosophically different approach to achieving the evolutionary goals envisioned for the project. The idea of "working to achieve" implies flexibility and inevitable compromise in achieving a goal. Taking this approach, along with Orr's statements noted above, it is clear that Orr saw the evolving Solar Village as an experiment that would need time to test its various concepts and components. It would move forward in phases, each phase learning from the previous one. This friction between a more flexible approach to exploring and achieving project goals, and a more mandatory and prescribed statement of them would endure as the project continued to evolve over the next years.

VISION OF THE BUILT ENVIRONMENT: THE FIRST MASTER PLAN

This new visioning process contained the first planning maps for the community. A preliminary version was approved by the State Land Administration in March 1992, and then modified and expanded later that same year. On the two previous pages are a series of preliminary and then evolved concept maps presented to the State Land Department.

The last three more refined plans lack much detail, but do show a general disposition of land uses that would remain a constant throughout the evolution of the project. Though giving a general feel for how the community would be laid out, there is little detail that would give a sense of how the built components of the future community would work together.

Notable is the middle plan on page 27. It attempts to show how then-existing Tucson zoning codes could be overlayed on the future community. It is an awkward application of zoning codes that were created for a very different vision of community building. Moody ultimately gave up trying to fit existing zoning onto the new concept.

The last plan on page 27 suggests an initial idea of street and lot layouts. Notable is the dependence on cul-de-sacs. Even recognizing that this is a conceptual layout, it does suggest—and other documents support this interpretation—that Moody envisioned what was called a "garden apartment"/"parkland" type of community. This is a 1960s and 1970s planning concept in which connectivity, both vehicular and pedestrian, takes a back seat to placing houses in open, park-like, settings. Paradoxically, the lack of pedestrian connectivity in these types of communities often leads to increased car use.

THE FORM AND SHAPE OF THE LAND AND COMMUNITY: ACCOMMODATING PASSIVE SOLAR

An interesting feature of these early conceptual plans is that the schematic lot layouts do not appear to favor orientation to maximize passive solar generation: a core goal of the 1992 Solar Village vision. One of the enduring criticisms of Civano as eventually built out has been that it "abandoned the solar initiative" by compromising home orientation for utilizing passive solar strategies. This is an idea promoted by many of the Solar Village's early advocates and has been accepted as truth in much of the published work about Civano. Specifically, the adoption of New Urbanist planning protocols is cited as "forcing" the lot sizes and orientation in such a way that it precluded passive solar and optimal implementation of active solar. However, a careful examination of Moody's own assumptions demonstrates that a strict adherence to land planning that fully utilizes passive solar strategies could never really have been a significant part of the Tucson Solar Village concept.

Moody's report contains an accounting of acreage allocations for the proposed land uses, and it bears careful examination. Of the 818 acres of project land, the report assumes 50% will be left as open space; 7% will be taken up by streets; 10% is set aside for the planned Neighborhood Center and other commercial and retail; leaving 33%, or 270 developable acres, for all residential components. Moody assumed 2,527 housing units of all types be built on this remaining land. Simple math indicates that, with these assumptions, a pro-rated per housing unit allotment of land of about 1/10th of an acre. However, Moody's report assumed a broad mix of housing types, specifically: 1,400 single-family homes, some detached and some attached. 137 townhomes were allocated 238 acres. This equates to roughly 0.15 acres per unit. Additionally, 697 apartments of all kinds were allocated 57 acres, or roughly 0.08 acre per unit. Assuming the majority of these apartments would be in two-story buildings, we could say each "stacked unit" would be allocated 0.16 acres. Going to a height of four floors—the standard walk-up height—would yield 0.32 acres per "unit stack."

However one sifts the proposed number and type of residential units—including a contemplated residential highrise—optimal passive orientation for the vast majority of the homes contemplated in Moody's report would have been difficult, if not impossible. The size of the land was just too small, especially after taking into account the proposed open space and land needed for even a minimal street system. Short of having a greater number of residential towers and low-rise residential buildings to accommodate a very large portion of the planned program, the proposed density articulated in the report all but precluded a massive application of ideal passive solar orientation. It would be appropriate to say, then, that from this early point on, the planning goals for what would become Civano all but precluded maximizing passive solar for every home. It would be fair to say that this was another demonstration of the cutting of connections to the old Tucson Solar Village in favor or a broader concept, a concept still focused on alternative energy but in the context of a broader social agenda.

THE NEED FOR SPECIAL ZONING FOR AN EXPERIMENTAL PROJECT

Moody stressed the need to create a Specific Plan going forward. These special zoning overlays could create new zoning guidelines for defined areas, which were new to Tucson planning. This is a critical moment in Civano's history, in that it recognizes that no manner of shifting and modifying Tucson's existing Land Use categories could achieve the goals of the project. Instead, an entirely new zoning and land use overlay covering all manner of development standards would need to be in place prior to the beginning of the implementation of the project.

THE LOOK AND FEEL OF THE COMMUNITY

Moody also created the first Design Guideline as a component of the Tucson Solar Village Master Plan Study. The version approved with the plan was meant to be a catalytic document—one that would be further developed and enhanced over time.

This guideline is a compendium of thoughtful observation on how to modify buildings to mitigate the demands of desert living. However, there is little in Moody's report that shows how to achieve a physical framework—both horizontal and vertical—in which the uses contemplated for the project would exist. The guidelines are silent on the subject of the formal relationships between built elements. The encouragement to use vernacular home designs noted in Kessler's 1982 memo is only indirectly addressed. There is no mention of the idea of creating a hierarchy of roads and travel ways, or about the relationship between homes and public buildings and the streets and public spaces they face.

COMMUNITY COMPONENTS AND ECONOMIC FEASIBILITY, THE FIRST INVESTIGATION.

Moody included in his report the first financial modeling based on a clear set of assumptions about the Tucson Solar Village. An examination of these assumptions, both general and in the details, is illuminating. Moody contemplated the following:

- The phasing of the project into three neighborhoods;
- Provision for additional land set aside for recreation;
- An assumption that 2,500 homes would eventually be built;
- Provision for a community school;
- A Visitors' Center, which would also be the welcoming/sales center;

- A Conference Center and Hotel;
- A Village Center with 250,000 sf of retail and commercial;
- An Industrial Park, with approximately 750,000 sf of commercial and light industrial space.

These components would, for the most part and in varying form, remain as program for the Civano project—and the living community it has become—to this day.

The schematic financial projections showed an assumed development cost of around $38 million, and a projected project income to the developer (over sixteen years!) of $29 million, *leaving a $9 million shortfall.* The total land development cost was assumed to be about $35,000 per acre, this at a time when the norm in Tucson was closer to $19,000. The financial projections assumed dwelling units in the Tucson Solar Village would cost between $100,500 to $176,000, this at a time when the median price of a home in Tucson was $97,500. Daunting assumptions to put before a private-sector developer thinking of implementing the Solar Village!

THE FIRST SUGGESTED ENERGY CODE AND THE EVOLVED ROLE OF METROPOLITAN ENERGY COMMITTEE

Concurrent with all of these developments, by the end of 1992, the Metropolitan Energy Commission had developed a "Model Energy Code" which they hoped would be adopted by the City of Tucson as the code used to measure compliance with the energy reduction goals of the newly named Civano, and eventually for the entire city.

This proposed code built on the then-current ASHRAE-created US Model Energy Code. It was prescriptive, and it took what is called a "building shell" approach. That is, energy-saving measures were focused on making the exterior envelope of a building as tight as possible and energy efficient. Little or no credit was given to the integration of tried and true vernacular responses to the Sonoran Desert climate, and there was no attempt to measure impact of the overall planning of the community in which a building was located. The proposed code was specific to each reviewed structure, and no thought was given to how a group of structures, if mindfully designed, might help decrease energy consumption.

There is no doubt that the Model Energy Code was a significant step forward from the then-current Tucson building code in terms of its addressing energy efficiency. It provided builders and designers a predictable way to achieve energy savings. However, one can say that the thinking that went into this suggested code had not made the same conceptual leap that the policy change represented by changing the name of the project from the Solar Village to "Civano, A Sustainable Community" had. The "building shell" approach of the code really demanded no fundamental rethinking of residential land planning. It just provided guidance on how to make a typical production house more energy efficient. Its focus on the single building and ignoring the larger street, neighborhood, and community scale really did not invite any consideration for a new approach to land planning that might create both energy-efficient and human-scaled communities.

It is notable that the 1992 model energy code was not formally adopted as a requirement of the Solar Village/Civano standards, though it was *tacitly* recognized as a recommended path for designers. It would not be until mid-1998 (when the Memorandum of Understanding was formulated between the City and the implementing private-sector developer) that a version of this code would be formally adopted as a requirement for the future Civano. It is our belief that the City wanted to leave open a broader path for designers to achieve the building energy savings anticipated for the project.

THE FIRST FORMAL GOVERNMENTAL ADOPTION

By the end of 1992, both Tucson's City Council and the State Land Department had reviewed and accepted the new Master Plan that came out of the public review process. The now named Civano's new stated goal, as it was announced on the City of Tucson's official website at the time, would be to: "demonstrate the marketability of sustainable community development on a large scale at affordable prices."[1] The older focus on solar of the Tucson Solar Village had become, officially from the City's perspective, just one of *many* components of the newly named Civano project. It was a critical component, no doubt, but no longer the driver of *all* aspects of the "sustainable community" vision.

SUMMARY

This was a remarkable and formative period in Civano's history. In two short years, after the City took the lead in formalizing the "visioning planning" of the Solar Village, much had happened:

- The stated purpose of the project had shifted significantly and its goals had been expanded and, to a degree, codified;
- There was an approved Master Plan; and
- There was an acknowledgment that the approved plan would need further work to address the project's goals.

The legacy of this two-year-long public planning process would reverberate throughout Civano's future development. Critically, the process gave a quantifiable definition of what the Solar Village would try to accomplish and laid the groundwork for the eventual set of measurable goals—the IMPACT Standards, about which much more later—that would become the guide for Civano's development. The long public planning process had created a sense of excitement and broad, general support for the project. This in turn had laid the foundation for the City of Tucson to begin to get serious about providing public support and investment for the project.

We would submit that the most impactful legacy of this planning process was to move beyond the singular solar focus of the history of the Tucson Solar Village. The idea of the Solar Village had moved from the advocacy of a small group, to a very public visioning process, to a total rework of its intent to include social and broad economic goals. With that, the newly named Civano, A Sustainable Community could become integrated into the City of Tucson's growing set of policy initiatives to address the challenges of containing sprawl. The components of the project had been identified, if not refined. Perhaps as important as any other achievement during this period was framing the Civano project as a multi-part experiment in a new approach to growth accommodation, an experiment in which each part would incorporate the lessons of the previous part.

1 Bauer, page 297.

The City Takes Charge, Concept to Policy Initiative 1994 to 1996

From the end of 1992 and for the next two years, the newly named Civano project was managed through the City of Tucson's Energy Office. Several Requests for Proposals were sent out to attract developer interest but without success, and frankly, the project languished. It was because, even from the most optimistic perspective, it seemed economically challenging. Anyone reading through the financial modeling done in 1992 would notice the $9 million gap in return as against costs. Will Orr had moved on, and there was no one person attached to the project within the City government to act as an advocate and catalyst.

NEW LEADERSHIP, NEW PURPOSE

Things began to change in late 1994. With Tucson's growth now accelerating and with it an ever-increasing demand for infrastructure expansion, City Council member Janet Marcus introduced a motion directing City Manager Michael Brown and City staff to "aggressively pursue" the expanded Civano initiative. Brown then assigned John Laswick, working under Deputy City Manager Luis Gutierrez, to assess the market and financing prospects for the Civano project and report on the feasibility of the project. Laswick had been a part of the City's Office of Economic Development and had recently returned from a sabbatical to earn a master's degree from Harvard's Kennedy School of Government. Laswick would focus on analyzing market demand and creating more complete financial models to motivate the City to consider providing financial support. He would also be tasked with evolving and codifying the performance goals for Civano. In early 1995, Brown created the Office of Special Projects, reporting directly to the city manager and headed by John Jones. Its primary responsibility would be to push the Civano project forward. Jones was an experienced and highly respected urban planner with a track record of getting things done within both City and County governments. He was recognized as a "can do" consensus builder able to break through institutional barriers. John Laswick eventually moved to the Special Projects office. Jones and Laswick made an effective team, united by shared traits of tenacity and a deep interest in finding innovative ways to address Tucson's growth challenges. (See portraits on following page.)

CREATING THE IMPACT STANDARDS: EVOLVING AND CODIFYING CIVANO'S GOALS

The critical first focus of Laswick's efforts was creating a more clearly delineated set of project environmental and social goals, all in the service of clarifying and better describing how to achieve the set of "performance targets" delineated in the 1992 Master Plan Final Report. Laswick formed an advisory committee that was given the charge to reformat the performance targets so that they were both "exemplary and feasible."[1] The City also stressed that the Committee's final version for the standards should "encourage innovation... through application of a range of techniques, rather than detail prescriptive standards that appear cumbersome or regulatory."[2] The old tension between exploratory flexibility and mandated means was coming to the fore again.

In organizing this effort, Laswick sought to address three key criteria relative to the standards:

1. They had to respect past ideas and initiatives, going all the way back to Kessler's original 1982 memo. At the same time, the goals needed to be re-examined to consider the current realities of the marketplace, based on new market studies for this novel type of community.
2. They needed to be aggressive, *but* achievable by a private-sector developer. Even with support from the public sector, in the end it would be the private-sector developer, working in the marketplace, who would be responsible for the project becoming a reality.
3. They had to be measurable but there would have to be flexibility in understanding how they would be achieved over time. Some, like building homes that met a certain energy use standard, could be measured on a house-by-house basis from the first moment. Others, like creating the employment envisioned for the project, could only be achieved over time.

Laswick advocated openness in considering how to achieve the goals. For example, rather than prescribe a process of designing a house to meet its energy use reduction goals, Laswick advocated precisely stating what the reduction target should be and then giving future developers and builders latitude on how to achieve that target.

This approach, supported by the members of the Advisory Committee made up of builders and environmentalists, encouraged experimentation and consideration of time-tested vernacular materials and home designs to decrease energy demands. This more open approach facilitated the City's approval of the proposed standards.

The final product of the Jones-Laswick effort was the *IMPACT* (Integrated Method of Performance and Cost Tracking) Standards. In October 1995, the IMPACT Standards were adopted by the City Council and became the official environmental and social performance targets for Civano. They were attached to the 1992 Master Plan, superseding the goals noted in the 1992 report. This version of the IMPACT Standards—with minor revisions and clarifications—would remain in place until they were revised in 2003, as part of the Civano project being split into two entities—but that is getting ahead of the story.

A standard-by-standard review, comparing the IMPACT Standards to the 1992 performance targets is illuminating:

REDUCTION OF ENERGY DEMAND

This goal was radically redefined. The old 1992 target of a 75% reduction in residential energy use was abandoned as being too aggressive and adjusted to 65%. A baseline from which to measure this reduction was defined: the 1990 average Tucson home energy use. A standard of 55% reduction for non-residential buildings was also introduced. The 1992 targets had never articulated any difference between residential and non-residential uses.

The final IMPACT Standards took a more open approach as to how energy savings could be measured. A suggested goal was achieving an average

1 Mayor and City Council Memo, Civano Performance Targets, page 2, 10/2/1995.
2 Mayor and City Council Memo, Civano Performance Targets, page 2, 10/2/1995.

John Laswick

John Jones

per-person per-year energy use in homes of 20,000 BTUs/sf/year, as compared to the then standard home average of 64,000 BTUs. The new standards were completely silent on how that energy would be produced, and encouraged builders and designers to explore how to achieve the energy savings.[3] Having said that, the IMPACT Standards did state that, "as a goal," the use of photovoltaics and solar thermal power generation was to be encouraged and emphasized, but their inclusion would be expected over a period of time. Importantly, the standards recognized that an aggressive implementation of solar strategies was a shared responsibility among the developer, the builders, local utilities, City agencies, and even the eventual Civano Homeowners Association. However, it would not be until 1998, in the drafting of a Memorandum of Understanding between the City and eventual developer outlining exactly how each of the IMPACT goals would be met, that the use of solar was explicitly stated as a requirement, though it was in the context of a broadly defined "beneficial use," a term selected to preserve the flexibility of the original IMPACT Standards.

WATER USE

The new IMPACT Standards called for a 53 gallons per-person per-day residential use goal, as compared to the norm of 114 gallons at that time. The new standard again made a distinction between residential and non-residential users by also setting a standard of 15 gallons per day per employee, but with case-by-case reviews for special needs and businesses. For the critical issue of irrigation, the new standard called for a maximum of 28 gallons per person per day for exterior use. Swimming pools were allowed, though discouraged by reducing the overall exterior water use budget. The developer would be required to provide community pools to offset the demand for private pools. Irrigation demand would be reduced by the aggressive use of natural drainage patterns, where possible. The project would promote xeriscape strategies and the use of native desert vegetation. Whatever its provenance, all landscape irrigation would be by non-potable water, and the project would incorporate access to Tucson's reclaimed water system.

This new IMPACT Standard did not differ that much from the old 1992 performance target in the degree of use reduction aimed for: 53 gallons per person per day versus 114 gallons.

REDUCTION IN CONSTRUCTION SOLID WASTE CREATION

The overall goal of waste reduction was readjusted to 30% of waste at the onset of the project but increasing to 60% once 1,250 residences had been built. The 1992 performance target had been 75% at start-up, and 90% once 50% occupancy was achieved. This adjustment was made in large part out of the recognition that Tucson simply did not have an existing recycling structure in place.

TRANSPORTATION/AIR POLLUTION REDUCTION

This new IMPACT Standard retained the old 1992 40% reduction in Vehicular Miles Traveled (VMT) but expanded the means by which that could be achieved. The 1992 performance target called for mostly prescriptive methods of achieving this goal. Two examples: all travel within the community would be human powered, with the exception of "permitted" electric golf carts; and energy used for off-site travel would be reduced by 40%, with the balance of energy used being solar generated or off-peak.

This new IMPACT Standard first noted that achieving this goal would be difficult in the early years of the project. This was a simple and honest recognition that the location of the project land on the far edge of Tucson would necessitate a higher VMT than desired. It further noted that no public transportation to the site existed or was planned. Given these realities, this IMPACT Standard called for:

1. Inclusion of commercial services from the outset of the project, with those services within walking and biking distance to most of the residences;
2. A general encouragement of pedestrian activity by creating a "pedestrian friendly" community;
3. Advocacy for extending City bus service to the project; and
4. "Consideration" be given by the developer and community HOA to the adoption of the California Clean Fuel Vehicle standards.

This last point bears some further commentary. One should question just how a private developer could mandate, much less enforce, adherence to a governmental clean fuel standard. The only thing the developer could do is to suggest and perhaps lead by example by installing electric charging stations and the like. Having said that, it must be noted that at this time Tucson Electric Power, the local utility, was building charging stations for General

3 Mayor and City Council Memo, Civano Performance Targets, page 3, 10/2/1995.

Motors EV2 electric cars, and CNG-powered fleet vehicles were becoming a common sight to see. There was some precedence for the private sector and Tucson Electric Power taking serious steps to explore alternative fuel sources for vehicles. Nonetheless, this part of the IMPACT Standard's articulation is in our view a departure from the more pragmatic tone brought to bear on the other standards.

What is extremely significant, and would have a lasting impact on the project, is how the Laswick memo on this proposed standard suggested that a "pedestrian friendly" community must be achieved. The memo called for the avoidance of cul-de-sacs in favor of a hierarchy of "through streets," a complete system of sidewalks and bike paths, designing non-residential uses with predominately non-vehicular access, and the provision for mixed retail and commercial uses from the beginning of the project buildout. The memo directly called for cooperation from the City Planning and City review agencies to help create a "concentra[tion] of high-density development and urban activities" in conjunction with Civano. And it urged the local public transportation agency, Sun Tran, to consider extending a bus line to Civano and locating a planned East Side Transportation Center be placed in or near Civano.

JOBS/HOUSING BALANCE

This new standard called for either the creation of 300 sf of non-residential space per every two residential units built, or the 1992 standard of one job created for every two residential units. As with reducing VMT, the new standard suggested a variety of ways to achieve this. For example, credit would be given for in-home offices, clearly anticipating and supporting the idea of a strong live-work vision for the homes built in Civano. By offering an option of square footage per house built, recognition was given that a developer can build a space but cannot guarantee that there will be a job to use it. Critically, the memo noted that city zoning would need to be modified to support this.

HOUSING AFFORDABILITY

The importance of achieving all the other IMPACT Standards, while maintaining affordability was once again made a key component of the project. The inclusion of affordability as a separate standard served to re-emphasize the City's stated goal of Civano being a model that would "demonstrate the marketability of sustainable community development on a large scale at affordable prices," a model that could be transferred to the larger residential production industry. The new standard recognized that the projected home prices for Civano would work for the middle home-buying market in Tucson but would be difficult for the lower-middle and working-class potential buyer. Accordingly, it set a goal of 20% of the "eventual total" number of all dwellings being designated as "affordable." Affordable was defined as being a house that someone earning 80% or less of Tucson's median income could afford. The memo called for a periodic review of this standard, with adjustments being made at 25/50/75% of buildout.

A GROWING EMPHASIS ON LAND PLANNING TO ACHIEVE CIVANO'S GOALS

Laswick brought David Butterfield to Tucson to be a member of the IMPACT Standards advisory committee. Butterfield was a Canadian developer who had done several well-regarded and resource-conscious projects in his hometown of Victoria, British Columbia. (See pictures on page 35.) He also was planning a small new community, Bamberton, that mirrored many of Civano's goals. He brought a valuable private-sector viewpoint to the evolution of the IMPACT Standards. As we shall see, Butterfield's role in the future of Civano would become larger and more critical to its implementation. For the moment, Butterfield's critical contribution was to make Laswick and Jones aware of the New Urbanism movement, and how its approach to land planning and community design could help achieve the project's goals. With Butterfield's urging, an exhibit was added to the draft development agreement: a document explaining "TND/Neo-traditional Planning" for the project's civil engineering. There was little in these guidelines that addressed the relationship of buildings one to another, to civic spaces, or the network of streets and pedestrian passages. Nor was there anything giving any guidance to building typologies, or a hierarchy of recommended densities within a neighborhood. Though far from a New Urbanist document, it pointed in a similar direction, and it was a departure from standard subdivision street design. Critically, this document, combined with some of the suggested means of achieving reduced VMT, further acknowledged that the form and details of the physical planning of the community would be important ingredients in achieving the IMPACT Standards and creating a model for sustainable growth. It seems clear that, at this critical juncture in Civano's evolution from the old Tucson Solar Village, a new and deeper emphasis was being put on how the built form of the community would, in itself, contribute to meeting the IMPACT Standards.

TWO STUDIES THAT BUILD GROWING OPTIMISM ABOUT THE FUTURE OF CIVANO

Two studies were published in 1995 that added to the growing momentum for the project. Jones and Laswick were able to convince the State Energy Office to approve funding for a formal market study to determine whether a market even existed for the concept of an affordable "sustainable community." Petersen, Jacuzzi & Green, a highly regarded mainstream Phoenix-based residential marketing research firm, was engaged. Their initial findings were very optimistic, with projected sales as high as 200 homes per year, competitive with any housing development in Tucson. Their preliminary survey reports found that well over 50% of surveyed homeowners found Civano's proposed features appealing, and a substantially higher percentage would pay more for a house that had them, especially if the energy savings offset some of that added cost. Their 1997, more extensive and segmented surveys of potential and likely homebuyers in Tucson supported these initial findings, if at somewhat lower percentages. This was strong evidence that the buying public was looking for an alternative to the standard choices the market offered. There were nuances and qualifications to these projections buried in their reports; chief among them was the fact that Civano would have to capture an extremely large percentage of its target market home buyers to meet that 200-a-year sales goal. However, for the moment, these reports provided an invigorating boost for the project's stakeholders.

A financial study by Laswick showed that the Civano approach to growth accommodation presented compelling cost benefits for Tucson, and for that matter, any local government. These studies indicated that the City could realize nearly $500,000 (1995 dollars)[1] in avoided infrastructure costs per year over the life of the Civano project. This detailed cost-benefit analysis created a context for advocating—at the governmental level at least—a compelling fiscal argument for Civano. This also was a good political advocacy point: decreased infrastructure costs could translate into a lower community tax burden, or potential funding for community amenities such as parks and improved services.

Together, the new market study and Laswick's financial analysis created dual advocacy platforms beyond anything that had been developed for the

1 Laswick, Benefits and Costs of the Community of Civano, 1996.

project previously. The encouraging sales projections from Petersen, Jacuzzi & Green had a special impact. If this level of sales could be achieved, that nagging $9 million shortfall in the old 1992 Master Plan Study pro forma seemed less ominous. That figure represented 18% of the projected land development budget of roughly $50 million. Sales at the level the Petersen, Jacuzzi & Green studies projected exceeded anything imagined before, and promised a stronger cash flow into the project could decrease, if not entirely erase, the old project shortfall.

The details of these two optimistic reports were of less importance to some Civano supporters, both in the City and among the public, who seemed to believe that this financial gap would somehow be bridged by an "enlightened" developer, who would pursue Civano's every goal regardless of cost. This expectation would ripple through the future of the project in subtle but important ways. It would lead to painting some future pragmatic development decisions as diminutions of Civano's goals, rather than painful financial choices required to address the 1992 mandate to "demonstrate the marketability of sustainable community development on a large scale at affordable prices."

A FRAMEWORK FOR DEVELOPMENT & RECOGNITION OF THE NEED FOR PUBLIC SUPPORT

To balance the requirements that the future developer would have to meet, along with their costs, the City began to think through a draft development agreement that would codify the responsibilities of the City and State in an effort to counterbalance some of those costs. This effort harkened back to Will Orr's statements that any project with all the goals and requirements being demanded of Civano would need public support. The draft development agreement proposed the following:

- Construction by the City of approximately $3 million in road and reclaimed water infrastructure in Neighborhood One. Additional financial help for infrastructure work by creating a Municipal Improvement District in part of Neighborhood One. This later mechanism allowed these costs to be a loan attached to the home purchase, rather than having the developer pay for them.
- Implementation of a building program for education and training in energy-efficient construction. This would become the Civano Institute, about which see more below.
- Agreement to request an Arizona Energy Office grant for a Sustainability Resource Center. This later became a $300,000 grant to cover the cost of the use of a variety of alternative and sustainable building materials in the Neighborhood Center. (See pages 150–151.)
- Agreement to grant the developer an option to purchase 325 acres across Houghton Road for the expansion of the Civano site at a future date. The eventual signed agreement would note that the incorporation of this land was, in the selected developer's opinion, essential for the overall financial feasibility of the project.
- Future issuance of a $4 million bond for a park/community center after 1,000 homes were built.
- Various measures to offset the cost to the developer of the required Neighborhood Center.
- Expedited review and approval by City Planning and Zoning agencies.
- City help in bringing employment possibilities to the project.

These were tangible commitments that added to the more aspirational hopes embedded in the 1995 Petersen, Jacuzzi & Green market study and Laswick's financial research. Obviously, the timing of each commitment would vary, and most would be dependent on the developer's ability to create and stay on a project schedule.

One effort that began in this period was the creation of the non-profit Civano Institute, whose mandate it was to facilitate education about more energy efficient and sustainable building practices among Tucson's builders, contractors, developers, and potential home buyers. As such, the Institute was carrying forward the long history of community involvement in the project, while attempting to help implement the new Civano protocols. Jones and Laswick were able to secure a $300,000 state grant for its initial funding. It was staffed by Doug Crockett, an energy specialist on loan from the Tucson School District, and Eileen Alduenda whose efforts would be focused on developing a design guideline for Sonoran Desert-appropriate buildings. (See bibliography.) Throughout 1966–1997, the Institute built awareness of Civano at a time when there was limited public visibility of its progress. The Institute was also an important bridge to the Tucson architectural and builder community, especially the alternative builders. The City and developer hoped that the Institute would also provide much needed on-site training for the builders in Civano, a hope that would be frustrated by the confluence of delays on the development side, and funding continuity issues on the Institute's side.

IMPLEMENTATION BEGINS

In October 1995, with Jones' guidance through the politics of the City, a new strategic plan for Civano was approved in concept when the Tucson City Council approved the IMPACT Standards detailing the specific performance goals for the project. In February of the following year, the City would issue a final RFP solicitation for the Civano project, with the auction for the set-aside land scheduled for June 1996.

The activity during this critical period marked an important transition of the Tucson Solar Village/Civano idea from an advocacy-based vision to a city policy. As a part of this transition, from this moment forward, all State and City funding would be channeled through the City and the Special Projects Office, rather than through the Metropolitan Energy Commission. For over sixteen years, this volunteer commission had dedicated their support for and given guidance to the evolution of Civano. The Commission's role now reverted to what it had been originally, that of an advisory body, without any managerial or implementation oversight. A detailed market study had been done showing that there was demand for the "sustainable community" concept. New Urbanism had been brought into the project as a potential planning protocol.

We should note that all of this was taking place in a larger political context that was markedly different than during the Tucson Solar Village days. The Clinton/Gore administration was in place, and a new and more proactive attitude towards addressing environmental issues, led by Al Gore's leadership within the administration, was emerging. Within a year of the Civano land auction, the administration would be announcing its Million Solar Rooftop initiative and begin formulating what would become the Partnership for Advanced Technology in Housing (PATH) program. Both programs mirrored important aspects of the Civano initiative, and their coming into being helped support the legitimacy of the project. All of this presented a hopeful context for the long-awaited implementation by a private-sector developer of Civano into a living urban development reality, a reality that would create a model for environmentally sensitive and traditional neighborhood development, preserve desert open space, and provide measurable savings to the City in infrastructure costs and ongoing public service delivery expenses.

HORIZON 4

The Handoff to the Private Sector Mid-1996 to Mid-2002

(opposite, left) David Butterfield on the right, leading a community event in one of his developments.

(opposite, right) David Butterfield, first developer of Civano

In February 1996, the City issued a Request for Proposal solicitation to qualify for and participate in the auction to be held in June for the 818 acres set aside for Civano. Only two companies replied: David Butterfield's Trust for Sustainable Development (TFSD) and Arizona Public Service, one of the three large Arizona power generation companies.

As part of any Arizona State Land Department sale, an independent appraiser must set the minimum land value for the public bid. As one can imagine, this appraisal was subject to considerable debate. On the one hand, the State Land Department sought the highest justifiable estimate. On the other, given the estimated $9 million financing gap in the then project pro forma, the City hoped to have the State Land Department establish the lowest reasonable valuation. Laswick worked with the appraiser to ensure that he fully understood the requirements of the IMPACT Standards. As a measure of just how ambitious the development requirements for Civano seemed to a conventional real estate expert in 1996, the appraiser asked Laswick if he realized that "it would be possible to assign the land a negative value." The appraiser's reaction shows the institutional bias against any development prospect that did not conform to standard sprawl development. An important corollary point is that, in the estimation of this experienced appraiser, innovative prototypes like Civano would require some form of subsidy to achieve financial viability.

There is also a "road not taken" story buried in the public bidding process. John Wesley Miller relates that David Case, who will be introduced in the next chapter, first approached Miller and Arizona Public Service about forming a development team to go after the Civano RFP. When APS could not come to terms with the City on pre-bid conditions, Miller made Case aware of Butterfield, and the two joined forces, but with Butterfield remaining in charge. The departure of APS left Butterfield/Case as the only bidder, allowing them to purchase the property at the minimum appraised value: $2.3 million. One can speculate on just how different Civano might have been if APS had been one of the development partners. The financial issues that plagued Civano almost certainly might not have happened. With Butterfield, a strong proponent of New Urbanism, as a partner, one can speculate that Civano could have happened with New Urbanist planning and design, but far better funded.

APS's interest possibly reflects that, in 1996, most large utilities were supporters of "alternative energy," especially solar. It was an infinitesimally small factor in energy generation, but it was good public relations. The public loved solar. As the price of alternative generation—especially wind and solar—came down over the next two decades, utilities began to see a threat to their monopolies on energy generation and distribution. APS is now considered to be a ferocious opponent of renewables—especially when owned by private users—and has been exposed financing the campaigns of candidates for the public utility commission who would support their position.

With a developer chosen, they and the City reviewed final revisions to the Development Agreement. Once terms had been agreed upon, the Agreement went to the Mayor and City Council for approval. That approval was far from certain. While the Council was quite progressive, two of its six members, who were ardent environmentalists, did not support the proposed Agreement. The primary reasons were its distance from the central city with its employment base, and Civano's middle-income market focus. The fact that there was no open land of Civano's scale any closer to established employment centers, and most jobs lay in a band about midway between downtown and the site helped, but did not erase the "distance from jobs" concern. The commitment to 20% affordable houses over the life of the project failed to sway one dissenter. After some tense debate, the motion to approve the Development Agreement and certify Butterfield/Case as the developer narrowly passed 4-3.

The sale of the land at the minimum "fair market" value and the fact that no bidding pushed it higher was significant. The winning bid equated to roughly $2,800/acre, or $4,000/acre of buildable land, if the mandated 30% open space set-aside is taken into account. At that time, buildable raw land on Tucson's far east side was valued at roughly $6,000–$8,000 an acre, resulting in an effective discount of at least $1.15 million to the developer, a discount that could be directly attributable to the development requirements for Civano. This discount was seen as another way that the financial challenges that had been implicit in Civano's planning from its conception were gradually being overcome.

Fifteen years after the Kessler memo first outlined the ideas that should be included in what would become the Tucson Solar Village, all the components were in place to begin making its evolved descendant, Civano, a reality. Land; a clear Development Agreement assigning public and private responsibilities; professional studies showing that there should be a strong market for Civano in the Tucson region; a committed private-sector developer; two exceptional City officials to help the project's passage through the regulatory and entitlement process: all these were in place. A public planning workshop, or charrette, was scheduled for September. Momentum could be felt, and optimism abounded.

And yet, not quite six years later, the last two neighborhoods of the project would be broken away, and the IMPACT Standards softened. All this, even though Neighborhood One, fully incorporating New Urbanism and on its way to meeting the IMPACT Standards, was showing sustained sales and growing success. A new builder/developer, Pulte Homes, would embrace sprawl production housing standards for Neighborhoods Two and Three. During those

six years, no less than six different entities had responsibility for managing the development of the project—a remarkable fact, the impact of which on the project was profound. Any development project of Civano's size would be negatively impacted by the frequency of management turnover Civano saw. In Civano's case, we submit that impact was leveraged by the special nature of Civano's history. Even if there had been one management group throughout the development of Civano, entitlement and development would have been a challenging process. What made this particular project so sensitive to the absence of continuity in the development process?

- Civano's long history and the legacy of open public planning lead to a sense of ownership by many parties. There had been nearly ten years of visioning, open meetings, and planning efforts. A broad coalition of people had been brought into contact with the project, and each left their contribution in their own time. Unfortunately, each step in Civano's evolution was too often seen as a diminution, if not outright abandonment, of the previous group's understandings and expectations. By the time that dirt actually started to be moved on the Civano site, there were many people who felt they were the holders of the true vision, even if they bore no responsibility for the emerging built reality of the project. While their adherence to a single issue or the concepts of the past may have been laudable, this limited focus was no longer in balance with the broader and more interlocked goals of the project.
- Lack of experience in developing a project like Civano. Civano was the first attempt to create a community of some 1,400 homes composed of three mixed-use neighborhoods to be planned and implemented with a combination of New Urban protocols and aggressive energy and resource conservation goals, and to be aimed at middle-market housing.
- Lack of experience in marketing a project like Civano at its scale. Contributing to this complexity was figuring out how to market a development that was so focused on new concepts like sustainability and the New Urbanism, concepts still emerging into the broad public consciousness. While there were other projects that incorporated some of Civano's environmental and social goals, none were of the same scale and none were aimed at the middle market, the province of production builders.
- The complexities of public/private partnerships. In this public/private partnership, like most, the public side formulated policy, and the private side was held responsible for implementing it in both its broad strokes and details. The policy makers and advocates were not constrained by the discipline and pressure of time, interest payments, and the search for financing. The importance of having both private and public representatives in a constant dialogue with each other, not just in times of crisis, took a while to learn.
- The limited financial resources of the initial development team.

A NEW SET OF EXPECTATIONS

With the Trust for Sustainable Development certified as the developer and the Development Agreement approved, a new era began: the project had entered the province of the private sector. With that passage came new expectations, some obvious and acknowledged, others more subtle and unspoken. The responsibility for "making things happen" shifted from the City to the developer. Along with that shift came expectations that key project goals and schedules would be met. It was the private sector that had the expertise to implement and build this ambitious community in the real world. The developer was dedicated to the core ideas of the project, experienced and respectful of people who had been involved in its history. For many of them, the moment had arrived when this evolving idea they had helped mold would become a reality, a place in which many of them wanted to live. They felt that the right developer was in charge, one who acknowledged past promises, real or perceived. In the following sections, we will track the constant changes in the composition and strategy of the development management team, focusing on the causes for those changes and the impacts they had on the implementation of the project.

It is important to remember Will Orr's admonition that this ambitious project was an ongoing experiment that would need to be adjusted in its early stages. It would be in the first neighborhood phase that the various ways to achieve Civano's goals would be explored. It was also during this phase that some of the key assumptions of this private/public partnership would have to be tested. Would the dual responsibilities, either stated outright or implied in the Development Agreement, be able to be implemented in the unforgiving and demanding world of the marketplace?

The Trust for Sustainable Development June 1996 to June 1997

Ownership Interest	**Lead Development Decision Maker**	**Lead Planning & Design**
David Butterfield; then Butterfield/Case Enterprises	David Butterfield; then Kevin Kelly & David Case	Wayne Moody

NOW THAT YOU HAVE WON THE AUCTION... THE SEARCH FOR FUNDING

In the months leading up to the June 1996 public auction, David Butterfield, knowing that he could not depend on his normal financing partners—primarily Canadian labor unions not allowed to invest outside of Canada—turned to venture capital sources. He found that they were interested, but their terms and expectations of financial return were onerous and simply unsupportable for this innovative project. Butterfield determined that he could self-finance only *the initial planning and entitlement* phases of the project. He began to search for a development partner that could bring additional financial strength to the project, and one that could also take the lead in day-to-day management.

In mid-1996,[1] he joined forces with Case Enterprises, a small Connecticut-based development company with a strong presence in Tucson as well. Case had many things to offer Butterfield. It had a solid development track record in historic rehab, urban revitalization projects, and a commendable record of developing affordable housing. The fact that Case Enterprises already had business interests in Tucson helped. Most important to Butterfield, Case also had established relationships with institutional investors. They could take the lead in raising development capital. Sadly, they quickly discovered that Case's institutional investors, like Butterfield's, were lukewarm at best. While they expressed admiration and general support for the Civano concepts, they were leery of investing in a residential development with so many innovative and untested aspects, and in a marketplace like Tucson, with "thin" demographics, as evidenced by the very low median income statistics.

Within months of the land auction, and as the project's design and planning was to begin in earnest, the expanded development team found themselves without a clear path for adequate funding for the entire project. Butterfield, Case, and Case's partner Kevin Kelly were left with using their personal funds and loans from a network of private individuals to cover the initial but growing costs of the project.

Three factors helped, to a degree, calm concerns. First, the Development Agreement provided financial support from the City for the early stages of the site work and guaranteed "expedited" reviews during the entitlement phase of the project. These promises helped support the view that, if the development team could just get through entitlements, funding would be more available for the early stages of site work. Secondly, at this early stage of the project, cash flow demands would be relatively low and could be covered by the internal funds the developers could raise. Thirdly, everyone was optimistic that the development time schedule discussed in the Development Agreement and with the City could and *would* happen. Within eighteen months, homes would be ready for sale. Once sales started, they would accelerate, generating cash flow for the project. This assumption was based almost entirely on the very positive and optimistic Petersen, Jacuzzi & Green market study. The obvious—but not openly considered—corollary to this thinking was how critical it would be to keep to this schedule, and how any delays could have financial implications.

PUBLIC PERCEPTION AND A SHARED VISION: JUST WHAT WAS THIS THING SUPPOSED TO BE?

Prior to joining with Butterfield, David Case was looking for a "legacy development project," one that would build on Case's established experience in small community development and his growing interest in issues of sustainability. He and his partner, Kevin Kelly, had been on a tour of innovative communities in the United States and had been especially taken by Seaside, Florida, the iconic and pioneering New Urbanist project. Their visit had an enormous impact on them, and they became converts to New Urbanist planning. To put it somewhat simplistically, Case wanted to do something as innovative as Seaside. Civano met those criteria, though overlooked was the fact that the complete Civano project was magnitudes larger than Seaside.

This shared conceptual framework for planning was an important connection that facilitated Case joining with Butterfield. Butterfield, Case, and Kelly understood that the "neo-traditional planning" requirement that had been attached to the Civano project was most compellingly achieved using New Urbanist protocols. The application of New Urbanist protocols would go far beyond the focus of the neo-traditional planning addendum, which was focused on horizontal planning and civil engineering. The addendum did not give any guidelines for the inter-relationship in three dimensions of all the built elements in a community. All three understood that the creation of a vibrant, compelling, and market-friendly community that would also address all Civano's proposed environmental and social goals would be easier to achieve using the concepts and planning protocols of the New Urbanism. And yet, events would soon test their commitment to a full New Urbanist planning and design agenda.

1 Bauer, page 296.

The Civano Charrette, September 1996. A meeting showing from the left: John Jones (City); David Butterfield (Lead Developer); Kevin Kelly (Case Enterprises); Unknown; Unknown; Wayne Moody (Consultant to Butterfield/Case).

LOOKING TO THE PAST AS A BRIDGE TO THE FUTURE: THE CHALLENGE OF PERCEIVED OWNERSHIP AND ITS CONSEQUENCES

As noted previously, it was John Laswick of the City's Special Project's Office who first identified Butterfield/TFSD as a potential developer for Civano. In the months leading up to and after the land auction, Butterfield publicly endorsed the then current goals of the project, as codified in the newly defined IMPACT Standards. However, he went beyond that, expressing a desire to maintain a strong continuity with the expectations of Civano's long history all the way back to the Tucson Solar Village days.

The consequences of doing so were subtle but important. We believe this created an expectation of an ongoing public "open planning" process for the project going forward, similar to that of 1991–1992. This expectation was buttressed by the number of working relationships the development team established with community advocacy groups and academics. Although these relationships were initiated with the intent of building on the experiences of these groups and individuals, many felt that there was an implied expectation of involvement in the continuing development of the project. All too often, they did not see themselves as experts to be *consulted* from time to time, but as having quasi-managerial oversight rights. Perhaps this is, on some level, understandable. Many of those contacted had a long history with the old Tucson Solar Village efforts. With some justification, they felt that their years of effort had kept the idea and project alive, and they were the guardians of the "original and authentic" vision. As such, it was up to them to remind "the newcomers" about original intent and push for its implementation. Lost on this group was the recognition of two inescapable facts. First, the original vision of the Tucson Solar Village never had any life other than that of an idea. Secondly, only with its reformulation into the concept of a "sustainable community," one promoted and supported by governmental agencies, had Civano begun to have a life beyond that of an idea.

A great signal of this desire to embrace the past of the Solar Village was the hiring of Wayne Moody to direct the entitlement and agency review process. Moody's long and deep history with the Solar Village made a strong and direct connection back past the current Development Agreement to the history of the Tucson Solar Village. Though never stated, and in spite of the fact that the new IMPACT Standards had modified the project's performance focus and metrics, among many of the "old TSV hands," there was an assumed reassertion of the primacy of the old solar agenda over the more nuanced sustainability goals of the IMPACT Standards and the Development Agreement under which the project would proceed.

It is our view that this well-intentioned engagement with local experts and advocates helped create a confusion about the identity for "Civano, A Sustainable Community," and even the rights of the development team to define and evolve the project's development protocols. This confusion would stubbornly persist through the following years. As Case Enterprises, and especially Kevin Kelly, became more deeply involved in the day-to-day management during this period of the project, they inherited these outreach efforts and expectations that Butterfield had established. At the same time, they began to bring a sorely needed discipline to the engagement with these groups and individuals. The first notes of potential limitations to their involvement and oversight that the project's implementation would require were struck.

This had the effect of creating a subtle friction between the more pragmatic needs of the project, especially as Case and Kelly became more visible, and the promises—explicit and implied—that many felt had been made before.

THE UNVEILING OF THE NEW ERA OF CIVANO: THE 1996 CHARRETTE

The charrette would be the first opportunity to announce the new directions that would be taken by the development team to fulfill the long history of the project and meet its current requirements. The development team wanted to gather all the possible commentary from legitimate stakeholders in the

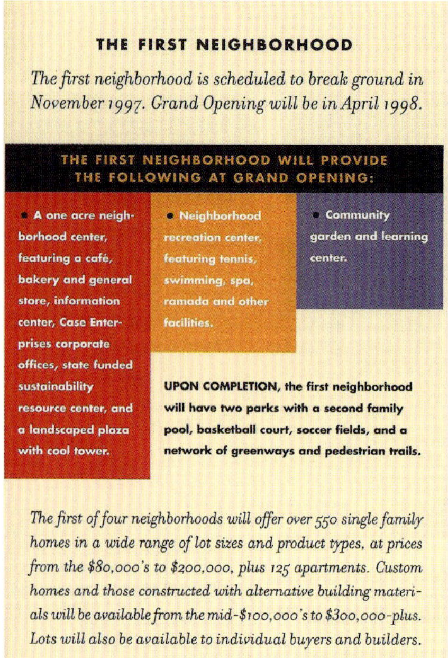

THE FIRST NEIGHBORHOOD

The first neighborhood is scheduled to break ground in November 1997. Grand Opening will be in April 1998.

THE FIRST NEIGHBORHOOD WILL PROVIDE THE FOLLOWING AT GRAND OPENING:

- A one acre neighborhood center, featuring a café, bakery and general store, information center, Case Enterprises corporate offices, state funded sustainability resource center, and a landscaped plaza with cool tower.
- Neighborhood recreation center, featuring tennis, swimming, spa, ramada and other facilities.
- Community garden and learning center.

UPON COMPLETION, the first neighborhood will have two parks with a second family pool, basketball court, soccer fields, and a network of greenways and pedestrian trails.

The first of four neighborhoods will offer over 550 single family homes in a wide range of lot sizes and product types, at prices from the $80,000's to $200,000, plus 125 apartments. Custom homes and those constructed with alternative building materials will be available from the mid-$100,000's to $300,000-plus. Lots will also be available to individual buyers and builders.

Section of a marketing brochure from late 1996. Note the optimistic schedule assumed for the project in the aftermath of the land auction. A grand opening was just a year away.

David Case

Kevin Kelly

project. After that, they would engage in a more efficient review and entitlement process: one that would not be open to the public.

Three design teams would participate. Two represented the forward-looking, new direction for the project, a direction in which New Urbanist planning and design would be the central organizing principle: Duany Plater-Zyberk and Moule & Polyzoides. The principals of these firms were founding members of the Congress of New Urbanism. Wayne Moody, with his long history going back to the Tucson Solar Village, would also take part.

The process of the charrette and what would come to be seen as its limitations are more completely covered later in this study. For the moment, it is important to note that there were two critical shortcomings in this charrette process. First, it was structured not to be as open and inclusive as a normal charrette. Only selected invitees could attend. This robbed the event of being the public announcement of a new direction in the Civano initiative. It also precluded active participation and commentary from the old Tucson Solar Village advocates: positive commentary which could have been accepted and negative commentary which could have been put to rest. Second, and perhaps far more critical, rather than create a master vision for all three neighborhoods planned for the Civano set-aside lands, only the first neighborhood, about 40% of the total land, would be addressed. This failure would have profound consequences in the years ahead.

Because of some fundamental differences in opinions about the design direction, the charrette package, created by Duany Plater-Zyberk, was not as complete as was the standard of practice at the time. This translated into delays in getting together a workable master plan for Neighborhood One, which in turn delayed the beginning of the review and entitlement process.

In the end and post charrette, Moule & Polyzoides was engaged to further evolve the master plan and produce a regulating plan that became the basis for the start of site engineering and the entitlement process. In a separate process, Moody started to work in earnest on the creation of the Specific Plan zoning for the project.

THE END OF THE BEGINNING

In June of 1997, David Butterfield suddenly announced to Case and Kelly that he would no longer contribute funding to the project, and frankly wanted to be bought out. He set the price for his buyout at about $1.468 million, basically what he had put into the project up to that point. If the buyout was not agreed to, Butterfield, as the development's managing partner, threatened to close the project down. Faced with this ultimatum, Case and Kelly agreed to Butterfield's withdrawal and his reimbursement. Thus, barely a year after the land auction, Case Enterprises found itself in a situation it had never anticipated. It was now the sole owner and developer of the project, and solely responsible for its financing. A principle source of funding was leaving the project and taking with him a significant amount of cash.

Looking back now, it can be argued that this moment in Civano's history was the genesis of many of the problems that would plague the project going forward. Case and Kelly had entered the project with the assurance that Butterfield would continue to be primarily responsible for funding through the entitlement phase. After that, it was assumed that bank loans would be enough to carry the project forward until site work was done, and the actual selling of houses begun. Based on Petersen, Jacuzzi & Green's market study, an assumption had been made that a high volume of home sales would generate substantial income from that point on. The prolonged post-charrette period—though not in itself that critical—was a preview of a series of delays that would wreak havoc with these assumptions of steady progress leading to funding.

Case and Kelly now found themselves facing a much larger and more challenging financial burden, having to commit to repaying Butterfield, a project cost that no one had anticipated. This would begin a constant and grueling search for sufficient and predictable funding that would eventually lead to a partnership with Fannie Mae, with many consequences to be discussed later.

The long-term financing of the project and the funding for its current work were becoming ever more complex challenges, with an increasing dependence on continuing short-term, higher interest loans from families and friends of Case and Kelly, and the principals themselves. Case and Kelly should be acknowledged here for the individual courage and commitment it took to continue despite the risks involved, and for putting their personal finances on the line for the project. Simply stated, without this commitment, Civano would have died.

It was an unfortunate time for the project to face this challenge. The entitlement process was beginning in earnest, along with civil engineering design and other City reviews. With that, it had begun to become obvious just how different the New Urbanist intentions of Civano's developers were from standard norms of development. With its multitude of planning and design concepts so different from "standard operating procedure," project reviews challenged the training experience of agency reviewers. The limitations of the promise of expedited reviews became very apparent.

The high optimism of the period immediately following the charrette had hit the solid wall of reality, and cracks in the structure of optimism so prevalent earlier in the year started to show.

Case Enterprises
June 1997 to December 1997

Ownership Interest	**Lead Development Decision Maker**	**Lead Planning & Design**	**Average Homes Sales per Month**
Case Enterprises	Kelly/Case	Wayne Moody	NA: Project under development

In the aftermath of Butterfield's departure, it was left to Case Enterprises to move the project forward. Critical Development Agreement deadlines were looming, deadlines that not only would allow site work to begin but were also essential for obtaining bank loans. Chief among those was getting the first phase of Neighborhood One entitled and having the Specific Plan for all of Neighborhood One approved by the City Council by late October.

In the aftermath of Butterfield's departure, Case and Kelly continued to rely on their own private resources. These short-term loans—providential as they were—did carry higher interest rates than standard bank loans, adding increased financial pressure to the project. They had been able to obtain a small operating loan, collateralized by the value of the land, from Bank One, but that institution was not willing to extend further loans. Finding lending sources was becoming a more insistent preoccupation for Case and Kelly as it would be impossible to start site work relying only on personal financial resources and short-term loans.

THE LIMITS OF PUBLIC-SECTOR SUPPORT

We remember Will Orr had rightly predicted that Civano would need public support and funding, and that it could be considerable. The Development Agreement addressed this with a long list of commitments to support the development team, among them two that were critical front-end supports:

- Contributing $3 million towards the installation of the sewer, water, and reclaimed water infrastructure. Another $2 million was granted to cover on-site utilities, but as a loan at an interest rate slightly lower than the then current commercial rates. A caveat of this support was that the City would act as the construction manager for all of this work.
- Agreeing to enter into a long-term lease for a significant part of the planned Neighborhood Center to be used as an East Side City office complex. There would be an assembly room that the City Council could use occasionally, along with City-related offices. The Neighborhood Center was a requirement of the Development Agreement, and this lease could significantly defray the costs of the Center's construction and operation.

It was during this six-month period, hard on the heels of Butterfield's departure, that some of those promises began to fade, and the details of these commitments began to be better understood; and with them some unanticipated issues for the development team were exposed.

While the City-funded infrastructure work brought critically needed funding, two downsides became evident. City personnel, acting as the construction managers, would bid out the work, adding a layer of cost. The management cost started as a 12% cost plus construction management agreement, at a time when 8% was more the common rate for this size of project. By the time this work was completed, the actual management fee approached 18%. The simple reality was that the "good" of the additional funding was partially outweighed by additional cost considerations. It was true that the City-covered costs were passed on to future home buyers as a second loan on a purchased lot in the first phase of Neighborhood One, relieving the developer of this cost. However, this complicated the sale of homes on those lots. The buyer would have to understand that there would be *two* loans for which they would be responsible: the mortgage they would obtain, but also their portion of the MID loan. This was another layer of complexity in a sales story that was already complex enough.

In August, it was announced that the City would not be leasing any space for an East Side City office complex in the Neighborhood Center. It had become clear that the optimistic schedule projections of 1996 were not going to happen. An East Side City complex was desperately needed, so another site was chosen. The income from renting the facility to the City—which could have been the earliest of the income streams into the project—could be forgotten. On top of that, there were added costs to change the design of the Neighborhood Center due to this new reality.

Throughout this period, as site plan reviews were underway, the limited reality of "expedited reviews" became ever more evident: they just were not happening. So much of what the development team wanted to do in pursuit of new urbanist planning was entirely new to the review staff, or worse, contradicted what they had been trained to accept as "the right way to do things." Just two illustrative examples:

- The proposed site plan had alleyways, lots of them. These were essential to the site plan concept and encouraging pedestrian life in the community. Alleys allowed car and service access to the house from the rear. The fronts of houses and their adjacent sidewalks were uninterrupted. Because you did not need a driveway taking up some part of a house lot, those lots could be narrower. These two factors created a more inviting pedestrian realm along the streets. However, alleys had been all but bled out of Tucson's zoning by the 1960s. It was enormously time consuming to get them reviewed, much less approved. In the end, they were, but as "non-conforming" streets, an unsatisfactory solution for all parties.

- A very important goal for the development team was utilizing xeriscape landscaping concepts. This is an approach to desert landscaping that emphasizes, among other things, catching rainwater where it falls and then letting it percolate down into the soil where it can nourish plants. Simple enough, and a potentially important part of meeting the reduction in water use requirement. However, the standard water absorption calculations that reviewers used assumed that home lots had the same absorption value as a concrete surface. Thus, the only way, by code, that rainwater could be accommodated was getting it off the home lots, to the streets, and from there into a variety of expensive site engineering elements whose purpose it was to get the water off site or just hold it until it evaporated. Water was treated as a waste product, not as a revitalization product. However favorably a reviewer might personally view the xeriscape approach, their review was wedded to then current code. This was another time-consuming struggle that delayed reviews, and sadly it was a struggle the development team lost for most of Neighborhood One. In later phases, things changed.

No matter the good intentions and efforts to make a reality of the promise of "expedited reviews," the City's reviewers—and for that matter the developer's consultants—were caught in a web of established standard sprawl subdivision codes and requirements. Whatever the commitments made in the Development Agreement and at the upper echelons of City government, the rank and file reviewers were being asked to review and approve land use concepts very different from their training and experience. The overlay of a Specific Plan only added to the complexity of the task. It would take time for the adoption of new ideas to work their way into the review process. It also can be said that with Butterfield's departure, there were doubts about the survivability of the project, abetted by a period of internal confusion among the Developer's staff about its direction. Reviewing agencies and their employees were that much less open to taking risks in approving site engineering that might never be built.

We should note at this juncture that the developer's two main site engineering consultants, civil engineers MMLA and landscape architects McGann & Associates, were critical allies throughout the entitlement and review process. Though their companies had grown successful on standard development practices for the Tucson region, they became dedicated students and advocates of the new planning protocols to be implemented in Civano. Critically, they became bridges between the developers and the reviewers. Their established local reputations gave them a credibility and trust that the new-to-the-area developers had not as yet gained. They were essential in the eventual common ground that was created around the project.

EXPLORING HOW TO ACHIEVE THE PROJECT GOALS AND PUBLIC PERCEPTION

Some of the tensions of the charrette between adherents to the history of the Solar Village versus those embracing the chosen New Urbanist path for planning re-emerged with Butterfield's departure. Moule & Polyzoides, designated to take the decisions of the charrette forward into the land planning effort, had been excluded from the initial civil engineering and master planning work. This exclusion was in part due to the simple need to keep costs down after the departure of Butterfield. But it also reflected a tentative embrace of the New Urbanist character of Civano, a factor that will appear again, and a theme we will explore more elsewhere in this book.

Then there was the complex task defining just what a "sustainable community" would be. At the time of writing this book, this would not be a difficult task, there is a wealth of thoughtful—and usually largely overlapping—definitions for sustainability. Its core protocols and components are generally recognized. In 1996, this was hardly the case. The concept of "sustainability" was emerging beyond a relatively small group of academics and advocates into the broader public marketplace of ideas. While there may have been a consistent academic understanding of the concept, there was great disagreement about exactly what it entailed in the harsh realities of "real world" implementation.

In Civano's case, there was the added challenge of achieving the sustainability goals, while staying within the rigorous mid-market price structure that was a part of the project's core concepts. Would the perfect compacting toilet from Australia be specified for every house—at a cost nearly triple of an American water-saving toilet? Would all the trees in Civano be food-bearing trees? If so, who would harvest them? Sorting out the *perceived perfect* answer to these and hundreds of other like questions exposed a fault line between old expectations, and the pressure to find *good* solutions that met a pragmatic balance between cost and achieving the various project goals. This friction had several consequences that would impact the project. First, the confusion around a clearly stated vision of the protocols for Civano's development was another subtle factor that slowed the City agency review process. Agency reviewers, already reluctant to step out of their professional comfort zone, were simply less likely to do so without being offered a clear and compelling technical reason. Secondly, without a clearly articulated set of protocols for accomplishing the IMPACT Standards, especially the energy reduction goals, the old Solar Village advocates and their allies, the Metropolitan Energy Commission, stepped in to fill the vacuum by promoting the "thermos bottle" approach to energy reduction as the primary standards by which efforts at Civano should be measured. As noted earlier, this approach looks at a building as a shell, in which actions are taken to achieve energy savings, primarily for heating and cooling. It does not take into account tried and true vernacular responses to heating and cooling, much less the way that internal spaces can flow into external mitigated spaces not requiring energy at all for heating or cooling.

Ideally, the summer of 1997 would have been spent on drafting and refining the Specific Plan (the zoning overlay document for Civano)—a fuller design guideline that tied back to the work of the 1996 charrette—and even creating a first draft of the Memorandum of Understanding which detailed just how the many interlocking responsibilities of the Development Agreement would be implemented. Sadly, during this unfocused period, none of these critical documents was pushed towards a final draft.

From an internal financial management point of view, money was pouring out the door without a clear sense of purpose. Scarce financial reserves desperately needed for design and entitlement work had been expended on searches for ideal expressions of sustainability. There was also a period of several months while Kelly was in the hospital that the very nature of what the project was trying to be wandered. Was it really a co-housing project? Should it emphasize aging in place? Once Kelly was back in the key management position, efforts and funds were redirected and refocused, but time and money had been expended on dead ends and frankly peripheral explorations.

In August, Lee Rayburn joined Case as Director of Design, and part of his portfolio was to manage the review and entitlement process. Through an intense effort and just plain diplomacy and engagement with the reviewing staff, concerns at the City were addressed and lessened. He also brought Moule & Polyzoides fully back into the ongoing design and site engineering work on the project.

Fortunately, as 1997 entered its last quarter, critical tasks had been accomplished for the project. The first tentative plat was approved by the City Council, and site work could begin. Simultaneously, the Specific Plan for Neighborhood One was completed and approved by the City Council. With this zoning document in hand, the review process in various City agencies became easier and less time consuming. Progress was being made on the design of some of the model homes and the Neighborhood Center.

With the approval of the first tentative plat and the Specific Plan, Bank One agreed to a small increase in its loan, enough to keep things going, but not for long. By mid-fall, the development team was in a constant state of crisis in terms of finding money to cover the increasing cash demands of the project. Whatever other progress was being made, the search for funding overshadowed everything and had become an almost monthly—if not weekly—challenge. The principals of Case Enterprises had come to the limits of what they and their small network of private investors could personally put into the project. The Bank One loan was only enough to cover the initial stages of construction costs. It is not an overstatement to say that the project would have ground to a halt if a substantial equity investor was not found and found quickly.

THE AMERICAN COMMUNITIES FUND AND FANNIE MAE COME ON THE SCENE

In what seemed to be a providential event, Case and Kelly were introduced by Fred Dreyfus, a senior administrator at the Department of Energy, to the key managers of the American Communities Fund of Fannie Mae. As most people became aware of later, in 2007 and 2008, Fannie Mae was a federally chartered private company whose original purpose was to buy up mortgages made by others. In so doing, they in effect guaranteed these mortgages. That is, banks and other entities knew that, if they chose not to keep the loan themselves, there was an entity that would buy it—as long as it met certain guidelines established by Fannie Mae. Fannie Mae was granted a number of special privileges by its charter, chief among them very considerable relief from paying corporate taxes. Fannie Mae justified this relief, and aggressively protected it, by stating that these special considerations were required in order to successfully fulfill its primary roles: to promote home ownership by as many Americans as possible and to encourage innovation in housing.

The American Communities Fund, which had been created in 1996, was at the vanguard of Fannie Mae's innovation efforts. They typically became secondary and passive equity investors in projects that would have positive economic impact on communities, or that demonstrated innovation in housing concepts, but simply could not attract enough traditional financing. Civano certainly met those guidelines! Case Enterprises represented the type of small, innovative developer that the Fund looked for: a company doing a project in which attracting the support of Fannie Mae could make the difference between the project going forward or collapsing. In hindsight, perhaps the fact of one giant, highly politicized institution, the Department of Energy, introducing another giant, highly politicized institution, Fannie Mae, to a small company focused on innovation should have given pause. It did to some, but that pause was overridden by the prospect of financial salvation for the project.

As the discussions began with Case and Kelly, the American Communities Fund/Fannie Mae were promising things they could bring to the project beyond desperately needed funding. There was the idea of "energy-based mortgages" and other home financing products that would recognize that energy-saving homes provided more day-to-day liquidity for families, liquidity that could be used to buy a larger home or to help underwrite a mortgage for a more financially challenged family.

The advantages of a relationship between American Communities Fund and the Civano project appeared to be obvious and many. For Fannie Mae, becoming involved in Civano would be a good story about housing and community development "innovation" that it could present to Congress during its periodic reviews of how well Fannie Mae was fulfilling its charter and justifying their special status. For Case Enterprises there were enormous—even stunning—advantages. This small development company, which had not been able to get its traditional financial partners to invest in Civano, could now claim the cachet of having one of the largest financial institutions in the world as its partner. To say that this would provide the project—and its developer—a magnitude of legitimacy would be an understatement. To say that Fannie Mae's involvement in the project would give the City of Tucson a huge sense of relief that the current financial instability of the project was about to become a thing of the past, was an almost immeasurable understatement. Finally, this alliance would give Bank One, the only bank willing to support the project, confidence to extend a much larger line of credit.

By early October, a general agreement was reached between Case Enterprises and American Communities Fund on a very advantageous combination of a large equity investment and smaller loan package for the project: in all, about a $5 million infusion of funding. With the critical City Council approval vote on the proposed tentative plat for the first phase of Civano just days away, the timing could not have been more providential. Optimism was justifiably high within the development team and the among City officials. All that remained was a final review and approval by Fannie Mae's central investment committee.

It had been observed that the American Community Fund was much more entrepreneurial than Fannie Mae as a whole. The leadership of the Fund was socially conscious and relatively activist by nature—a subtle but highly important difference from the more conservative and institutional general leadership of Fannie Mae. In late September of 1997, this seemed an interesting organizational observation, but little more than that. In early December, the importance of the difference between the American Communities Fund and the broader culture of Fannie Mae became starkly apparent, as did the first inklings that maybe this marriage made in heaven would have some darker undertones to it. When finally acted on by the executive investment committee, the original commitments agreed to had changed dramatically. Rather than the promised $5 million in an equity infusion, $3 million *in total* was approved, and $2 million of that would be a loan at a market-plus Interest rate. The remaining $1 million would be an equity investment, but with Fannie Mae gaining a 16% ownership position in the project. Yet another layer of debt, and another "interest clock" was added. Critically, an institution that was just about as different as could be from the development team now had an ownership position. This would have growing consequences.

Entering into reasoned conjecture, one could speculate that the Fannie Mae lending committee pulled back on the initially promised, and much larger, equity funding because they reflected Fannie Mae's institutional culture and the concerns and biases of its board. Fannie Mae as an institution and its individual board members were deeply intertwined with large national builders and the post-WWII dominant sprawl development. One can reasonably imagine their likely reluctance to become too deeply involved in a model of development which was attempting to be the antithesis of that well-established growth model, a model which had brought considerable wealth to Fannie Mae.

Whatever the motivations and regardless of the diminished commitment, this cash infusion was welcome and critical to the project's continuing. Without it, Civano would have come to a halt by the end of 1997. The passage of time would yield a deeper understanding of just how different the development team's expectations were from those of Fannie Mae.

Funding was received just as the New Year began, and with the funding, Fannie Mae became a partial owner. There was much to celebrate: site work had just begun, critical entitlement approvals had—despite odds—been obtained, financial stability seemed to have been achieved, and schedules were being made and met.

Case Enterprises/Fannie Mae 1998

Ownership Interest	**Lead Development Decision Maker**	**Lead Planning & Design**	**Home Sales**
Case Enterprises (84%); Fannie Mae/American Communities Fund (16%)	Kelly/Case	Rayburn	NA: Project still under development

HIGH HOPES AND NEW ENERGY

The year 1998 was a pivotal one in Civano's history. Site work would begin in earnest and the first phase of Neighborhood One would be completed by the fall, bringing 125 lots online, about a fifth of all lots planned for Neighborhood One. Builders would be signed on and a variety of home plans would be created. By the end of the year, the first model homes would be started, and construction on the Neighborhood Center would be well underway. (See image opposite.)

For the first time the project had what appeared to be a dependable source of financing. Fannie Mae's infusion of cash had been quickly followed by Bank One agreeing to a larger line of credit for the project. All parties believed that, with site work picking up pace, the projected income stream from sales of 100 to 200 houses per year—the rate that the Petersen, Jacuzzi & Green market studies had projected—would guarantee a steady stream of funding into the project.

BUILDERS

The first months of 1998 saw the signing on of the home builders. They were, along with their primary reason for wanting to build in Civano:

- KE&G, headed by Karol George, a very well-established regional homebuilder. Geroge wanted to build in a project that emphasized quality building and community making.
- Bednar Homes, headed by Ted Bednar, a smaller, well-regarded local builder. Bednar saw an opportunity to learn new building techniques and liked the emphasis on building homes that had a strong regional character.
- RGC Homes, headed by Jim Murrar, was an award-winning California-based builder. Murrar was attracted by the emphasis on building affordable, energy-efficient homes.
- Frog Mountain Homes, headed by Gail Marsland, one of Tucson's best-known advocates for solar energy and an established, if small, custom home builder.

It is notable that the project attracted this diverse and significant group of local builders who in their collective intent reflected the core goals of Civano. Kevin Kelly would, in 1999, also create First Homes to build homes stressing alternative materials as a pathway to more energy-efficient and healthier homes.

A RELATIONSHIP BETTER UNDERSTOOD

In February, Fannie Mae's initial cash infusion, some $3 million in both equity and loan funds, arrived in the working capital account of Case Enterprises. Almost as quickly as it came in, it flowed back out to cover outstanding debts and to pay down the short-term "mezzanine" loans that had just barely kept the project going up to now.

Along with that cash came the qualifications the development team needed to acknowledge and accept as a condition to that investment. There were twenty-two pages of them. Among the qualifications was language discouraging the use of the following words and concepts in the marketing of the project: sustainability, environmentalism, and New Urbanism. This was a "suggestion" that the development team decided to honor by ignoring it. Another requirement was the signing of four production builders within three months. On the surface this did not seem unreasonable. After all, site work was underway, and two builders—KE&G and RGC—had committed verbally to coming into the project. However, the need to *quickly* sign up additional builders and lock in their lot option agreements had several subtle but important and lingering consequences. First, the builders' contracts were set long before a full set of project design documents were in place. Had they been, they could have been made part of the contract. As it was, the development team spent a lot of time and money getting the builders up to speed on the core design concepts of the community. Any attempt to create the regulating documents so vital to a project like Civano was delayed or just outright diminished, partly out of budget concerns and partly out of fear of "asking too much of the builders." What had originally been a deficiency largely due to a lack of resources became a deficiency of commitment increasingly institutionalized in the project without the development team quite realizing it.

As the year went on, the development team would continue to learn exactly what a partnership between a highly innovative and entrepreneurial small developer and the nation's (then) largest financial institution would look like.

A NEW TREND EMERGES

Within a month of this initial cash infusion, the development team found itself once again facing a looming cash shortage. Old short-term debt and lingering bills had been retired but had claimed virtually all the Fannie Mae cash. The costs of planning and entitlement work were higher than had been budgeted for, and it was just taking longer to get the work done. Horrific construction weather had plagued attempts to get the site work going for the first phase of

CIVANO[SM]

UPDATE | Case Enterprises TUCSON ARIZONA | MARCH '98 No. 3 http://www.civano.com

Civano salvage tree storage – see page 4

FANNIE MAE JOINS CIVANO PARTNERSHIP: A HARBINGER FOR GROWTH IN SUSTAINABLE LIVING

The world's largest diversified financial company, Fannie Mae, announced that it will join Case Enterprises as co-owner of the Civano[SM] community. "...Over the last 6 months, we've talked to leaders all across the country to determine how important this kind of development is," explained Linda Davenport, managing director of the Fannie Mae American Communities Fund. (continued on page 7 – Fannie Mae)

Building Begins

(above) The Neighborhood Center under construction, early spring 1998. The Center, organized around a central courtyard, incorporated a variety of "alternative" building materials. In the lower image, straw bale is shown, while the gray building is being constructed of Rastra blocks. The upper image shows the use of fired adobe for what would become the Welcome Center and meeting facility at the Center.

(left) A quarterly information newsletter announcing Fannie Mae becoming part of the development effort. These newsletters were sent out to a growing list of potential buyers interested in Civano and to media outlets in the run-up to sales beginning.

Neighborhood One, creating cost overruns and pushing back the point that houses could be built by three months.

In late February, Kelly made a forceful presentation for additional funding to senior Fannie Mae management, and they agreed to increase Fannie Mae's initial equity in the project. In some ways they had little choice; more funding was needed if the project was to move forward. There was one caveat: the additional cash influx would be in the form of a loan that would require eventual payoff and would accrue ongoing interest payments. The interest pressure on the project just continued to grow.

Throughout 1998, Fannie Mae would continue to increase its funding of the project, and by the end of the year, it had reached a total of $4.525 million, approaching twice what they had originally approved. With that increased financial support came increasing oversight, both from the American Communities Fund and from the Fannie Mae central board. It is fair to say that from this period on, the project became as much about managing Fannie Mae as trying to get it built. This was the moment that marked the entry of the impact of *institutional ownership* into the Civano project. With that came all the demands and expectations of a giant financial institution, one that had a deep and wide relationship to many of the major companies wedded to the status quo of production building and subdivision-based sprawl.

The rippling effects of this growing presence were many and important. Not all of them were bad. For instance, Fannie Mae brought in the national consulting firm The LaSalle Group to study the varying project phasing and sales assumptions to understand what Fannie Mae's exposure might be in a worst-case scenario. The study was telling. For the first time, a realization was dawning that the project—and thus its income stream—might drag out far beyond what had been imagined in the heady days of 1996.

The combination of the focus on LaSalle's pushing a much more cautionary set of assumptions about probable sales rates, and Fannie Mae's realization that there would be continuing pressure on them to bring more funding to the project, led to a consistent questioning of the project's commitment to its New Urbanist vision. To both Fannie Mae and LaSalle, New Urbanism represented the untried, in stark contrast to the dependably consistent standard "cookie cutter" sprawl development they knew and could easily quantify and predict. That the latter had virtually no relationship to the stated—and mandated—goals of the project seemed a fungible point to Fannie Mae.

All of this created an increasing and escalating tension with David Case. This friction came from two critical factors. Case was a "big idea" person if ever there was one. He had entered into the Civano project for a combination of motives, financial and deeply personal. With the growing presence of Fannie Mae, he saw his vision slowly but increasingly becoming enmeshed in their institutional realities. Beyond this conceptual dissonance, Case also saw that Fannie Mae's increasing involvement would slow the project down. As the principal *private* investor, project slowdowns impacted Case more than anyone else. Case became increasingly the odd man out in the tense management discussions between Case, Kelly, and Fannie Mae. He was finally forced out. Fannie Mae purchased his ownership share in the project, with payment partially in the form of an ownership interest in the area that was

Construction in Phase 1 of Neighborhood One, Early 1999 Models

A variety of building materials other than standard wood framing were tested in the first phase of Civano, and their advantages publicized. A combination of limited availability, uncertain supply chains, and substantially higher cost limited their use. The logistic demands of a large project and keeping within the price parameters mandated for the project simply overwhelmed the development team's attempts to make these materials more of a standard for home construction. Nearly all homes in Civano ended up being constructed of wood framing. It was hardly standard construction, though. Better construction detailing and joinery combined with constant testing ensured significantly better performance.

(from far left)
Upper: Two rowhouse models from the Neighborhood Center being constructed of Rastra block. Rastra block, as seen in the right image, is a large block made of recycled plastic material and concrete. Hollow cores inside the block can be filled with concrete for strength.
Bottom: A model being constructed of recycled steel framing and a model being constructed of SIPS: Structural Insulated Panel System.
This page, upper: A model being constructed of straw bales. The bales are made of a special type of straw that can be compacted and holds virtually no moisture. This is a rigorously modular system of construction.
This page, bottom: Three models grouped together. From the left: one made of standard wood framing; one made of SIPS; and at the right edge, a model being built of Rastra block.

slated to eventually become the Town Center. With his departure at the end of the year, the second of Civano's original development partners had left the project, with this departure a forced one. Fannie Mae was now the majority owner of the project. Kelly remained the managing member of the newly aligned ownership team, but with the ownership percentages skewed so much in Fannie Mae's direction it would be unrealistic to expect for them to remain passive partners.

There was one other disappointing development. The general master plan for Civano envisioned a town center, and the Development Agreement called on the developer and City to cooperate to create "employment centers" in and around Civano.

High hopes had been raised about the possibility of creating employment centers at an early stage in the project. Global Solar, a solar panel manufacturer, opened in the fall of 1997. Civano Nursery started operations in 1997 at the entry into Civano along Houghton Road, the major highway which formed the western edge of Civano. Their presence in what was then largely empty desert landscape helped fix in the public's mind Civano's location. Importantly, each of these enterprises reflected an important aspect of Civano's goals. It was hoped that more like-minded enterprises would be drawn to the Civano area.

With City support, from mid-1997 and into 1998, the development team contracted with Cornell University's Work and Environmental Initiative, a consultancy that offered assistance in marketing innovative and purpose-driven commercial, retail and light industrial centers. With their national scope, it was hoped that they could bring more businesses like Global Solar and Civano Nursery to Civano.

Despite eighteen months of focused effort, a reluctant but direct conclusion become inescapable. The market demand just was not there to support the concept. The University of Arizona had purchased the abandoned IBM manufacturing plant about 5 miles to the south of Civano and was aggressively promoting it as a "technology center" and business incubator. Whatever demand there was for commercial or light industrial space was sucked into that complex. At the same time, there simply was not enough residential development in the immediate area to support much, if any, significant retail presence.

This episode put a spotlight on an aspect of the Civano project that many of its supporters did not want to fully acknowledge. Civano existed in the realities of a market: it could not create those realities, most certainly not on its own. Minimized in the excitement about Global Solar and Civano Nursery, was the fact that each of these enterprises was heavily subsidized: Global Solar by its owner, Tucson Electric Power; and the Civano Nursery by the developer. Without significant additional subsidy funding, the full attainment of Civano's employment goals, along with the connected reduction in car use, could not be met in the early years of its implementation. Time would make a difference: some twenty years later. If Civano was being started in the past five years, it's job creation ambitions could have been easily met. Commercial and retail growth along the Houghton Road corridor has been strong and consistent from about 2010 on and a town center would have filled up. Happily, much of Neighborhood One's employment goals were met by what became a robust in-home and accessary unit business presence. Neighborhood One's special zoning allowed for this. The lack of the same in what would become Neighborhoods Two and Three precluded this same employment phenomenon from developing.

Herein lies a critical lesson. The creation of the Town Center, and its employment potential, was one of the most challenging of the goals of this public/private partnership. In a perfect world, mechanisms would have been included in the development agreement that would have allowed for this land to lie fallow until there was enough market demand to make the creation of a town center feasible, if still ambitious. These mechanisms could have included the State or City holding the land in trust; tax abatements; bonds to subsidize businesses located in the center. This was further than the City was willing to go in its support for this critical element.

NEVERTHELESS, PROGRESS NOTED: DESIGN

Amid all these worrisome events, some important and positive things were being accomplished, or begun, during this period. With Lee Rayburn, a new convert to New Urbanism, now the director of design for the project, Moule & Polyzoides's scope of work continued to expand. They were engaged to participate in the civil engineering reviews for phases Two and Three of Neighborhood One, and some—but not all—of the planning deficiencies of the first phase were addressed. Builders were brought together with Moule & Polyzoides to review, if not entirely design, the proposed model homes for the project. Two builders, RGC and TJ Bednar, embraced this help. Others did little more than listen politely and then proceeded with their own models with no site plan coordination. Detailed site plans were developed for several, but not all, sections of the neighborhood; and it is those sections—the Desert Country and Neighborhood Center Courtyard Housing—where the concepts brought up in the 1996 charrette are most completely implemented. There was an effort to bring *all* the New Urbanist ideas from the charrette back into the project and to create a complete document framework for the future. It must be said that this effort was not seen as an essential task by the directing management. What was accomplished was done was through the efforts of Rayburn and Moule & Polyzoides, but never made a mandatory requirement for the builders by project owners. The fear of "asking too much of the builders" made its presence known again and became a growing project reality.

THE IMPACT STANDARDS

As the builders began to work on model home designs, the development team was put in touch with the Department of Energy's Building America program, a program that provided assistance to home builders in designing and building more energy-efficient and healthier homes. The development team was partnered with IBACOS (a name derived from Integrated Building and Construction Systems) and set up what amounted to a builders' guild that focused on building energy-efficient homes, while not increasing costs significantly. As with the design engagement effort, some builders took to IBACOS's training with dedication, others not as much. Three of the five builders at this time did, and it would later be determined that their models were significantly more energy efficient than the two builders who did not participate. Suffice it to say, IBACOS provided much-needed technical help at a cost carried by the Department of Energy.

This and other partnering activities helped to offset expected public and private-sector funding through the Civano Institute which did not materialize. Having expended virtually all its initial funding on education and community outreach efforts, creating a Civano Builder Handbook, and holding three training workshops, the Institute could not provide the on-site training now needed by the Civano builders. By the end of 1997, key personnel had left the Institute, there was no new funding on the horizon, and its activity as a whole was winding down, with the fortunate exception of the completion and publishing in early 1998 the book *Sustainable Design: A Plan Book for Sonoran Desert Dwellings.* This book became an oft-used component of Civano's marketing. In addition to that valuable contribution, three of the home designs featured in the book became, with further development by local architect Paul Weiner's firm, Design Build Collaborative, well-received models in the first years of Civano's build-out.

SETTING UP CENTRALIZED SALES

As site work began and builders began their model development, a critical marketing component was created, staffed, and began operations: the centralized sales effort. In centralized sales, all salespeople are hired and trained by the developer, and then present the various builder models in a central sales and information venue. All site visitors are channeled through the information center, where they are exposed to the *entire* story of the community, before proceeding to individual builder models. This is a way of guaranteeing that a complex but compelling project story was told consistently "on message." The centralized sales effort was paid for by charging a percentage of each home sale. Though resistant at first, all the builders came to realize that the deeper training and more complete messaging that centralized sales offered was to their advantage.

DEMONSTRABLE PROGRESS, HIDDEN TENSIONS

Whatever tensions were becoming more apparent within the project management, the City and most on the outside of the project saw demonstrable progress and apparent stability. This was especially true within the upper echelons of City management. The confidence at this level that the project was stabilized began to be reflected in the zoning and plan reviews. Getting all the innovative site engineering and land-planning aspects of the project through review was still a struggle, and it most certainly was not expedited, but a corner had been turned and the development team was in continuous dialogue with reviewers.

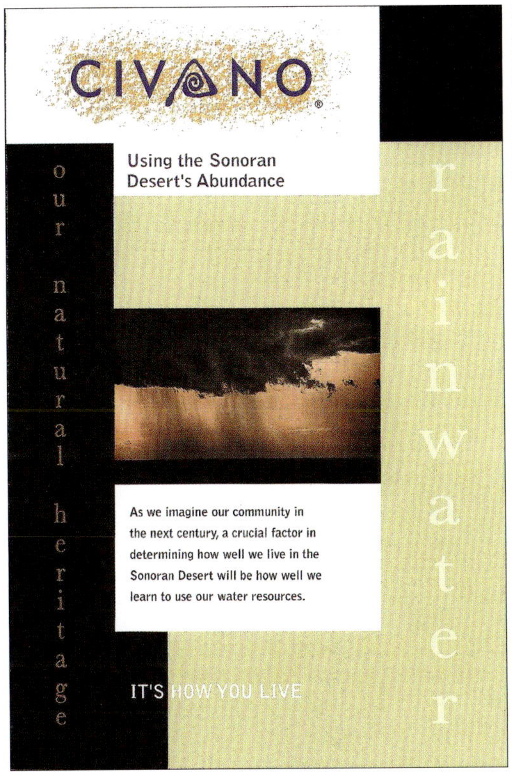

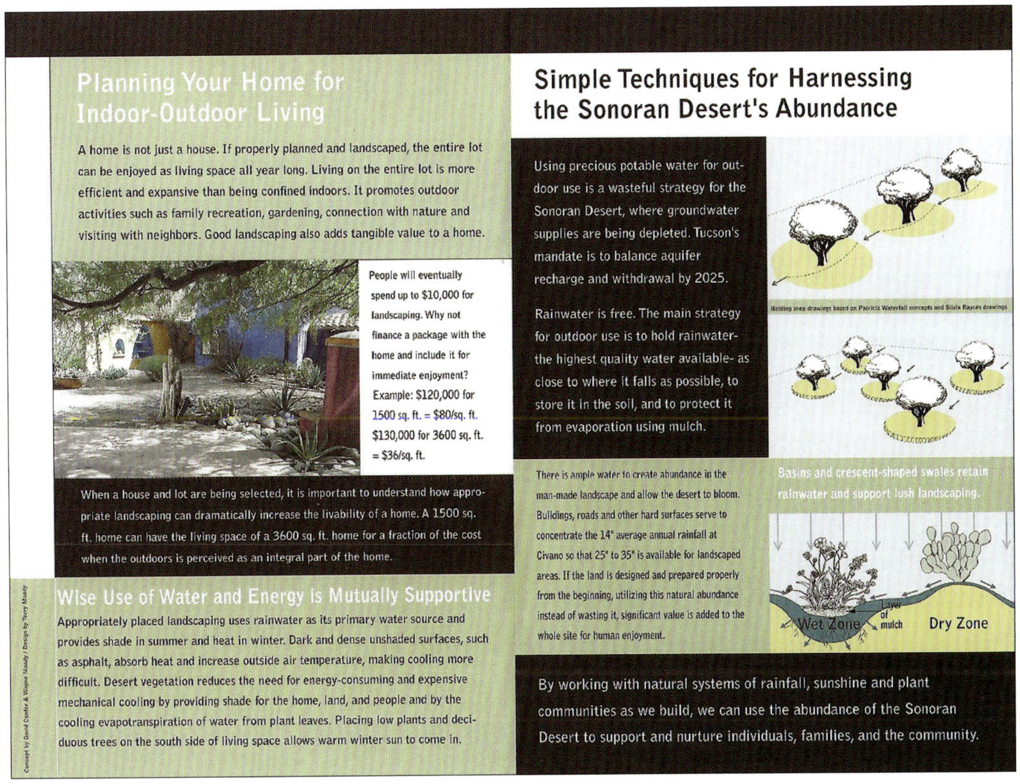

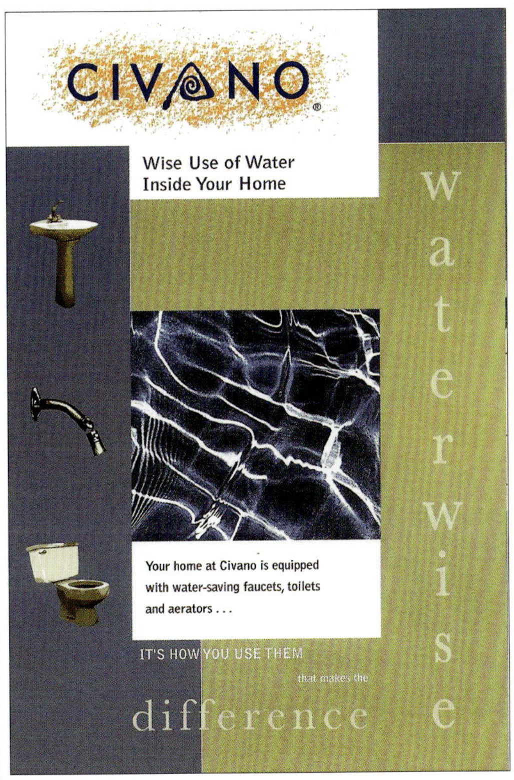

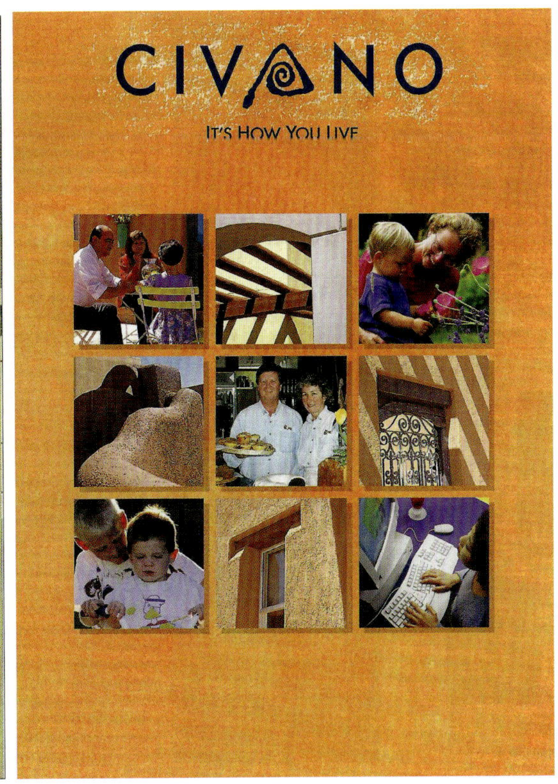

Early Sales Brochures for Civano

A series of brochures were created to explain important environmental aspects of Civano. The upper images are of a brochure exploring living in abundance in a desert environment. The lower two images to the left are the covers of brochures on permaculture landscaping and residential water conservation.

On the lower right is the cover of a pamphlet with articles about the lifestyle being promoted for Civano, along with information about the builders.

All of these were used for pre-opening publicity, and as handouts to visitors to the Civano Welcome Center.

Civano Development/Fannie Mae 1999

Ownership Interest	Lead Development Decision Maker	Lead Planning & Design	Total Homes Sales for This Period (began in April 1999)
Fannie Mae/American Communities Fund (66%); Civano Development (34%)	Fannie Mae/Kevin Kelly	Rayburn	118 contracts by the end of the year; 13 per month on average

BECOMING A REALITY

1999 was the year that Civano finally became a living reality. The first section of Neighborhood One was completed. Site work began on the remainder of Neighborhood One, and the project site was a beehive of activity. Home models opened for sales, and the public response was enthusiastic. There was a general feeling, both within the development team and the City government, that sales momentum would overcome the delays of the last eighteen months and provide a steady and increasing cash flow to the development. No one could imagine that by the middle of fall, the project would once again be at a virtual standstill and in crisis.

THE BEGINNING OF HOME SALES AND THE GRAND OPENING

In early April, the public was invited to a "pre-opening" view of the nine model homes that had been completed. On the first day, over 600 people showed up to walk through the models and there was enthusiastic coverage in the local media. This was an astounding number for a housing development in Tucson, and the first indication that the project would, in fact, find success even in Tucson's challenging housing market. The formal grand opening of the first neighborhood of Civano was held on April 16th. Fannie Mae senior management was there in force. Although invited, Vice President Al Gore could not attend, but did send a very appropriate and supportive letter that emphasized Civano being a model for the future. (See page 2.)

By the end of the year, 118 contracts were written for new homes. About thirty were for people who had been following the Tucson Solar Village / Civano project for years, and their "pent up demand" was finally met. The remainder of the sales were to buyers without a long association with Civano but attracted by its "different" look, the energy savings features, and by the ability to customize their home to a greater extent than was the norm for national production builders.

The strong sales were an enormous confidence booster for all the project stakeholders, though how those sales were interpreted differed widely. For the City, the strong sales did much to erase earlier frustrations that the grand opening was behind by months, as well as concerns about the impact of Fannie Mae's ever greater presence and ownership position. With some frequency, doubts had been expressed about whether the development team would continue on or whether Fannie Mae would take over completely. The strong sales pushed those doubts to the background, and there was a newfound confidence that the project would generate an income stream that would make for a future far less turbulent that the past two years.

The benefits to the project of this new confidence were immediate. The entitlement reviews for Phase Two and Three of Neighborhood One were accelerated. Optimism based on the strong sales was a factor, but now, as homes began to be constructed, reviewers could go the project site and see what they were being asked to approve. This tangible "look and feel" won many over. The promise in the Development Agreement of expedited reviews looked to finally become closer to a reality.

With the enthusiastic sales, the City started to look beyond Neighborhood One and began pressuring for the start of planning for Neighborhoods Two and Three. In May and June, a series of workshops were held to start outlining the general approach to be taken for the next phases of the project. The workshops were notable for their inclusive nature, and especially for the strong support and attendance by City planning, zoning, and engineering personnel. There was general agreement that Neighborhoods Two and Three should build on the protocols of Neighborhood One, while adding on some of the more challenging site engineering concepts that just did not have support during the earlier entitlement reviews, notably those addressing surface water management.

In Neighborhood One, Rayburn and Moule & Polyzoides continued their efforts to create a body of design codes that would solidify the new urbanist intent started in the 1996 charrette. Street standards and the first form-based codes were drawn up. But as with the earlier formalization of the site planning process, their formal adoption as project guidelines or requirements ran into resistance from the senior members of the project ownership.

DARKER CURRENTS: MONEY TALKS

With Case's departure from the project at the end of 1998, Fannie Mae became the majority owner. Kelly remained the managing partner, in charge of day-to-day decisions and general strategy. Technically, Fannie Mae was to be a passive partner; but with greater frequency Fannie Mae used its majority ownership position to insert itself into day-to-day operations. This tendency only accelerated as Fannie Mae's continuing funding contributions grew throughout 1999.

The downside of the unusually large and discounted lot options that had been used to lure builders into the project at its inception now came to the fore. Though the strong home sales were accelerating builders' takedown of their optioned lots, the locked-in prices were just covering the project's land development costs. There was little left over to cover the development team's

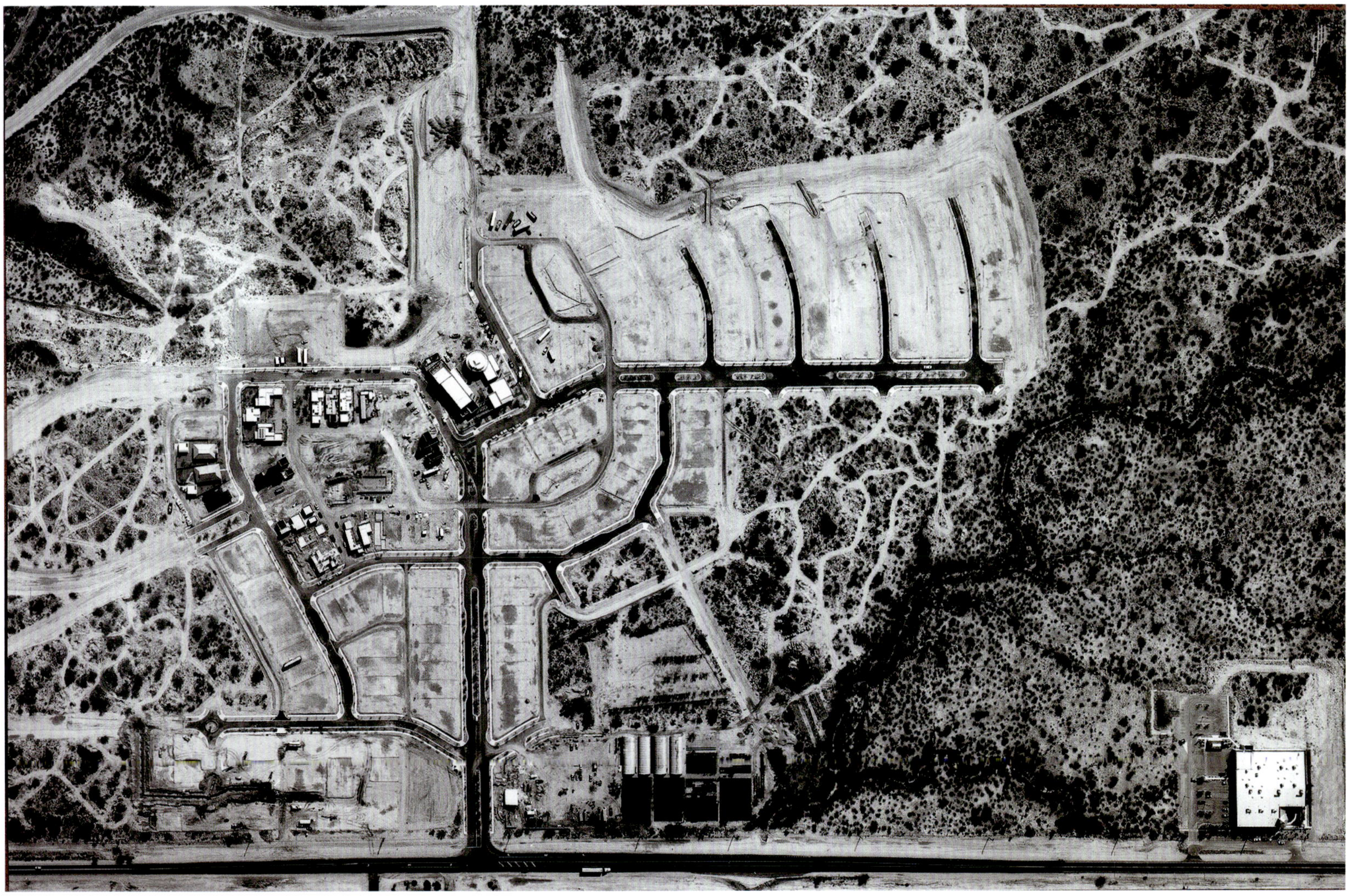

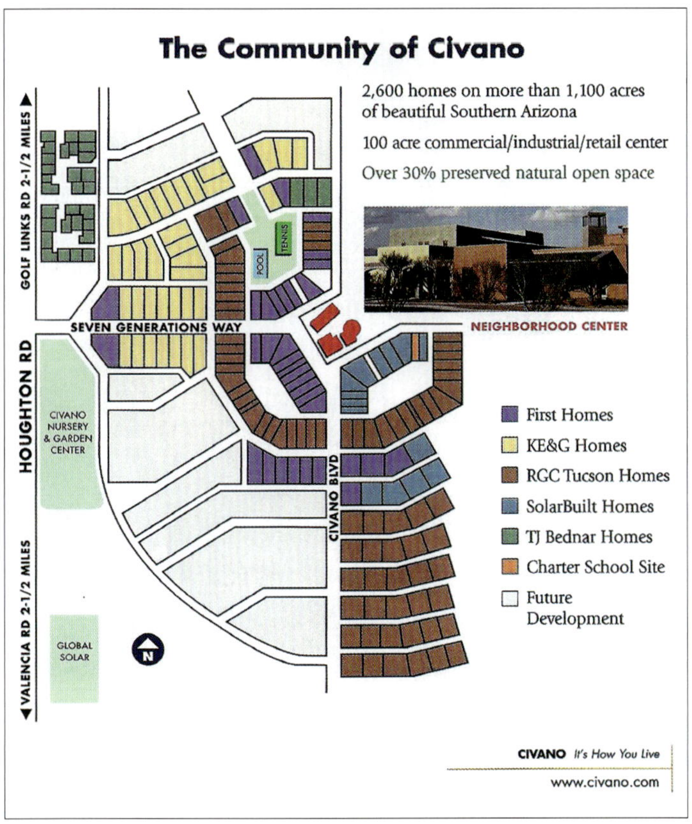

(top) An aerial view of the site with the Neighborhood Center in the middle and builder model homes under construction to the left of the Center. North is to the left.

(far left) A map showing the first phase of Neighborhood One, with the homes being built by the various builders.

(left) The first sales advertisement for Civano once model homes were ready. It stresses quality and the difference between Civano and standard production homes.

overhead and general operational costs. By the end of the year, Fannie Mae's cash contribution would increase to about $10.5 million, now in excess of three times their original commitment.

Unfortunately for the project, the model of residential land development that Fannie Mae best understood was the standard sprawl model. As they became increasingly concerned about the escalating funding it was putting into the project, they turned to this comfort zone with greater frequency. This tendency was made more frequent and insistent once the management of Civano as a Fannie Mae asset moved from the relatively innovative American Communities Fund to the core of Fannie Mae's senior management team. The development team faced ever-growing pressure from Fannie Mae to modify and "soften" the core ideas embedded in Civano, especially its adherence to New Urbanism. This, despite the growing evidence that the marketplace was, in fact, embracing the very aspects of the project Fannie Mae considered worrying.

A clear signal of a shift in Fannie Mae's attitude towards the management of the project was their engagement in the spring of LaSalle to do a full *forensic* audit of the project. Charitably, this could be seen as a new majority owner wanting to take stock in an asset. As that may be, this action also sent at the very least a message of doubt about the development management team, if not outright suspicion. It is not improper to say, as Kelly claims to this day, that this was a punitive and aggressive action on Fannie Mae's part to undermine Kelly's reputation in the business world and was the first step in increasing pressure on him to leave the project. There is no question that the audit was intrusive. It certainly raised concerns with the project's major non-Fannie Mae financing partner, Bank One, slowing down their consideration of expanding their financial support of the project. This in turn made the project team more dependent on Fannie Mae funding.

A second clear signal of Fannie Mae's attempt to steer the project into its comfort zone was their insisting on the appointment of a Phoenix-based "marketing consultant," at great cost to the project, to take over marketing and sales. She was an advocate for abandoning the new urbanist planning for the balance of Neighborhood One and the future neighborhoods, substituting it with "cul-de-sac" planning—her code word for standard sprawl practice. At her direction, centralized sales were abandoned and all sales activity given over to the individual builders. With that, marketing messages became erratic, and core messages about the design intentions of the neighborhood were muddled.

Troubling as all of this was from inside the project, to the public and the City, these ominous occurrences went virtually unnoticed, hidden by the project's growing sales and evident popularity with the buying public.

THE FALL 1999: A REVERSAL OF FORTUNE

At the beginning of the fall, that sales-based optimism began to show some cracks as the result of growing awareness of three troubling events.

RGC, the leader in the first wave of home sales in Civano, was not completing homes and turning them over to the buyers. During late summer, this was explained away by the builder as the result of "coordination issues." By October, it had become apparent that it wasn't just a matter of some homes not being completed; many had not even been started. Virtually all RGC's sixty buyers were growing more vocal regarding concerns about delays.

What came to light was deeply troubling and multi-faceted. RGC was simply not able to complete its homes at the contract sales price because of several factors; chief among them was that their construction methods involved practices that were far from the norm in Tucson. These are reviewed in detail on page 112. These were technical problems that with some foresight and training, RGC might have been able to address. Moreover, as a California-based builder, they faced some resistance from the local trades because they were an unknown quantity. No one was quite sure what their payment performance would be. All this translated into RGC not receiving the most competitive of bids for construction. Sadly, they did not compensate for this and continued to sell homes at prices they increasingly knew they would not be able to meet. As the situation worsened, a few contract holders contacted local media—and the story began to have a public life. Fannie Mae, understandably, was especially troubled by anything that would cast a bad media light on the development, and by extension, their increasingly public involvement.

As RGC's growing failure was becoming rapidly more public, Fannie Mae was negotiating with Kevin Kelly about his departure from the development, and Fannie Mae's taking over full ownership of Civano. There was concern, justifiably, that the departure of the last of the three original development principals (Butterfield, Case, and Kelly) would be seen as a signal that the project was, again, in trouble. Kelly had been the most visible and verbal of the three, and had never shied away from accepting the role of the "enlightened developer," one who—in the minds of many Civano advocates—would work to achieve all of Civano's goals without consideration of cost. His departure, it was feared, would be seen as a signal that Civano would back away from its goals and become a more typical subdivision, one that would now be owned by the largest financial institution in the United States.

The coinciding of RGC's growing failure and public knowledge of Kelly being forced out once again threw shadows on optimism about the project. Just as the project's home sales seemed to be taking off, it was stumbling again. Civano's supporters in the City government were disheartened. It must be said that there was a growing weariness with the near constant state of turmoil that the project could not seem to escape. There was a feeling that with Fannie Mae as the complete owner of the project, at least finances would be stable and there would be an end to constant management changes that had been so much a part of the project up to this point. This longing for stability went a very long way towards assuaging concerns about Fannie Mae's commitment to continue to embrace and implement the project's goals. Representatives of Fannie Mae gave the City officials many assurances on this critical topic. The City was further encouraged by the fact that a component of the Kelly buyout discussions and final agreement was that key development team members, other than Kelly, would stay on with the project. Project operations and goals, the City was assured, would not change, even though the on-the-ground development management team would now be reporting directly to a Fannie Mae-appointed asset manager.

All this turmoil certainly did not help the public perception of the project. Sales slowed dramatically. From a high of twenty-five sales per month at the beginning of the summer, they fell into negative territory by November as RGC cancellations began to mount and overwhelm the slowing number of sales from other builders.

THE FUTURE POSTPONED

There was one other critical casualty of all this tumult: the pre-planning for Neighborhoods Two and Three came to an abrupt and complete halt. It would be over a year before the development team would be able to get this going again, and by that time much would have changed. The impacts of this were many. Continuing forcefully with the planning for Neighborhoods Two and Three would have shown both a strong commitment to, and faith in, the project's continuing despite the current turmoil. It would have helped the overall project stay on schedule, thus giving a better chance that the income streams from lot sales could (once the temporary difficulties and challenges of the RGC collapse had been resolved) support the development management of

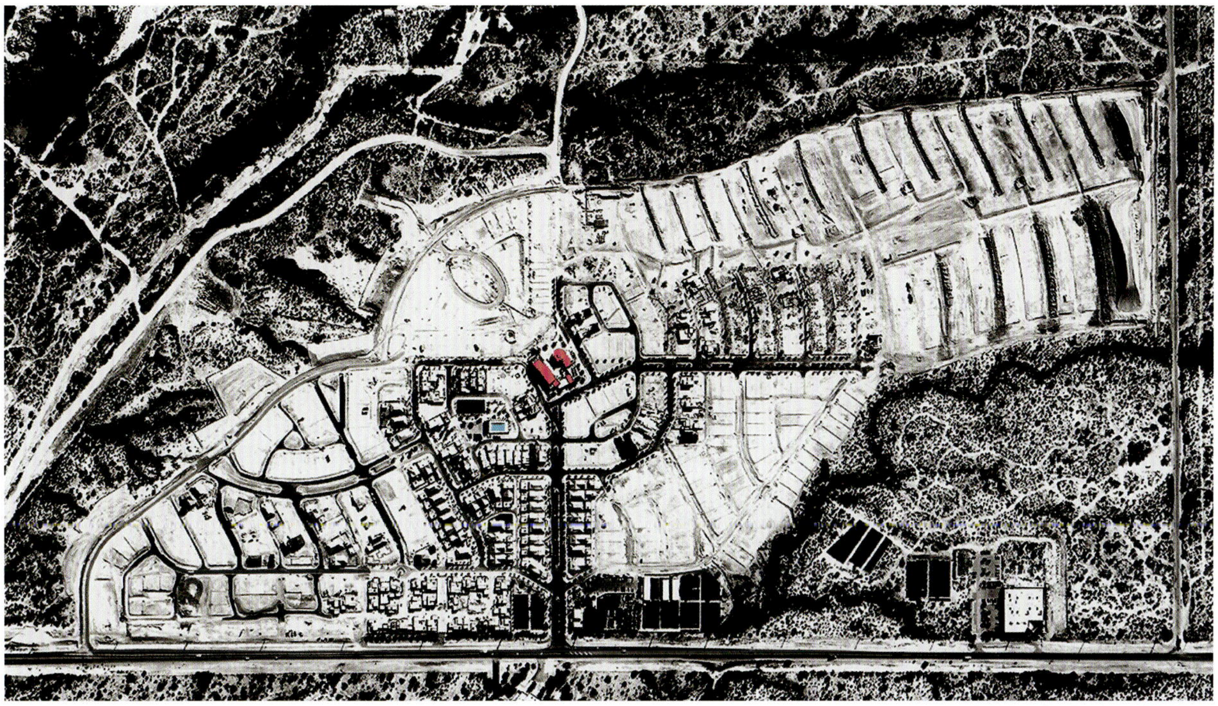

(top) Aerial view of Civano in early 2000. The first phase of home construction is well underway, and infrastructure for the entire neighborhood is almost completed. North is to the left.

(bottom) A panoramic view from the top of the Neighborhood Center, looking north; late 1999.

the project. These were legitimate points, and in a rational business environment could have prevailed. Sadly, the fall of 1999 at Civano was not a time that could be described as a rational business environment.

What was clear was that Fannie Mae was suffering from "project fatigue." Civano had become a project that they saw as a torrent of red ink, one where they had stepped far out of their normal role of passive investor. Fair enough, but perhaps more telling was that Civano was a project in which they felt they had been forced into accepting land planning policies which they felt were not "market tested." It could be more accurate to say that Fannie Mae, with their many relationships with national builders, simply did not feel comfortable with a planning and land development approach that was so different from the subdivision norm, and in fact was adversarial to what can be fairly called "typical production sprawl housing development." Fannie Mae, a huge institutional entity, simply wanted to stop and assess everything, including what they perceived as runaway costs, before moving forward. They were not thinking about long-range planning or keeping on schedule to ensure a future stock of developed lots. They simply wanted to bring the Civano development into their institutional context before moving forward. The collapse of RGC only served to strengthen and focus this desire.

The year closed with many questions and much doubt in the air. In late December, a meeting was held with all the RGC contract holders. It was not a happy meeting. It was clear that RGC would not be able to finish the homes under contract. Many of the RGC contract holders voiced their strong expectation that the developer would ensure that their homes would be finished and turned over to them. The correct explanation that the developer did not have any contractual relationship with the buyers, *only* the builder did, limiting what the developer could and was required to do, fell on deaf and unhappy ears. Years of expectation built up over promises that too often exceeded what was likely and even possible were coming home to roost. It would be management's task in the next year to figure out how to move through this time of trouble and push the project forward. At year's end, Kelly's buyout was complete, and a new management company, CDC Partners, was created with the remaining development staff—especially Rayburn in his role as director of design and liaison to the City and Larry Lamy, the chief financial officer—continuing to work under contract to Fannie Mae.

Fannie Mae Sole Owner/CDC Partners Managing 2000 to June 2002

Ownership Interest	**Lead Development Decision Maker**	**Lead Planning & Design**	**Total Homes Sales for This Period**
Fannie Mae (100%)	Fannie Mae with day-to-day management by CDC Partners	Rayburn	210; or average of 7 per month

The year 2000 began as a time of transition, turmoil, and concern for all of Civano's stakeholders. There was the ongoing RGC bankruptcy, with its attendant negative publicity. All homeowners in the community had been shaken by the collapse of RGC, wondering what this would do to the value of the homes bought from other builders. Operating costs had mushroomed, largely due to the cost of the Fannie Mae-installed marketing director. Costs needed to be diminished and stabilized if there was to be any chance of the project turning an operational profit. The City wondered what Fannie Mae's full ownership would mean. Would it lead to stability? Would Fannie Mae adhere to the project's stated goals and the IMPACT Standards? Would the timetables for the development of Neighborhoods Two and Three be met, ensuring continuous sales? It was clear that Fannie Mae would not be likely to embrace in the future neighborhoods the New Urbanist approach that had been such a critical core component of Neighborhood One. While many in the City held the principals of the new on-site day-to-day managers, CDC Partners, in high regard, no one misunderstood that it would be Fannie Mae controlling the direction of project decisions. Fannie Mae's goals were clear:

- Stabilize and reduce, if not stop, their escalating funding of the projects;
- Immediately address the RGC situation, and get beyond its financial, legal, and PR potential impacts; and
- Make the future phases of Civano more national-builder friendly.

CDC Partners shared with Fannie Mae the first two goals but took exception to the third. As the inheritors of, and the last link to, the original vision of the project, CDC would pursue some goals that Fannie Mae in fact might not fully support, those being:

- Restarting the planning for Neighborhoods Two and Three, and to make that planning continue new urbanist protocols of Neighborhood One;
- Creating a fully developed set of planning and design documents for Neighborhood One, based on new urbanist protocols, in order to create a documented contextual legacy that could be transferred forward in the future neighborhoods; and
- Recreating some version of central sales as a part of re-establishing a consistent marketing message on the special nature of Civano.

CDC's principals firmly believed that pursuing these would help *correct* the imbalances of the immediate past, while moving the project towards stability and profitability, two things of benefit to Fannie Mae.

2000: A YEAR OF STAGNATION AND THEN STABILIZATION

The first quarter of 2000 was dominated by Fannie Mae's desire to take stock and understand Civano in a context more familiar to them, which is to say in metrics common to large-scale production housing. This was the first step in preparing the project for sale, and almost certainly to a large national builder. This last assumption was bolstered by Fannie Mae directives to halt all activity that would deepen the New Urbanist imprint on the project.

Once again, the LaSalle Group was brought in to do a new "buyers audit," with a central focus on density assumptions for Neighborhoods Two and Three. Underlying this new assignment was Fannie Mae's assumption that New Urbanism equaled lesser density and thus fewer lots, leading to significant loss of value. CDC argued that this assumption was no more than just that, and should be tested. Somewhat surprisingly, they were able to convince Fannie Mae to engage Moule & Polyzoides on a limited basis for the focused task of developing density studies for Neighborhoods Two and Three based on new urbanist principles. As they had done previously, Moule & Polyzoides's studies showed a density as good as, or better than LaSalle's. CDC was able to use these studies, which LaSalle acknowledged as being well thought out and objective, to bring Moule & Polyzoides back into the project as the master land planner.

In April, Fannie Mae decided to reset the financial accounting for the project. By this time, Fannie Mae had invested around $16 million, a far cry from their original commitment of $3 million, but not an unreasonable sum considering the size of the project, especially considering some its "special costs" like partner buyouts and a builder failure. An artificial accounting start at zero was set, along with the goal of showing a $3.4 million profit by the buildout of Neighborhood One. For internal consumption at Fannie Mae, this was a way of saying, "we are now in charge, so let's measure only what we are responsible for." It was also a way of measuring the performance of CDC Partners. No doubt there were tax advantages to be had. But there was also this: by setting the financial clock to zero, Fannie Mae was announcing its intention of selling the property unburdened by the troubling accounting of the past.

DIAMOND VENTURES THE FIRST PROPOSED SALE, AND ITS AFTERMATH

In late spring, nearly everything came to a halt when Fannie Mae decided to attempt to sell the entire project to Diamond Ventures, a Tucson-based land developer with a decades-long practice in standard subdivision development and extensive political influence in Arizona. The firm typically bought large tracts of raw land, entitled them, and then sold them to home builders. They were well-funded, extremely professional, and deeply capable. It is, however, an understatement to say that they were not interested in anything but standard development protocols. Maximizing lot sales and minimizing development costs was the core of their business plan.

Diamond's due diligence period began in May and would run on through the summer. Very quickly, it became clear how they saw and wanted to present Civano: as a failure needing to be saved, at any price, specifically, at the price of a softening of the IMPACT Standards and other requirements of the Development Agreement. Both Fannie Mae and Diamond openly stated that their goal was to make the next neighborhoods of Civano a standard development with more attention paid to energy efficiency and leave it at that. The IMPACT Standards would be made more aspirational than mandatory and have much lighter reporting requirements. Changing the IMPACT Standards and the Development Agreement would require approval by the City Council. The politically powerful Diamond felt confident of their ability to convince the City Council to make the changes they desired.

CDC refused to accept, much less advocate, this story of failure, especially as spring turned into summer, there was growing evidence of Civano's success. A near total revamping of the marketing and sales programs for the project had finally put the RGC failure in the background. Home sales were rising dramatically and had begun to compete with the best "sprawl" developments in Tucson. But success was also being measured by the fact that the quarterly IMPACT reports were showing that the standards that could be measured at this point *were* being met. A significant number of senior City officials saw this success and began to push back on the story that the standards of Civano needed to be diminished in order to achieve sales.

While fulfilling their contractual obligations to faithfully represent Fannie Mae in their dealings with Diamond, CDC began meeting with City staff and City Council members to lay out a clear vision for the development of the future neighborhoods, one based on the growing evidence of Neighborhood One's emerging success. Two key ideas were emphasized:

1. Expanding and revising the existing and approved Civano Neighborhood One Specific Plan, rather than starting a new Master Plan process for the next neighborhoods. This would save considerable time for the development of the next neighborhoods, while ensuring the extension of the planning protocols of Neighborhood One.
2. Creating, for the first time, a complete set of regulating plans for Neighborhood One, along with other design and engineering standards that would act as a guide for future street layouts, lot sizing, density distribution, and house type allocation. And have all of these linked to a mandated design review process based on these documents.

On the day of the City Council, Diamond's very experienced political operative predicted the vote would be 7–0 in favor of their requested changes. It turned out to be a 7–0 vote against. This was a stunning surprise for DVI and an equally stunning vindication of Civano's public/private partnership. Perhaps the simplest to way understand this unanimous endorsement from the Council was that it represented a broad public and administrative desire for a new way of building in Tucson, one that tread lighter on the land and created desirable physical communities. In short, it was an endorsement of the original and ongoing intent of the Civano experiment: let Neighborhood One be the test bed and ensure its successful features would be incorporated in the following neighborhoods.

Hard on the heels of the collapse of the effort to sell the project to Diamond, there was a complete overhaul of the American Communities Fund, and every person inside Fannie Mae who had been associated with getting Fannie Mae involved with Civano ceased to have decision-making involvement with the project. Importantly, there was a long period—over a year—while Fannie Mae considered their next steps and there was no on-site Fannie Mae asset manager. CDC seized on this opportunity to revitalize the project.

MARKETING: FINALLY ACHIEVING THE HOPED-FOR SALES FIGURES

At the beginning of 2000, the marketing program for Civano was under stress from multiple directions and causes. The RGC crisis was in full bloom and very public. The other builders were nervous about how they would be impacted. Visitors to the sales center and the individual builders' models were asking as many questions about the future of Civano as about the houses being sold. Complicating developing a consistent and appropriate response to all of this was the fact that the central marketing effort had been abandoned, along with any unified sales agent training. Each builder was effectively on their own to develop a sales presence.

The marketing budget had ballooned out of proportion to the number of homes being sold, spending over twice that of the average development, and consuming a disproportionate amount of the projected profit from lot sales. Nearly half of this bloated budget went to the Fannie Mae-appointed Phoenix-based marketing consultant. After over a year on the project, she had failed to develop any marketing message, collateral material, or coherent advertising program, but had billed the project close to $400,000. Using Fannie Mae's mandate to reduce overhead costs, CDC at first opportunity removed this consultant, and the excessive cost, from the project.

A well-regarded local PR firm, Gordley and Associates, was brought in to totally rethink marketing. Gordley's new campaign and marketing material emphasized the "look and feel" of Neighborhood One. In their new ad campaign, the words "choice," "quality," and "enduring value" were prominent. This was all in notable contrast to the more typical message of "low cost for lots of space" and a limited number of builder upgrades that the typical production subdivision offered.

Fannie Mae continued to adamantly oppose re-instating centralized sales. In a workaround, mandatory salesperson training was implemented. CDC hired Joan Tober, an experienced and successful Tucson realtor who believed deeply in what Civano stood for, to organize these weekly sessions. They quickly became eagerly anticipated information-sharing sessions among the builders' salespeople and the development team's own sales and marketing staff. In effect, something very like centralized sales had been re-established.

As the new marketing program really took hold in late 2000 and on into 2001, the results were notable. Monthly sales consistently improved, with the project achieving 77 sales by the end of 2000 and 110 homes sold by the end of 2001. This was a sales velocity to match the most successful of the standard production home developments in Tucson.

EXTERNAL FACTORS IMPACTING SALES

Contributing to the sustained increase in sales at Civano were two critical external events that were true "paradigm shifts," one regional and the other national.

In the spring of 2000, stories began to come out of California about unexpected spikes in electricity rates, followed by instances of brownouts and even blackouts as summer heat waves hit the state. This was, of course, the beginning of what was then called the "California Energy Crisis." The causes of this crisis are not the subject of this book, but it had a significant impact on Civano.

The "crisis" awakened the residents of California, and much of the American West, out of their complacent assumption that energy for their homes and businesses would always be available and affordable. Very quickly, understanding a home's energy consumption became an important concern of potential home buyers. There stood Civano with documented proof that its homes used 50% less energy than its competition. The market found Civano, and suddenly buyers were asking about energy efficiency, and builders and realtors from other developments were contacting the Civano development team to ask about how to make homes more energy efficient.

The other externality that had an impact of Civano, and indeed on everything else, was the aftermath of the events of September 11, 2001. Those traumatic days and their rippling impact made us all think in a new and deeper way about what "safety" meant. The ideas of "home" and "community" resonated in a new way both individually and in our broader culture. So many aspects of Civano's physical reality spoke to those very human desires. The street fronts, unbroken by driveways with porches leading to front doors spoke to a sense of connection. The more compact lot layout along those streets, and the way the landscaping of one front yard flowed into another, gave off a physical sense of the continuity of community and connection to nature. In the aftermath of 9/11, as every sector of the economy reeled, home buying was hit very hard. Civano spoke of "home" and "authenticity" and "connection" at a time when the nation hungered for tangible demonstrations of those core human values. Civano home sales paused, but quickly recovered and remained strong.

BECOMING PART OF THE TUCSON REALTOR COMMUNITY

There was one other important marketing action taken in early 2001 that benefited the project. Typically, about 25% of home sales in a new community could be attributed to an unaffiliated local realtor bringing a client in. At Civano, it was closer to 2%. A much bigger pool of potential buyers—those represented by outside realtors—was not being tapped in any significant way. CDC expanded Joan Tober's role, tasking her with a special outreach effort to local realtors, with the purpose of educating them on what Civano had to offer. It was a very successful program. Within three months, outside realtor sales had increased to 12% of all sales and would continue to increase. Rather than seeing Civano as "different," realtors began to see this community as a "different buying opportunity," one that offered what their buyers wanted that no other local and regional builders were offering.

We have gone into some detail on all these marketing and sales efforts for three reasons. The first is the most obvious: they were remarkably effective. We believe that this effectiveness rested on the second reason: for the first time since Fannie Mae had taken over the project, Civano was being marketed in a disciplined and comprehensive manner that embraced its New Urbanist nature and its special energy saving and sustainability aspects.

The third was that the renewed sales success gave foundation to a new faith at the City level. There was renewed pressure from the City to start planning for the next neighborhoods. If sales in Neighborhood One proceeded at the 2001 pace, it would be sold out within two to three years. This meant that the initial planning for Neighborhoods Two and Three had to start almost immediately if there was to be seamless transition to those future neighborhoods at the buildout of Neighborhood One. Fannie Mae's initial reluctance to proceed was overcome by pressure from the City and the realization that moving forward with planning would make the Neighborhoods Two and Three land more valuable than unentitled land.

THE RE-ENGAGEMENT OF THE NEW URBANISM AND ENVISIONING THE FUTURE

As noted above, Moule & Polyzoides had been brought back into the project during the LaSalle study on density, but that re-engagement was limited. In the aftermath of the Diamond Ventures failure, as Fannie Mae turned its focus inward, and without a day-to-day "handler," CDC expanded that re-engagement as it responded to the City's pressure to get on with Neighborhoods Two and Three planning.

Moule & Polyzoides were engaged to complete for Neighborhood One a set of codified planning and design documents typical for a New Urbanist plan. They set about creating site plans for all the housing types in Neighborhood One, and the neighborhood sections in which they were found. Form-based codes were developed, and while by today's new urbanist standards, these early attempts seem somewhat simplistic, they were far better than anything contemporaries were doing. They were an important addition to understanding the spatial relationships of homes to streets, and differing types of buildings to each other. While directly related to Neighborhood One, all these documents would act as templates for the next neighborhoods. There was little expectation that these same codes would become a *formal* part of any design review process for the balance of Neighborhood One. As in the past, Fannie Mae refused to make them mandatory design review documents, out of fear of pushing the builders "too far." In the aftermath of the RGC fiasco, Fannie Mae was optioning lots to builders as quickly as possible and allowing them close to free reign. Only perfunctory design reviews of new home models were tolerated.

The first detailed efforts at laying out Neighborhoods Two and Three began in the second quarter of 2001 and gained momentum through the summer of 2001. It was recognized that Fannie Mae would never agree to a true New Urbanist charrette, both for cost reasons and because they frankly did not want to have an open venue that they felt they could not sufficiently control, especially when that venue would be managed by advocates for the New Urbanism. Largely due to pressure from the City, they did agree to a number of smaller meetings with experts in land planning and conservation, and with the builders. CDC Partners was also able to convince Fannie Mae to hold a number of meetings with members of the community to solicit their ideas and recommendations for the new neighborhoods. These meetings were "facilitated" by non-design professionals. Their comments were codified for future detailed planning. How these comments were to be incorporated into the future design process was left unspecified. (See images on following page.)

By early fall, a schematic master plan for Neighborhoods Two and Three emerged from those meetings and follow-up work. (See plan on following page.) The plan:

- Rigorously respected the topography and special environmental aspects of the site. Great care was given to the location of major collector roads and the layout of streets and neighborhoods so that grading was kept at an aggressive minimum. This was both environmentally sound and dramatically reduced the cost of site work.
- Dealt more aggressively with water runoff issues than had been done in Neighborhood One.
- Ensured a proper New Urbanist hierarchy of streets, from boulevards to alleyways.
- Ensured the incorporation of neighborhood centers. Discussions with the local school district and Pima County Library were initiated to bring amenities such as recreational facilities, libraries, and meeting rooms shared with schools into these future centers. Retail and commercial activity would be primarily reserved for the Town Center planned for the area at the heart of all three neighborhoods.

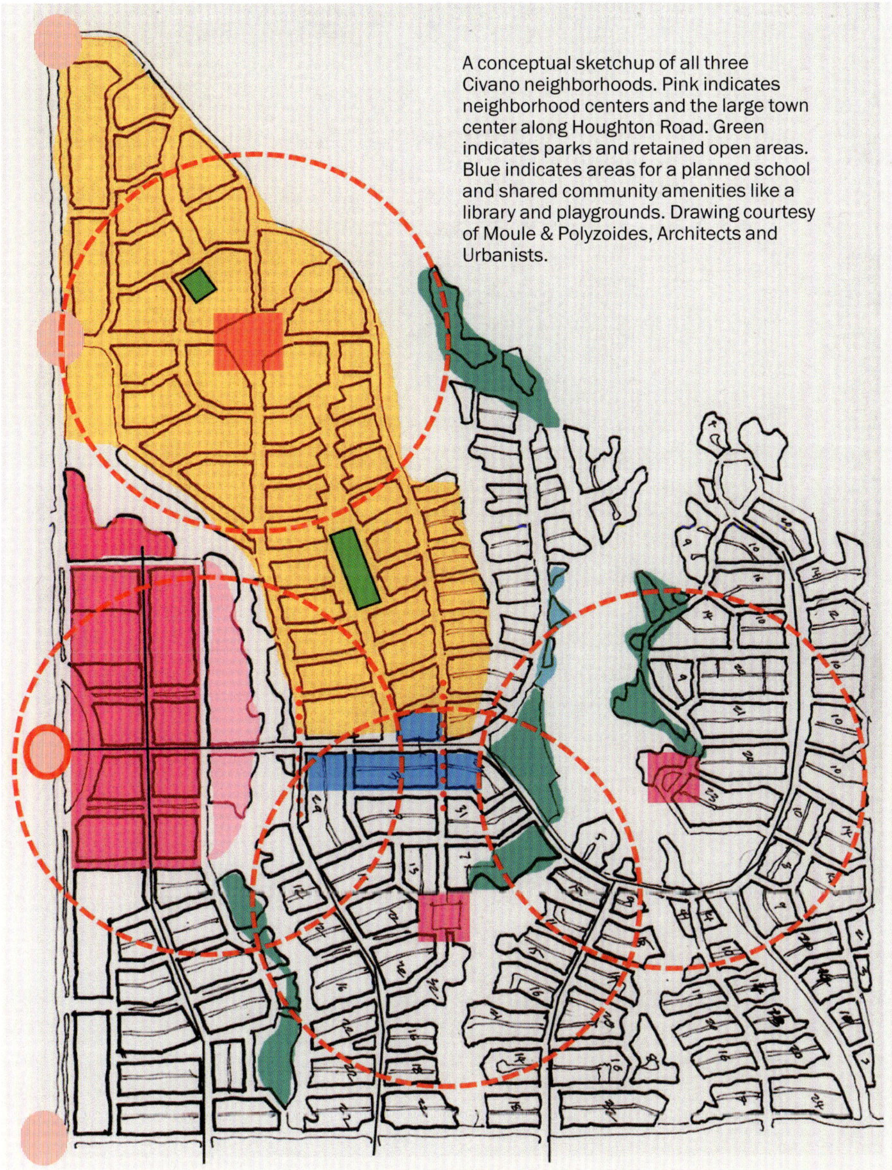

A conceptual sketchup of all three Civano neighborhoods. Pink indicates neighborhood centers and the large town center along Houghton Road. Green indicates parks and retained open areas. Blue indicates areas for a planned school and shared community amenities like a library and playgrounds. Drawing courtesy of Moule & Polyzoides, Architects and Urbanists.

Two of the community workshops held to solicit Neighborhood One homeowners' ideas about the future neighborhoods; April 2001.

- Ensured that the neighborhood blocks were of a dimension that would accommodate a variety of lot layout sizes and housing types, and a variety of streetscape schemes.
- Created densities that matched or were higher than LaSalle's.
- Assumed a variety of housing types.

In support of this forward-looking planning, the City began to consider creating a formal inter-departmental "Civano Group" that would consist of code and zoning review officials and staff. Its role would be educating its members on the concepts implemented in Civano and coordinate their review and enforcement of them going forward. Furthermore, an informal agreement was made between CDC and the City planning agencies supporting an expedited review process, *based on the success of Neighborhood One.* Rather than the normal twelve-month time period to obtain approval for a Planned Area Development (special zoning district), there was a commitment to reduce that to seven months. This meant that it would have been possible to start site work in Neighborhoods Two and Three by mid-2003, at the latest. Given the rate of Civano sales, inventory in Neighborhood One would start running low by that time. This timetable would have enabled the market-tested builders in Civano Neighborhood One to move on into new inventory without a break in sales.

FINANCIAL SUSTAINABILITY

From 2001 and on through the remainder of CDC's management, operational overhead was reduced dramatically, by about 35% from what it had been in 2000. By late 2000, the steadily increasing home sales were offsetting a growing portion of operating costs. By the end of 2000, the project came very close to breaking even for the first time, and by the end of 2001, the project was able to turn a modest profit for the first time in its history. This trend continued through June 2002. Will Orr's statement from the late 1990s about the true goal of Civano—to test whether a middle-market, production housing community promoting sustainability in the Sonoran Desert context could work—could begin to be answered in the affirmative.

THE BEGINNING OF THE END

The last quarter of 2001 was a complex time for Civano. On one hand, all the currents of hope discussed above were becoming more obvious. On the other hand, a newly appointed Fannie Mae asset manager arrived on site, ending nearly fifteen months of no on-site Fannie Mae presence. Her background was in the workout (real estate language for "disposal") of distressed, problematic properties, and her agenda quickly became evident:

- Revamp the key project documents to make them "softer" and more acceptable to a mainstream large-scale production home builder.
- Keep the Civano homeowners quiet, as it was the view from inside Fannie Mae that their activities had contributed to the collapse of the DVI purchase.
- Re-engage with key City officials, offering financial support for special City-backed projects in a quid pro quo for their support for making the Civano protocols more "builder friendly."
- Keep as much distance as possible from the New Urbanist characteristics of the project.
- Accelerate Fannie Mae's discussions with Pulte Homes—who had been identified as a potential buyer—about buying the remaining two neighborhoods and replacing Fannie Mae as the designated master developer of the entire project. Pulte Homes, the largest national home builder, had been identified as the best option among national builders. They had a very good reputation and notable energy savings programs for their homes.

In February 2002, three Fannie Mae-approved "workshops" were held to show all the work done on Neighborhoods Two and Three planning to date: one for environmental experts and City agency reviewers, one for the builders, and one for the residents of Civano. They took the form of presentations with extended question and comment periods. A lot of work was shown, and many comments gathered from each of the groups.

It was all for show. There was never a time when all the project's stakeholders were able to meet together. The cross comments and more freewheeling engaging of opposing points of view, typical of charrettes, could not happen. There would be no culminating and summarizing work that integrated all the comments, and around which the project stakeholders could rally. Significantly, Fannie Mae representatives, while they attended the workshops, never participated in them. By standing back from involvement, Fannie Mae could claim that it had never committed to anything in these public forums. It was a charade, as events would soon make clear.

In mid-March, Fannie Mae brought virtually every aspect of the planning for Neighborhoods Two and Three to a halt. Nothing was to be done. It was announced that Pulte Homes had signed a letter of intent to purchase Neighborhoods Two and Three and there would be a ninety-day due diligence period. In response to efforts by CDC to convince Pulte to recognize and build on what worked in Neighborhood One, it was made clear that whatever Pulte needed, they were to get. And Pulte, as a large national builder, was not about to change the business protocols they knew.

SUMMATION

In this thirty-month period, Civano had gone from the low points of the RGC bankruptcy and the abortive Diamond Ventures sales attempt to a period of rebuilding that had brought Neighborhood One to a stabilized level of success. The project was for the first time profitable. It now had strong support from City government planning and review agencies for a clear vision of how to proceed in Neighborhoods Two and Three. Strong and consistent sales were, by 2002, the expectation. The project was demonstrating success, as could be measured on four critical fronts:

1. The number of homes sold and gaining control of costs (economic sustainability).
2. The effectiveness by which the project met the energy, resource management, and growth accommodation goals (environmental sustainability).
3. The ease with which New Urbanism and environmental goals could be applied to production housing. With the proper institutional tools and documents in place—some of which had been created for Neighborhood One—those protocols could be brought forward into Neighborhoods Two and Three, freed from the missteps of the first, more experimental, phase of Civano. Indeed, a model was being created that could be duplicated many times over and adapted to other regional situations (conceptual sustainability).
4. The fact that the builders embraced the IMPACT Standards and were ready to carry them forward into the next neighborhoods, and in their work beyond. This new level of acceptance was in no small measure due to their recognizing that the buying public had embraced these standards.

In spite of Fannie Mae's actions, a foundation on which their own financial success could be built had been created, a foundation based on strong sales, sales that could be realistically expected to flow over into the Neighborhoods Two and Three development.

There can be no denying that the earliest years of the Civano project can be—must be—seen as financially challenging and disappointing. Certainly, from 1996 through mid-2000, a lot of money flowed out of the project, far more than flowed in. As we have stated elsewhere in this consideration, it took some time to figure out how to integrate all the IMPACT Standards into middle-market production housing, and then find builders willing to take on the challenge. The constant management change took its toll. An adjunct to that management turmoil was an inefficiency or ineffectiveness in using the money available. This was especially true in marketing.

Having said all that, we come back to this reality: by early 2001 the project was beginning to perform as hoped. It was, in fact, fulfilling the stated goal of the entire experiment: to see if an environmentally responsible and affordable production housing model for growth could be created for Tucson, and by extension the Desert Southwest.

The operational, marketing, and design protocols developed by early 2001 could have been continued on into the complete buildout of Neighborhoods Two and Three. Based on the available evidence, the City and Fannie Mae would have seen a project very well received in the marketplace, and one that would meet the IMPACT Standards. It is not unreasonable to believe that the total buildout of all three neighborhoods would have occurred before the housing and financial crisis of 2007/2008.

A community of some 1,400 homes, with multiple community centers and a growing commercial center could have been in place. It could have stood as an alternative model for growth accommodation, one that created value by any measure at its implementation and one that would have held its value.

Experiments often have false starts and need to have their components readjusted. That is the very nature of experiments. But once those components begin to point towards a successful outcome, it would be foolhardy to focus on the false starts. That, sadly, is what happened in mid-2002. While success was building in Neighborhood One, Fannie Mae had decided to extinguish the Civano experiment, and with it, the people of Tucson's ambition to take on the senseless pattern of sprawl in the Sonoran Desert.

HORIZON 5

Betrayal & Abandonment June 2002

To end all possibility of any resistance to this final and complete abandonment, on June 26, 2002, Fannie Mae abruptly ended CDC's engagement in Civano. With that, the last links to the original developers and the New Urbanist ideals of the project were expunged. Day-to-day management was taken over by Fannie Mae. CDC's departure was quickly followed by Moule & Polyzoides's. Fannie Mae and Pulte would spin a tale that Neighborhood One was, at best, a noble attempt, but that the future success of Neighborhoods Two and Three would depend on moving forward with standard large-scale production planning and building practices, somewhat modified to recognize some version of the IMPACT Standards. The idea of taking the existing Neighborhood One Specific Plan and revising and expanding it to become the basis of zoning for Neighborhoods Two and Three was abandoned, along with all the preliminary work on those two neighborhoods that had been done up to that point. A new planning and design team was brought in, and a complete restart commenced, even though taking this action added one to two years to the planning and entitlement process for the future neighborhoods.

The new master plan that would emerge from this process embraced the general sensibility and typical practices of sprawl development, tweaked a bit to deflect any complaints that the Civano experiment was being betrayed wholesale. The home designs for Neighborhoods Two and Three would be mildly adapted standard national builder models, houses that could be from anywhere and yet, evoke nowhere.

Fannie Mae hired a local architectural firm, noted for their institutional work, to review new construction. While this firm claimed a general knowledge of traditional architecture and urbanism, their lack of understanding of the basic ideas that had made Neighborhood One so appealing in the marketplace would be manifested in many of the houses they approved for the project. Too often, they were lot-consuming and inward-looking, with little attention paid to how they fit into a larger neighborhood pattern.

A more serious and flagrant act of abandonment was the acceptance of a proposal by a local builder to place over eighty-four homes along the edge of Neighborhood One. This was a narrow section along the northeastern side of Neighborhood One previously planned for about twenty-one homes. Beyond the inflation in the number of houses, the proposed plan made no attempt to relate to the adjacent street grid. Its entry roads cut through a dedicated pedestrian walkway no less than six times. Rayburn, now dismissed from the project but a homeowner in Civano, intervened with the Tucson city planning director. The number of approved homes was reduced to seventy-four. The streets entering the area were reduced to three, and they were aligned with adjacent streets in the existing neighborhood.

Anything resembling centralized sales or sales training was abandoned, and each builder's sales staff had free reign to say whatever they wanted to their potential buyers. It did not take too long to discover that buyers had bought homes without being told there would be children's playgrounds and a mixed-use center near them. This was a shocking discovery for some buyers.

SEEING ONLY THE FIRST STAGES OF AN EXTENDED EXPERIMENT

The accepted story became that Civano's Neighborhood One, unto itself, was an experiment that took too long and cost too much. With corrections, Neighborhoods Two and Three could be the practical new version of the project. Lost was the ability, and perhaps even desire, to see that Civano Neighborhood One was the initial phase of a longer process in which the challenges of the concept would be tested and worked out so that the next phases could build on the solutions resolved there. The missteps of Neighborhood One could more accurately be considered the trial and error of the first part of a complex and long experiment, with the next phases learning from that trial and error. The stabilization and profitability of the Neighborhood One phase in 2001 and 2002 showed that this view was not a hopeful thought, but rather a rational appraisal.

Fannie Mae and Pulte justified their decision to undo the project by casting the years immediately after the 1996 auction as a period of missteps and an undisciplined pursuit of overreaching goals, all of which lead to ever-increasing demands for more equity infusions on Fannie Mae's part. Fannie Mae had originally committed $3.5 million to the project, but by mid-2002, their equity in the project had mushroomed to about $20 million. On the surface this was a shocking number used as a proof of Fannie Mae's dark view of the project to that point. Much was ignored under this simplistic explanation of the project's history. The fact was that the majority of that $20 million in equity had been invested prior to CDC's stabilization of the project in 2001. In that year and the following, Fannie Mae's contributions had slowed to a trickle and were beginning to be offset by income. Furthermore, much of that $20 million would be eventually returned to Fannnie Mae through lot sales. Fannie Mae had also just walked away from substantial profits that would have gone a long way toward reducing the net amount of their investment. Pulte paid for $9 million, or about $21,000/acre for the usable land in what would have been Civano Neighborhoods Two and Three, but was renamed Sierra Morado. This was at a time when raw land in the general area of Civano was going for about $30,000/acre. How to interpret this discount? One could see it as the fire sale price for a troubled project. Or it could be explained as a sweetheart deal between two closely allied business interests. The reality no doubt lies somewhere in between. It does, however you look at it, represent Fannie Mae walking away from about $3.45 million.

We have only mentioned in passing Parcel Two, a 300-plus-acre site across from the Civano parcel, which the City had held aside as a potential Civano Neighborhood Four. Fannie Mae had optioned that land, with the right to buy it for about $9,000/acre. If they had done nothing more than purchase the land and then hold onto it until the height of the housing boom, when it could have been sold at a price of $32,000 per acre, they could have generated about $7 million in profit. It is easy to be critical of them for not doing this. Any entrepreneurial developer would have done it. But the fact is that from 2002 on, Fannie Mae was abandoning its commitment to the development of Civano and returning to what it was most comfortable being: a passive institutional investor, the type of investor most comfortable with the tried, true, and predicable, not the innovative.

Conceptual layout of Neighborhoods One, Two, and Three, but also showing Parcel Two across Houghton Road. Parcel Two could have become Neighborhood Four of Civano.

Aerial showing the abrupt transition from the southern edge of Civano to Sierra Morado, a transition from planning that focuses on the integration of the public realm, an appropriate hierarchy of streets and byways, and a diversity of housing types to one that depends on street systems that put the car first, and a limited number of housing typologies.

LOSS OF INSTITUTIONAL MEMORY AND POLITICAL INDIFFERENCE

Given the City's past role in adopting and promoting Civano, it might seem surprising that Pulte's limited view of the project found acceptance among the members of Tucson's political hierarchy. But much had changed by mid-2002. The City personnel with the longest history with Civano and the most passion for its goals had moved on. John Laswick had left the City government altogether. John Jones had moved on to a key role in the Rio Nuevo Redevelopment District, a major new Tucson downtown revitalization effort. Luis Gutierrez, the city manager who had been such a strong supporter of Civano and all its goals, had retired. Many voices that could remind everyone that Civano was a long-term experiment that would demand patience before showing success were gone. For a new City leadership, especially a new city manager hired from California's Bay Area, the idea of a major national builder with virtually unlimited resources coming in to "save" the Civano project was appealing, especially if some version of the IMPACT Standards remained in place, even if softened and made more aspirational than required.

In a curious irony, this represented a flip in the history of the project. At Civano's inception, with the City aggressively sponsoring the project, it was a top-down, policy-driven public initiative that met with resistance at the City's staff level. By 2001, commitment at the top had faded, but as the enthusiastic support the planning and engineering departments had given to expanding the protocols of Neighborhood One into Neighborhood Two and Neighborhood Three demonstrated, the rank and file in the reviewing departments had become strong, even enthusiastic, supporters.

We will remember that the City Council had voted unanimously against the proposed Diamond Ventures acquisition of the Civano project. The unanimous rejection by the City Council of the Diamond Ventures takeover was largely based on opposition from city planning, zoning, and engineering staff professionals, in combination with a lobbying effort by a number of Civano residents.

In this instance, overcoming the Council's possible opposition to Pulte's takeover was deeply aided by Fannie Mae and Pulte's success in gaining support from a tiny group of Neighborhood One residents who presented themselves as representing the entire community. This group of four, appointed by a small segment of the community's residents, was recognized as being the official and only spokespeople for Neighborhood One. They were then invited into a series of closed sessions with Pulte management to discuss how Neighborhoods Two and Three would be developed. Verbal promises were made that the IMPACT Standards would not be changed, and that the look and feel of Neighborhood One would be carried over, with only minor modifications, into the new neighborhoods. Assurances were made that the home designs for the future neighborhoods would be more than lightly modified standard national models. There would be parks and amenities to match those found in Neighborhood One. In a quid pro quo for this private dialogue, these community leaders agreed that there would be no public review and discussion by Pulte regarding all of these critical issues. There certainly would not be anything approaching a community charrette, nor even the imperfect and truncated public presentations that CDC had hosted in early 2002. The leaders further agreed to support Fannie Mae's subtle but significant modifications to the IMPACT Standards.

Pulte encouraged this small group to believe they had achieved a virtually equal status with management in terms of defining how the future neighborhoods would be developed. Lost on this group of community representatives was the fact that there was no documented record of Pulte and Fannie Mae's assurances, no master plans, no concept drawings, and no attempt to present a coherent vision for the future neighborhoods. There were no records of any kind of the private meetings between these representatives and Pulte.

The City Council members looked at this group of individuals and assumed that, as in the past, their support for the proposed changes had been vetted by a community-wide open discussion. If the community members, who had shown themselves to be vocal advocates during the Diamond Ventures misadventure, were approving of what Pulte and Fannie Mae wanted to do, why should council members push back?

Aerial view looking to the northwest from Sierra Morado, with Civano along the upper right side of photo. The Catalina Mountains are in the upper background.

Sierra Morado is a planning form imposed on the desert.

Civano is a planning and community form that acknowledges its place and grows out of the desert.

On the ground the dominance of the car in Sierra Morado is bluntly apparent. Major streets become highways for cars, with houses turned away from them.

A MORE NUANCED VIEW: AT HEART, A FUNDAMENTAL CONFLICT OF VALUES

Putting aside all of the above, there were more fundamental and deeply embedded institutional reasons that, after three years, Fannie Mae did all they could to sell Civano to the largest, and generally regarded as the best, national production builder in America. It was true to the nature of who they were as an institution, and what their staff knew and believed in.

It is no exaggeration to state that the core goals of Civano were in fundamental conflict with the values of the suburban sprawl model, a key component of the economic engine at the heart of Fannie Mae. Civano took Fannie Mae far away from their normal role, that of passive equity investors. They became far more involved in the day-to-day management and funding of Civano than in any other concurrent project of theirs. When an institution as strong as theirs drifts outside of its normal roles, that institution will eventually correct its course. By the end of 2000, it had become a dangerous thing to be associated with Civano inside Fannie Mae. Some of the early staff who genuinely tried to make Civano work paid a price for that association. The Fannie Mae representatives who became the active asset managers and overseers by late 2001 were far more representative of the true corporate culture of the institution. They had little interest in pushing forward the Civano agenda and were focused on getting back to what would be more recognizable and understandable roles for them and their institution.

There is a deeper inquiry that can also be made. Gretchen Morgenson's research into the workings of Fannie Mae in her book *Reckless Endangerment* is generally considered to be the most detailed and insightful study of Fannie Mae's activities in the years running up to the housing collapse of 2008. Morgenson's investigation demonstrated that their engagement in projects like Civano was, to a large degree, a public relations program aimed at diverting too much oversight into how the company operated and to protect their partial tax-exempt status. Fannie Mae had become adept at fending off congressional oversight questions about their status by stating that without it, they could not encourage and support innovative programs and projects. It proved to be an effective strategy on their part.

The fact is that in the pre-2008 world, Fannie Mae was a key participant (not the cause or even primary driver, as some would claim, but certainly an essential component) in the vast, national financial leveraging scheme that used housing as its commodity. That commodity's supply, in ever-increasing numbers by 2004, fueled an out-of-control sprawl development and sales model, to the point of eventual financial collapse. The model promoted and depended on doing business based on a very well-established, conventional process, one that depended on the following:

- Buying up land as cheaply as possible;
- Planning mono-zoned, car-dependent subdivisions;
- Using civil engineering that depended on mitigating environmental impacts on the land that a lowest-cost land development model created;
- Building standard national production home models that could be constructed without really paying attention to local climates and cultures;
- Completely depending on mechanical systems for heating and cooling rather than integrating vernacular, passive building elements that had been developed over decades, if not centuries, in those environments;
- Being able to do this because of cheap, subsidized energy and road systems, and a political and financial system deeply interwoven with the above; and
- Securing cheap mortgages, whether a buyer qualified or not.

We now realize that this system had, by the mid-2000s, become divorced from any sense of lasting value and was dependent on creating more of the same impermanent, mediocre, subdivision-based architecture and urbanism. There was little or no desire on Fannie Mae's part for innovation, especially if that innovation slowed down the pace of planning and production of sprawl communities. The entire sprawl industry was fueled by commissions and other financial incentives based on the highest possible production numbers.

A series of typical houses found in Sierra Morado. Virtually all houses there have front-loaded garages, and driveways become the element along the sidewalks, all but destroying them as a pedestrian realm. Gone are the porches found throughout Civano, a design element that helps enliven the sidewalks and signal a desire and opportunity for social interaction and community. The house models in Sierra Morado are national models slightly modified to hint at a specific location. They could be almost anywhere.

As *Reckless Endangerment* and other studies have shown, Fannie Mae, had benefitted for years by underwriting an increasingly larger stream of home construction to the ever-growing demand for financial instruments that could be packaged, marketed, and sold to investors. These were the now-infamous mortgage-backed securities, CDOs, synthetic CDOs—the whole list of increasingly leveraged and irrational instruments leading to a worldwide financial disaster. Profound innovation in production housing, especially innovation that aimed at creating true and lasting value and questioned nearly every precept of sprawl development, had little or no utility in the system in which Fannie Mae had become so enmeshed. By simply declaring Neighborhood One a "noble, but failed experiment" and passing on the project to what was generally and justifiably considered to be the best of the national builders, Pulte, Fannie Mae was able to create a story that fit into their self-promotional, institutional world view:

- They had supported this overly aggressive, innovative project, spending millions on it;
- They had deciphered the best lessons to learn from it;
- They then passed those lessons onto the nation's largest production home builder, who promised to meet the very same IMPACT Standards as Civano Neighborhood One ; and
- It had been the New Urbanist protocols that had added to all the other factors to create the runaway costs for the project.

A pretty good story if what you are interested in is perpetuating the standard industrial-scale production housing system and wanted to reduce any real innovation to a mere tweaking of a few elements of that system.

It is a simple fact that, in 2002, key members of Fannie Mae and national builders' upper management sat on each other's boards. Having Pulte come to be Civano's white knight was not at all surprising. From Fannie Mae's point of view, and for many others, getting a national builder of Pulte's stature was a victory. In the dominant view of that time, adoption by "bigness" signaled success. The largest national production builder agreeing to develop the remainder of Civano had to be a sign that some more streamlined and regularized version of the "Civano noble experiment" was achievable, and that Fannie Mae's support had been worth it.

It is also important to note that in 2002, there was a profoundly different national political landscape than the one in which Civano had received so much help from the federal government. After the much-disputed 2000 election, the Bush administration was in power and especially emboldened in the aftermath of 9/11. Bush famously declared that the rich and powerful were his constituency. However we have come to acknowledge the fundamental decency of the man at the time of the writing of this book, there was little doubt during his presidency that big, and preferably unfettered, business was to be ascendant. There was no support for the strong environmentalism so deeply represented by Al Gore. In the aftermath of Bush's disputed victory, this passionate defender of the environment and proponent of new approaches to housing and community building was politically marginalized. Simply put, there was no meaningful support for experimenting with alternatives to industrial-scale homebuilding and the system of sprawl that it engendered. Civano had played out its public relations use for Fannie Mae. By June 2002, it was time to end the story.

One can question, with ample evidence for this view, whether Fannie Mae wanted Civano to succeed. Did they really want the lessons learned from Civano Neighborhood One and its emerging market success expanded to the future phases of the project and to the Tucson region and Southern Arizona as a whole? That scale of success would have been noticeable in a way Civano Neighborhood One, the testing part of a larger experiment, wasn't. A different, one-off community of 600-plus homes is an item of interest; a community of 1,400 homes with neighborhood centers, plus an eventual mixed-use Town Center would be hard to ignore. The planning and development of a polycentric, new urbanist, and environmentally progressive pattern for the State of Arizona would have been something even more noticeable. It would be national news. The political and economic repercussions of that day of reckoning are yet to come.

THE AFTERMATH

On December 8, 2003, the City Council approved revising the Development Agreement to record Pulte's purchase of the remaining Civano lands, and its designation as the new master developer responsible for implementing the Development Agreement with the City. Other changes in the Development Agreement were approved. Most had to do with resetting deadlines to bring them up to date after the delays of the previous years, and the life of the agreement was shortened from twenty years to ten. This last point was the final assault on the idea of Civano being an ongoing and evolving experiment. By the time the life of the Development Agreement, and with it the master developer's responsibilities, was shortened to ten years, seven of the ten had already passed. Pulte would be out of this deal and relieved of all responsibilities within three years or less, it was assumed. The IMPACT Standards were, on the surface, largely left intact, though the language for each of the standards was generally changed from a "shall be achieved by" context to "striving to achieve."

Gone entirely was the old Development Agreement requirement to adhere to anything resembling traditional community planning, to say nothing of requiring the New Urbanist planning and design protocols of Neighborhood One.

Over the next months, the full reversal of planning, design, and engagement of the IMPACT Standards that Pulte and Fannie Mae would incorporate into Neighborhoods Two and Three became apparent. Belatedly, the same community leaders that had engaged in what they thought was a co-equal dialogue with Pulte expressed their shock and dismay at how different the emerging reality of Neighborhoods Two and Three was from what had been promised or, more accurately, implied to them. They were informed that the Pulte management team with whom they had negotiated was no longer associated with the project, and the new team, the one that would actually implement it, was in no way beholden to the undocumented discussions had with the previous Pulte team.

This was a stark and brutal lesson in the necessity of insisting upon open meetings; reviews, if not formal charrettes, that are inclusive of all stakeholders; and documentation of intent, to say nothing of promises. As the oft-repeated Russian proverb goes, "Trust, but verify." In retrospect, Fannie Mae and Pulte's strategy was seen clearly. Avoid at all costs any public review of what they wanted to do. Make general promises in closed, undocumented meetings. Mask the return to something approaching standard sprawl development, far from what had been accomplished in Civano Neighborhood One.

THE LONG HISTORICAL PERSPECTIVE

From the perspective of the long history of the Tucson Solar Village, which became Civano, A Sustainable Community, this City Council vote marked an ending. Whatever the turmoil and delays of the past seven years, the development implementation of Civano had always sought to reflect and honor the original goals of the project, its advocates, and the many people who had worked to try to find a way to make its goals come to life in the very demanding world of middle-market production housing. The intent was ambitious but direct and unwavering: to find a realistic alternative to the status quo in market-rate community making. This City Council vote had the effect of handing over that idea to perhaps the best example of that status quo, but to the status quo nonetheless. The ongoing experiment that Civano was meant to be had been abandoned and reduced to tweaking and modifying a few elements of standard American production housing development.

Fannie Mae could have capitalized on the emerging success of Civano Neighborhood One. Ultimately, they chose not to because, at the deepest level of their corporate culture, the truth of the matter was that they had no desire to see or support any form of development that would divert them from their established business practices and those of the housing industry in which they were so entwined. Key to the continuing supremacy of the sprawl development cartel was making it so dominant that home buyers could not discern any other house-buying market alternatives, chiefly because they would not even be aware that they existed. Extinguishing the Civano experiment would remove the possibility for the emergence of a countermodel of development, one fundamentally opposed to Fannie Mae's entwinement with that dominance. Watering down Civano's ideals, declaring the project a financial and design failure, and removing it from currency and public awareness would guarantee the continuing success of their monopolist but deeply unsustainable practices. This kind of business and communications strategy may have succeeded then, but sooner or later will prove to have been a Pyrrhic victory.

One can look on all of this as a final and sad step in the journey of the original Tucson Solar Village from being a pure vision, though unobtainable; to its adoption by the City as a policy initiative; to the testing of its assumptions and goals in the marketplace with all the imperfections and trial and error that went into that; to its final abandonment in favor of a more predictable and less radical version. It is fair to say that most of what has been written about Civano to date has focused on this narrative. But there is a far more revealing way of interpreting this history.

The trap that Civano fell into was to assume that once its goals were articulated and it was handed over to the private sector, the market forces that the private sector lives or dies by could be modified, or just plain overcome with the momentum of the laudable ideas embedded in the project goals. This was a profound, even fatal, underestimation of the relentless economic and political influence and power of standard development interests, even if only experienced as systemic inertia.

Being overwhelmed by conventional reality has been the fate of many "cities on a hill." We accept the fact that Civano– especially Neighborhood One—was an experiment, one whose outcome was much different than hoped. However, it is also important to note that if one thing had changed—the way the project was financed and the land initially acquired—the outcome of the experiment could have been radically different. This fact should not be forgotten. Ultimately, the most important contribution of the Civano experiment is that it has illuminated the path to future successes by showing how land planning, design, and construction need to be changed to prevail over the sprawl industrial complex.

In the following chapters we will examine what was actually built and compare the urban and environmental performance of what became two split communities—Civano and Sierra Morado. A comparison that offers a glimpse into what might have been if the protocols of Civano Neighborhood One had been rolled into Neighborhoods Two and Three. We will then offer a summary of the lessons learned from the successes and failures of designing and developing Civano; lessons that can positively affect the framing and execution of similar projects in the future. We will conclude with a presentation of Civano as a model of sustainable development, outlining the deep policy changes that need to be implemented in our country to modify how we plan, finance, design, and build our towns and cities, new and old, in the decades to come.

We believe that it is important to focus on both the history of Civano and the observable data from the community as it is now. Together they offer an example of post-sprawl urban expansion that has great relevance for today's climate change challenges. Doing that is the best way that we can think of to lift this noble vision and place out of a clouded and obscure past and bring it into the present and future, seeing it with the clarity and honor it merits.

Having said this, the first step in gaining a clearer understanding of Civano is to first go back and examine in detail both the thinking behind its design and planning and the built reality.

DESIGN PROCESS & THE BUILT PROJECT

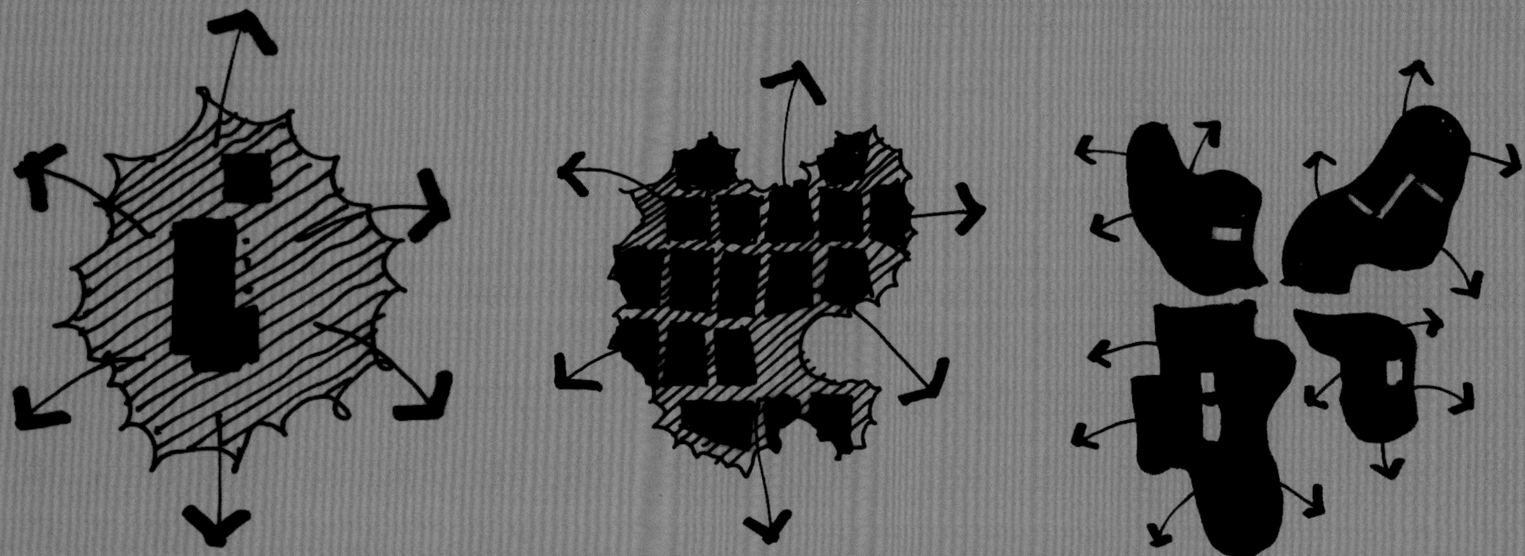

Sketches explaining the relationship, from the left, between nature and the single dwelling; between a neighborhood and nature; and between a set of neighborhoods and nature. Prepared for a public lecture on Civano in the early 2000s.

Courtesy of Moule & Polyzoides

The Birth of an Idea

The environmental movement in the United States was born in the 1960s and was formally launched through the establishment of an annual Earth Day celebration in the spring of 1970. In the glow of the anti-establishment protests of the Vietnam War era, many young architects were attracted to the pro-nature arguments of a burgeoning environmentalist community. It was a reaction perhaps to the rationalism, corporatism, and command-and-control militarism so nakedly practiced by the U.S. government at the time.

Of the many strands of policy and design initiatives to spring from environmentalism, the passive solar movement was an early and significant one. It was focused on the design of individual buildings, most typically single-family houses and sometimes multi-family housing. By designing with nature, these pioneering activists were hoping to reverse the damage done to the environment through the development process. A typical passive solar set of architectural patterns included proper building location, building shape and orientation, location of interior spaces relative to the outdoors, window and skylight size and placement, use of local materials, etc.; all now familiar ingredients of many of Civano's later architectural design practices.

The idea of Civano was also born at this time as a Solar Village by people who were acutely aware of passive solar practices and often involved with this movement. Wayne Moody was one of them. He clearly understood the importance of the sun as a force both enabling and threatening human life in the desert. He was an enthusiastic advocate of the passive solar agenda, and the most energetic promoter of the need to create new eco-sensitive desert settlements as an antidote to sprawl.

His first 1991–1992 Civano Master Plan was groundbreaking because it transcended the passive solar focus on single buildings and instead embraced a place- and climate-based approach that, for the first time, combined social, architectural, urbanist, and environmental performance in unison. The social agenda of Moody's Master Plan was based on a set of ambitious programmatic values:

Community: Familiarity, belonging, proximity to and interaction with neighbors, pride, shared activity, and responsibilities.

Identity: Distinct visual characteristics and associations appropriate to the desert ecology.

Privacy: Home as shelter and retreat from public life, personal and family focus, a sense of distance from public social interaction and business, quiet and peacefulness, visual and auditory seclusion.

Respect for Place: Views, respecting the natural site vegetation and features, the local climate, and the prevalent cultural patterns and values.

Diversity: A variety of individual as well as subcultural expressions that bring a rich mosaic of life to the community.

Security: Safety, protection, visual access, and the fostering of trust and openness.

Moody's urbanist agenda also promoted a genuine neighborhood structure, a radical move, preceding the publication of the Charter of the Congress for the New Urbanism by eight years. It was based on five key principles:

Organizing of Land Uses by what we now call transect zones, from the highest intensity in each neighborhood center to the lowest at their edges. Prescriptions for walkability and the definition of neighborhoods by nature corridors were also included.

Preservation of Natural Open Space Systems that included the conservation and management of the highest-value natural areas within the site, made accessible to all neighborhoods and the Village Center, and to explicitly support community recreation, agriculture, and recycling. These natural areas were also to be utilized for drainage, water harvesting, and pedestrian circulation.

Neighborhood Diversity that allowed residents a broad range of living experiences at all scales, through a choice of all kinds of house types, lot sizes, and ownership patterns, with a variety of street types that provided access by car, bike, and on foot to the diverse use offerings of the Village Center.

Hierarchical Circulation that was multimodal and included easy access to residential, civic, commercial, and employment activities, with a broad range of thoroughfares that were balanced by mode and carriageway dimensions, and with a higher concentration of modes at points of higher density and complexity of uses.

Balance of Land Uses in Each Phase that was meant to provide an adequate number of residents and locate them near a full complement of community uses, residential densities, on-site job opportunities, commercial services, recreational facilities, and institutional uses.

The strengths of the 1992 Moody Master Plan were mostly focused on elaborating the broad site-planning principles of the passive solar movement and extending them to the scale of neighborhoods. Among them were: solar access and cross ventilation for all buildings; providing ample exterior space for house patios and yards; favoring maximum shading throughout; advocating for extensive water management, especially reclaiming and reusing water, and recharging the aquifer; and a strong preference for xeriscape and the planting of landscape with species and size to enhance the livability of houses. There was also a clear bias expressed for prescribing houses of varying types, assembled into clusters and placed in identifiable parts of neighborhoods. Most of these ingredients happily found their way into the constructed Neighborhood One of Civano.

The weaknesses of the Moody Master Plan were concentrated in one key area: the absence of a clear vision for organizing the project around the form of a coherent, traditional town plan. The urban design deficits in this respect were considerable. The open space and drainage network were too intrusive and eroded the block and building fabric of the neighborhoods. The Village Center was located away from Houghton Road and was disconnected from passing traffic. The thoroughfare network was unbalanced. Its vehicular cul-de-sacs dominated at the expense of pedestrian connectivity and a unique street-based townscape. The constant singular orientation of buildings at 22 degrees south from west undermined the idea of a street-based urbanism, and rendered the public realm of each village residual and dominant over its building fabric. This was based on the false belief that every picturesque design move would deliver relief from conventional, restrictive suburban growth patterns. The entire project at the scale of neighborhood, block, streets, and lot was rendered in wiggly, naturalist form. Ironically, in the end, the Master Plan's disinterest in traditional geometries rendered it more like the unintegrated urban form of suburban sprawl than not.

In the end, there was plenty of planning by bubble diagram, superficial biomorphism, and loose site-planning geometries, and no emphasis on defining a robust town form, derived from the ideas of traditional neighborhood design. There were also no architectural styles proposed based on concrete historical desert construction and environmental design precedents. It was these two perceived shortcomings of the 1992 Moody Master Plan that eventually precipitated the shift into the New Urbanism once the Tucson Solar Village evolved into the broader Civano, A Sustainable Community.

It should finally be noted that the other 1991–1992 Master Plan deficit was the generality of its environmental design prescriptions, and by extension the absence of a method for measuring positive performance and progress on the road to environmental redemption. To Moody's credit, the document did include a set of environmental goals. And these must be seen as the beginning of a planning process that eventually led to the standards outlined in the Civano environmental protocols as enshrined in the IMPACT Standards.

Consistent with the practices of the time, when most planning ideas were conveyed through bubble diagrams and rough sketches, the illustrations of Wayne Moody's 1992 Tucson Solar Village Design Guildelines are not very informative.

The perspectives (above right and left), although graphically undistinguished, nonetheless convey a strong sense of the place character of the Desert Country Home Greenways. They served as an inspiration to the charrette team in adopting the idea into the final Civano plan.

The diagrams (right) illustrate four of the two dozen guidelines that were part of the Solar Village Design Guideline document. Divided into various subjects, they served more as objectives on the interface between human life and building in the desert, than as clear direction on the form or imagery that the final design of the project may have taken.

They also foretell the eventual battle of wills on the design team between Moody, who was a planner at heart, and the New Urbanists who were architects. Happily, their common interest in the environmental design of the project kept the design team together.

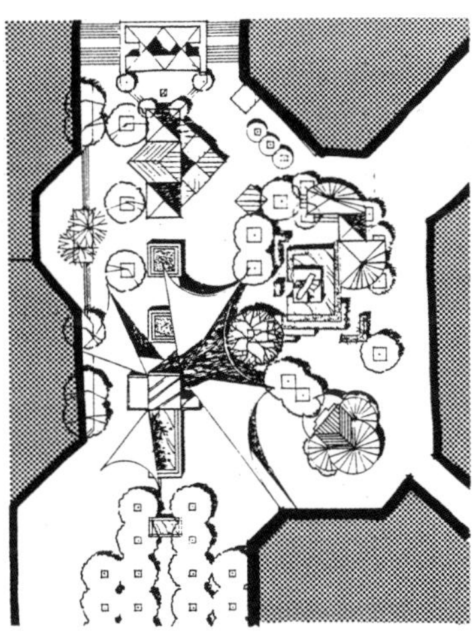

"**Urban Oasis:** *The village plaza should be designed as a shaded and cool microclimate for summer enjoyment and natural warmth for winter use. The oasis should educate about sustainable food, water, and shelter system in the desert environment."*

From 1992 Tucson Solar Village Design Guidelines

"**Interior and Exterior Design Integration:** *Common outdoor spaces should be provided in the form of shared courtyards throughout the work environments. These gathering places will serve as informal working areas, places for work breaks, and sites for office parties and celebrations."*

From 1992 Tucson Solar Village Design Guidelines

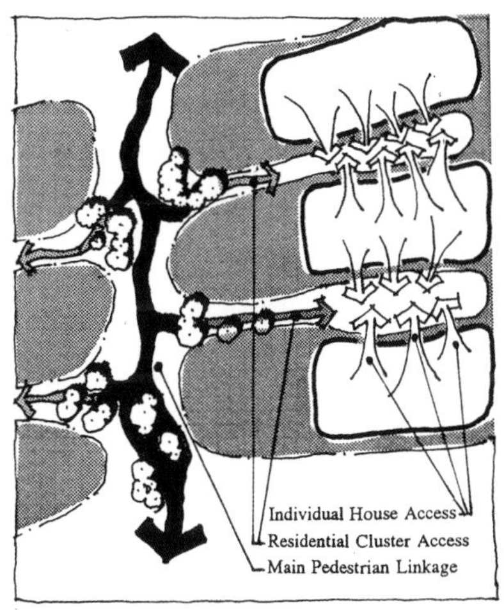

"**Common Spaces and Facilities:** *A network of pedestrian paths and bikeways must be designed to be integral with all residential areas. This network connects each home and neighborhood to all other parts of the Village (Neighborhood Center, Employment Center, Recreational Open Space, etc.) reinforcing the residents' access to and participation in the larger community".*

From 1992 Tucson Solar Village Design Guidelines

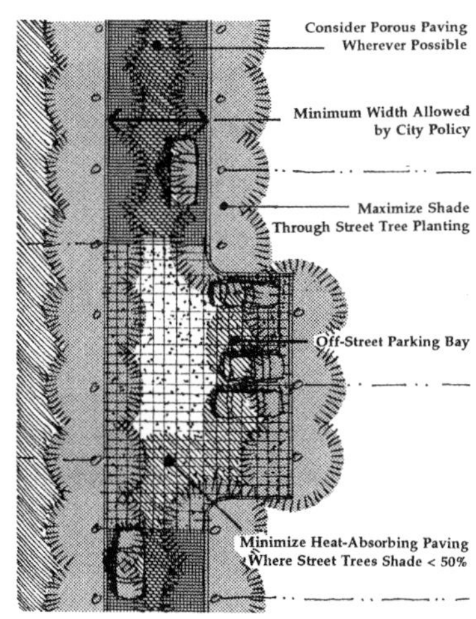

"**Albedo Issues:** *The width of street pavement is kept to the absolute minimum allowed by local codes, in order to minimize the use of heat-absorbing asphalt and maximize shade from tree cover. Parking areas are not added to the street width except in small, shaded areas and in separate parking bays. Alternative paving materials to asphalt which are less heat-absorbing and more porous should be considered whenever possible."*

From 1992 Tucson Solar Village Design Guidelines

A Bold New Direction

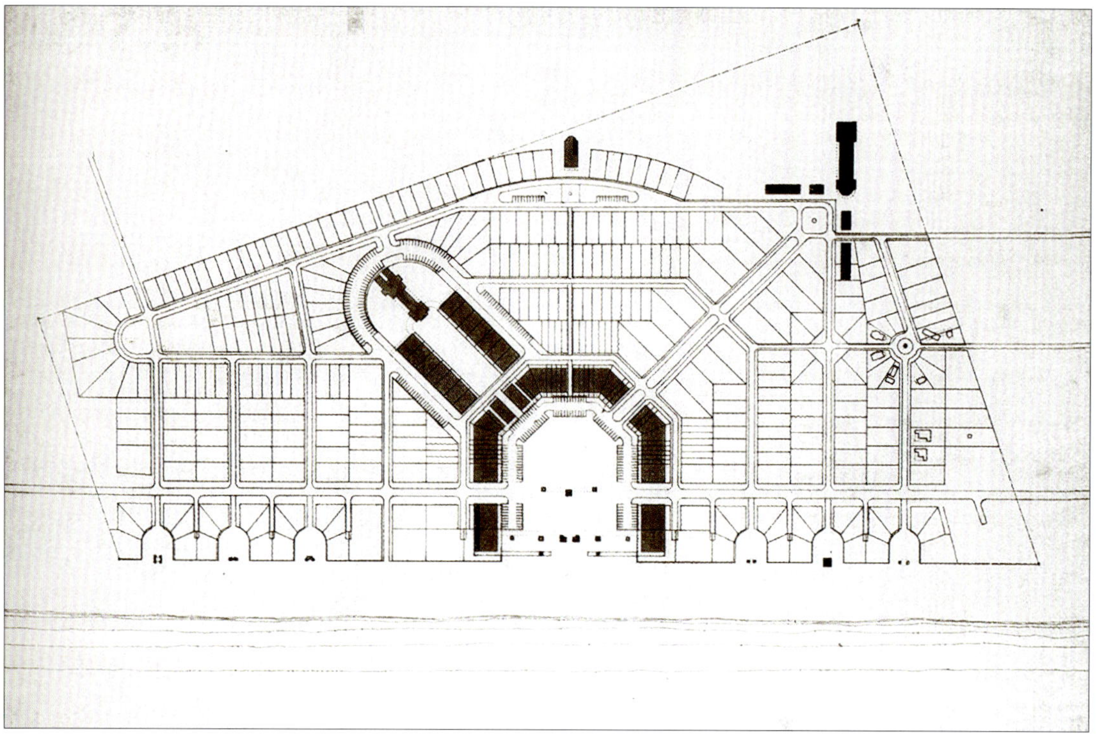

By 1996, the principles and influence of the New Urbanism had spread nationwide, with many projects underway, in various stages of design and construction. The earliest operating principles of the Congress for the New Urbanism were focused on neighborhood design. They emphasized the re-introduction of street, block, and lot/building patterns as the basis for all urbanism. Streets were interconnected, of many types, multimodal, and of reduced dimensions to favor pedestrians. Blocks were built out in a harmonious building fabric that defined a well-shaped and well-landscaped public realm. Buildings of many types, uses, densities, sizes, and styles provided market choices for a broad range of residents. All of this was in service of creating more resilient and diverse communities.

It is not surprising that in 1996, the developers that won the bid to develop for Civano, David Butterfield, David Chase, and Kevin Kelly, would bring the then latest and best community design ideas and practices to the project by hiring Duany Plater-Zyberk of Miami and Moule & Polyzoides of Pasadena, California, as co-leaders for the design of their project. Elizabeth "Liz" Moule, Stefanos Polyzoides, Elizabeth "Lizz" Plater-Zyberk, and Andres Duany were, after all, four of the six founders of the Congress for the New Urbanism.

Between the initial 1992 Wayne Moody-designed Civano Master Plan and the 1996 land sale of the Civano property, the City of Tucson had become increasingly more involved in decisions regarding the incorporation of environmental design ideas into the Civano project. As the City's general support evolved into potential public support, their involvement morphed into an advocacy for the definition of a concrete environmental protocol, one that would both justify and safeguard their investment. With the tacit support of Wayne Moody and the wider environmental community, the Laswick/Jones IMPACT Standards set six goals with metrics that targeted both the social and environmental performance of the proposed buildings and neighborhoods.

The bold, new direction in community design that Civano pioneered aimed to reform suburban sprawl by seeking a new urban form through social and environmental objectives, with an eye to both improving the human habitat and mitigating the effects of what was then called global warming. This was the first time ever that such a radical step had been taken in designing a mid-market development project.

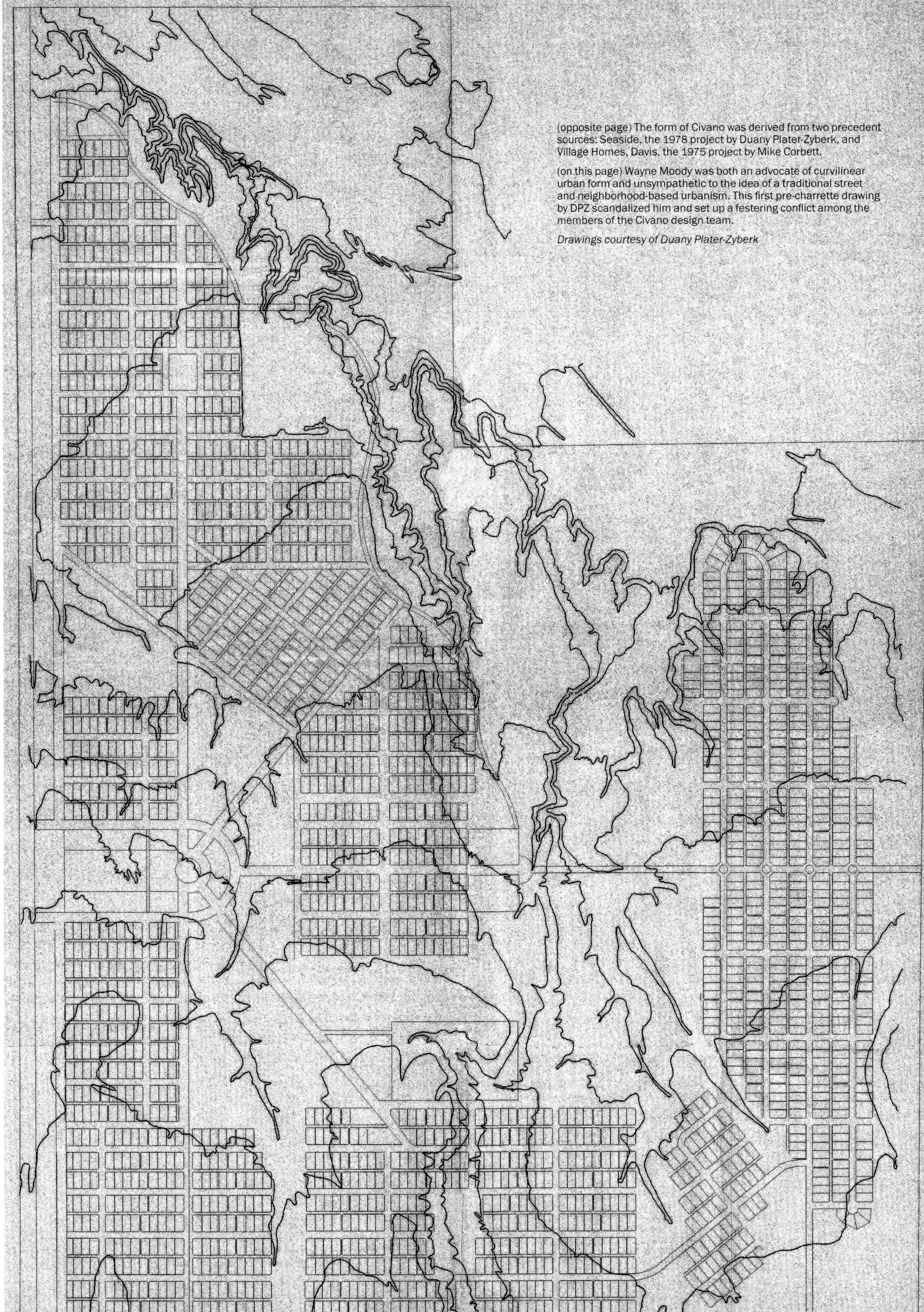

(opposite page) The form of Civano was derived from two precedent sources: Seaside, the 1978 project by Duany Plater-Zyberk, and Village Homes, Davis, the 1975 project by Mike Corbett.

(on this page) Wayne Moody was both an advocate of curvilinear urban form and unsympathetic to the idea of a traditional street and neighborhood-based urbanism. This first pre-charrette drawing by DPZ scandalized him and set up a festering conflict among the members of the Civano design team.

Drawings courtesy of Duany Plater-Zyberk

Preparing for the Charrette

In the 1990s, Tucson was a difficult place to undertake the experiment to recast suburban sprawl. The charrette process was meant to address urban development challenges in a region where national builders were operating with seeming impunity, producing cookie-cutter houses in out-of-control subdivisions, with most small and medium-size local builders following them on the same path. They produced modest homes with a sole interest in their first sale, not the eventual social, economic, or environmental value to their buyers and the community as a whole. At the time, there was also little substantive experience, sympathy, or support for the anti-sprawl cause among the ranks of most practicing engineers and architects.

Like many other early New Urbanist projects, Civano was led by a developer team high in ideals, but inexperienced, impatient, undercapitalized, and not particularly knowledgeable about the charrette process and the design of complex projects. Three errors were committed at the inception of the design process for Civano that ended up frustrating the proper evolution and execution of the project, and negatively affected the chances for its success.

THE TEAM

The team hired to run the charrette and design the project eventually included three firms: Moule & Polyzoides, Duany Plater-Zyberk, and Wayne Moody. Moody, having led the long effort to establish Civano as an environmentally driven community, was unhappy, even perhaps resentful, of relinquishing his leadership position to a couple of out-of-town Young Turk firms. He was also a Modernist at heart and was unsympathetic to some key New Urbanist positions. He did not believe that the street was an appropriate expression of the public realm of a neighborhood. He did not support the study or practice of house design based on traditional form precedents. He was emphatic on the need to orient all buildings optimally for maximum solar access. He was clearly more interested in seeing to it that the final form of Civano coming out of the charrette would follow the one he had envisioned during the 1992 Master Plan process.

By contrast, DPZ and Andres Duany were recognized as the chief evangelists of the New Urbanist movement. Duany advocated with a verve that riled Moody. His interests were in the realization of the key principles of the New Urbanism: a diverse street network; a Laws of the Indies-inspired, orthogonal grid of streets and blocks; block patterns that included alleys throughout; and buildings that were unabashedly traditional in precedence. His open-ended leadership style, generalist ideology, and interest in constantly challenging the 1992 Master Plan made Moody uncomfortable.

Moule & Polyzoides were cast in the role of defining a Civano New Urbanism and architecture that were desert-appropriate. During the pre-charrette and charrette, the role of Moule & Polyzoides was directed at designing all the project's building types and the Neighborhood Center, advising on the design of the neighborhood street/block network, and keeping the peace among team members. Their contributions strayed occasionally from New Urbanist orthodoxy and aligned with positions held by Moody.

This design in trio proved ultimately to be a confusing and unsuccessful process.

THE SCOPE OF WORK

The Civano program was initially framed as a 818-acre town of three neighborhoods and a mixed-use district. It was the charrette team's recommendation to pursue the project as a whole new town, in the context of polycentric desert urbanism for Tucson. Unfortunately, and for a variety of reasons, the charrette covered the first neighborhood only. A lack of resources by the developer, a lack of political will and foresight by the City, and a lack of understanding of the promotional and political advantages of a transformative, large-scale proposal for the future of Tucson ruled the day. This proved to ultimately be the Achilles heel of the project.

When, in 2002–2003, Fannie Mae decided to first water down and then terminate the Civano experiment, it took advantage of the fact that the 1996 visioning was only one neighborhood deep. Fannie Mae claimed it had completed the experimental first phase of the project and proceeded to sell the rest of the land to a national sprawl builder who first diluted and then abandoned the project's essential contribution: the linkage of social and environmental ideas with place-based urban and architectural form.

THE ROLE OF THE DEVELOPER

The incompleteness of the scope of work, paired with the incompleteness of the charrette documents, allowed the developers unusual wiggle room in the implementation process of the 1996 Plan. There was no overall illustrative plan of Neighborhood One ever drawn, and no code to direct basic decisions about the location, massing, and frontages of individual buildings. There was never a town architect officially assigned to the project.

Despite determined efforts by various individuals associated with both the design and the management process, serious errors were repeatedly made by the development team during the process of implementation. Almost always of immediate necessity, financial considerations took precedent over design and planning priorities. Only a short-term consideration was given to the consequences. Little by little, this led to accepting formally and materially compromised design submissions, in locating buildings inappropriately, and in not properly monitoring the work of builders. The parts of Neighborhood One where site plans were drawn for the production housing construction by individual builders, and where designs were more properly reviewed, are very much superior to the places where a more arbitrary process prevailed.

1896

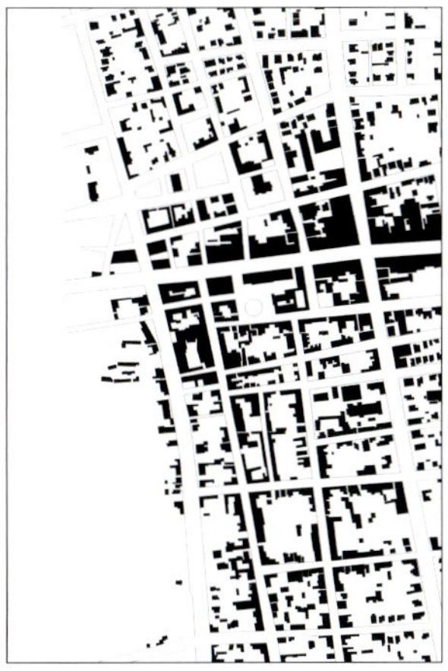

1919

1962

2002

(left) The analytical work done preparing for the charrette included the study of the urban history of Tucson. The figure/field documentation drawings of downtown, highlighting the horrors of the Urban Renewal of the 1960s, were produced by Moule & Polyzoides.

Aerial photograph of a fragment of Sam Hughes, one of Tucson's most beloved traditional neighborhoods. It served as a local model of neighborhood design for Civano. Note the components present of a complete neighborhood: interconnected and walkable blocks, rich landscaping along the streets, a variety of building types, and the presence of alleys inside each block providing service and garage entry while preserving the street frontages as pedestrian zones.

Learning from the Southwest

By mid-1996, when Civano became an active development, it was already quite common for New Urbanists to be studying the cultural and physical context of their assignments. By then, New Urbanist theory had firmly established the value of focusing on regional precedents in order to extract applied design lessons for transfer to new projects. Charrette-based projects were then a relative novelty. Charrettes put a premium on design speed and decisive decision-making. Time to think was compressed and limited, so designers were obliged to enter the process well-versed in the knowledge of key, project-particular social and design patterns. Most of this prep work typically involved firsthand documentation, as there were, and still are, so few books that explain existing vernacular and classical form as source material for Sonoran Desert design, or for that matter, for any other part of the country.

It was proposed early on by the design team and accepted by the client group that this latest urban and architectural incarnation of Civano would have to be place- and climate-specific, rooted in a deep understanding of desert environmental conditions, as well as Southwestern living design and construction traditions. It was not, therefore, surprising that at the launching of the project, it was decided that the first order of business would be gathering evidence of successful, inspiring, regional architectural precedents for the project to be modelled on.

The desire to discover the authentic character of placemaking in the Desert Southwest led to a number of trips through Arizona and New Mexico in the summer of 1996. The trips were led by Liz Moule and Stefanos Polyzoides, and initially included David Butterfield and later Lee Rayburn. Through interactive observation, documentary photography, measurement, sketching, and discussion during and after meals, a number of key formal ingredients of the Civano project emerged.

Selected pages from the sketchbooks of Stefanos Polyzoides illustrate these. Some of his sketches explore the nature of unique regional building types, such as the Santa Fe Compound, a housing format that collects detached homes around a rural yard. Others describe the geometry and environmental performance of Tucson adobe houses, buildings that provided a substantial degree of living comfort in an extreme hot/dry environment, without expending dramatic amounts of energy or material resources. Any evidence of well-thought-out design responses to unique Southwestern cultural and environmental challenges did not escape the attention of the design team. For example, new Anglo 19th century immigrants dealt with their disdain for adobe houses by wrapping them in wooden roofs and frontages. They added trumpet scuppers and stone bases for the exterior walls of adobe buildings to protect them from rainwater erosion.

Explored as well during these trips were open-space types, such as the signature streets and plazas of the region, principally in Albuquerque and Santa Fe. Their geometry and dimensions were carefully measured and drawn. The unique monumental building form of the Arizona missions and the equally figural and poetic form of the Arizona desert landscape also captured the imagination of the developers and designers of Civano and are carefully illustrated here as well.

In classic architect-think, the sketches often veer from what is being observed to what is being imagined and proposed. After examining the historical evidence, and composed after returning from one of these trips, a great single sketchbook page (see page 75) provides a comprehensive description of the elements of a Civano architectural style, understood as a living language with its own grammar and syntax. Another describes the ideal asymmetrical form of narrow, signature Southwestern streets, formed in section, by exterior walls stepping to the south and vertical to the north. (See page 73.) Taking after the famous historical precedent at Acoma Pueblo, this sectional pattern provides access to sunlight for passively heating the southern side of houses in the winter and generating cool shade on the north sides of streets during the summer. These sketches eventually became the basis for the design of both the rights of way and the building fabric of the blocks containing the Civano attached patio homes.

This urban and architectural research, taken together, promised that through transformational, inventive, contemporary design, and through typological repetition, native precedents could become the source of a new and place-rooted, genuine Southwestern project. Importantly, this process of documentation happened in real time and place, with clients and architects traveling together, sharing lots of time describing impressions and reaching first conclusions. This created a shared basis of understanding about the emerging architectural and urban form of Civano that eventually helped streamline the entire design process.

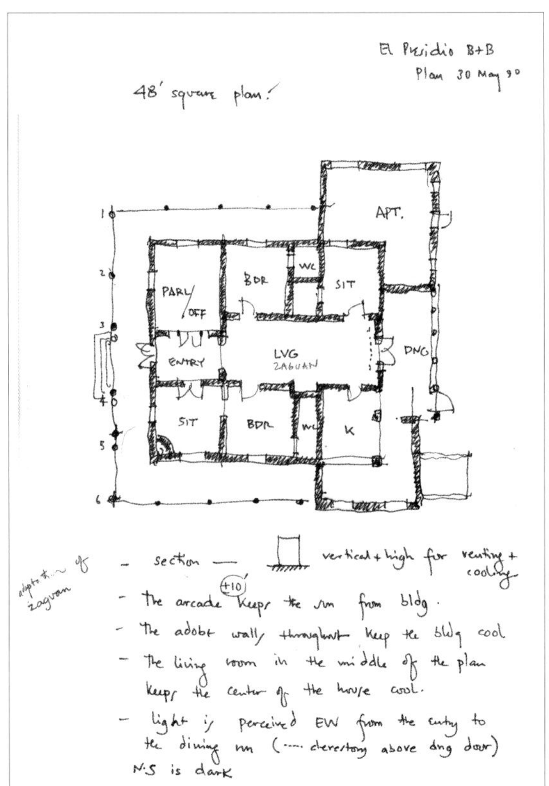

Tuscon, Arizona, late 1800s: A typical square plan Hispanic adobe house. Its central living room is fireplace-heated and clerestory-lit, to provide a balanced temperature through all seasons. The wooden porches, expansive roof, and addition of garden rooms are all frontages designed to satisfy the living expectations of a newly arrived Anglo American elite.

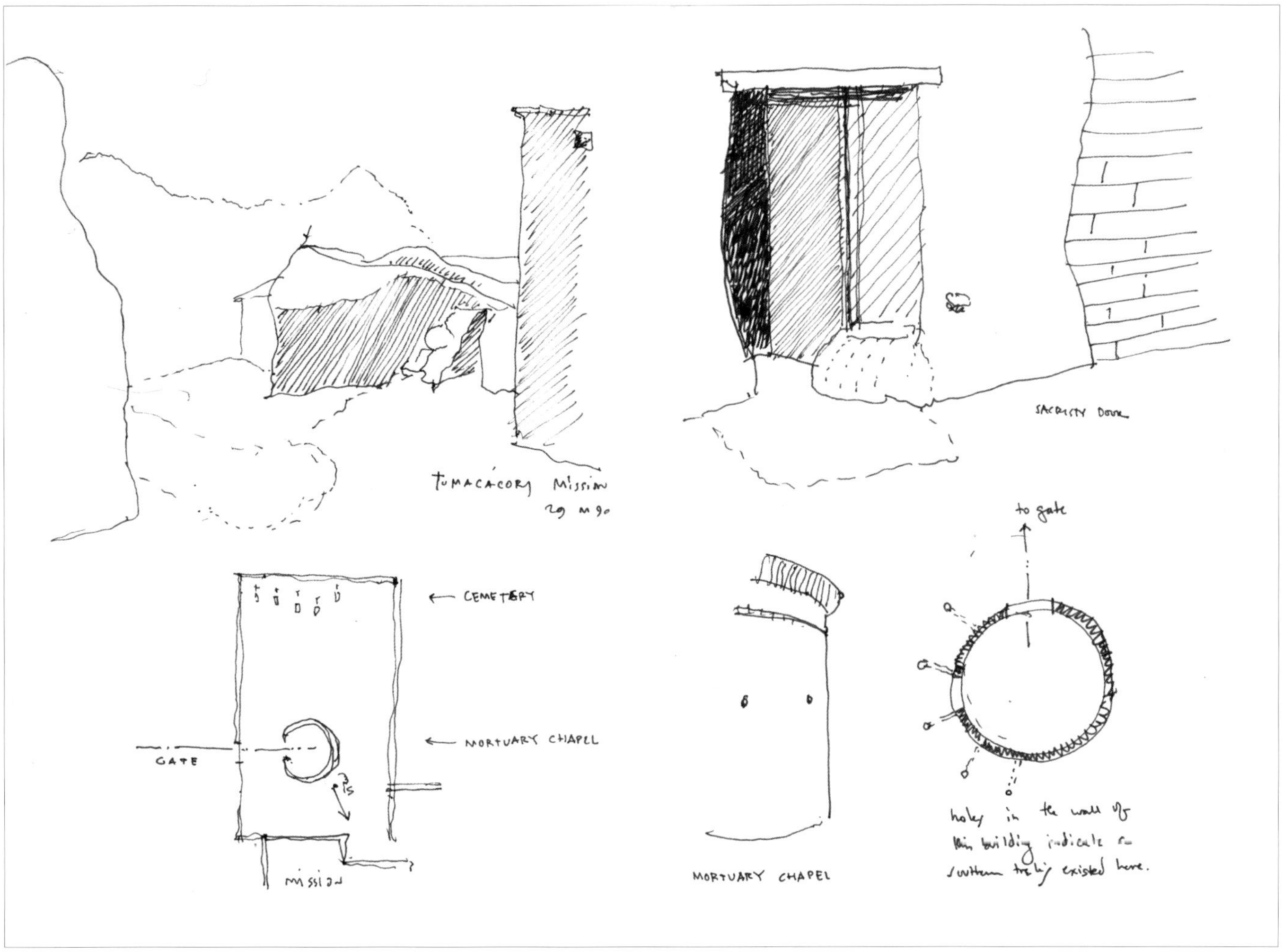

Cemetery, Mission San Jose de Tumacacori, Arizona, 1691: A cylindrical room contained within a walled cemetery yard.

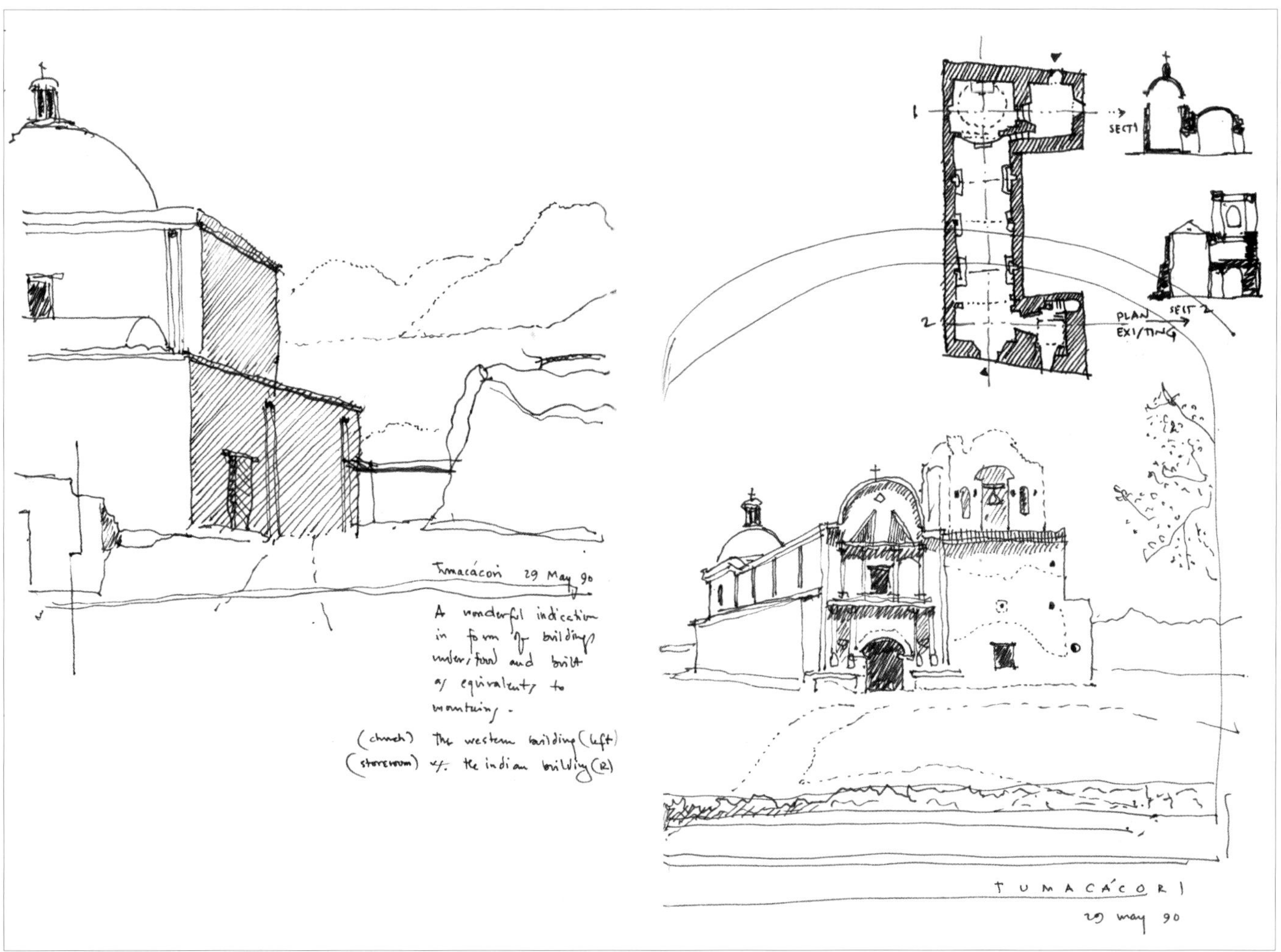

Cemetery, Mission San Jose de Tumacacori, Arizona, 1691: Plan, sections, and perspectives of the Mission church.

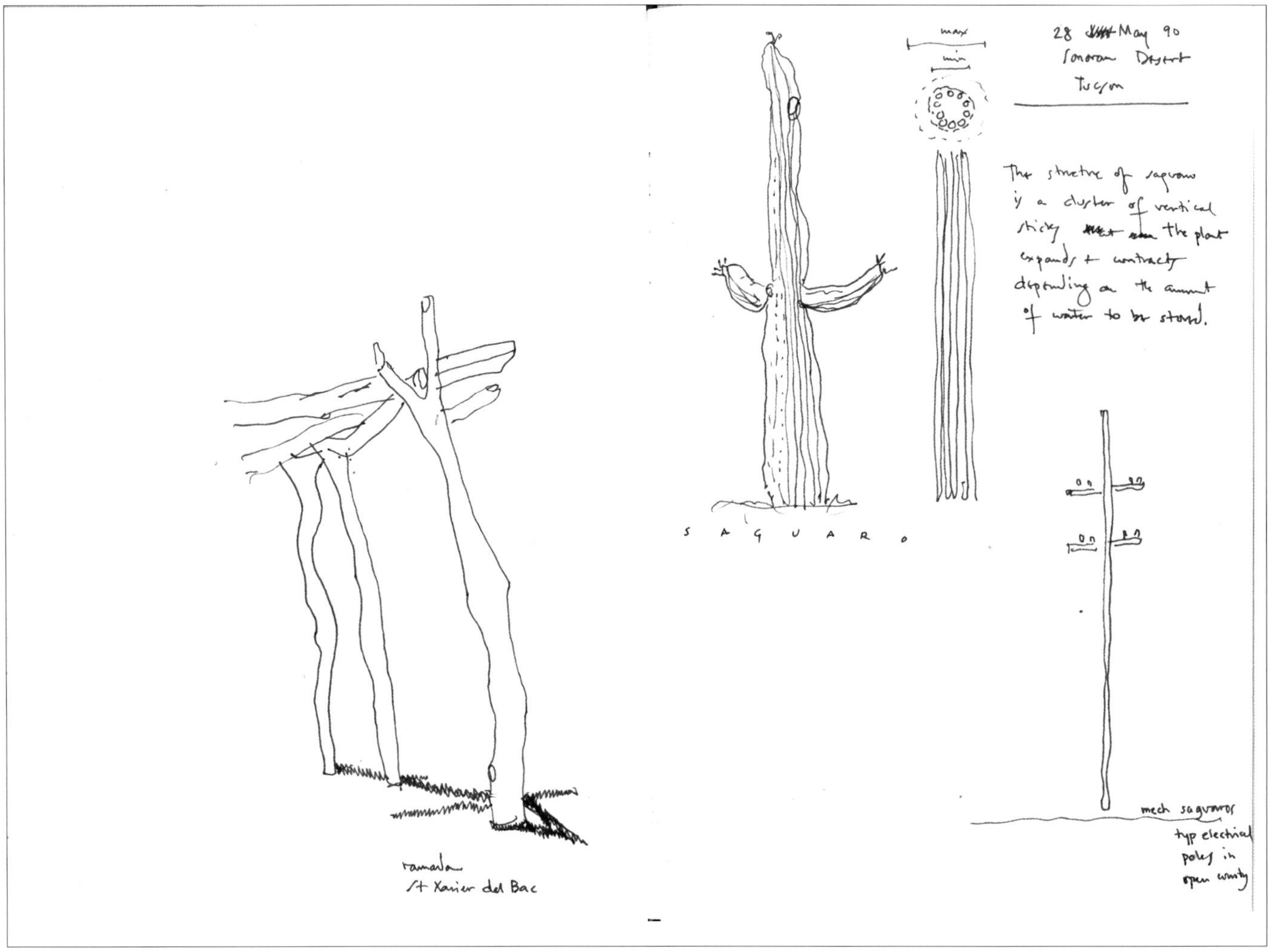

Sonoran Desert, near Tucson, Arizona. Vertical markers in the form of Ramada supports, saguaro cacti, and electrical transmission poles.

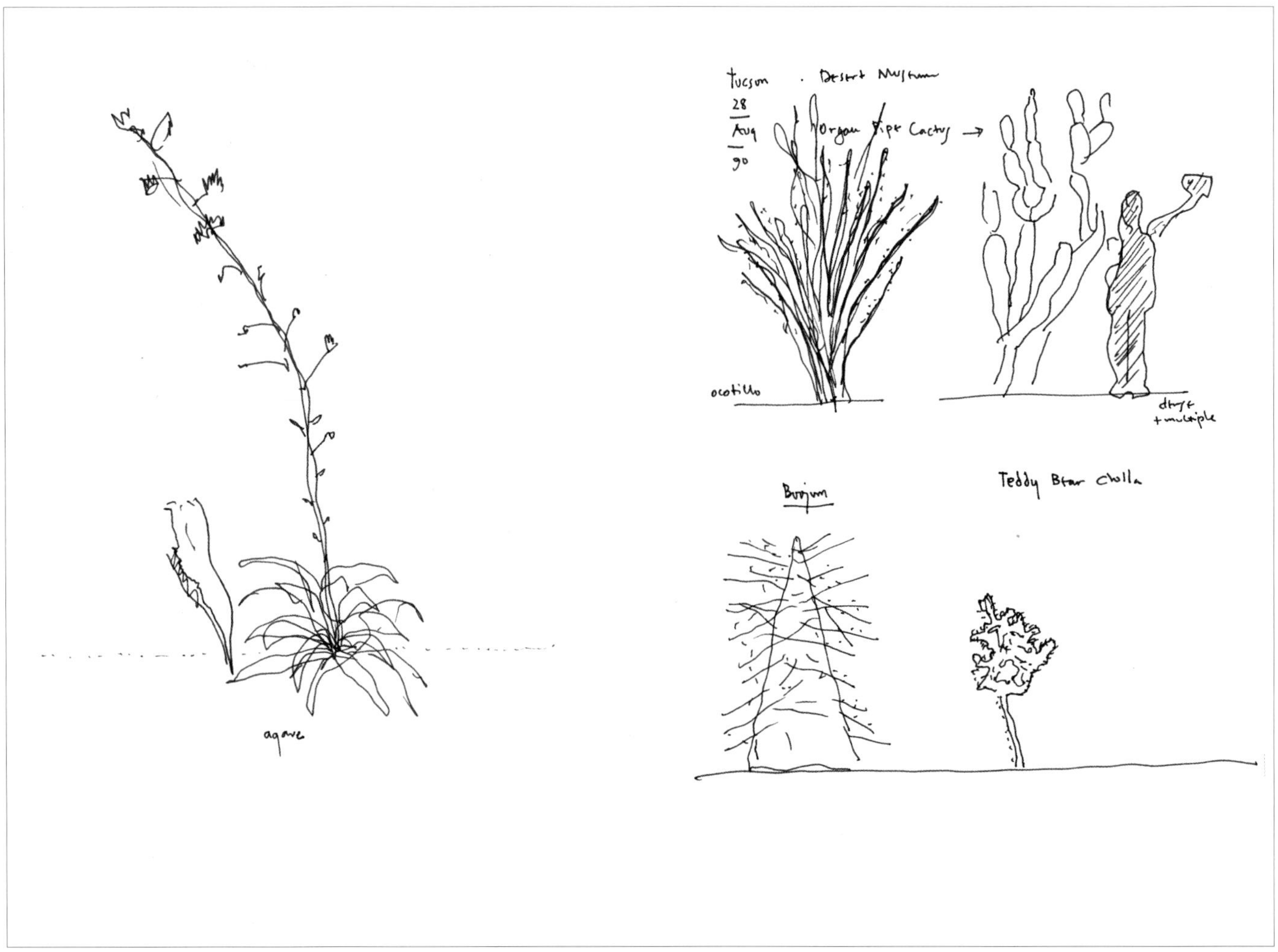

Sonoran Desert, near Tucson, Arizona. Cacti and succulents emblematic of the desert landscape.

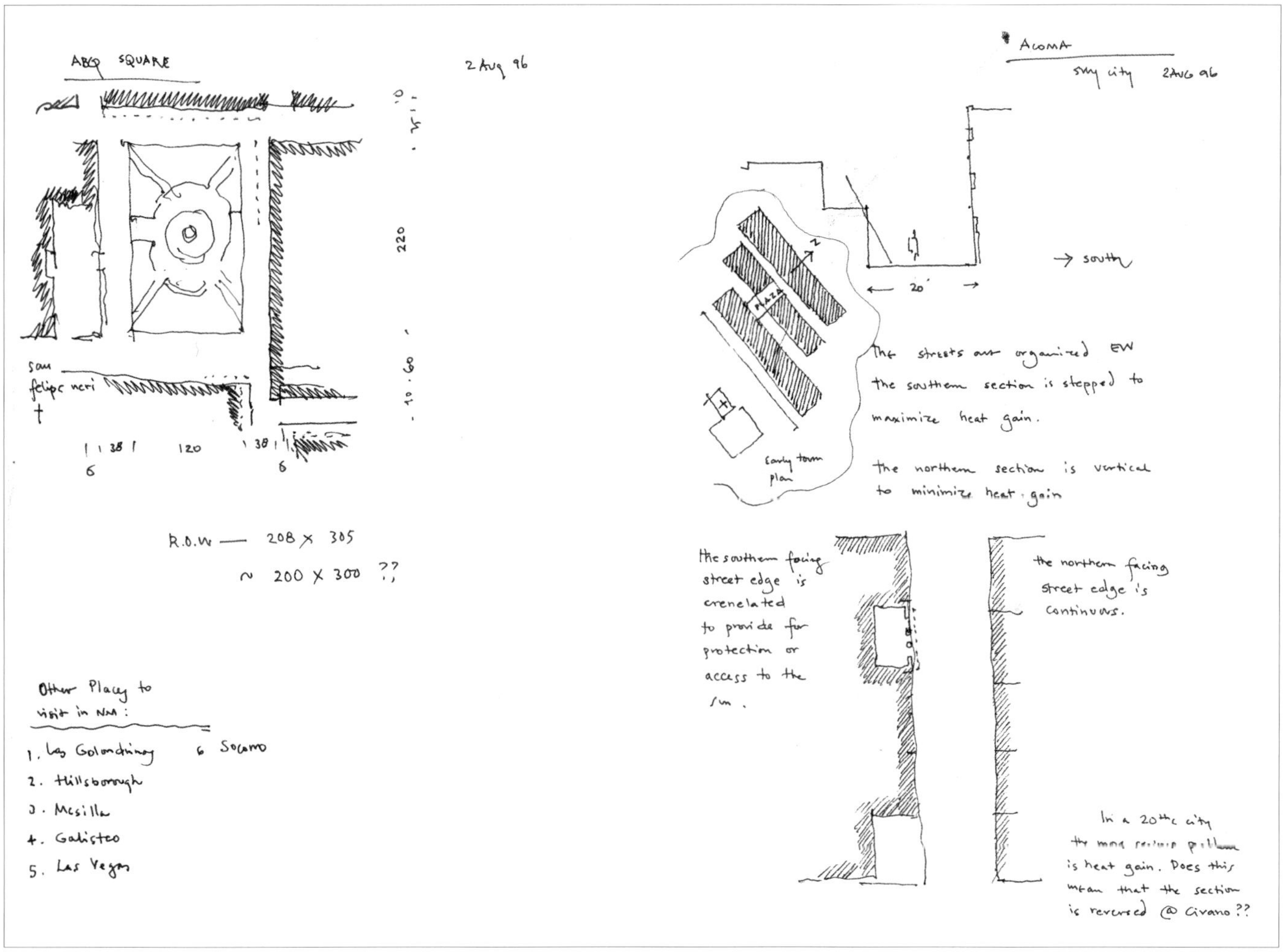

(left) Albuquerque, New Mexico, established in 1706: Plan of the Plaza.

(right) Acoma Pueblo, New Mexico, established in 1100: The quintessential southwestern street section, stepped on the south-facing portions of buildings to take advantage of solar access.

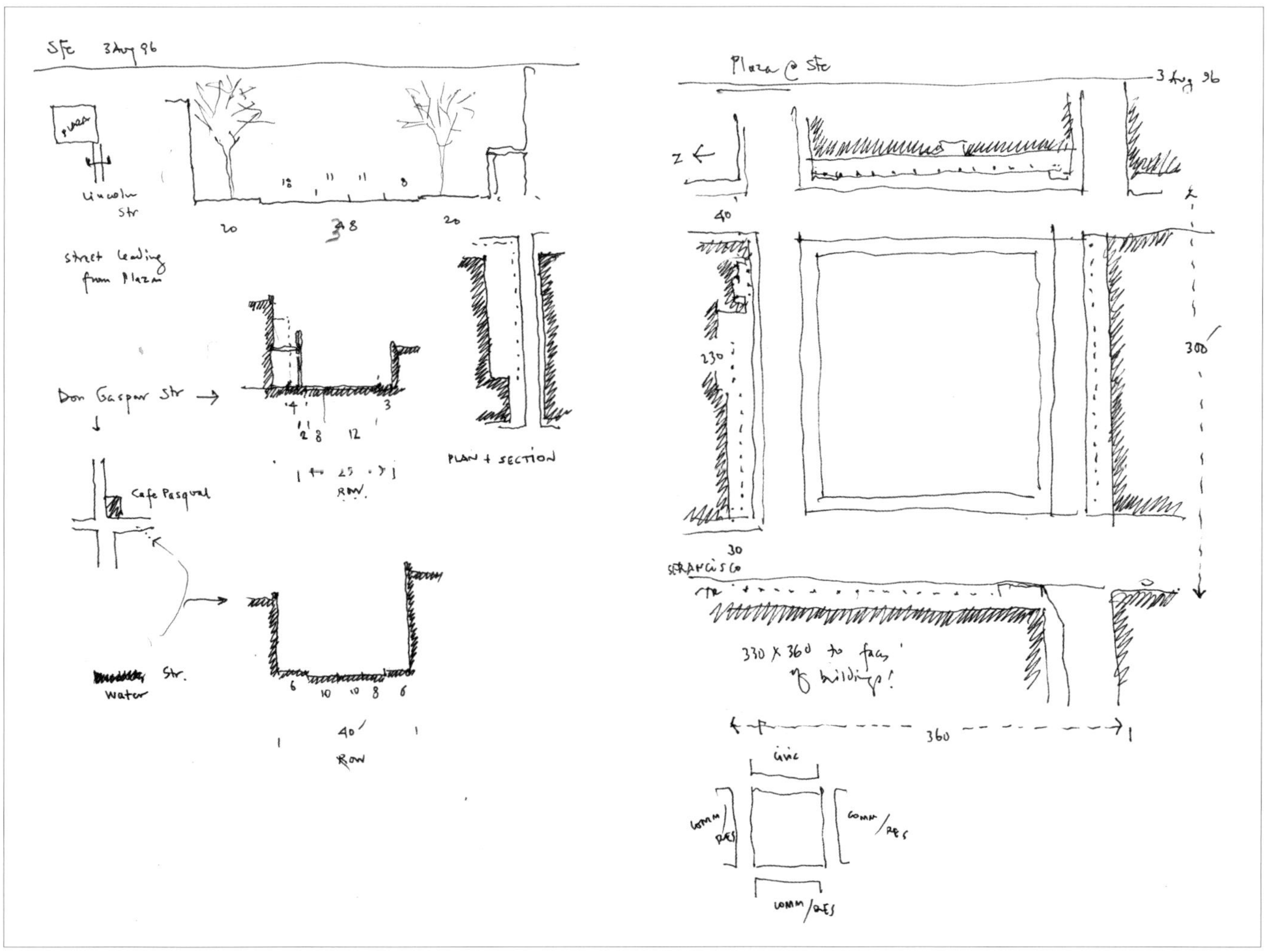

Santa Fe, New Mexico, established in 1610.

(left) Measured street sections around the Plaza.

(right) Measured plan of the Plaza.

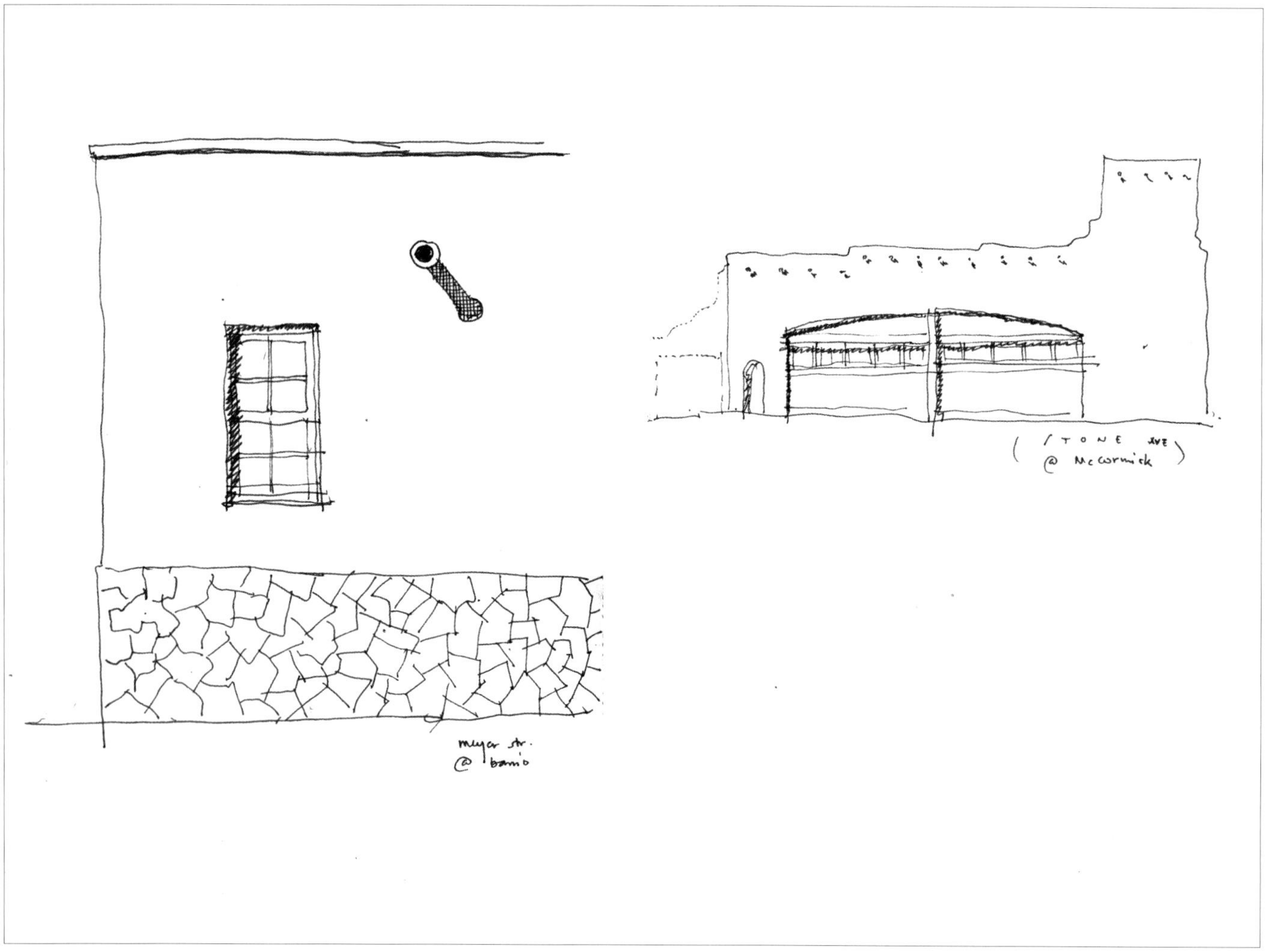

Downtown Tucson: Sketch of an adobe house and a commercial building.

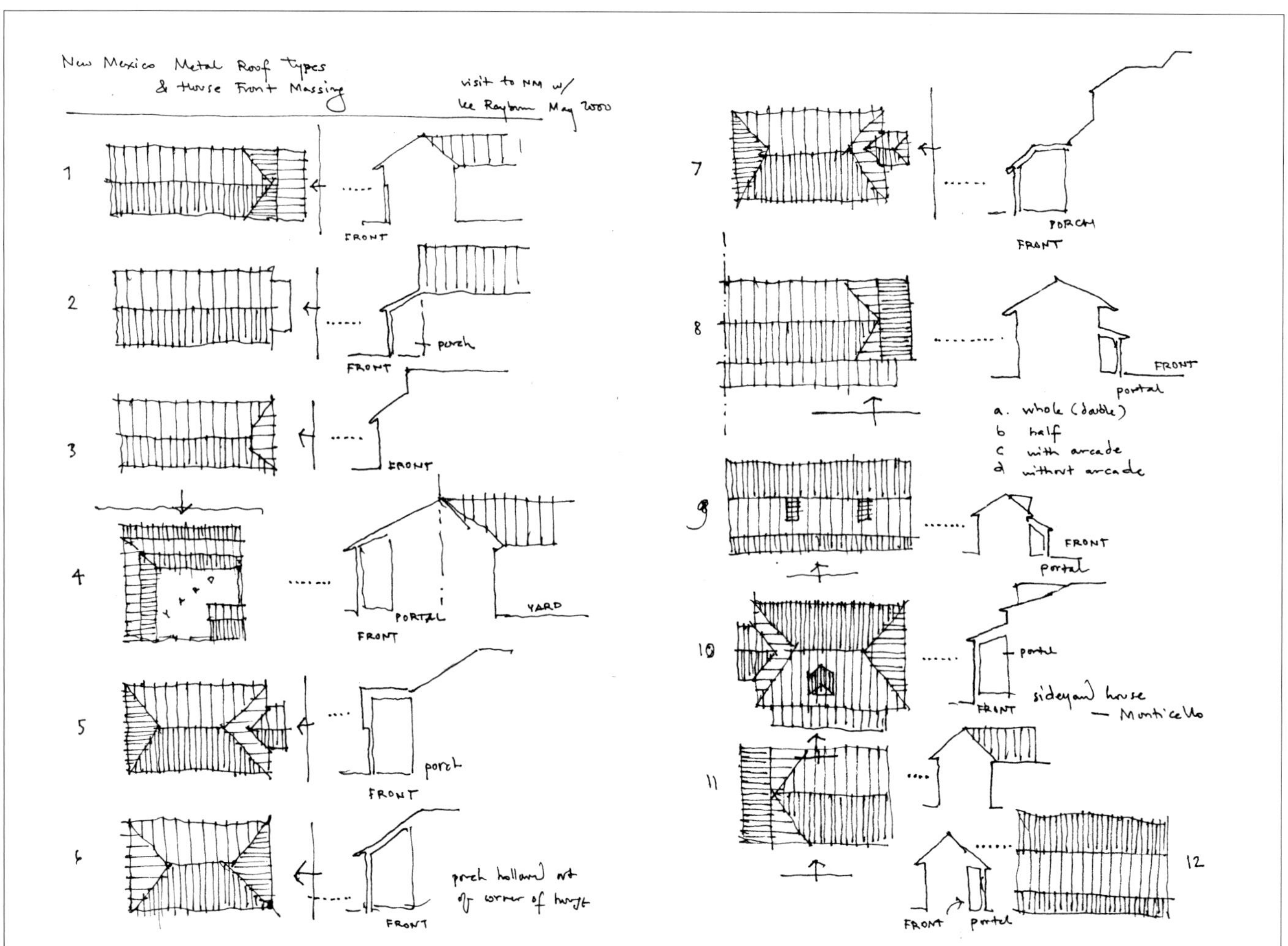

(left) Cordillera Villages of Central New Mexico: Roof form variations at the frontage of detached adobe houses.

Sketching during a trip by the authors in May 2000

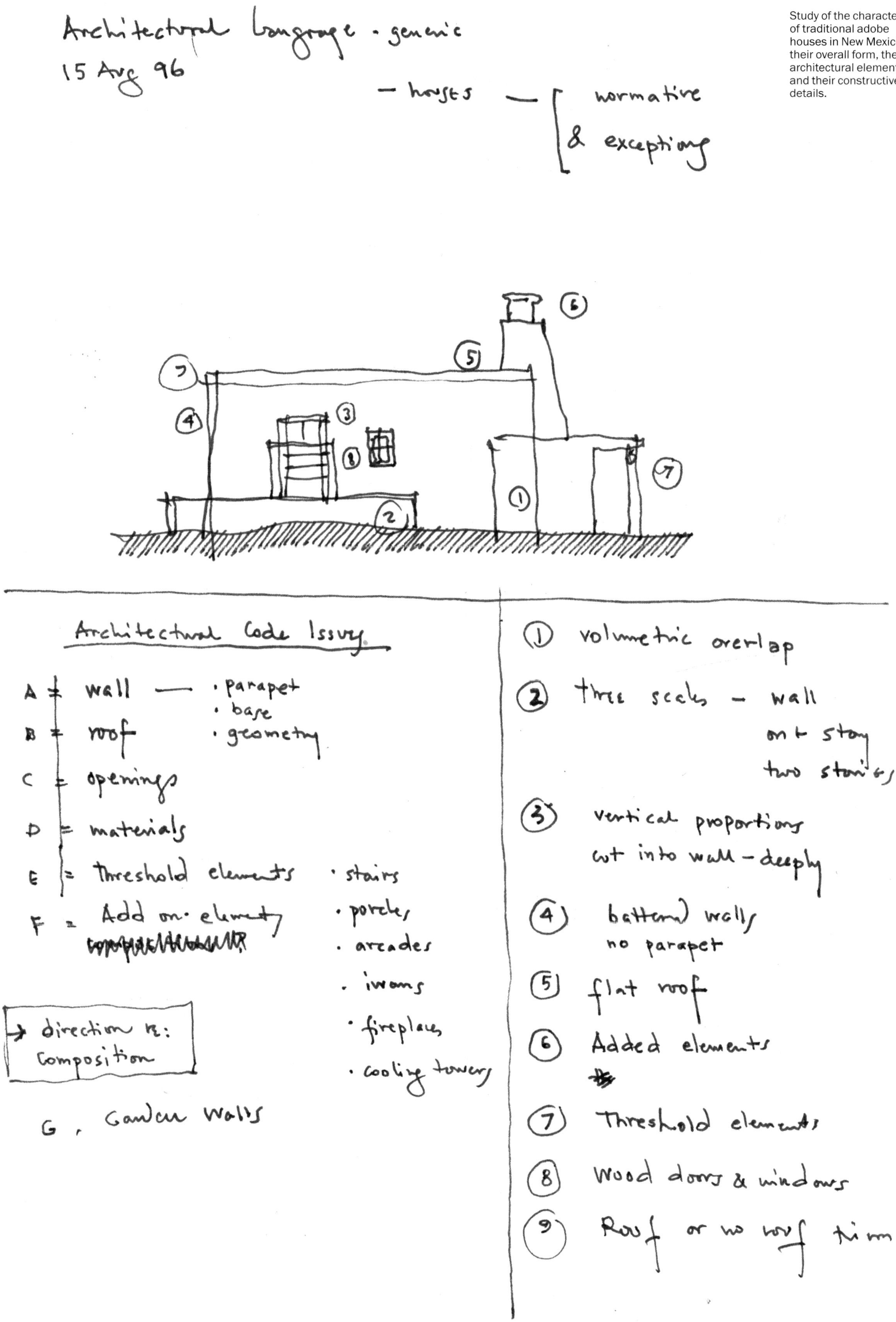

Study of the character of traditional adobe houses in New Mexico, their overall form, their architectural elements, and their constructive details.

The Charrette preparation process focused on the study of traditional and new traditional adobe and rammed earth buildings in the 19th century Tucson neighborhoods that they were built in. Before the senseless demolition of 300-plus historic buildings and two plazas during the early 1960s, Downtown Tucson was the equal of Santa Fe in terms of its built heritage. Happily, in 1996 there were many historic adobe houses to study still standing in the Presidio, Barrio Historico, and Barrio Viejo neighborhoods.

Over the centuries, Tucson's traditional form had been developed in response to living in the desert with limited material and energy resources. Its lessons had been abandoned since the 1950s. It was providential that the Civano charrette team would have recognized the urban and architectural principles that had enabled sustainable living in this climate and culture over the centuries. They adopted them as the basis of developing the image, place-character, and environmental performance of the most ambitious sustainable project.

These modest, one-story buildings had been built before the petroleum era. They were arranged along walkable streets and packed tightly around well-shaded private patios on urban blocks. They were highly energy and material efficient. Their neighborhoods featured a jobs-housing balance, diverse building types and uses, high affordability, and excellent service by various transportation modes. After studying them in detail, the architectural team concluded that their performance exceeded the standards of the Civano Protocols by 50% and the typical subdivision production house standards by 100%.

The 1996 Charrette: Master Plan

A three-day Civano design charrette was held in September 1996. The charrette was meant to focus the considerable experience and skills of the three chosen design firms on one overarching design objective: to generate a vital new desert urbanism, rooted in social, environmental, economic, and aesthetic objectives, that would stop sprawl dead in its tracks.

The social and aesthetic objectives were gleaned from the TND (Traditional Neighborhood Development) and architectural projects of Duany Plater-Zyberk (DPZ) and Moule & Polyzoides: a walkability shed, a mix of uses, interconnected multimodal streets, a well-configured open-space network, a diversity of residential types and architectural styles based on local materials and construction techniques, and climate-specific practices.

The environmental and economic objectives were based on the decades-long advocacy of Wayne Moody, as it was finally incorporated and codified by John Laswick and John Jones, on behalf of the City of Tucson, into the IMPACT Standards. The two sets of standards together would eventually come to be known as the Civano Protocols, a historic accomplishment by comparison to any other initiative going on in the United States at the time.

As was discussed earlier, in some ways, the charrette was a normal one. But in other and more significant ones, it proved to be nothing but. Wayne Moody and Andres Duany, along with various of their staff members, were assigned by the client group to develop neighborhood design alternatives through different street, block, and lot design configurations. Stefanos Polyzoides was asked to lead a team that envisioned the house and housing types and the Neighborhood Center building. This proved to be an unfortunate division of both subject matter and firm responsibilities. This led to a conflicted and incomplete project.

Moody and Duany never saw eye to eye during the charrette. It was a matter of design ideology, personal chemistry, and understanding of the desert context. Duany promoted a typical New Urbanist charrette method of town planning, acted as the impatient outsider, and did not fully appreciate the deep history of the Civano idea: the special emphasis of this project to build a new kind of desert settlement in order to sustain human life in balance with nature. On his part, Moody was uncomfortable with his assigned, limited role. He thought of himself as the master of place-sensitive desert design and most certainly as the keeper of the promise of Civano's previous versions. He could barely control his anger at being displaced as the leader of the overall project by a bunch of outsider novices. He was annoyed by the speed and inclusiveness of the charrette design process and with the common understanding by all others of the principles of traditional urbanism that it entailed. He acted more as an architect than an urbanist. He understood planning as a series of small design interventions eventually adding up into a whole fixed master plan, rather than setting up a typical urbanist framework of streets, blocks, and lots meant to allow others in the future to operate within them and generate a final project and place form.

After four days of intense design arguments and unsuccessful attempts at converging design alternatives, the semifinal review on the evening of day four of a five-day charrette was an unmitigated disaster. Duany and Moody argued and contradicted each other in front of the assembled developer clients. The project was headed for collapse when Duany decided to follow an unprecedented, brilliant strategy. He stood up and delivered his famous, endless Fidel Castro speech, referring to the revolutionary leader of Cuba. He spoke in monologue for two and a half hours, well into the night. He first defended the general approach to the project he preferred by describing in crushing detail the entire neighborhood design canon of the New Urbanism, which he had pioneered and knew inside out. He then described in extraordinary depth his preferred alternative in terms of its precedents, its design principles, its references, its potential form, and its economic and environmental consequences. Finally, he went on to outline the shortcomings of all the urban design efforts that had been proposed during the charrette and the calamities that would befall the project if any of these schemes had been taken seriously and implemented. After hours of brilliant, cogent arguments and impressive oratory, he was poised for as yet a further line of argument. But the clients would have no more and threw in the towel.

Exhausted and unclear about the depth of such arguments, hungry and thirsty, they interrupted Duany and directed DPZ and Moule & Polyzoides to work overnight to produce the final neighborhood design scheme for an ultimate final review the day after. Wayne Moody was excluded from this effort, although his organic grid scheme was the one that the clients instructed the New Urbanist leaders of the charrette to further explore. This poorly developed, final, compromised scheme was accepted by the client group at the conclusion of the charrette. (See page 81.)

The Moule & Polyzoides architectural contribution proved to be the most decisive and valuable of the materials produced during the charrette. Their work was a lasting response to the very unusual social program for the Civano project: creating a range of house and housing types that would produce a New Urbanist neighborhood, while addressing the needs of the workforce or middle-class tiers of the demographic scale of the Tucson market. It also combined architectural form issues to the construction of the exterior shells of houses as necessary ingredients in reaching exemplary environmental performance in a desert environment, and of a kind that would eventually meet the goals of the Civano Protocols.

Not only did their charrette designs accomplish this, but in the process they also created a distinct form language of local building, public space, and landscape, based on the knowledgeable application of the lessons of the long history of desert Southwest building and town design. For the first time, there emerged an unambiguously authentic look and feel for a sustainable Tucson architecture and urbanism, at least since the abandonment and destruction of Tucson's Barrio and El Presidio by urban renewal in the 1960s.

The charrette ended with great dissatisfaction all around. The developers were unhappy because there was no decisive charrette product. The professional team was fractured, and the final report that was eventually produced by DPZ was incomplete by the common service standards of that time. It included a Neighborhood One Regulating Plan that indicated the location of various house and housing types by development intensity. But it lacked three key sets of instructions that would establish the definitive, integrated form of this initial portion of Civano and would mandate its future development: thoroughfare standards, an illustrative plan, and a code. What Duany and Polyzoides did not know then is that they had won a decisive battle, but had planted the seeds of an eventual distressing loss in a much bigger campaign against Sonoran Desert sprawl.

The Civano charrette was inconclusive, and the developers opted to not continue by filling in the gaps that were left unaddressed during the charrette. This was a grave mistake. Street parking standards were never properly considered. The absence of a fully designed and explained street network, in

Duany Plater-Zyberk, Moule & Polyzoides, Community Design Associates (Wayne Moody): Diagrams of the Civano Charrette Scheme.

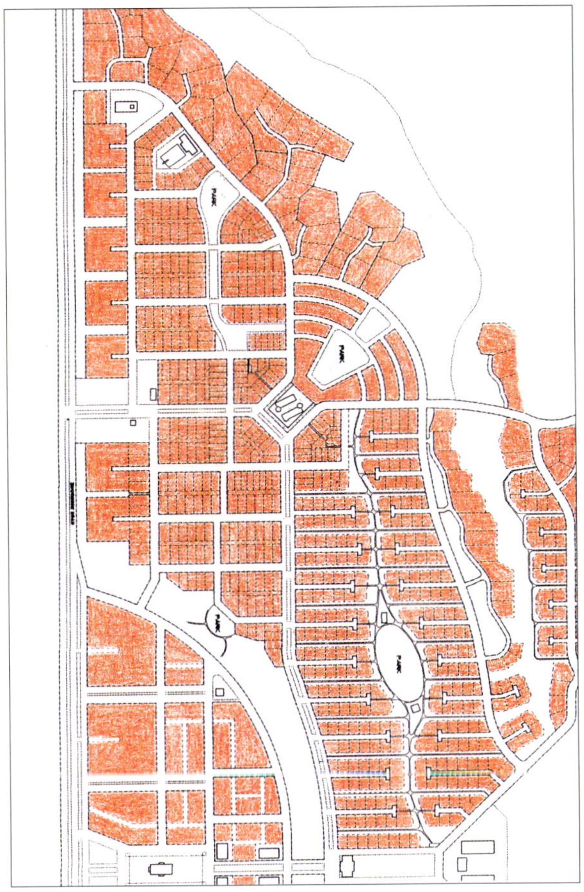

Street and block pattern

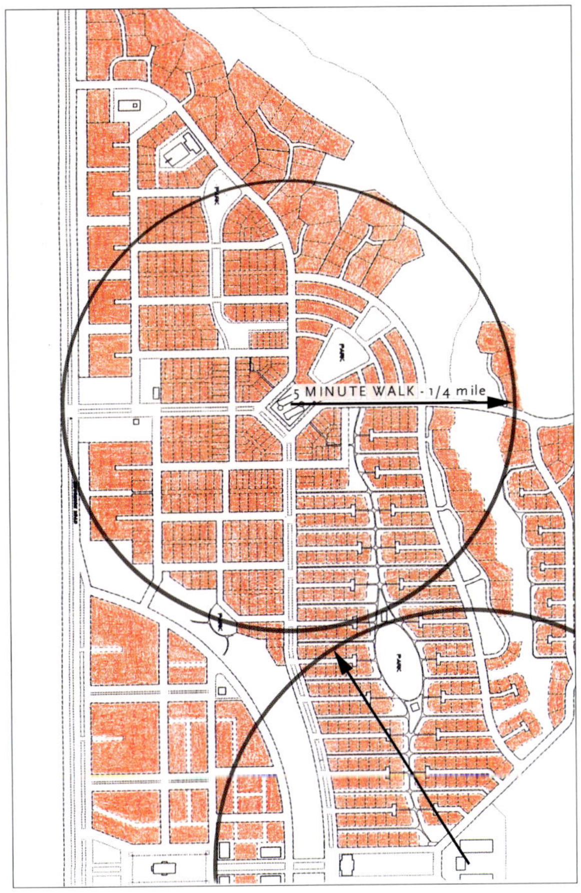

Neighborhood structure defined by walkability sheds

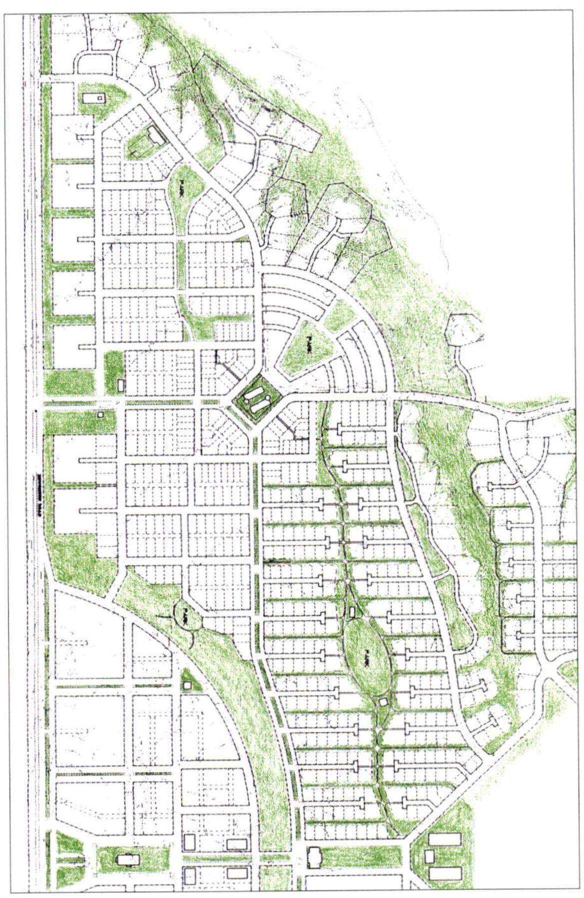

Open space network

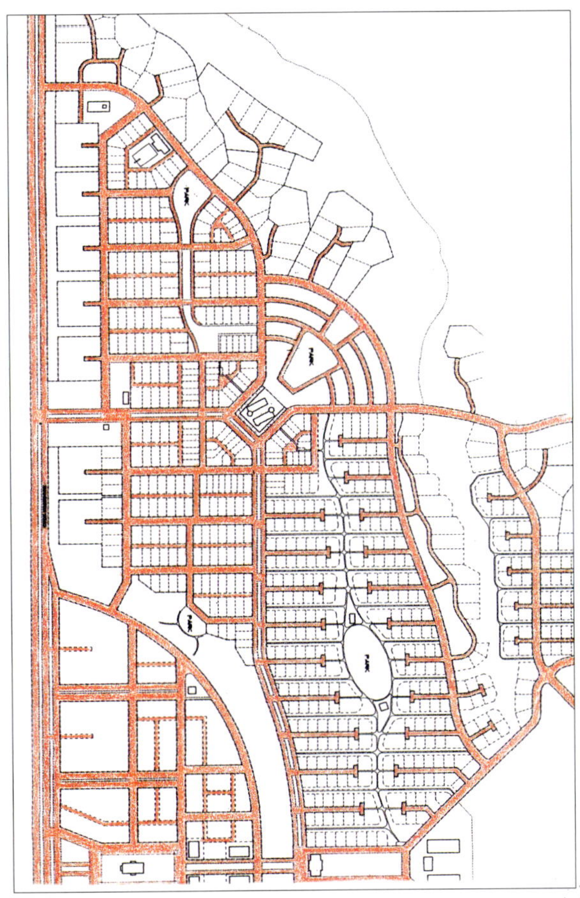

Street network

Community participants during the final charrette presentation. Wayne Moody is standing in the back row, far right.

(top) David Butterfield and David Case addressing the community participants before the beginning of the final charrette presentation.

(bottom) Andres Duany scaling a drawing.

plan and in section, meant that there was no coherent traffic agenda to present to the City of Tucson in order to proceed with the appropriate design of the street grid of the project.

At this time, the City's technical departments were openly hostile to the transportation priorities of the design team. Pressed for time, and without a coherent thoroughfare framework to base technical arguments on, the development team had to accept unnecessary compromises regarding the character of Civano streets.

The absence of a charrette-generated illustrative plan meant that there was no clear direction given for builders to produce an appropriate block-scale building fabric that would generate the robust streetscape urbanism necessary to meet the project's community and environmental goals. Moule & Polyzoides eventually worked with most of the builders in some fashion to better organize the siting of their houses. Those efforts, however, were often thwarted or compromised by decisions made by the development team giving concessions directly to the builders, the perceived necessity of the moment obscuring larger objectives and concerns. The best designed parts of Civano are the ones where the builders became so personally interested in exploring the urban form of their buildings that they sought some direct architectural help. The less compelling parts were the ones where the builders ignored all outside advice and continued with their standard subdivision practices and house designs.

Operating without an enabling code was a particularly serious challenge. The Civano charrette predated the introduction of "form-based codes" that later became a central part of standard New Urbanist practice. This kind of code typically give guidance to builders on how to locate their models relative to each other in terms of their height, width, length, street frontages, materials, details, or colors. Even prior to the formal creation of this critical tool, New Urbanist charrette documentation would usually include some such information for the use of builders to resolve such issues. Nothing like this was prepared for the Civano project. This lack of crucial technical and design documentation and instruction was a never-ending challenge during the implementation of Neighborhood One.

After the delivery of the charrette report, Moule & Polyzoides was eventually hired to reconcile the ideological gaps between the DPZ and Moody teams. Moule & Polyzoides produced a final design for a regulating plan and incrementally filled in some of the missing technical portions of the final project report. But with diminishing resources available to do any meaningful further planning work, it often fell upon the development team to negotiate many of the key formal dimensions of the project directly with the City and with the builders. Mixing technical advocacy with development economic pressures is always an invitation to compromise, which if not addressed can lead to disaster. This hit-or-miss process was fraught with errors and damaging accommodations that usually favored the short-term needs over the long-term benefit of the project.

The ultimate negative consequence of the Civano charrette was that it was executed as a private, closed-door design process. It involved just some City participation, a few chosen passive solar warriors, and a handful of City staff. The developers were overly controlling and apprehensive about engaging with the wider Tucson community. In that way, they missed the once-in-a-project chance to educate the wider public on this new and much more articulated epic vision of Civano. When public help was eventually needed to overcome the many moments of political and economic crisis that followed, it was too late to harness community understanding and enthusiasm into support for Civano.

(top) Andres Duany and Stefanos Polyzoides concerned about the charrette's impasse.

(bottom) David Butterfield welcoming charrette visitors.

(right) Duany Plater-Zyberk, Moule & Polyzoides, Community Design Associates (Wayne Moody): Regulating Plan of the Civano Charrette Scheme. Note the total geometric orthogonality of the street and block pattern.

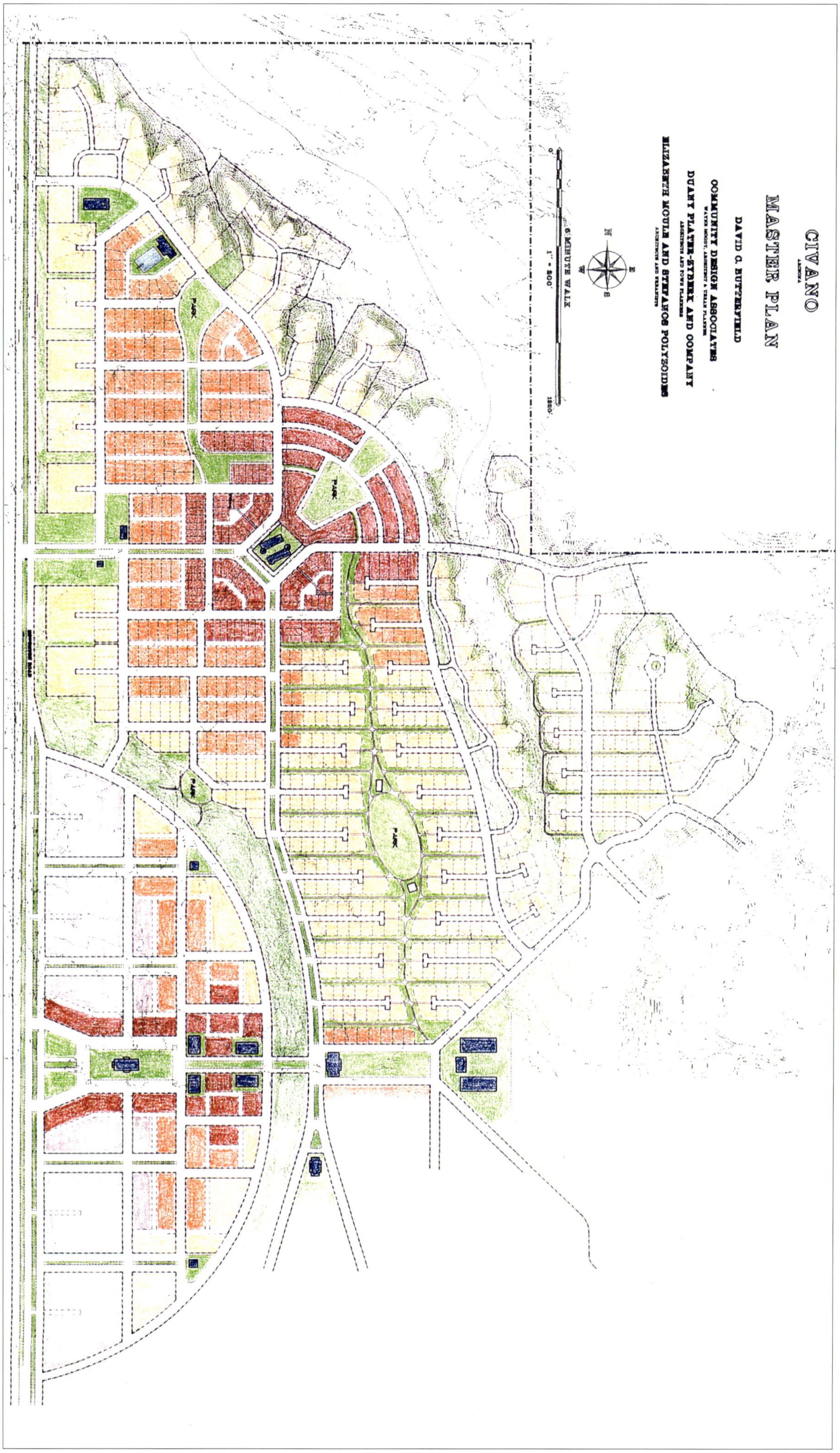

The foundational sketch of Civano's image: The Neighborhood Center viewed from Seven Generations Way.

Courtesy: Moule & Polyzoides

The Charrette: Generated Architectural Prototypes

COMPOUNDS

The compound is a historic Southwestern house form that is typical of the rural areas of the region. It is characterized by the internal picturesque subdivision of a large land parcel into individual land parcels and the incremental construction of houses on each. What gives a compound its unique form is the pattern of the residual spaces between houses, not the houses themselves.

Each house is organized around a patio that affords it access to nature and safety away from the central space of the compound, which is dedicated to parking and service uses. This loose definition of the central yard is reminiscent of agricultural traditions and practices.

Civano compounds consist of four unit types organized within a block of approximately 270 ft x 270 ft. A combination of single- and double-story homes, each unit has its own front, side, or rear "yard" defined by a compound wall.

The compounds are organized to face south to capture the winter sun, and the south-facing walls of the units are bounded by exterior walkways. Each compound unit has an attached garage accessed through the community space between the clusters. The various units are clustered so as to share garage walls and sometimes house walls to shade the various patios and mitigate heat gain.

Houses are designed as a collective fabric, not as individual objects. The landscape is informal, its form and location accentuating the residual nature of the shared space of the yard.

All drawings courtesy of Moule & Polyzoides.

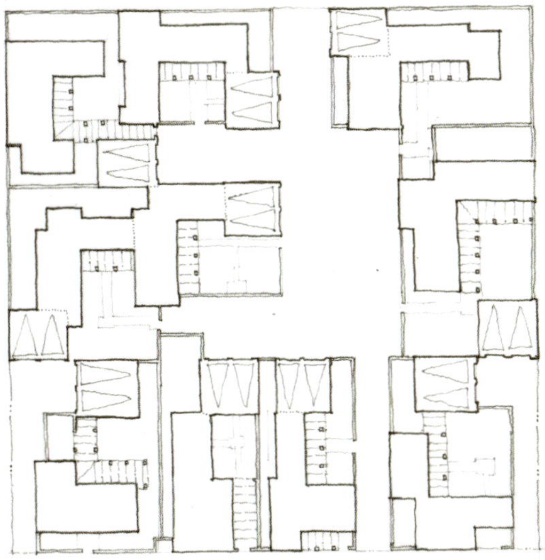

The yard provides access to garages and allows service vehicles to reach each unit for garbage collection and utility repairs. The ground plane is not paved and is finished in gravel.

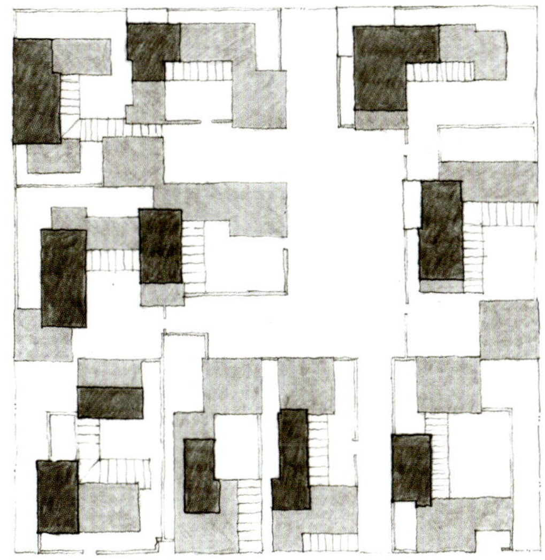

Second floor plan, Compound 1.

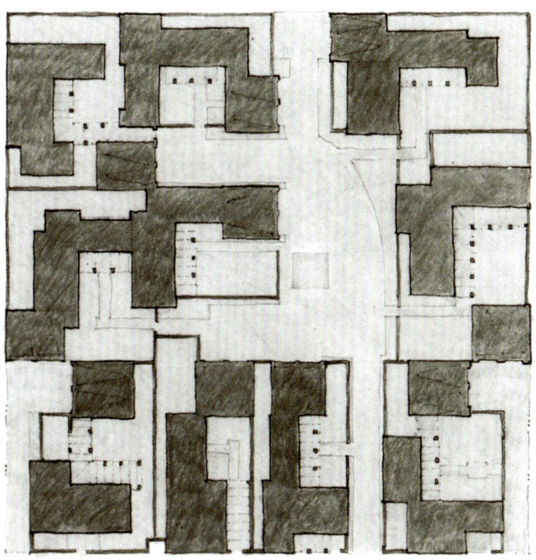

Site plan illustrating the vehicular interconnection between compounds.

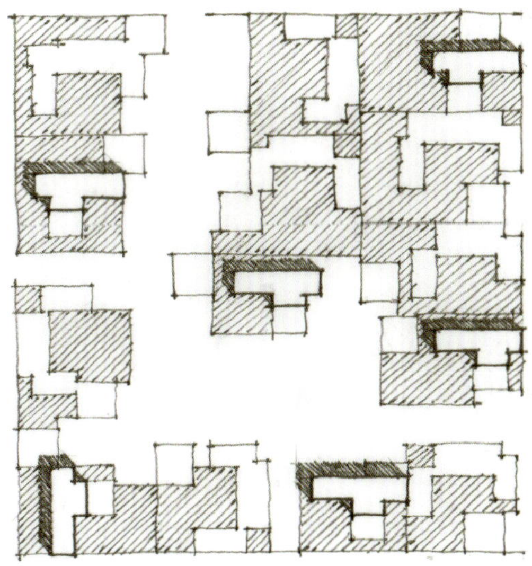

Private versus shared space, Compound 2.

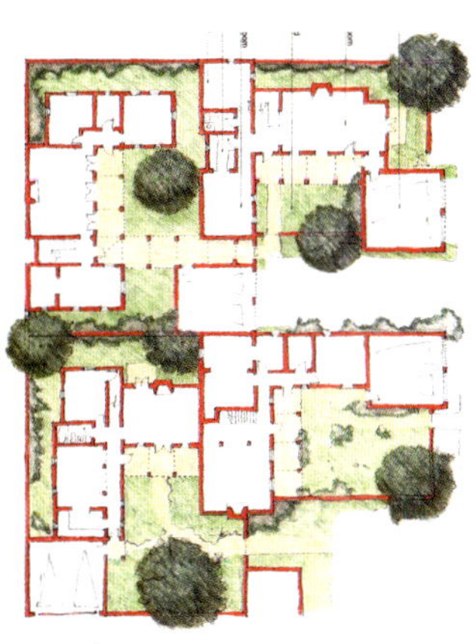

Houses are designed to define and enclose individual patios.

The walled portions provide an intense sense of privacy.

UNIVERSITY HOMES

The University Homes project was inspired by the urban patterns of early 20th century single-family detached houses in the neighborhoods near the University of Arizona in Downtown Tucson.

This particular project consists of four single-family cottage types organized within lots of approximately 44–60 ft x 110 ft. Whether a single- or double-story home, each unit has its own front, side, or rear yards, defined by a wall. The University Homes are organized to face south to capture the winter sun and the south-facing walls of the units are shaded by arcades or galleries to provide transition elements into and from the house into the yards.

Each unit has a detached garage accessed through the rear allée.

(above) A typical neighborhood street defined by single-family houses and their unique building and garden wall frontages, so characteristic of the architecture of Civano.

(left) The design of individual houses was imagined in a southwestern vernacular language of simple volumes, small openings, sparse materials and detail, and a high degree of visual continuity from building to building, creating a uniform neighborhood fabric.

All drawings courtesy of Moule & Polyzoides.

The large house type was envisioned as an assembly of small volumes. These connected building parts presented a small face onto the street, while extending into their lots to generate a variety of well-shaded yards and a central patio. This compositional strategy rendered large-, medium- and small-sized houses compatible on the same street, located side-by-side.

The size of these houses was determined by keeping their public rooms the same and varying the number of their bedrooms, extending them into the length of their lots.

The plan variation of the large house type was limited. The issue of variety in the drawing of their images was resolved with the common vernacular manner of using roofs, building, and garden frontages as distinguishing formal characteristics.

View of residential alley.

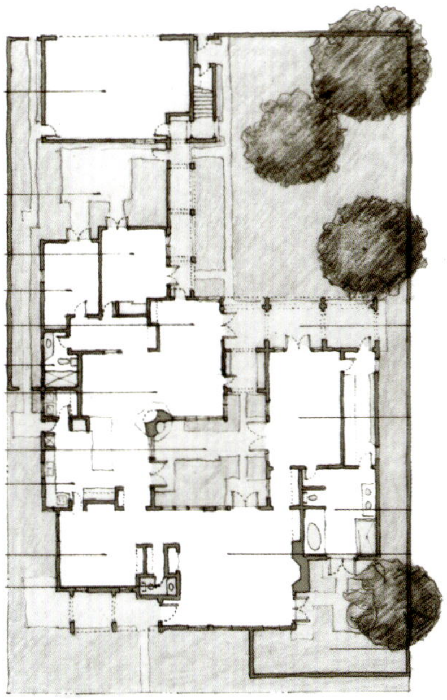

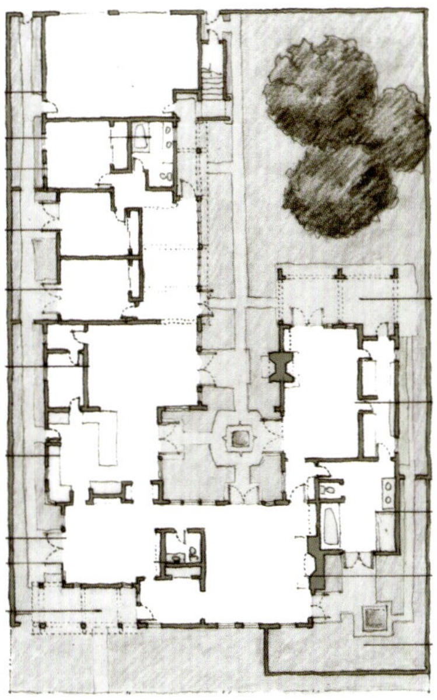

(top and middle) Alternative elevations on the same plan with a flat or pitched metal roof.

(left) Plans: Three- and four-bedroom house type.

All drawings courtesy of Moule & Polyzoides.

ATTACHED PATIO HOMES

The attached patio house is long and narrow, a single-family type that actively defines the public realm street through walls and building faces. Their patios, protected and little visible, provide a private place of repose for their owners.

These patio houses consist of three unit types, each occupying a lot of approximately 30–36 ft x 100 ft. The single- and double-story units are designed with lower massing to face south to capture the winter sun into the patios. The private patios are defined by a variety of building frontages that allow for year-round indoor-outdoor living. The various units are sometimes connected through landscape walls that enhance the continuity of the street front. Each patio house has a rear garage accessed through the alley.

The design of these buildings was carried out as an overlay on conventional builder plans. A 15-foot depth from the sidewalk to the front of each house was designed specifically to modify house volumes and set back landscape and porches to provide a better definition of the space of the street. The chosen style was an interpretation of traditional adobe forms with flat roofs, plaster walls, wooden porches, and high-quality windows and doors.

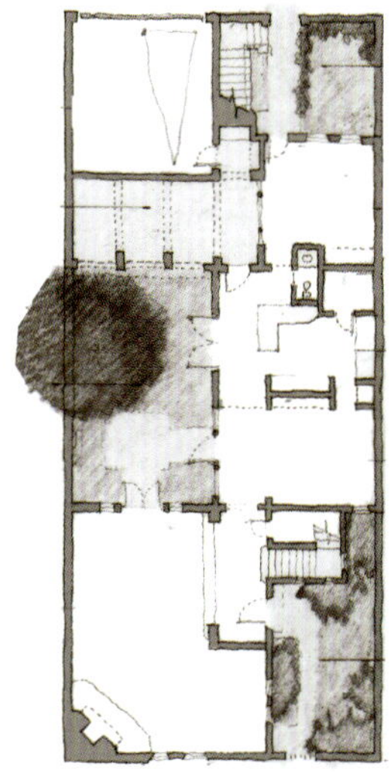

Ground floor

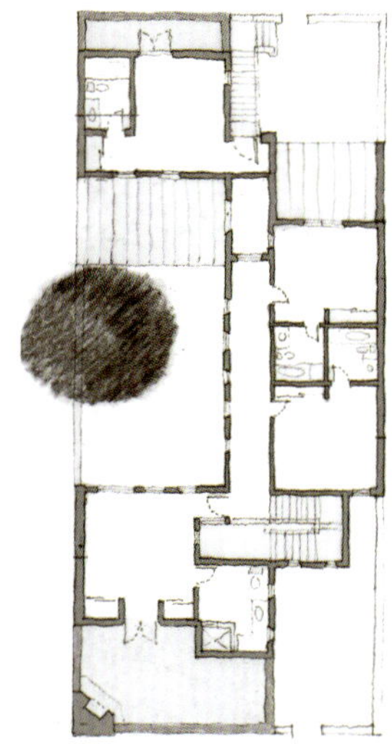

First floor

(above) Ground and first floor Plans, Attached Patio Homes

(below) The massing of each city block was calibrated by the design of each building relative to the four cardinal points, in order to balance solar access into courtyards during all seasons.

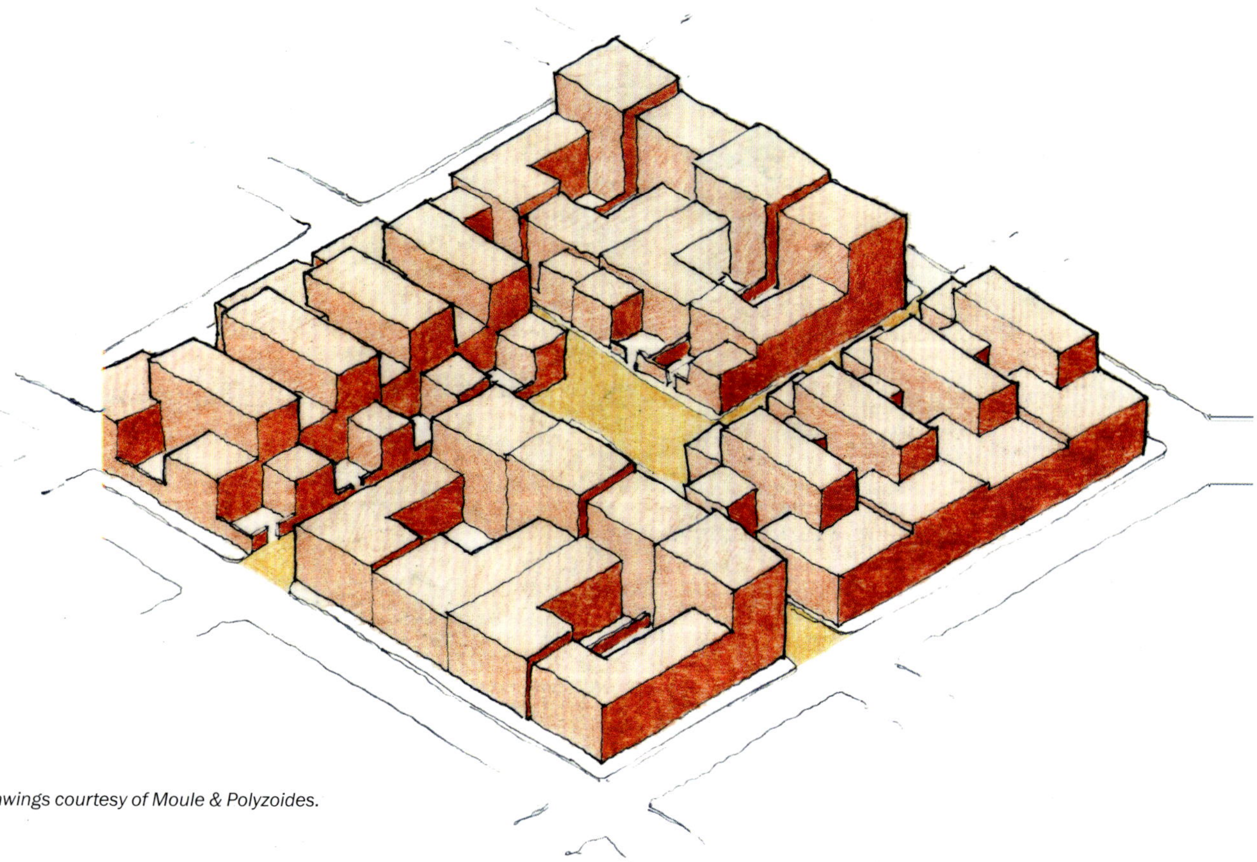

All drawings courtesy of Moule & Polyzoides.

North elevation

South elevation

(above) North and (below) south elevations, Attached Patio Homes. In the tradition of attached dwellings in ancient Southwest settlements, like Acoma in New Mexico, north-facing walls are tall and straight to provide street shade in the summer, and south-facing walls are stepped to receive the sunlight in the winter. In the summertime, balconies are shaded. This was the first time that the Acoma street section was applied to a contemporary project in the Southwest.

DESERT COUNTRY HOMES

The Desert Country Homes were derived from two historical sources: typical house types of the Radburn neighborhood plan in New Jersey in the 1920s and the Village Homes project in the 1970s in Davis, California. Both projects are organized around houses located on lanes, with their principal rooms (living rooms, dining rooms, etc.) facing a greenway in the back. Characteristic of these two historical precedents is the confusion between house fronts and backs, entering from the service side of houses, and the ensuing lack of identity and visibility of each unit and of these projects as a whole.

This part of Civano consists of four single-family cottage types organized within lots of nominally 80 ft x 80 ft. All homes, single- and double-story, are entered from a service lane and front a shared, pedestrian, linear desert garden that serves as a natural ecological zone between rows of houses. Each unit is carefully sited so that its patio is oriented to capture the winter sun.

The Radburn dilemma is resolved in this design by directing everyone, residents and guests alike, to enter these houses from the service side directly into a living room, and then to exit also directly into a walled patio that borders the linear desert garden.

Service lane elevation: The service lane is fronted by garages, carports, and service rooms. Their presence is mitigated by patios and the planting of a four-foot trellis. It is the intention of the design that the form of these houses be shared so that their ensemble is more important than any of them individually.

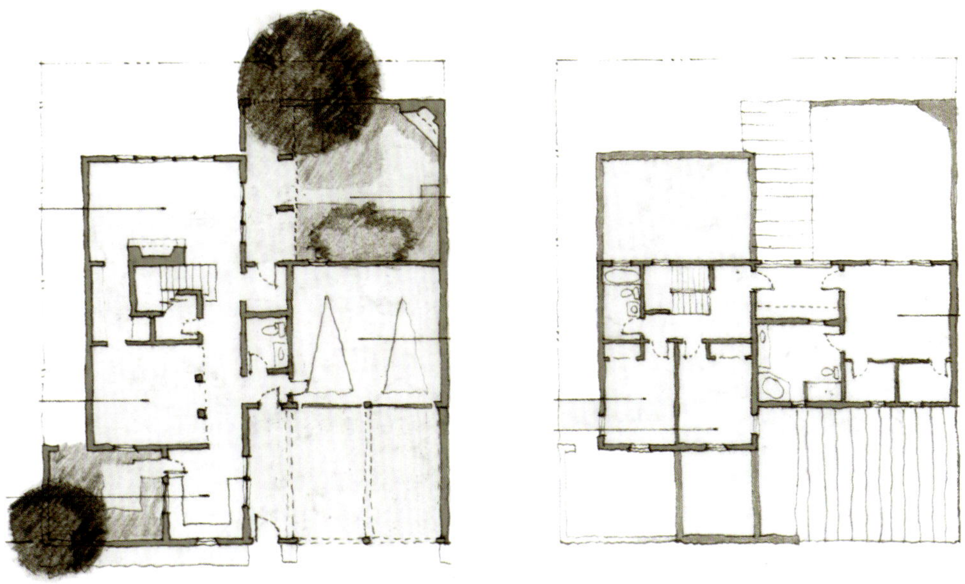

(left) Ground floor plan
(right) First floor plan

All drawings courtesy of Moule & Polyzoides.

COURTYARD HOUSING

The courtyard housing typology was utilized as part of an affordable housing strategy at Civano. Typical L-shaped units containing their own patio were arranged in a row and then replicated in a symmetrical pattern. This operation rendered a linear courtyard between the two rows. Parking was located in the back of the lot in attached carports. An alternative kind of courtyard housing had the L-shaped patio units arranged in back-to-back rows. Each unit in this arrangement was entered through a side yard. Both kinds of courtyards were to address the public realm through a combination of massing and frontage designs.

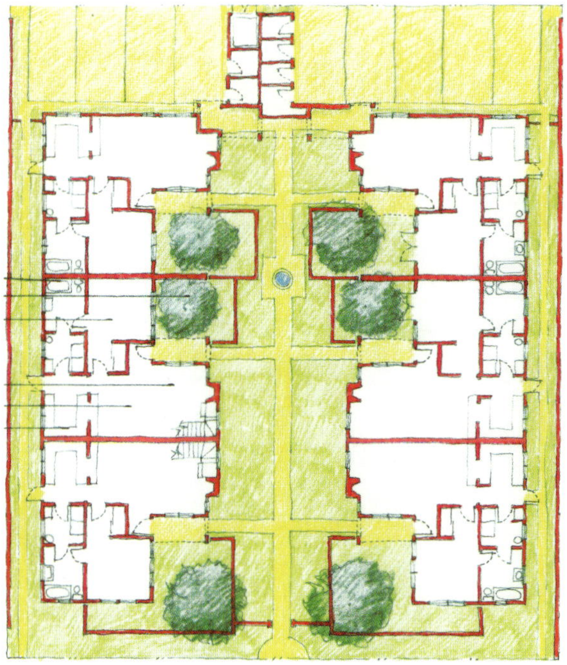

Courtyard housing Plan A: Units arranged across from each other.

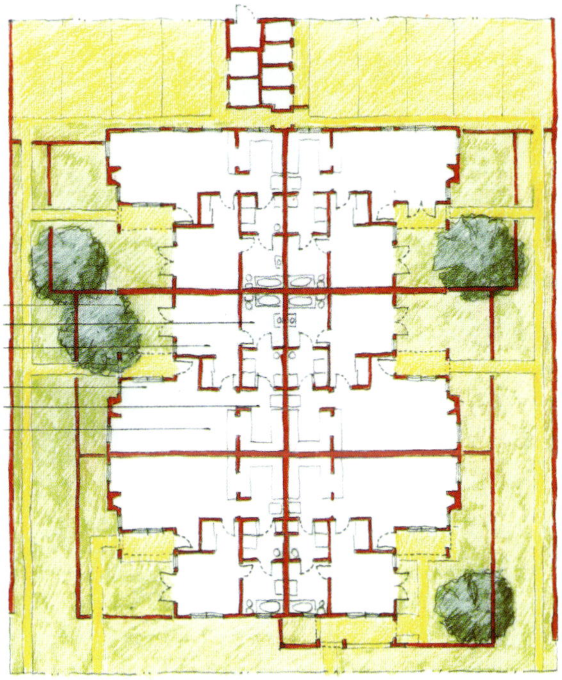

Courtyard housing Plan B: Units arranged back-to-back.

A courtyard housing front on a neighborhood street design at the scale of a large house.

NEIGHBORHOOD CENTER

The Neighborhood Center was conceived during the charrette as an active social magnet at the core of Neighborhood One. It was imagined in terms symbolic as an expression of a seven generations commitment to sustainability as community well-being. Unlike typical suburban buildings of its kind, it was designed less as a sales center and more as a combination of community and small commercial/retail facility.

So strong was the belief that this had to be a building of civic function and form that it was located away from Houghton Road and closer to the daily movement patterns of residents going about their lives by bike, on foot, or by car. Its design inspiration was Southwestern and its monumental character the result of siting that made it visually distinct and present from every part of Neighborhood One.

The courtyard was imagined as a year-round community gathering space, protected from the desert sun by balconies, arcades, and trellises. A cooling tower loomed over the complex. It provided outdoor temperature control over the summer months and also air conditioning for the Kiva, the cylindrical meeting room, the most distinctive and spiritual place in the building. The construction of the Neighborhood Center was designed to illustrate various natural ways of building that were alternatives to standard wood framing. These included walls that absorbed heat throughout the day and released it at night; a focus on natural ventilation; daylighting; shading tailored to building orientation; etc.

Frontages, trellises, and trees that shade openings, water harvesting, xeriscape, sustainable materials and building components were all meant to combine to turn this building into an icon of climate-specific, mostly passive environmental design.

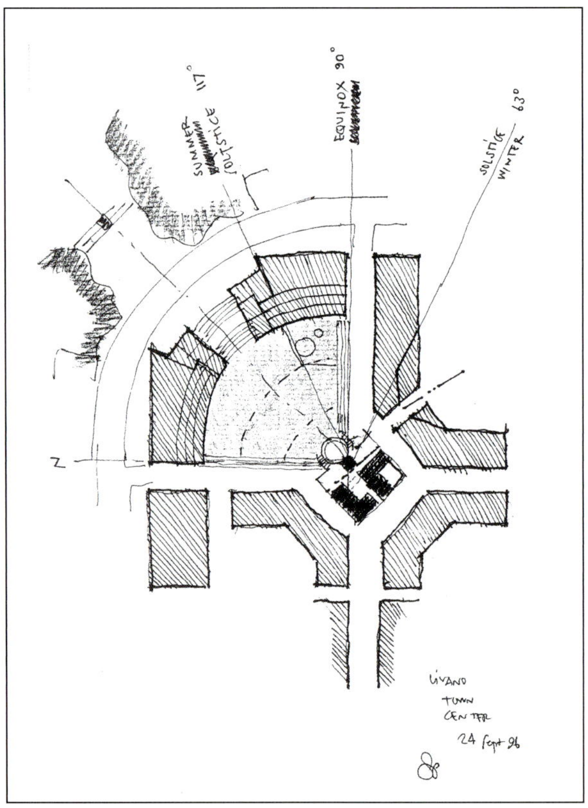

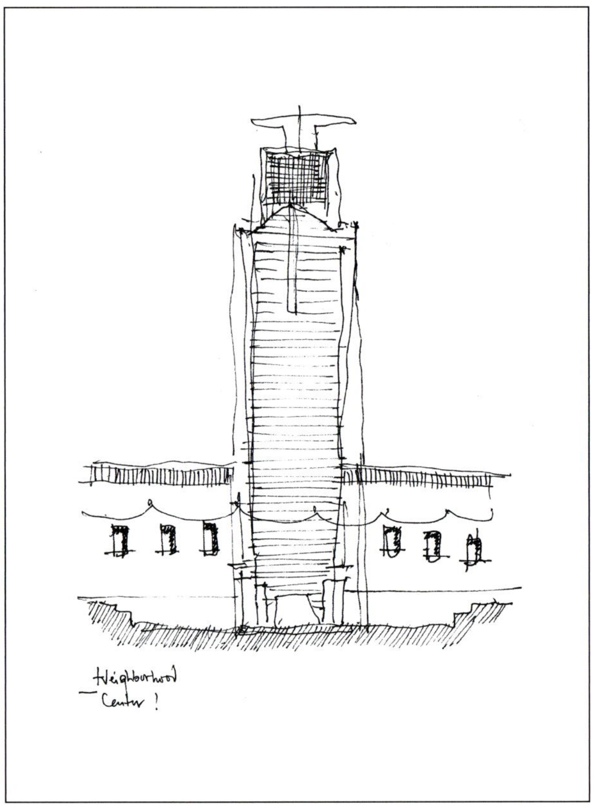

(left) Site plan illustrating the building's location in the pivot point of the first neighborhood.

A cooling tower dominates a quarter circular square to the northeast.

(right) Cooling tower with depressed courtyard for collecting cool air.

(above) Perspective of the entrance of the Neighborhood Center.

(below) Perspective of the Neighborhood Center courtyard.

All drawings courtesy of Moule & Polyzoides.

Aerial view of Neighborhood One at Civano.
Photograph courtesy of James Nicholas Polyzoides.

The Evolution of the Regulating Plan

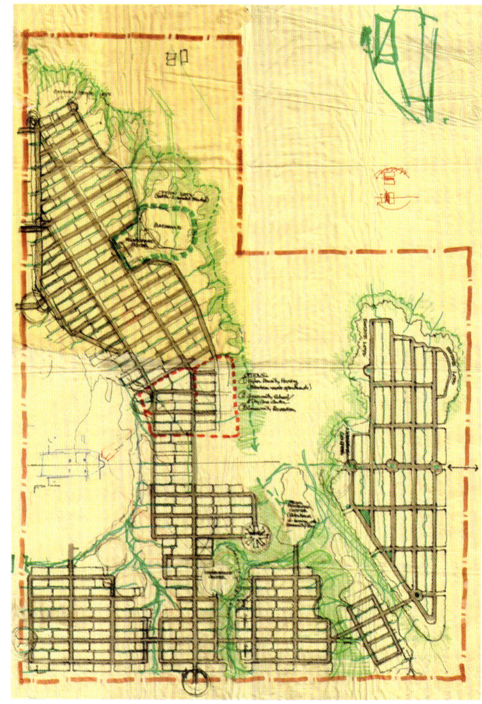

(above) A sketch by Wayne Moody modifying the extreme orthonogality of the first schemes by the New Urbanist members of the charrette team.

As discussed previously, the Civano charrette concluded without team agreement about the eventual form of the project, and without client acceptance of its partial recommendations. Duany Plater-Zyberk (DPZ) was asked to put together what ended up being a relatively incomplete, thin charrette report, one that did not include any of their customary sections on landscape, mobility, infrastructure design, or a code. There were no perspective images produced either. Their report did include a Regulating Plan that incorporated the initial street and block version of the Neighborhood One design, in a generally orthogonal grid form. It proposed the distribution of development intensities per block, into three zones: Neighborhood Center, General, and Edge. These zone designations were early, formative steps towards what was later developed by DPZ as the theory of the transect. This brilliant planning tool proposed that within neighborhoods and towns, uses, densities, and forms be distributed in zones of distinct form character, typically arranged from their center to their edges.

Post-charrette, Moule & Polyzoides were asked to complete their typological studies on houses and housing, and to illustrate them in context through a series of perspectives. Wayne Moody was given the assignment to produce the Specific Plan for the project. A Specific Plan is the kind of planning document that establishes the development standards for a project, including its land uses, thoroughfares, building types, design guidelines, landscape, utility infrastructure, implementation strategies, etc.

The Civano Specific Plan was eventually approved a year later, on October 20, 1997. Moody continued in his stance as chief critic of the work of DPZ with such vehemence that the developers eventually decided to give the subsequent steps for designing Neighborhood One all the way to satisfactory conclusion to Moule & Polyzoides. This became for Moule & Polyzoides an assignment as much in urbanism as in diplomacy. DPZ was out of the picture, but Wayne Moody was widely respected as the godfather of the Civano idea, and his opinions carried the weight of wide public support. No successful scheme could possibly be designed just by him, nor without him.

The definitive Regulating Plan designed by Moule & Polyzoides combined three key ingredients of the work preceding it. It established a grid of interconnected streets and blocks that balanced orthogonal and picturesque geometries. In effect, it resolved, through design, the DPZ-Moody deadlock. The Neighborhood Center remained at the center of the Neighborhood One composition, located at the intersection of the two principal and orthogonal project streets arranged on the four cardinal points. The blocks parallel to Houghton Road also followed the orthogonal geometry. The Neighborhood Center was inflected in its siting towards views of Reddington Pass in the Rincon Mountains. The pattern of streets that followed its rotated geometry, and those intersecting them in plan, constituted the picturesque portion of the grid. The two geometries taken together established the final gestalt of the project.

The streets were designed in plan and section with walkability and livability in mind. They included sidewalk, planting strip, parking lane, travel lane, and occasionally median dimensions and streetscape patterns that highlighted the differences in character among the various parts of this neighborhood. The street details were designed to accommodate a pattern of surface drainage that would maximize water detention and absorption. The Regulating Plan was now clearly readable as a neighborhood defined by an internal network of varied streets and blocks, and surrounded by a potent, preserved desert nature. It was a completed image of place, but also with potential connections to the future phases of the Civano project, then anticipated to take a New Urbanist form.

The other most important contribution of the Moule & Polyzoides Regulating Plan was the accommodation of their charrette-defined house types and styles into the DPZ three initial development intensity zones: the Row Houses, Courtyard Housing, and the Neighborhood Center building incorporated into the Neighborhood Center zone; the University Homes into the Neighborhood General zone; and the Compounds and Desert Country homes into the Neighborhood Edge zone. All blocks were also calibrated in their dimensions by reference to the lot sizes necessary for each building type. This proved to be an extraordinary contribution to the eventual success of the project, enabling the design and construction of every one of the models that builders brought to Civano. And it provided a stable framework for land sales and the evolution of an integrated and highly imageable neighborhood form, a rare point of order in an otherwise bumpy development process.

Wayne Moody eventually blessed this design approach and process. He incorporated the final Regulating Plan into his rather skeletal 1997 Specific Plan. The current form and operational order of Neighborhood One can only be understood as an outcome of the Moule & Polyzoides Regulating Plan and the Wayne Moody Specific Plan, in combination.

(below, top) Diagram of parks, greenways, and boulevards prepared in 2020

(below, bottom) Diagram of Housing Type Distribution by Zone, prepared in 2020

(below) Final Regulating Plan illustrating development intensity zones, 2006

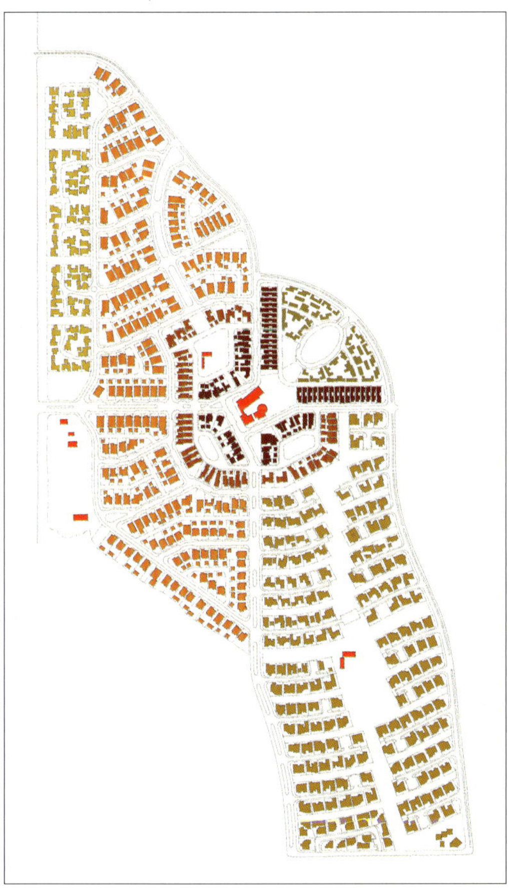

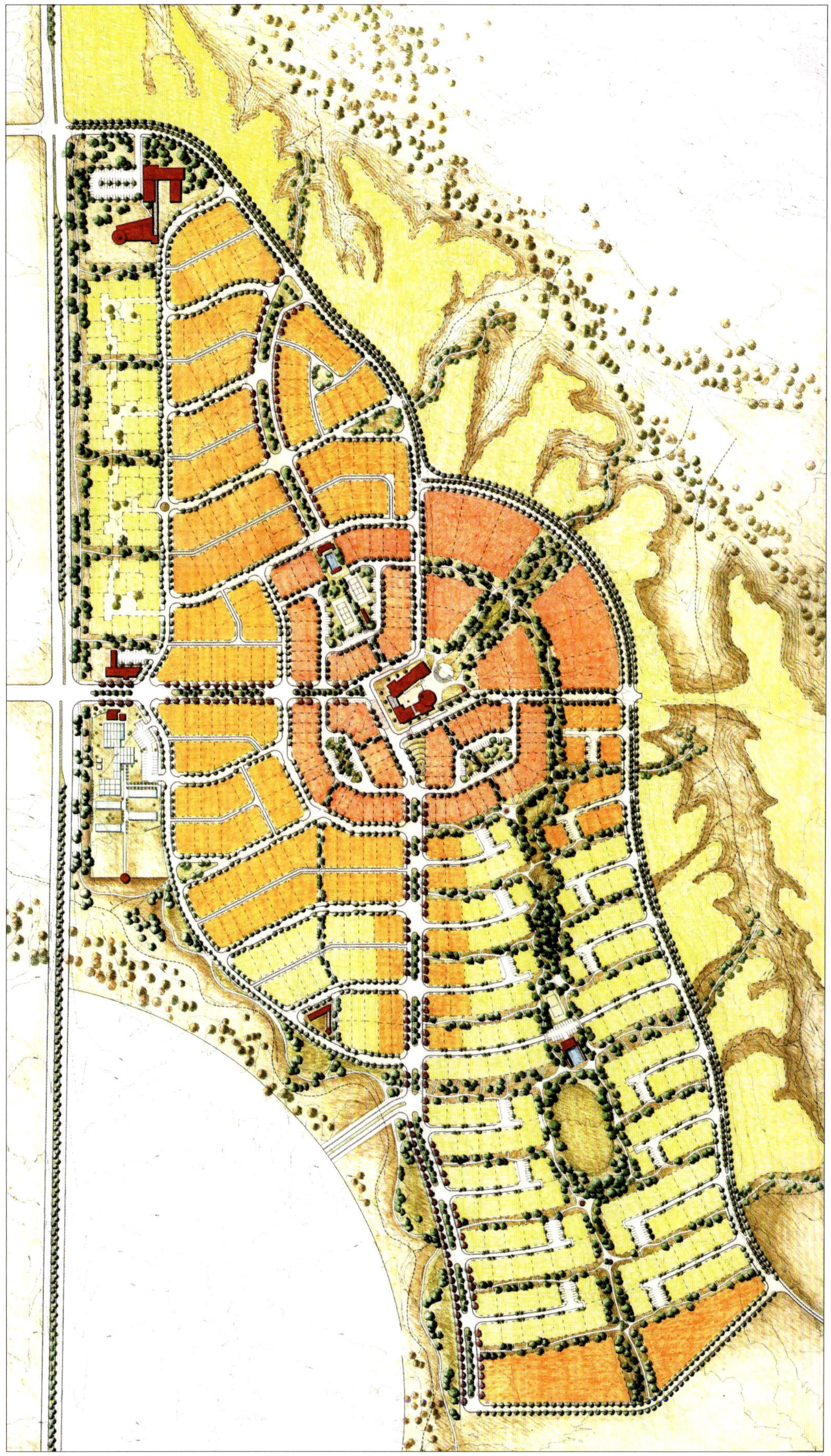

All drawings courtesy of Moule & Polyzoides.

The Illustrative Plan

No overall illustrative plan was ever drawn for the design of Neighborhood One, not during the charrette or during the development process itself. As a result, there was no comprehensive site plan available to direct the development team towards a vision for completing the project in a preferred urban and architectural form. As a consequence, the buildout of the project was episodic and marked by the random design preferences of each builder and the economic circumstances of each land sale deal. The illustrative plan shown here was recently drawn up to describe the scope and final form of Neighborhood One, as it has evolved through a twenty-year development process.

In the absence of an approved illustrative plan, and throughout the initial stages of development, Moule & Polyzoides produced site plans for some of the projects proposed by individual builders, and held design consultations with them. Some were more successful than others. Many of the builders had never worked with an architect before and did not enjoy receiving any kind of design advice. Others embraced the opportunity, working with Moule & Polyzoides to mutual advantage. That is, until Fannie Mae took the project over, when all such attempts at transforming common-practice house designs by builders into well-integrated neighborhood fragments were diminished and then suspended. Today, even the untrained eye can discern where these town architect-builder interactions were the most successful, where they were marginal, and where they did not take place at all. This is evident in the quality differential among various home ensembles: site plans, massing, interaction with the public realm, use of porches, stoops, and other frontage devices, and parking arrangements. Over the last couple of decades, the best designed and constructed sets of homes and their streets have commanded the highest real estate values within Civano.

The Civano initiative faced a number of extraordinary challenges. Chief among them was the differential between the cost of producing houses under an ambitious combination of environmental and new social protocols, and the project's targeted market. Civano was directed at the middle to upper-middle home buyer in the regional marketplace, with the important caveat of about 10% of the homes over time being priced to meet an "affordability" standard. Between 1999 and 2007, the homes produced for Neighborhood One sold between \$99,000 and the low \$300,000s.

A profitable balance between development production costs and lot and home pricing proved largely elusive. Even as home prices went up, the development team was locked into its discounted and large option blocks of lots, options that could not be adjusted easily. Income from early sales, which favored the lower end of the pricing structure, and the discounted lot sales could not readily support the high initial costs associated with setting forth on a new paradigm of suburban development, one that emphasized value building, durability, resilience, and affordability. Towards the end of the development cycle, pricing eventually addressed upper-middle-income families as well, providing a richer stream of profit to the home builders and, to a lesser degree, the developer.

A different approach to lot option pricing could have addressed this issue more successfully. Had the lessons learned about pricing in Neighborhood One been carried forward into Neighborhoods Two and Three, things would have been different for the development entity.

There were many other challenges, beyond pricing, that the project faced from a technical perspective. The sprawl paradigm, dominant for two generations, had generated a well-honed set of regional design and construction practices supportive of it. Unlike Civano, these were socially isolating, environmentally unsustainable, and house- and place-quality deficient. Tucson, as a small city, provided the developers of Civano with a limited professional group to help them realize their vision.

Local builders reared in producing stucco cracker boxes were unprepared to build houses in a variety of types and styles and of an advanced environmental performance. There were very few architects that were interested in vernacular architecture, believed in its social and environmental advantages, or knew how to design under its principles. Civil engineers who throughout their careers had subdivided land for rapid sale were not aware of or sensitive to the task of subdividing for distinguished urban and environmentally sensitive development. Bankers were concerned and nervous about the profusion of untested house types being proposed. Municipal regulators in the planning, public works, and transportation departments of the City of Tucson were concerned about and resistant to the prospect of approving projects that contradicted the standards developed over many decades of their practice, however questionable and destructive these may have been.

The absence of a coherent illustrative plan became a serious handicap in communicating at a glance the project's goals, intended form, performance, and technical needs. Finally, the house-buying public had to be invited to embrace the new aesthetic and new living ethic embodied in the Civano house and neighborhood form. This focused their attention on the typical market-driven issues of price and house features, and a great deal more. A 2001 Civano sales document presented to potential buyers by the development team described these extra choices thusly: "Buyers have the right to a healthy, safe, comfortable, durable, environmentally safe and energy efficient home." We would add another whole set of choices: the right to a neighborhood that enables walkability, beauty, and social interaction; allows live-work activity; and promotes access to nature and to recreational, commercial, and community amenities.

At the time, most of these ingredients were unheard of in the subdivisions being built for the middle class in Tucson, and they are still rare. As the buildout of Neighborhood One progressed, it not only attracted a set of enthusiastic buyers, but it also inspired the Tucson professional class to support its form of new urban development, a form more demanding and more sensitive to addressing the key social and environmental issues discussed above. As the project began to be realized, and its lots were slowly filled in with houses, the technical consultants learned to collaborate, design, and build according to the Civano Protocols. In the process, by studying and working with the best buildings and neighborhoods that had been built in decades in Tucson, many broadened their reception to innovative ideas. The results of this kind of probing, comparative, analytical work were transformative.

Neighborhood One Drawings

(below, top) Positive figure/field diagram illustrating the built fabric.

(below, bottom) Negative figure/field diagram illustrating the figure of the open space network

Prepared in 2020.

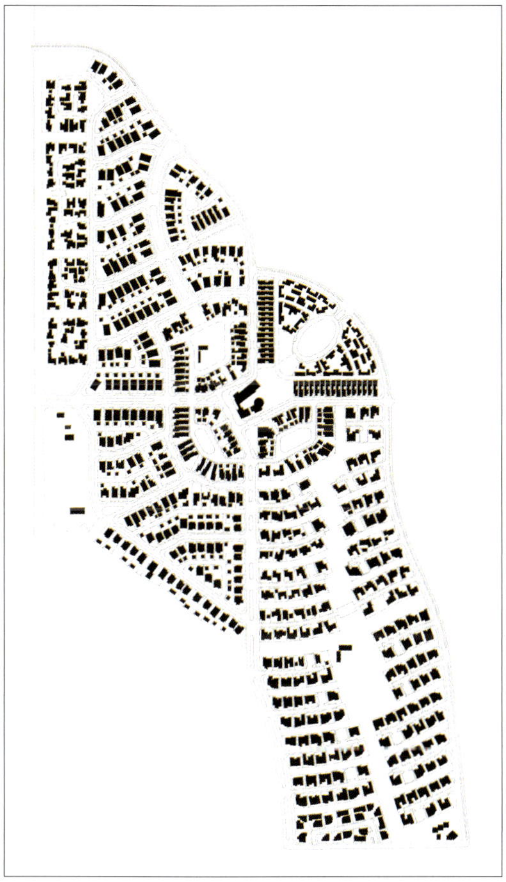

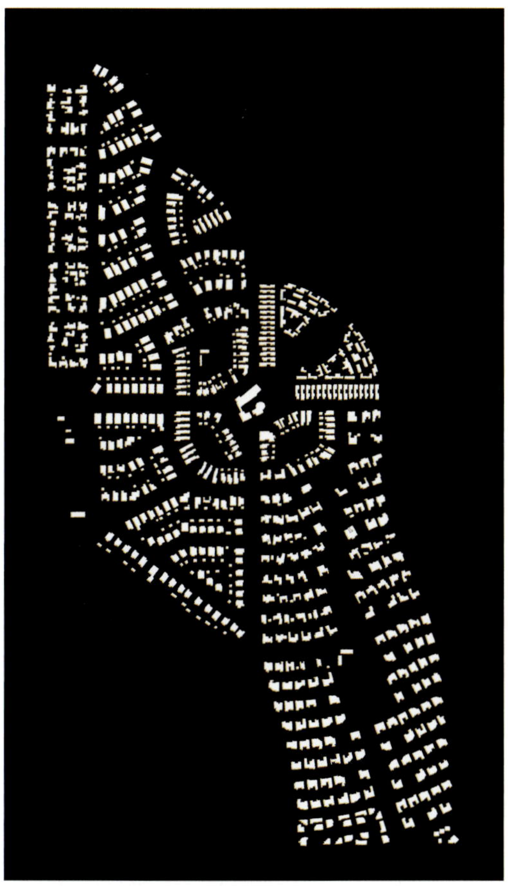

Drawings courtesy of Moule & Polyzoides

Final Illustrative Plan describing the urban configuration of the project.

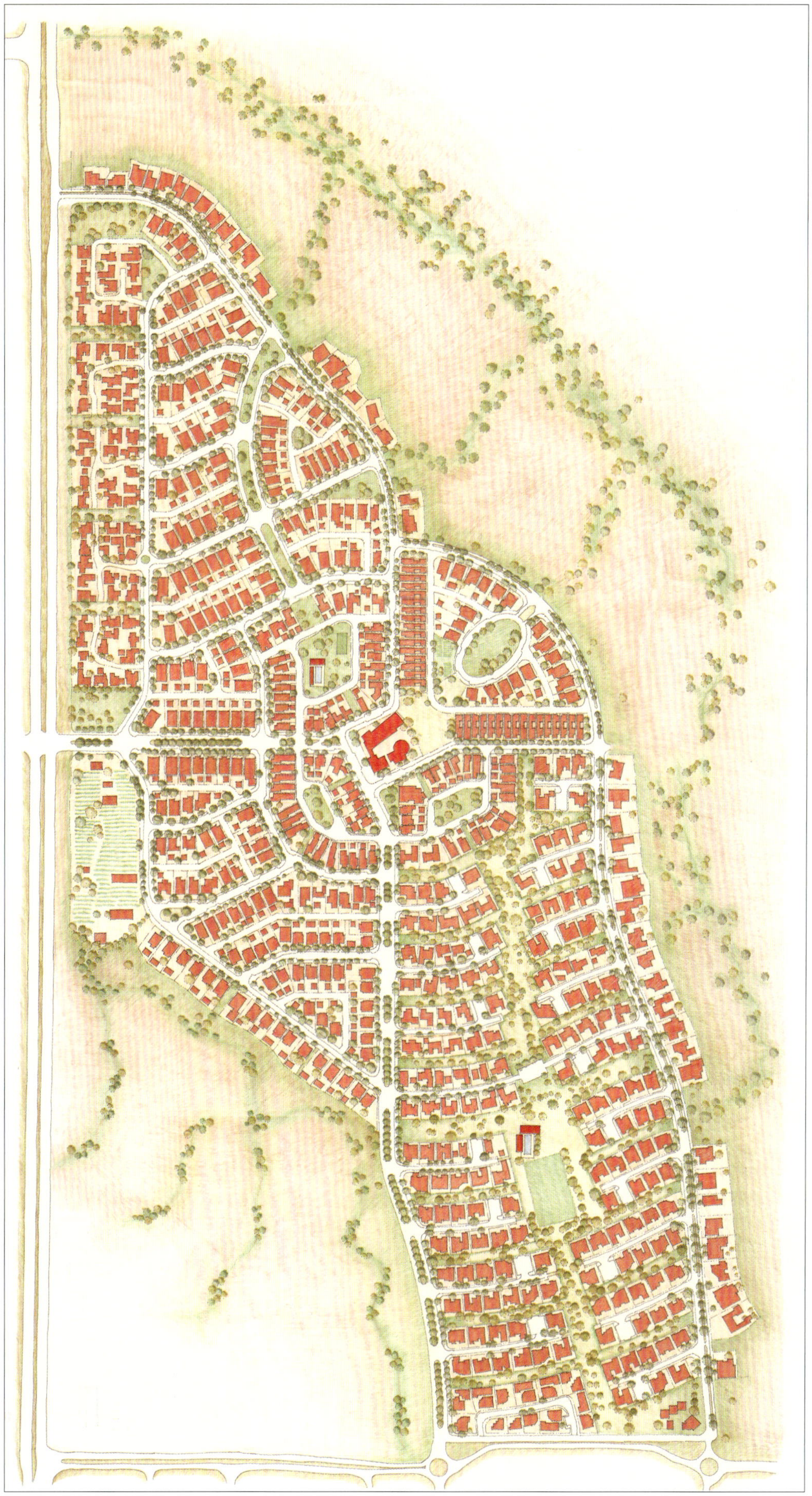

Compounds

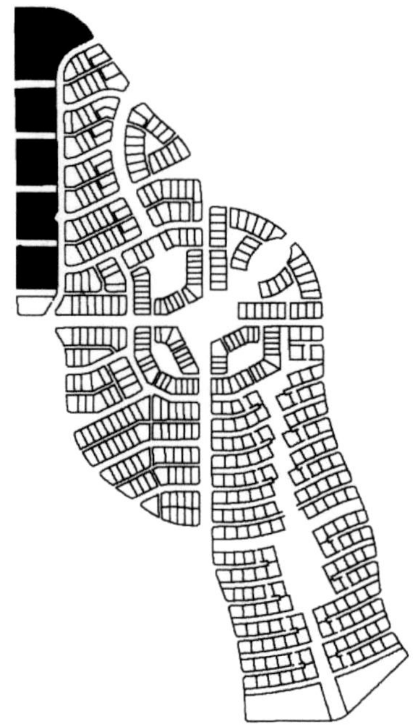

Density:
10 dwelling units/acre

Number Built:
68 anticipated
68 actual

Size:
1,385–1,566 square feet

Selling Price:
$111,300–147,000

Ted Bednar was a well-established local builder. At the time of his engagement with Civano, he was producing about twenty homes per year. He was drawn to the project because he really liked the emphasis on creating a community with homes that looked like they belonged in the Sonoran Desert. As a smaller builder, he was most open to trying to build experimental home types. In that spirit, he took on the risk of building the Neighborhood One compounds, a Southwestern type that until then could only be found in Santa Fe, New Mexico.

Buying lots of an unproven type in bulk allowed Bednar to option land at a discount price. That, in turn, helped him to steadily grow his business over time. There were three models used in the compounds: two one-story homes, and one two-story home, ranging in size from 1,230 sf to 1,566 sf.

His houses held the middle position in overall home pricing in Civano, and their simpler design reflected this. The compounds were an initial tough sell, until five had been built in a one cluster. They were then fully understood and appreciated by the public, and sales proceeded very well. The success of the compounds was a combination of their compact and well-resolved house plans, being offered at an excellent price point, and the organization of each house around a walled patio that was attractive to young families and downsizers. Once it could be experienced, the uniqueness of the compound lot layout itself could be appreciated for its distinct regional style. Bednar's regional style details inside his homes were also an important attraction to the buying public.

The compounds were the most innovative housing built at Civano, a valiant attempt to regenerate a traditional residential type of great character and dignity for families of modest income. Ted Bednar deserves a great deal of praise for having taken this challenge on. He accepted the direction provided by the Master Plan charrette drawings regarding this type, and had Moule & Polyzoides both adjust the designs of his houses and draw the complex site plans of all of his compounds. He followed these design changes and the overall design direction quiet faithfully. The differentiation of compound homes by massing and color was very successful, as was the quality of the desert landscapes in his walled home gardens and in the residual spaces among houses.

Despite their modesty, the compounds of Neighborhood One are remarkable in their variety and uniqueness of form and are one of the most distinctive recent projects completed in the region. As a small home building firm, Bednar readily accepted the expertise and construction input from IBACOS, and his homes also became good environmental performers. The developer made several attempts to use alternative paving materials that would mimic compacted dirt; all failed. The City then insisted on using asphalt paving. This insistence destroyed the rural character of the internal streets and compromised the essential quality of differentiating between the external and internal reading of the compound ensemble.

After the compounds sold out, Bednar bought lots in the University Homes area, lots that had originally been optioned by other builders who left the project for various reasons. Bednar used transformed and larger versions of the compound models to great success in the University Homes area.

Aerial perspective of the final scheme for the first Civano compound.

All drawings courtesy of Moule & Polyzoides.

The Stewart Compound in Santa Fe, New Mexico, was the key precedent for designing the Civano compounds. This is a first sketch illustrating the residual, service yards shared by all homes. Note that the material finish of these yards was meant to be gravel and not blacktop.

Drawing courtesy of Moule & Polyzoides.

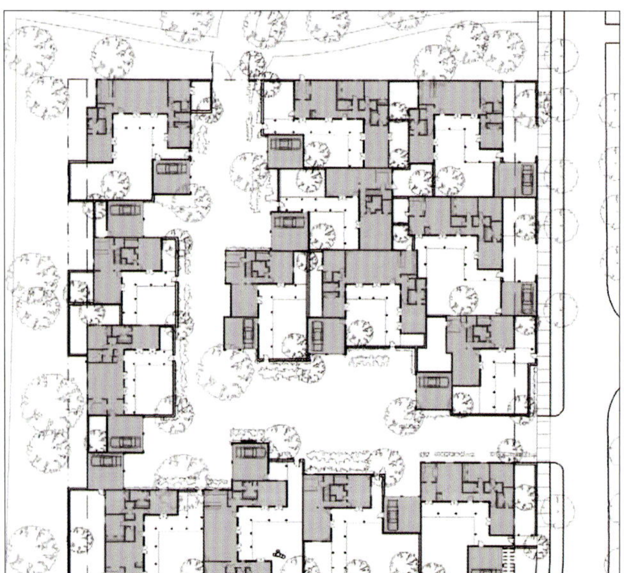

(above) Aerial view of a compound. Houses facing the street are entered directly from there. All other houses are entered from the service yard in the inner portion of the compound.

The configuration of the space of the yard is a reflection of the agricultural precedence of this type. Compounds in the American Southwest often started with one house. They were then grown by accretion as family needs dictated. New insertions into a compound were programmed unpredictably. They may have started as regular house forms, but typically grew by a room at a time. The result was that over the years, both the building fabric and the figure of the space among houses ended up irregular in shape.

(left) Plan of a compound that illustrates both the figure of individual houses and the residual nature of the service yard. Note the private walled patio space for each unit and the manner in which garages are accommodated.

Drawings courtesy of Moule & Polyzoides.

The houses of the compounds are modest, but their livability is enhanced by having access to a principal patio and various yards. Their form is distinctive and unique. As a result, their owners have landscaped their private realm with unusual xeriscape gardens that give this small part of Civano an intense desert character.

Aerial view of the Civano Compounds.
Photograph courtesy of James Nicholas Polyzoides.

Patio Homes

RGC and Jim Murrar, its owner, were price-point-aware and battle-hardened Southern California builders. In 1998, they were the first to sign up to build in Civano. That said a lot about their commitment to the ideals of the project. They were not afraid of innovation; they sought it. They understood and cared about how to build houses well beyond sprawl subdivision design stereotypes and they had already won many awards for their work. They decided to build in Neighborhood One for a host of reasons: the chance to expand outside of California; the challenge of building under the Civano community and environmental protocols; access to IBACOS training; and if successful, the potential national recognition that would follow.

RGC opted for the design of zero-setback, side-yard patio houses. There were three models offered to the market: two one-story homes, and one two-story home, ranging in size from 1,280 to 2,050 sf. The design process was exemplary. Jim Murrar was both interested in architecture and also open to learning how one could build sustainable, comfortable, and beautiful houses in the desert. He sought the advice of Moule & Polyzoides from the beginning. Builder and architect collaborated throughout the period of the design of these homes. RGC introduced the basic house designs in plan and section. These layouts were spatially fluid and very efficient, their great rooms extending laterally into well-shaded patios.

Moule & Polyzoides contributed three important site-planning ideas. The first was to carefully distribute the placement of the three models along any given street front so that they would relate to each other by the diversity of their massing and the figures of the spaces between them. The second was placing them to terminate vistas and generally produce the kind of visually superior streetscapes that would enhance the character of Neighborhood One. The third contribution was more radical yet: generating a unique Southwestern image for the entire enterprise. Murrar agreed to have Moule & Polyzoides design the three-dimensional frontages of his patio house models to a building depth of approximately 15 feet, as well as their hardscape and landscape, all the way to the front property line. The rest of the Patio Home architecture was of modest design, derived from models that RGC had built elsewhere.

The Patio Homes came the closest to following up on the architectural ambitions for Civano proposed during the 1996 Charrette. The built results were impressive. The interface between buildings and streetscapes produced a sense of both community and privacy, the hallmark of great residential design. Twenty years later, it is evident their residents continue to treasure them, by adding bright colors to their exteriors, improving their landscape, and customizing their porches.

The smallest of the three models was initially priced at $99,000, coming into the range of qualifying as "affordable" for the median-income family in Tucson. These were meant to be the lower priced housing options in the community, small homes on small lots. The RGC homes sold very, very well. They were especially popular with down-sizers and singles. Their price point helped a lot, but it was their street appeal that made them so popular.

RGC had no building or field staff in Tucson, and no experience building in Southern Arizona. They outsourced the construction of their homes to the local trades. Murrar worked closely with IBACOS, and the IBACOS crew eventually became his virtual on-site team. IBACOS was based in Pittsburgh and did not have any experience working in Tucson either. This lack of dedicated on-site management, failure to relate to the local building culture, and slow decision-making eventually doomed the project. Three decisions were particularly fateful:

- The first was the use of SIPS (Structural Insulated Panel System) construction. This is an extremely energy-efficient construction system, but new at the time. Tucson-based carpenters had never seen the system before. RGC failed to attract their loyalty and attention, and they also failed to educate them and deliver the respect that the subs thought they deserved. The result was that RGC never received from them the reasonable bids that they expected. Construction costs went up.
- The thin-set stucco that was used on the exterior of the houses began to telegraph every joint in the panel system after about six months. Lots of warranty work had to be done. RGC finally switched to a thicker, more pliant stucco system and the problem went away, but it took a while. This was not good from a PR point of view. Construction costs went up even more.
- Finally, they insisted, against local advice, that mechanical equipment would be placed in crawl spaces, in a town where nearly every home is built with on-grade slabs. The reason for this being the prevalence of caliche, a concrete-like lime/rock underground substance that is virtually impenetrable. The crawl spaces had to be jack-hammered away. The entire first phase of homes was built with crawl spaces. At this point construction costs went through the roof.

As a consequence of these and some other minor construction complications, when sales started in April 1999, RGC was selling homes at prices about $10,000 to $15,000 less than it had cost to build them. RGC thought they would "fix the kinks" in the first ten homes. They didn't. They kept on selling their very popular houses. A total of about sixty contracts were signed before their world came crashing down in late fall 1999. The result was a $900,000 loss to RGC, and they had to declare bankruptcy.

Voyager Homes would later take over RGC's models and Neighborhood Center lots, and build somewhat stripped-down versions of the old plans.

(opposite, center) Street perspective of a row of Patio Homes.

(opposite, bottom) The first sketches for models of the Patio Homes produced for Jim Murrar's company, RGC.

Drawings courtesy of Moule & Polyzoides.

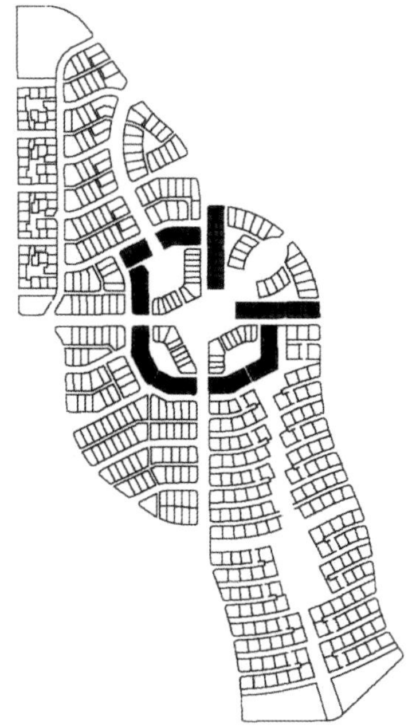

Density:
11 dwelling units/acre

Number Built:
75 anticipated
62 actual

Size:
1,144–1,641 square feet

Selling Price:
$99,000–106,000

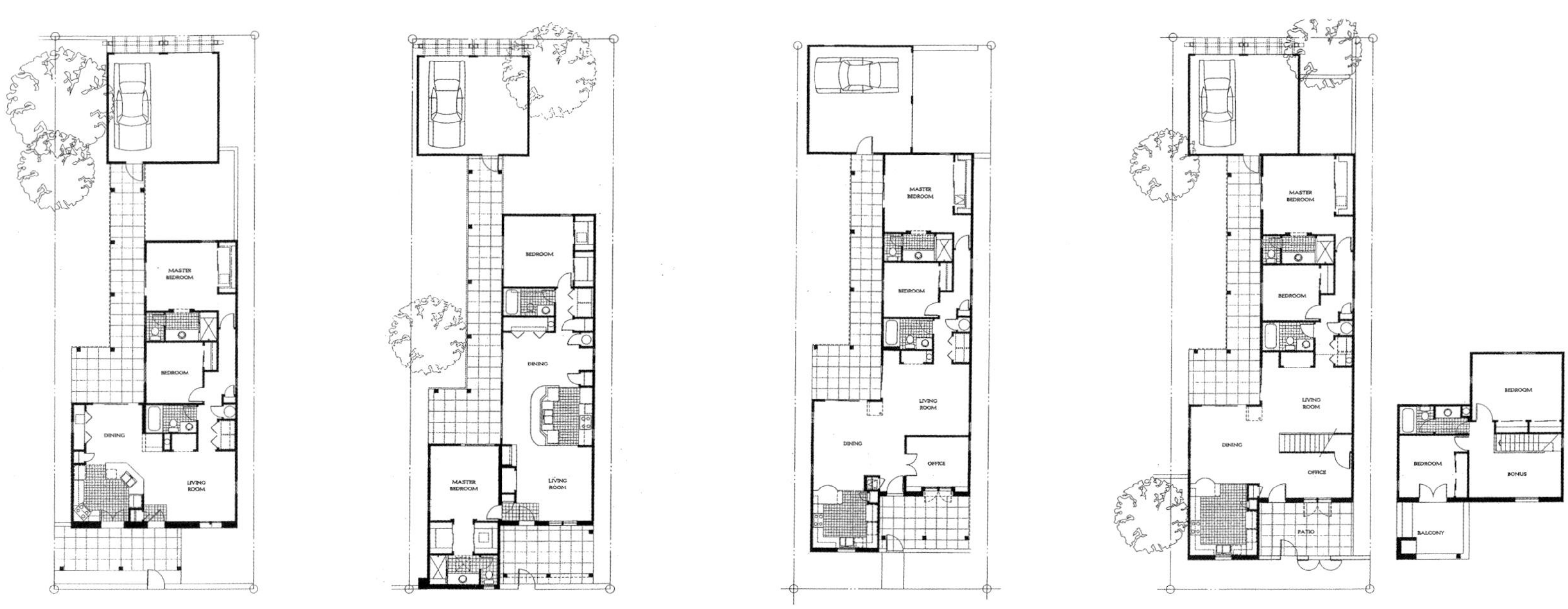

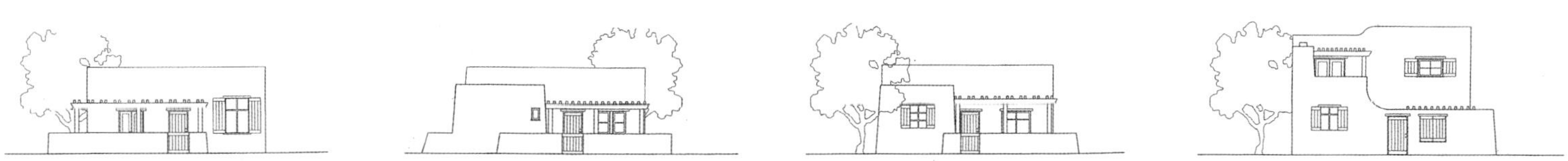

(above) Site plan of a row of Patio Homes. Note the proper distribution of side yards within the block and the well-defined frontage of every building to the street. The garages in the back allow a high-quality streetscape uninterrupted by driveways. Coordinating site plans like this are rarely, if ever, drawn for subdivision houses, and were not drawn for all of Civano's buildings in Neighborhood One.

Drawing courtesy of Moule & Polyzoides.

(left) A street view of a typical row of Patio Homes.

(opposite) The curving geometry of the streets in this part of Neighborhood One reveal the volumetric difference between one- and two-story houses to best effect. The frontages present walled but elevated trellised terraces that animate the pedestrian realm to a remarkable degree. The streetscape and xeriscape of the front yards is also very well attended by owners who evidently love living here.

These are the most architecturally distinguished houses and best streets in the entire project.

(above) Photo by Simmons Buntin

Aerial view with the Civano Patio Homes in the foreground.

Photograph courtesy of James Nicholas Polyzoides.

Desert Country Homes

The Desert Country Home type somehow survived the New Urbanist design bias of the 1996 Charrette. These were homes that were Radburn-inspired. Radburn was a new town designed in New Jersey in 1929, famous for its modernist urban patterns: houses arranged around shared greenways, in mega-block configurations, without alleys, and with access to front doors from service lanes. The Radburn pattern was anathema to the New Urbanist team, as it violated one of their key principles: the judicious mixing of all modes of transportation, including cars and pedestrians, in well-integrated street designs. Not surprisingly, the Desert Country Homes were vehemently defended by Wayne Moody. He imagined them as he had in the 1992 Master Plan: the embodiment of the ideal homes of the passive solar movement, consistently oriented to the south, self-shading, integrated into the landscape, amply connected to the outdoors, walkable to the neighborhood center away from car traffic, etc. He promoted them as the truest desert rendition of the fabric and public realm of Village Homes, his favored Radburn-inspired, visionary, eco-friendly community in Davis, California. In the end, Moody insisted and ultimately won out.

Final arguments for their incorporation and design elaboration into the house production phase of Civano were left for later stages in the implementation of Neighborhood One. They were impacted by the project's increasing financial challenges and Fannie Mae's increasing toxic presence in leading the implementation of the project. Despite that, the Desert Country Home area remains one of Civano's best thoughtout and beloved parts, despite its imperfect execution. In retrospect, the homes' informal siting and massing, surrounded by dozens of acres of desert greenways, was the right response to their location on the outer edges of Neighborhood One, and also to Civano's setting on the outer edges of the Tucson basin.

Moule & Polyzoides produced their best work on the Desert Country Homes at Civano for RGC, who initially had the option rights for the first batch of Desert Country lots released. Their site plan honored the Radburn and Village Homes, Davis precedents. Responding to different market needs, spatial variety was accomplished by introducing three kinds of central patio homes and mixing them on each lane. Every building shared in the formal language of both the traditional Hispanic and Anglo-American architecture of the region. Some buildings were to have metal roofs, and others flat ones, yet all of them were organized in a manner that allowed a reading of a collective form larger than any one building. The front-back dilemma was beautifully resolved allowing entrance into each home from the access lanes directly into their living room and then exiting directly on the other side of the same centrally located living room, first into a terrace, and then into a greenway.

Overall, the architecture of each Desert Country Home was proposed as a series of picturesque building volumes arranged tightly in a small lot, providing for the kind of self-shading that is necessary in the climate of the Southwest during both the winter and summer. As with the RGC patio homes, attention was paid to how an entire row of these homes would relate to each other, using the garden walls, courtyards, the geometry of the main body of the houses, and the rest of the kit of parts of Southwestern house architecture to interconnect them into a homogeneous fabric. The project was rendered in a poetic Southwestern style that resembled rural hamlets, an ensemble of houses that dissolved the difference between building fronts or backs, service or formal sides.

After RGC went bankrupt, the Desert Country lots were given to others. As Fannie Mae became more active in management, they rushed to engage any willing builder, especially those they thought would bring higher home pricing for Desert Country lots. Their hope was that such homes, either contracted or built, would create an immediate overall higher valuation for Neighborhood One. The new builders were allowed to bring their own house models, of their own chosen sizes, features, and architecture. All previous site planning and architectural model work that had been done before was set aside. The Master Plan as initially conceptualized was now officially seriously threatened, and with it a major component of the decades-old Civano vision. In retrospect, this was a first dire indication of the process that was to follow: Fannie Mae's slow unraveling of the Civano experiment that would eventually lead to selling the remaining land portion to Pulte Homes, the nation's leading practioner of sprawl development.

Fannie Mae brought ContraVest Builders into this part of the project. They had already been optioned a handful of lots in the University Homes area, and those had sold well. ContraVest was not sympathetic to the social or environmental goals of Civano. They were, simply and plainly, just regular builders. From day one of their involvement in Civano, they were behind on every aspect of their obligations to the development team. Luckily, they did not last long. They built few homes in the Desert Country area, as even Fannie Mae was finally convinced that they did not fit the profile of a Civano builder.

The next two builders to step in and take over a good number of lots were Doucette and Bednar. Most of the homes in the center of the Desert Country area, were built by one of these two builders. Like ContraVest, they also ignored the RGC site and architectural designs, and reverted to the building practices they were accustomed to. They took some of their own models, reworking them and siting them in individual lots, without any thought given to the relationship of each house to their neighbors. Even the most cursory review of these designs was squashed by Fannie Mae. This was disappointing because Bednar had previously delivered excellent Civano Compound projects and had actively collaborated with Moule & Polyzoides to produce them. Doucette took over a handful of lots from Bednar and used modified versions of Bednar designs.

Fannie Mae later decreed that a certain number of Desert Country homes would be set aside for custom builders. In all, about fifteen lots were given over to custom builders. Pepper Viner was the best of these, a Tucson-based builder with experience in building higher-end homes of good quality. Virtually the entire southern half of the Desert Country area was optioned to Pepper Viner. The process followed by the custom builders was similar to the case of Bednar and Doucette's: no design review, no particularly strong emphasis on a continuous building fabric, and a random mix of house models, forms, and colors.

Throughout this time, there was growing confusion about the character of this area and continuous criticism that the Desert Country Homes were not "Davis-like" enough. The people making these criticisms were looking for a number of ingredients that never came to be: the desert greenways to be landscaped with fruit-bearing trees, the vehicular lanes to be narrower, and this area to be a socially unique, co-housing-like area, recalling some of the earliest stated goals of the Tucson Solar Village.

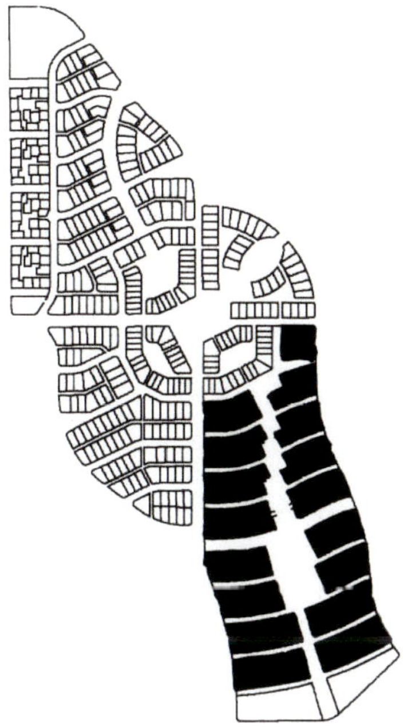

Density:
6 dwelling units/acre

Number Built:
177 anticipated
176 actual

Size:
1,734–2,500 square feet

Selling Price:
$135,000–205,000

Aerial perspective view of a lane at the Desert Country Homes area of Neighborhood One. Garages are set back and walls are used throughout to define the boundaries of private properties. The continuous building fabric is accomplished by the judicious placement of four different house types. All four allow direct access from the lane to the greenway behind the houses, though a patio or a living room.

Drawing courtesy of Moule & Polyzoides.

Perspective view of a lane at the Desert Country Homes area of Neighborhood One, illustrating it as a curbless and unpaved thoroughfare. Note the extremely picturesque character of the adjacent houses in the adobe style. They are massed asymmetrically by combining a variety of room-scaled volumes.

Drawing courtesy of Moule & Polyzoides.

The first sketches for models of the Desert Country Homes produced for Jim Murrar's company, RGC.

Drawings courtesy of Moule & Polyzoides.

Despite all the development difficulties and some resident discontent, and with the passage of time, there is a lot that is positive to note about this fully realized part of Neighborhood One.

The square configuration of the lots allowed for implementation of what was one of the big ideas for homes in this area: different kinds of gardens that would extend interior rooms into the landscape. In the desert, and for temperature control, these kinds of gardens needed to be small and here they were: an entrance patio, a courtyard off of the main living room, a patio off the master bedroom, a small garden/utilitarian courtyard adjacent to the garage, etc.

While all the homes were supposed to be of one color and compatible forms, and have their primary living spaces on the greenway network, some didn't. While all the houses were supposed to be of a related form, many now are not. Yet, even as an incomplete idea, the varied house ensembles, unified by the greenways, give the Desert Country Homes area an extraordinary image of place and a complete access to nature that is absent in typical single-family subdivisions, and also in the rest of Neighborhood One.

The greenway network did finally connect all the homes to each other and the Neighborhood Center with a very beautiful linear desert garden. It is heavily landscaped to create shade and encourage walking. It has managed to retain its original intent to be a wildlife corridor. It is common for coyotes to pass through it in the middle of the night. It is a functioning water catchment basin. The northern half of that network is an area where a lot of xeriscape water management ideas were implemented—gabions, heavy landscaping, dams that also were pedestrian bridges—all serving to slow water down and let it absorb into the ground. In the southern half, there is a soccer field that is also a public gathering space and a water catchment area.

This is surely one of the most unique, if not iconic living places in Southern Arizona.

Typical Desert Country Homes viewed from the desert greenways. These greenways are so extensive and their landscape so well-grown that they dominate these mostly single-story homes.

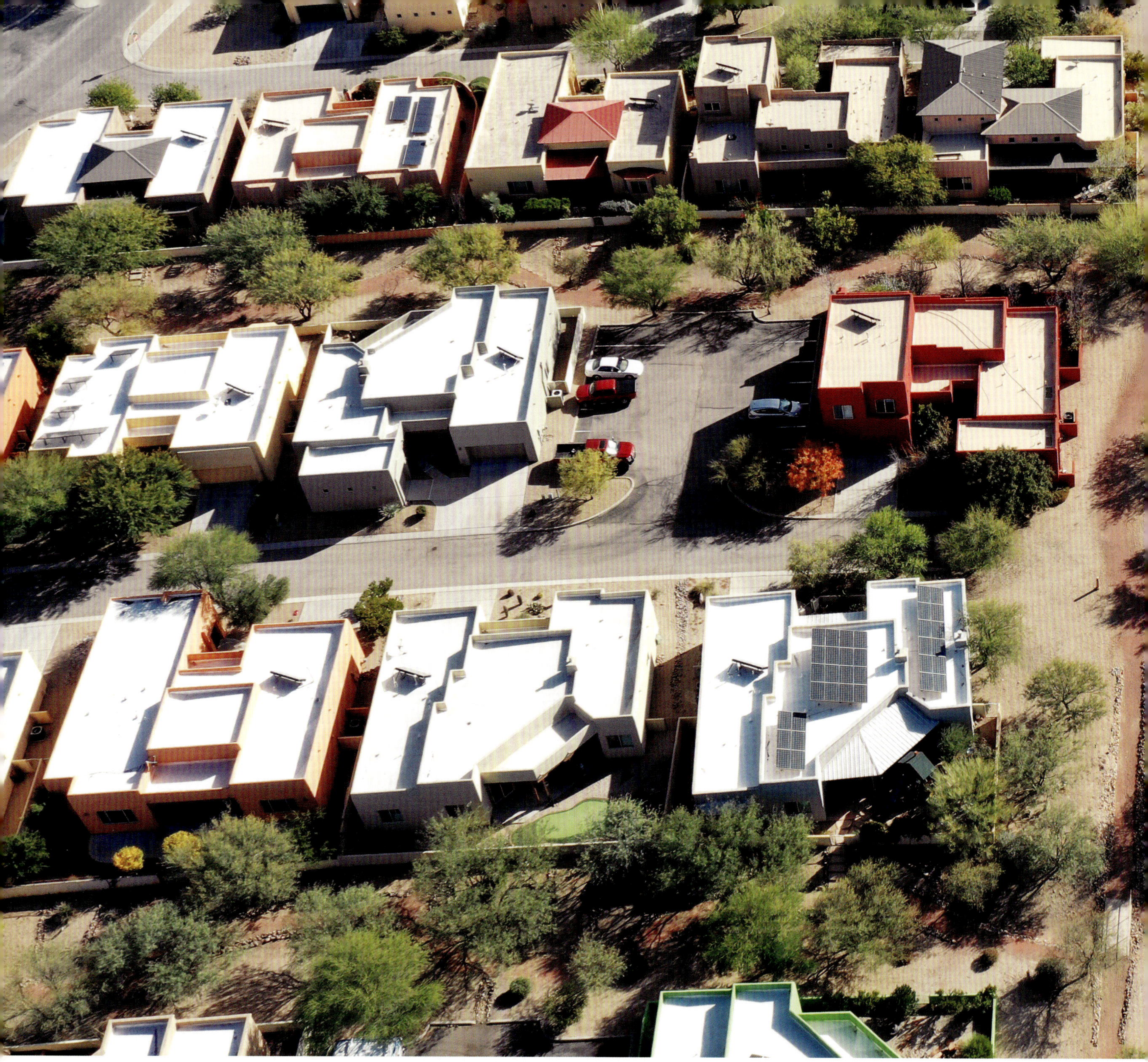

Aerial views of the Desert Country Homes. Note the north-south principal greenway, and the alternating east-west minor greenways and lanes.

The curving of the site plan pattern of these lanes and minor greenways enhances the plasticity of the homes when viewed in perspective.

Photographs courtesy of James Nicholas Polyzoides.

Townhomes

One of the great contributions of the New Urbanism to the culture of American suburban development was the idea that new development should be accommodated under a neighborhood-based, place-making model, that multiple neighborhoods should be joined to produce the form of a town. And that such towns should be located in the periphery of existing cities and should result over time in a polycentric, multi-use, and multi-density metropolitan form. Civano was designed under this general urban design theory.

Part and parcel of this idea of generating genuine neighborhoods and towns is that their residential program should include a diverse variety of house and housing types. This is especially true of single-family houses, with stacked flats, duplexes, triplexes, quadruplexes, townhomes, and courtyard housing being examples of that diversity. Located in the middle of the density range, from ten to forty dwellings per acre, these types were rarely, if ever, built during the reign of sprawl.

The packaging of a small percentage of houses into multi-family projects and their assembly into occasional dense urban fabric within neighborhoods can produce a number of desirable effects. It can conserve land. It can also generate a cluster of mixed-use buildings that encourage walkability, access to commercial services, and transit. The inclusion of row houses into the development menu of Neighborhood One at Civano was a fundamental step toward achieving a tangible neighborhood pattern with a strong visual presence, and in positioning the project as an alternative to senseless subdivision-based development.

The Townhouse type and its exact place in the Civano plan was anticipated, but not well-developed during the charrette. In the implementation phase of the project, the Townhouse type was designed to be incorporated into the denser core at the center of Neighborhood One. By being smaller in size, these homes were targeted to provide workforce and generally more affordable housing. It turned out that this was one step too far for the project to take. The developers were immersed in the struggle of setting a consistent pace of production of the simplest single-family houses and selling them at a steady annual clip. Dealing with an unproven residential type for Tucson seemed at the time an insurmountable challenge.

To their credit, the development team eventually formed a company called First Homes and seeded the market for producing townhouses. But the economic pressures were too intense for this small but important enterprise to succeed. Two houses were built adjacent to the Neighborhood Center. They were rather plain and not particularly well-received. In the meantime, other builders had come forth willing to construct attached housing of this kind. Unfortunately, they were allowed to design and build in an uncoordinated form and to lower design and style standards than those that prevailed throughout the project at the time. Eventually, after Fannie Mae took over, the townhouse lots were filled with arbitrary building types, not conforming in any way to the initial Civano vision.

The plans, elevations, and perspectives illustrated here are for projects that were commissioned by First Homes. They reflect the development team's ambitions for how the Neighborhood Center should have been developed. This vision was unfortunately never realized.

(right) Site plan of the townhomes illustrating their frontages. Arcades and buildings are set back on the street sides, and garages are set at zero lot lines at the alleys.

(below) Perspective of a Townhouse street. The original proposal for this portion of the project envisioned them as an interconnected and arcaded, continuous fabric.

Drawings courtesy of Moule & Polyzoides.

Density:
6 dwelling units/acre

Number Built:
27 anticipated
22 actual

Size:
1,300–2,500 square feet

Selling Price:
$205,000–270,000

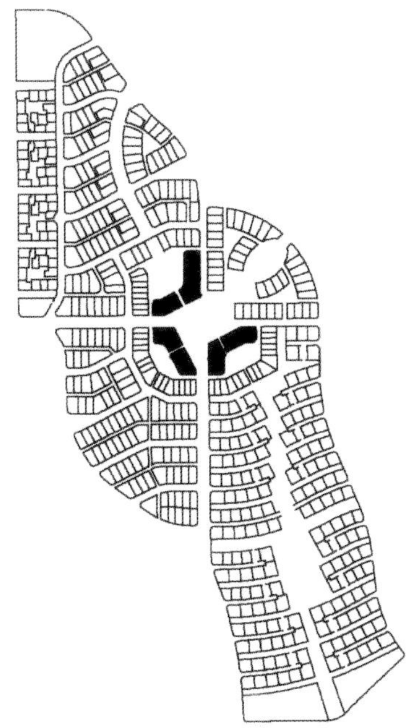

Elevations of two different versions of a Townhouse street. One features a frontage of walled front yards, and the other a frontage of arcades. The first produces a very picturesque ensemble of houses (above), and the other a more sober and controlled singular building composition (below). Neither of the two kinds of townhouses were produced as envisioned. With Fannie Mae in control, townhouse lots were sold individually, and buildings were built without any care taken as to their aggregate form.

Drawings courtesy of Moule & Polyzoides.

Aerial view of the Townhouse area of Neighborhood One, framing the Neighborhood Center building.

Aerial photograph courtesy of James Nicholas Polyzoides.

One of the features of Civano's special zoning is its encouragement of auxiliary and mixed-use spaces, especially around the Neighborhood Center. Shown in the images above are: at the top, a rowhouse with a café on the first floor, and small meeting rooms on the second; in the middle, a ballet school; at the lower left, a rowhouse with offices on the first floor and living space on the second; and bottom right, an above-garage unit used as a B&B.

University Homes

The name of this house type was derived from the single-family neighborhood houses to the east of the University of Arizona built in the 1920s. Karol George and his company, KE&G, took on the task of building in this particular type. He and his firm were established home builders in Tucson. They had a reputation for well-built houses and also did land development work for others.

During the mid-1980s housing boom, when IBM came to Tucson to build hard discs for its new personal computer business, KE&G went big time, offering houses that would appeal to the "out-of-towners" that were then arriving to Arizona. They got overextended when IBM pulled out less than five years later. They vowed to never get beyond the average market again, and just offer what were then tried and true sprawl subdivision houses.

What attracted them to Civano was the project's emphasis on community and quality, and by implication, the creation of a place that was good for families. As a local builder, KE&G offered more options and a greater ability to modify their plans than national builders, and that was an important factor for their eventual success. Their experienced field crews believed in quality construction and were ready to learn new techniques. They were also intrigued by the development team's promise to bring in experts to help their builders to build in an environmentally responsible way.

Of all the builders in Neighborhood One, KE&G was the most open and welcoming to the training that IBACOS offered. They produced three models: the Classic bungalow, which was loved by the market and was their bestseller at 1,835 sf; the Zaguan bungalow, their moderate seller at 1,556 sf; and their split courtyard entry home, which was not well-received by the market because these homes proved to be too expensive, at 1,850 sf. Two of this last model were built as part of a developer deal with the American Lung Association.

The design habits of KE&G, like those of most builders, were developed through years of standard development practices and were hard to break. The architectural designs produced during the Master Plan charrette were not considered by KE&G. There was no cooperative design process with, or by phase site plans drawn by, Moule & Polyzoides. As a result, there was no attention given to the frontage of the houses to the public realm or to their relationship with each other. The developer had received $30,000 from the State to aid in home design. There was a hard demand that only local architects be used to design these houses. Well-regarded local architect Paul Weiner had worked with the City on plans for a book called *Sustainable Design, A Plan Book for Sonoran Desert Dwellings.* It was decided to use some of these plans for the University Homes. While the model plans were good in principle, they were conceived as individual dwellings, rather than as ensembles, and suffered when placed next to each other and against the public realm of the street.

The final construction quality of the buildings was high. These were probably the best-built homes of Neighborhood One. They tested very well in terms of energy efficiency. They incorporated many local architectural elements: pitched roofs, outdoor spaces that extended indoor rooms, front porches, etc. But there was little or no variety in design from building to building, and their intended break with uniformity was forced. For example, they mixed metal and tile roofs. The tiled roof buildings seemed unresponsive to Barrio, El Presidio, and other Southwestern precedents, and unconvincing in the pattern of their application to particular sites.

While working at Civano, KE&G got sued over some ridiculous construction issue on another local development. They decided they were done with home building and abandoned their further interests in Neighborhood One. They sold their lots and home designs to Richmond American, a small national/regional builder. Quality went down a bit, as Richmond American was never on board with the Civano development and design approach. They also abandoned the project after about a year. Bednar homes then bought up the remaining lots and completed the construction of this portion of the project.

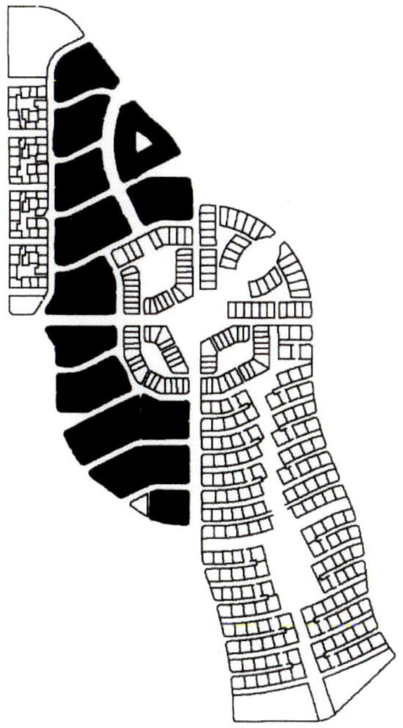

Density:
6 dwelling units/acre

Number Built:
192 anticipated
192 actual

Size:
1,566–1,834 square feet

Selling Price:
$149,000–175,000

Perspective view of a street lined with University Homes. Three key initial designed intentions for this part of Neighborhood One were never delivered: the balance in roof design between flat and hipped roofs, the preference for corrugated metal roofs, and the defining of individual lots by stone walls.

Drawing courtesy of Moule & Polyzoides.

(above) Aerial view of streets lined with University Homes.

(opposite) Typical University Home plans. The key to these single-family detached houses was the variety of their porches and patios and their unusual distribution in each plan, relative to bedrooms and living rooms.

Aerial photograph courtesy of James Nicholas Polyzoides.

Plans by Paul Weiner and Design Build Collaborative

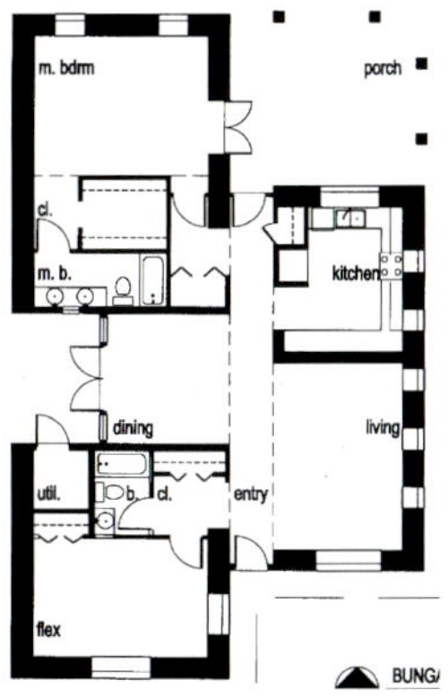
m. bdrm
porch
cl.
m. b.
kitchen
dining
util.
b.
cl.
entry
living
flex
BUNGA

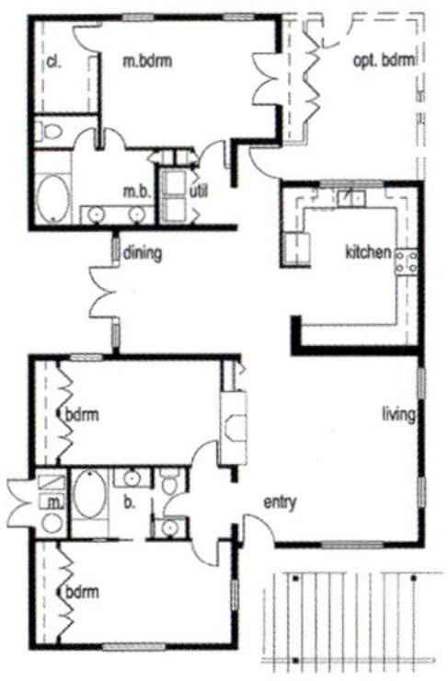
cl.
m.bdrm
opt. bdrm
m.b.
util
dining
kitchen
bdrm
living
b.
entry
bdrm

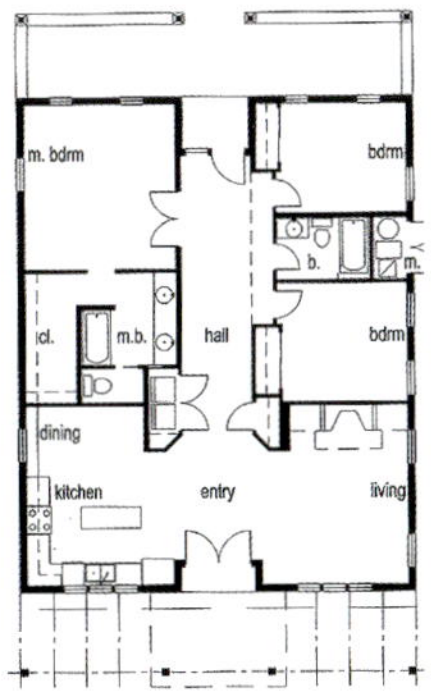
m. bdrm
bdrm
cl.
m.b.
hall
bdrm
dining
kitchen
entry
living

m. bdrm
hall
bdrm
cl.
m.b.
b.
bdrm
kitchen
entry
living
dining
COURTYA
floor plan

(above) The best-looking University Homes are the few that were constructed with corrugated metal roofs. The greatest distinguishing characteristic of streets lined with these kinds of houses is their richly xeriscaped front yards.

(opposite) The entrance to Civano is through Seven Generations Way, a magnificent desert boulevard. It is lined with University Homes and has its terminus on the Neighborhood Center.

Aerial photograph courtesy of James Nicholas Polyzoides.

Courtyard Housing

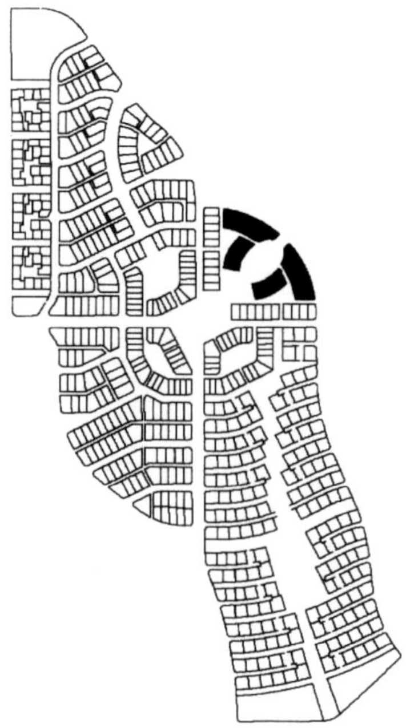

Density:
22 dwelling units/acre

Number Built:
67 anticipated
0 actual

Size:
N / A

Selling Price:
N / A

Courtyard housing is a Southwestern American multi-family type that is Hispanic at its root. It is particularly common in California, but examples of it are also present in Southern Arizona. The type is organized around a central shared space, with direct access to the homes surrounding it. Direct access refers to the fact that the homes are entered directly when located on the ground, and by direct stair access when they are located on a second floor. There are no common lobbies, corridors, or elevators to be found in the purest form of organization of this type. Sometimes an elevator is included as a means of convenience, but is not strictly necessary. Parking and service access to the homes is typically through their side and back yards. The simplest form of courtyard housing is the bungalow court, where the homes are detached. In a denser configuration, the homes are attached, creating a U-shaped or fully enclosed courtyard. In the densest version of courtyard housing, the homes are both attached and stacked.

Courtyard housing was the one housing type that was not built in Civano. There were manifold reasons for that. This was the densest of the charrette-proposed types and the one that was meant to be built towards the end of the design and construction process for Neighborhood One, after most of the other types had been fully tested and sold. It was the most unfamiliar residential multi-family type to all the members of the home production chain, developers, architects, engineers, builders, and of course, the public. It was the one type that was discarded under Fannie Mae's leadership, at the time when most of the ideals, principles, protocols, and market strategies of the Civano initiative were also derailed. This was a shame, because by both unit size and density, this building type was the last best hope for creating housing in Neighborhood One that could come close to meeting the IMPACT Standard affordability requirement.

The plans, elevations, and perspectives depicted here are for projects that were commissioned by the development team but never realized. They illustrate the team's interest in completing Neighborhood One as a genuine New Urbanist project containing a full range of types from low to middle density. The courtyard housing is of a rather unusual kind, where all of the units are arranged as duplexes around a central shared open space, but on sites that are irregular in shape. By rotating these U-shaped units in each duplex, their plasticity and picturesqueness is enhanced and every one of the courtyards is rendered different in architectural massing and imagery.

Drawings courtesy of Moule & Polyzoides.

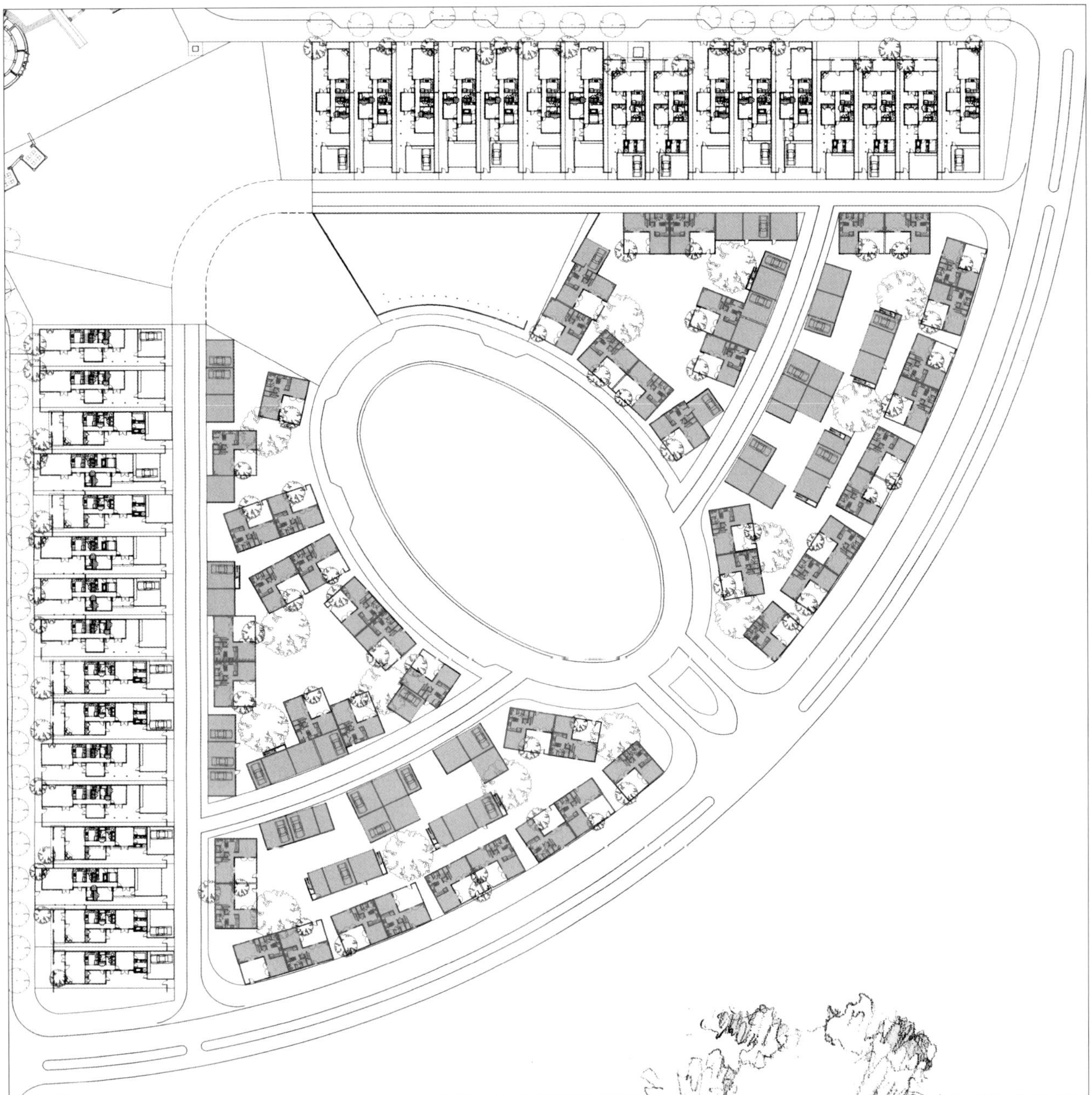

Plan of Courtyard Housing illustrating the arrangement of duplexes around gardens. The variety in the design of these in site plan, massing, and elevation render them and the entire project exceptionally picturesque.

Elevations of various clusters of duplexes.

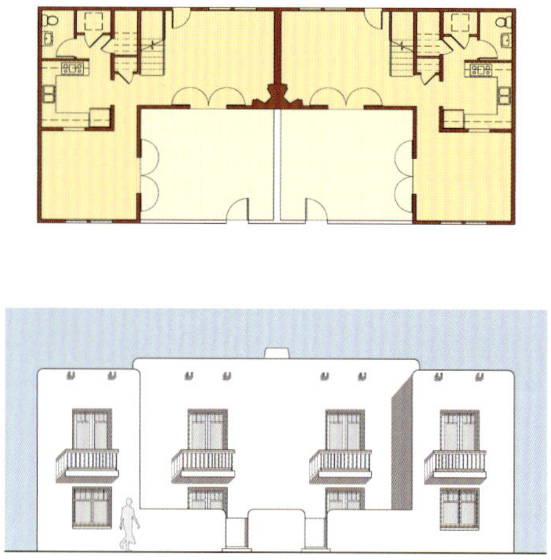

1

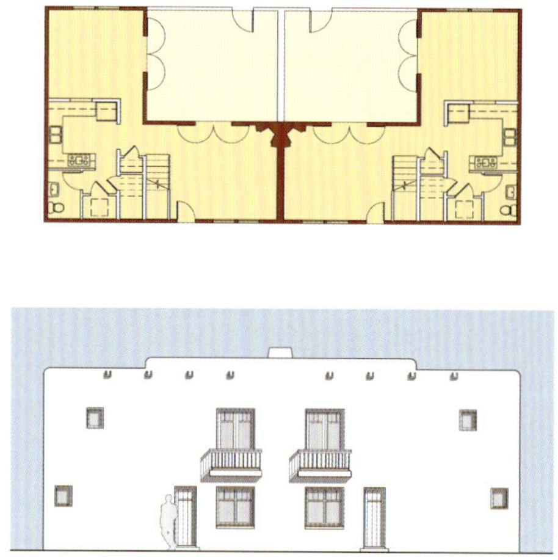

2

3

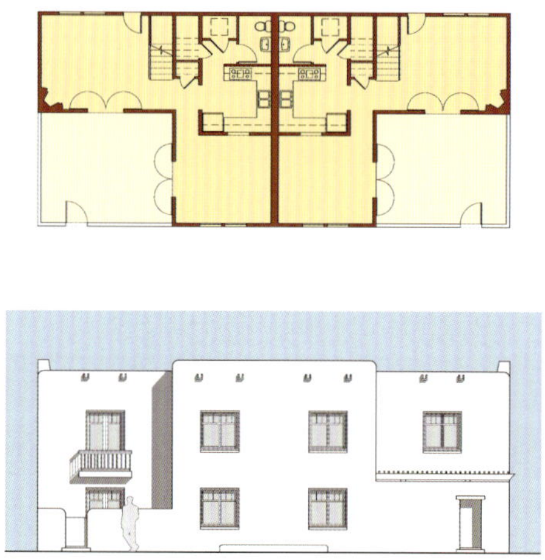

7

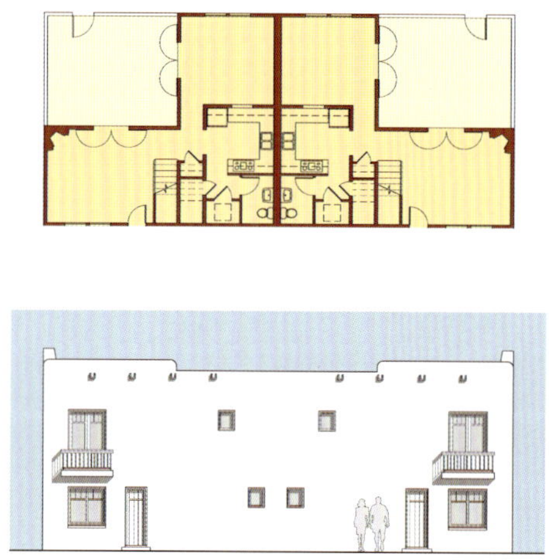

8

9

13

14

15

4

5

6

10

11

12

16

This is an illustration of a method that was generated during the design of the Courtyard Housing project for Civano. The project was composed of a set of duplexes. An initial duplex consisted of two identical L-shaped dwelling units enclosing a walled patio. This seed building was also elevated in a definitive building form.

By rotating each unit of the initial duplex in plan and elevation, it was possible to generate sixteen distinct duplexes, and to incorporate them into a courtyard housing complex. Unfortunately, this very unusual, simple, and intelligent project was never realized, as was the case for most of the best unconventional ideas at Civano.

Drawings courtesy of Moule & Polyzoides.

The Civano Neighborhood Center

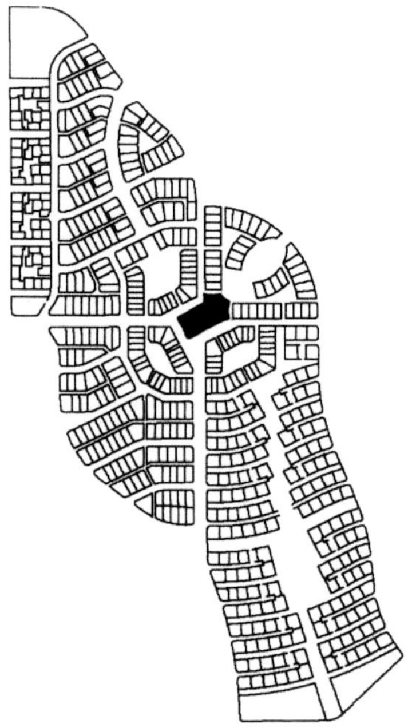

Size:
1,800 square feet

Cost:
$1,890,000

Cost per square foot:
$105

The overlap of social and environmental ideals that are the hallmark of Civano can best be understood in the context of the design of its Neighborhood Center. On the social side, the building occupies the focal point of the first neighborhood, within easy walking distance from all the families living there. In its form, particularly the kiva-inspired cylinder and enclosed courtyard, it embodies a sense of community and the pursuit of a lively local culture. It provides a place for the citizens of Civano to gather in public, and symbolizes the timeless struggle of human beings to live in balance with the awe-inspiring power of nature in the Sonoran Desert.

The Neighborhood Center building's mix of uses, such as offices, a café, art gallery, other retail stores, and a meeting hall, invites residents and visitors to occupy it throughout the day. It also accommodates a great variety of occasional special events. The passive and active solar design elements that are incorporated into the building respond to the local climate, the movement of the sun, the wind direction, the local winds, the native desert landscape, and the availability of common, local construction materials. The expressive use of adobe, wood frame, straw bale, and Rastra block to build its various form components combine to provide a rich illustration of the potential of building well in a challenging desert setting.

The form of the building was conceived from both the inside out and the outside in. From the inside out, the functional program was purposefully divided into distinct volumes. These were arranged around a central courtyard that provided respite from the relentless summer heat of the desert and was conditioned by a cool tower. The open end of the courtyard was composed to frame a view northeast, towards Reddington Pass in the distant Rincon Mountains. This alignment had a mystical power for Wayne Moody and should be considered a gesture dedicated to him.

From the outside in, the building was located at the crossroads of the two principal Neighborhood One boulevards. And as a result, it is easily accessible by car, bicycle, and on foot. The great variety of the massing and the porousness of the many passages into the courtyard render the view and pedestrian approach from every direction unique and unusual. The architectural style employed was based on traditional regional building types and Southwestern imagery. All these design responses, directly or indirectly, help maximize the building's energy efficiency and place-specific environmental performance.

Even before the 1996 Charrette, the need for a Neighborhood Center was firmly recognized, and the vision for it was established early. It would be a combination commercial, retail, and service center. The draft Development Agreement recognized that a facility like this would entail a major cost of construction and management, one that a typical urban neighborhood could not possibly bear. As a result, and as part of public support for the project, the City decided to contribute the idea of a satellite City Hall to be housed in the Neighborhood Center. The satellite City Hall would also attract department offices there, where suburbanites from the wider area could come and pay their bills. Once per quarter, the City Council would gather in its large meeting space. This civic function would help draw outside traffic to the Center in the interest of generating a heightened demand for the retail and commercial services the Neighborhood Center provided. Rent from this facility would help defray its construction cost and ongoing maintenance.

The developers had received a $300,000 grant for "solar and alternative building" demonstrations. The money was directed to building the Neighborhood Center. Eventually the roughly 18,000-square-foot building cost $1.8 million. It was a bargain compared to what it has since contributed to the life of Civano. Moule & Polyzoides were the architects of the Neighborhood Center. Their work was an excellent translation of the programmatic intentions and key images produced during the charrette into reality. Importantly, the internal courtyard and the passively cooled rotunda remained, as did the general massing and the Southwestern traditional style.

The battle to sustain the Civano Neighborhood Center since then has been epic. The cost complications and management realities of generating a relatively large mixed-use, neighborhood-scale building piled up fast. The promised satellite City Hall never materialized. In the end, the developers managed to save the building by initially occupying it themselves. The Rotunda became the Welcome/Sales Center; the attached offices became a marketing hub; the upper floor of the two-story building became their offices. They were able to rent out some of the commercial/retail space, but not all of it.

The developers were obliged by the Development Agreement and Memorandum of Understanding to produce a café and an art gallery from the get-go. They solved the art gallery problem by setting up a family-run art business. The tale of the café turned out to be as adventurous as it was risky. They attracted LeBuzz, a successful coffee shop/café with a very hot location over by the Catalina Mountains, and convinced them to come to the Neighborhood Center building at Civano. LeBuzz was massively subsidized to effectuate this move, but this was a subsidy that did not exist anywhere in the project budget. They tried everything they could, but could never make their business work. There were too few homes in place to generate a steady flow of users and cash, and their location was too far off South Houghton Road. They finally closed down and left. The café space was converted into a fitness facility.

Under Fannie Mae ownership and management, the Neighborhood Center declined rapidly. Under the original development team, the interior courtyard had remained a beautiful and vital place. Café tables and chairs were spread all around all to encourage people to casually gather. The fountain was kept running, the cool tower remained operational, and the small carpets of grass were kept green and growing. These efforts were directed towards inviting

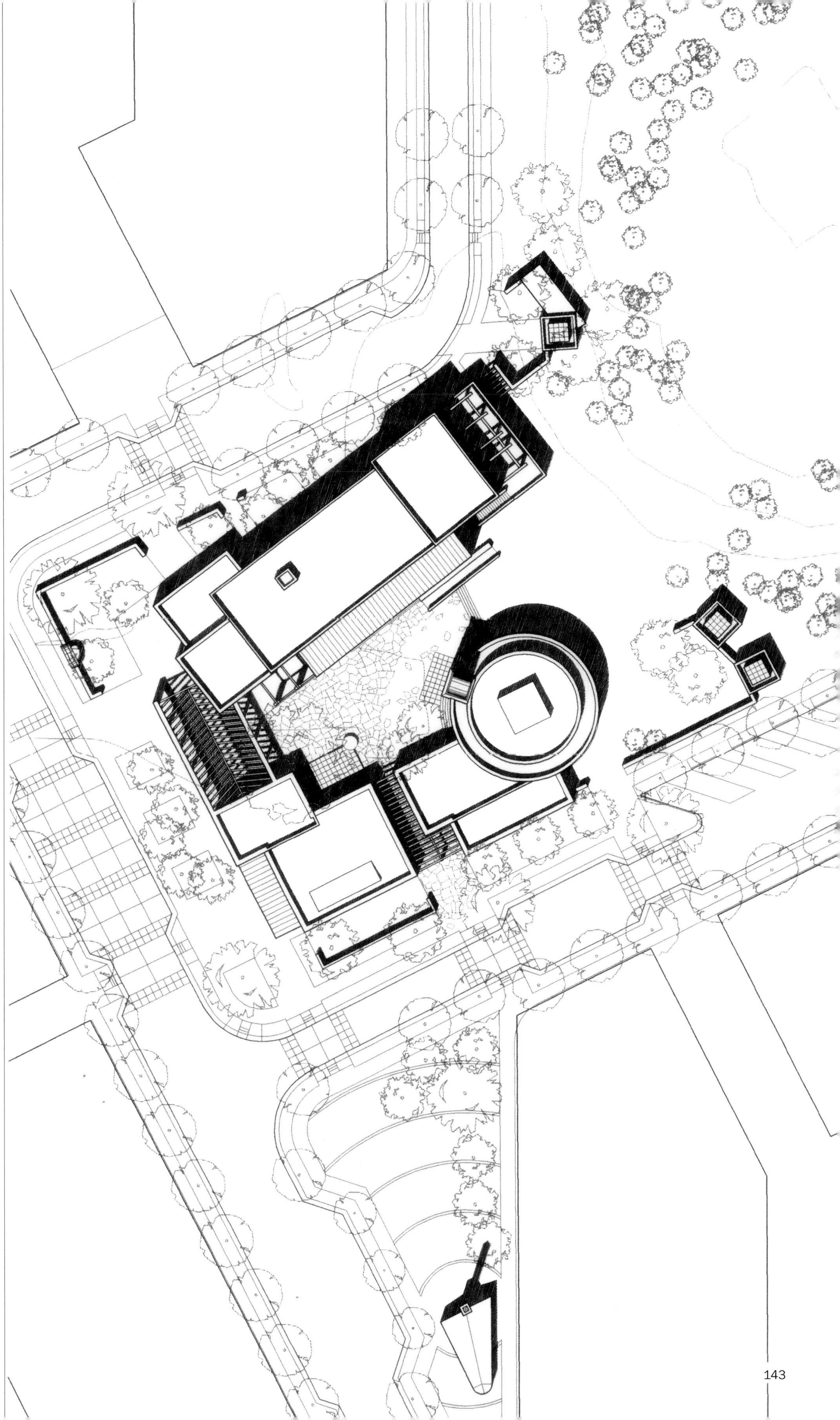

Site plan of the Neighborhood Center, Civano Neighborhood One.

Drawing courtesy of Moule & Polyzoides.

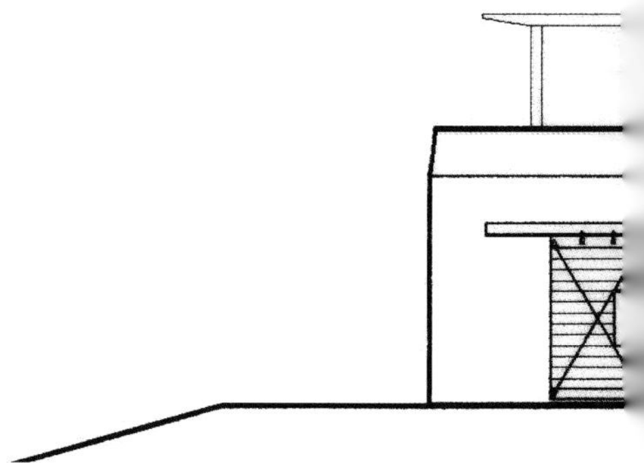

people to use and love the place. Sprawl-based economic and cultural impoverishment did not need a local civic institution to support its daily and ritual life. Fannie Mae abandoned all efforts attending to the mission of this building. They stopped minding it and also managing it. Soon all chairs and tables were gone, and signs were up warning about no loitering or skateboarding. The cool tower was shut down, a subtle but devastating change.

Soon thereafter, the entire complex was sold to Les Shipley for a bargain price. Fannie Mae considered it a lost cause. Happily, Shipley, famous for his ownership of the Civano Nursery, thought otherwise. A veteran of turning lost causes around, like the harvesting of the desert at the Civano site, he turned out to be the person that proved Fannie Mae wrong. He deserves a great deal of credit for working hard to get the Neighborhood Center complex filled up and in good repair. He put his offices in the lower floor, made the upstairs an incubator space, kept the Homeowners Association in the Rotunda building, and kept this large room in use by community groups. The building is now vital, well-used, and well-loved again.

Slowly but surely, national retail experience and rules prevailed as well. A café at Civano finally arrived when about 600 homes in Neighborhood One were fully occupied. It has maintained its relevance by becoming highly attuned to community needs. It has several successful websites, and is generating enough money to continue to maintain its relevance to the daily lives of the residents of Civano and its vicinity. Surprisingly, the café is not located in the Neighborhood Center building itself, but in a row house across the street, a welcome enlargement of the use flexibility that is beginning to spread in buildings all around the Neighborhood Center.

One of the big differences between Neighborhood One and Neighborhoods Two and Three is that the latter two were designed absent of a positive view of community life. They are not neighborhoods at all; they are subdivisions. Their more isolated residents can gather in a small community room, attached to a pool complex. There are no living, ranking community places there to draw people together. In the meantime, the original Neighborhood Center in Neighborhood One now stands as the principal monument to the Civano idea.

The following is the text taken from a document written by Moule & Polyzoides, Architects and Urbanists for the Neighborhood Center building. It was printed and handed out during the inauguration of the Neighborhood Center on April 16, 1999.

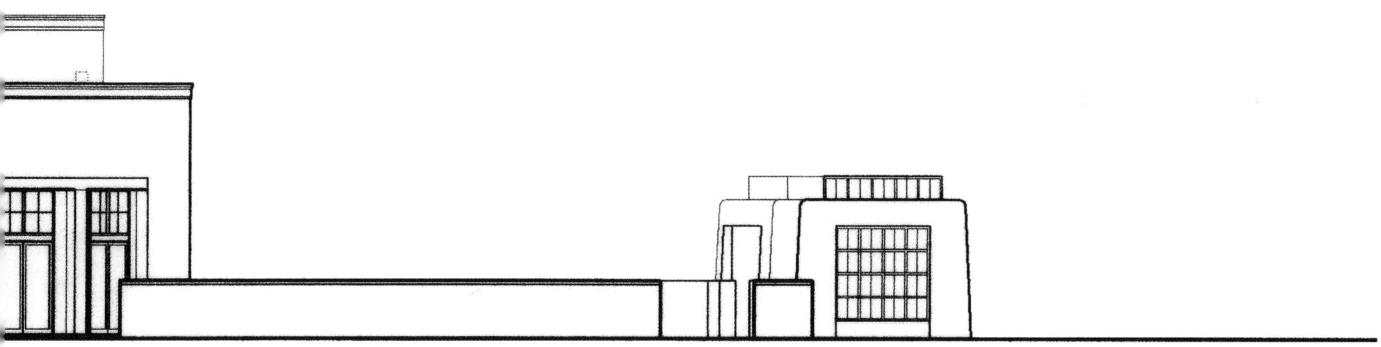

"By intent, the Neighborhood Center responds to the design challenges of environmental sustainability. The design endeavors to introduce resilience and durability into its architecture and urbanism. It creates a complete environment in the desert that is both familiar and new. Leading us toward a special kind of innovating, framed by cultural memory and also powered by the genius of an evolving form tradition. The following are the specific environmental design attributes of the Neighborhood Center that can be observed during your visit today. Please follow the numbers that are shown on the plan centerfold of this printed program (see pages 150 and 151)."

(above) West elevation of the Neighborhood Center, Civano Neighborhood One.

(below) South elevation of the Neighborhood Center, Civano Neighborhood One.

Drawings courtesy of Moule & Polyzoides.

Aerial views of the Neighborhood Center, Civano Neighborhood One. The cylindrical room was designed as a community hall. It was built out of fired adobe block and was cooled by a cooling tower. The room does not need any form of active environmental control, despite the extreme hot and cold cycle of Tucson's climate. The long, two-story block was designed as a mixed-use office and retail building; the short, one-story blocks as retail/commercial ones. The courtyard, an intimate gathering place, is serviced by a cooling tower and is accessible from all four streets around the building. This is the most expansive architectural expression of the social and environmental vision of Civano. In that respect, it is a monument to the optimism, ambitions, and Herculean effort of all the people that led its development team. They spared no effort or treasure trying to make it true. They deserve our admiration and appreciation.

Photography courtesy of James Nicholas Polyzoides.

(this page) A view into the Neighborhood Center courtyard with the adobe Rotunda meeting building to the left. A view of the balconied arcade that defines one side of the courtyard. Offices are on the upper level with retail and service offices on the ground floor. A view from the courtyard looking at the Rotunda building at the holidays. The Rotunda cooling tower is at the center.

(opposite, top) A view of the Neighborhood Center terminating Seven Generations Way. The coloration of the different volumes of the building is meant to signify their method of construction: gray for reinforced concrete, red for RASTRA block, yellow for straw bale, and tan for hyper-insulated wood frame. The colors have been modified over time.

(opposite, lower) Images of the Neighborhood entry arcade and interior courtyard being used for community meetings and celebrations. The Neighborhood Center courtyard is a social magnet. The coolness and shade provided by its orientation, form, and landscape attracts people for daily visits, community events, and special celebrations during the day and night, and through all seasons.

MODEL

10501

CIVANO NEIGHBORHOOD CENTER

1 | Adobe Construction Thermal Mass

This building is constructed of adobe, a traditional Southwest building material that requires little energy to make. The mass of the walls helps moderate seasonal heat extremes by slowing heat penetration during hot weather, and holding interior heat during colder weather. Passive solar energy can be used as the heat source.

2 | Cool Tower

Cool towers are a traditional method of cooling in arid climates. Water is forced over baffled filters, creating an evaporative effect that cools the moving air. The heavier cool air then drops into the space at the bottom. Cool towers use significant amounts of water, but this is offset by extremely low energy consumption. The grass plaza helps hold the cooler, moister air to create a micro-climate.

3 | Water Harvesting

Water from the roof is collected and stored in underground cisterns. This water is used in the decorative fountain and the Cool Tower. Harvesting water decreases the depletion of the water table, and captures an arid climate's most valuable resource.

4 | Millennium Windows

The windows in the adobe buildings are Millennium brand windows by Andersen Window Company. They are Andersen's most sustainable window product. They are made from recycled wood waste and environmentally friendly glues, and are extremely stable and resistant to heat transfer through the frame.

5 | Cooling System/ Fountain

The Neighborhood Center uses a water-based heating and cooling system. It is more efficient than typical heat pump systems which are air-based. Heat dissipation is achieved by passing the system's treated water through heat exchangers. The fountain is part of that heat exchange system. As it operates, the fountain water is aerated and cooled.

6 | RASTRA Construction

This wall system is made of cement-coated postconsumer foam plastics, with 85% of the material recycled content. The cementations block has a 4 hour (UL) fire rating and R-22 insulation quality.

7 | Photovoltaic Panels

Photovoltaic panels on this building convert sunlight into electricity. No fuels are used, little machinery is needed, and little energy is lost in its generation. With Arizona's abundant sunshine, this technology offers the promise of sustainable energy production. Recent developments offer the promise of significant price reductions in household sized systems.

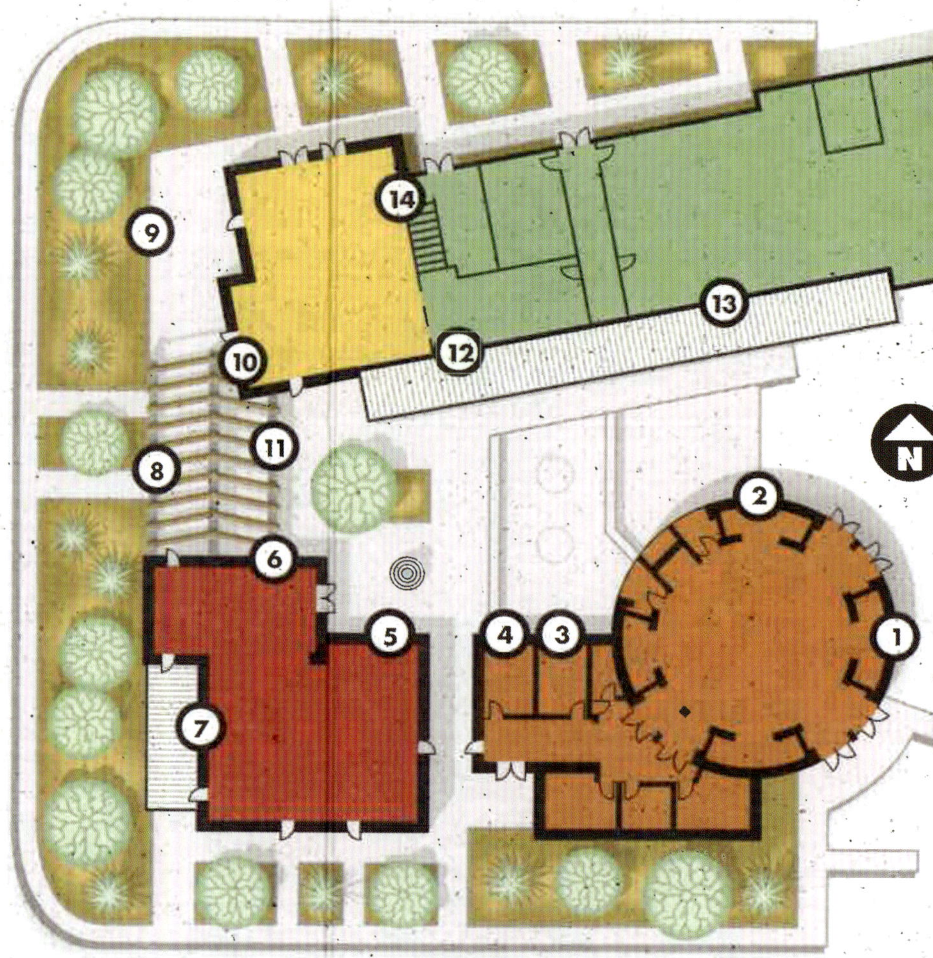

8 | Xeriscape

This is a method of landscaping that focuses on using native plants that are drought tolerant. The landscaping in the Neighborhood Center is designed utilizing this principle with the exception of the grass plaza. Xeriscaping can be inviting and colorful.

9 | Passive Solar: Winter Heat

In winter, the concrete patio collects solar heat. The deciduous trees allow winter sun to enter the interior space.

10 | Straw Bale

This building's wall system is made from the by-product of a wheat harvest – straw. This cellulose product is used as a construc material due to its insulation ities and thick, beautiful app

11 | Tree Salvage

This 100 year old Palo Verde over 3,000 other plants were vaged from the site before con

Some of the technologies used in the Neighborhood Center, and portions of the Center itself were made possible through financial support

COMMUNITY OF CIVANO 10501 E SEVEN GENERATIONS WAY TUCSON AZ 85747 | INFO CENTER 520-**885-6930** | CORPORATE 520-298-8900 |

This paper contains 100%

egan. This means mature are part of the project from ginning; providing shade and rving native plants which in helps to preserve native wild-

Solar Hot Water

olar panels located on the of the Straw Bale building ne sun to heat water, which n stored or used. This is the widely known and used ac- olar energy technology. Active hot water systems can be as le as preheat systems that ent fueled systems, or can be elaborate and generate all ot water needed for a building.

Passive Solar: Shading

ong porch helps shade both s from southern exposure, es- lly during summer months o creates a pleasant and invit- utdoor living and work space.

Sustainable Flooring

nium flooring is manufac- in a way that allows it to be ed. It is made by Interface, a er in sustainable manufactur- and is the company's most essively sustainable product. looring materials can be en- recaptured, radically reduc- waste, manufacturing energy nd costs.

Department of Commerce.

24-8266 | www.civano.com

ing of 100% post-consumer waste

A brochure developed for the Grand Opening and then handed out as part of the marketing information at the Welcome (sales) Center. The development team sought opportunities to demonstrate project goals and innovative ideas in the buildings they could control.

The Neighborhood Center was envisioned and built as a demonstration of how both new technologies and old traditional building traditions could come together to create a modern and compelling place.

CIVANO

IT'S HOW YOU LIVE.

TAKE A SELF-GUIDED TOUR of the special features throughout the Neighborhood Center. These features demonstrate active and passive solar technologies, alternative building materials, and other sustainable strategies. We hope this brief introduction of Civano's innovations will stimulate your interest in thinking about sustainability.

Ecological Stewardship & Regeneration

SITE ENGINEERING: STREET DESIGN

The 1996 Civano Master Plan was organized as an interconnected network of thoroughfare types taken out of the New Urbanist playbook. They are illustrated on the Street Classification Diagram in the next page. They ranged from formal north-south and east-west boulevards intersecting at the Neighborhood Center, picturesque streets at the edges of Neighborhood One with an open view to nature, typical neighborhood streets, and alleys intersecting every block. Atypical and included at the insistence of Wayne Moody were the cul-de-sac streets that are the means of accessing the Desert Country Homes. These were loosely interconnected across the central greenway by extensive pedestrian paths.

While the thoroughfares were designed consistently and proportionally to the uses and buildings that they serve, they were inconsistent in the design of their details, in part because they were never well-coordinated and refined as part of a technically succinct mobility chapter in the charrette Master Plan. The design and development team's valiant efforts to have this neighborhood-supportive thoroughfare network properly designed and built were ultimately frustrated by various City of Tucson departments. At the time, many municipal policies and approval procedures reflected a pro-vehicular traffic, pro-sprawl bias.

As a result, a number of major form deficits were incorporated into the eventual engineering design and construction of the Civano thoroughfares. While reducing the traffic lanes from 10–14 feet to 8–9 feet was unprecedented and a remarkable achievement, the rolled curbs, a compromise with city standards that helped achieve the width reduction, also ended up giving drivers the visual cue that travel lanes were wider than they in fact are, encouraging speeding. This sense of wideness was further enhanced by the absence of continuous accommodations for street parking that limits easy access by residents and visitors to homes and Neighborhood One destinations. Absent of parked cars, there is a sense of emptiness and excessive separation between the two sides of many streets. Paving of streets through the inner, shared spaces of the compounds dented their rural image and compromised the livability of their individual homes. And so on.

There are a few exceptions of successful Civano thoroughfares. In the Desert Country Home area of Neighborhood One, the short cul-de-sacs are dominated by a landscape of trees arranged in a picturesque pattern. These are lanes used mostly for accessing and servicing houses, allowing most walking to happen along meandering paths in the parallel greenways located on the opposite side of houses.

Overall, these design deficits are serious and not to be dismissed, but there is also a rather simple explanation for them. Twenty years later, there is a much more expansive understanding of multimodal and neighborhood-compatible street network design among urbanists, civil engineers, and to an extent, reviewers. In fact, Civano was a state-of-the-art thoroughfare design for its time.

SITE ENGINEERING: HONORING THE LAND

It is not a secret that in conventional sprawl development, the topography of the land is approached as an inconvenience. Natural profiles are typically removed, the land is flattened, the native flora is discarded, and stereotypical subdivision patterns are imposed upon it: discontinuous cul-de-sac-dominated streets; high-impact engineering for utilities and site design; endlessly repeating lots with deficient provisions for yards; the imposition of non-native tree and plant species in sparse landscape arrangements. There is no streetscape in this kind of development.

The site engineering of Civano followed a radically different path: regenerative design rather than mitigation by engineering design excess. The regenerative approach emphasized respecting the site's topography and disturbing it only as a matter of last resort; fitting roads and utility infrastructure to topographic conditions; harvesting and reusing displaced plants on the site; seeing rainwater as the precious resource it is in the desert; and approaching hydrological engineering to capture and reuse this resource, rather than manage it as a constraint that gets in the way of "efficient" land planning.

Two main approaches to rainwater management were used in Civano. To the extent possible, rainwater is captured where it falls and is infiltrated into the ground with the intention of nurturing adjacent plant life and, to some extent, recharging the aquifer. What runoff cannot be captured is directed to the arroyos to the east and west of Neighborhood One. This is accomplished through an elaborate drainage network centered on the three longest north-south conveyors of surface water within the plan: the central greenway of the Desert Country Homes, Civano Boulevard, and Thunder Sky Way.

On the thoroughfares, inverted curbs on the upslope side of their medians, and gabions placed along the medians, collect and hold water, nourishing the trees and plants in them. On the central greenway, the surface water follows a winding course that slows its flow down, also supporting the life of the flora all over it. Water is eventually directed to flow into the natural arroyos surrounding the site. Depending on topography, a number of streets also directly discharge water into surrounding arroyos. This elaborate, inexpensive, and remarkably effective drainage system is one of the earliest illustrations of what came to be called an LID (Low Impact Development) standard. It is described in more detail on pages 156–157.

The development team made a concerted effort to add capturing greywater from residential use for irrigation on private lots. Despite strong support and advocacy from their civil engineers, the efforts were not successful. At the time of this effort, local and state regulations regarding reusing greywater were contradictory to the point of being impossible to follow, much less achieve.

THE PUBLIC REALM: PLANT SALVAGE AND REUSE

The shortcomings of the engineering design of Civano thoroughfares are brilliantly mitigated by its streetscape design. During the 1996 Charrette, there

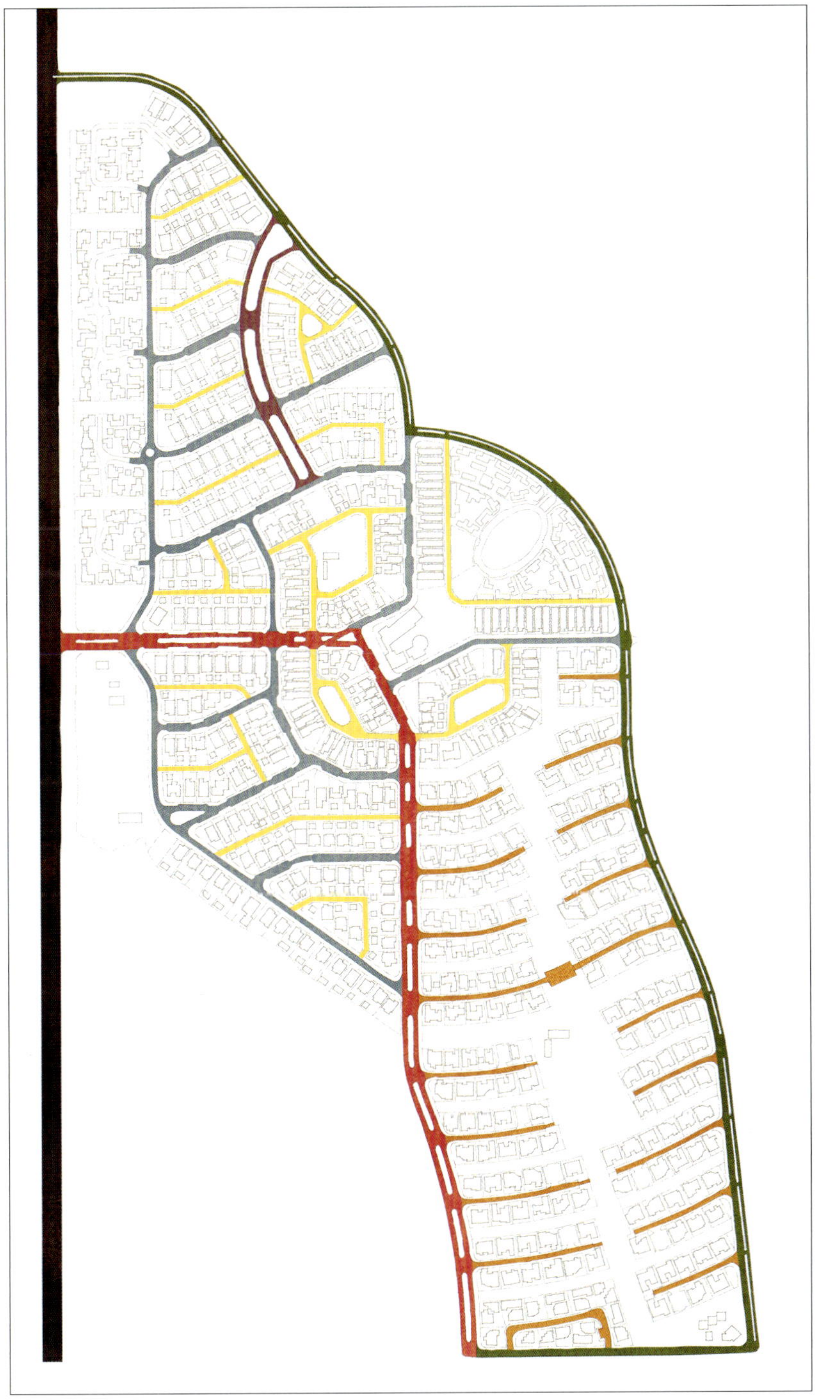

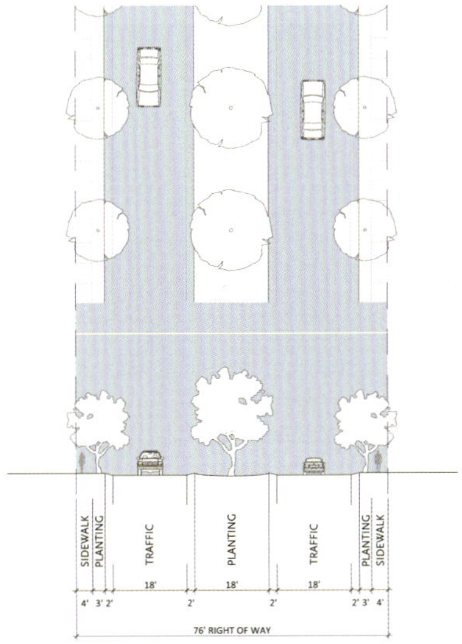

Neighborhood Access Street

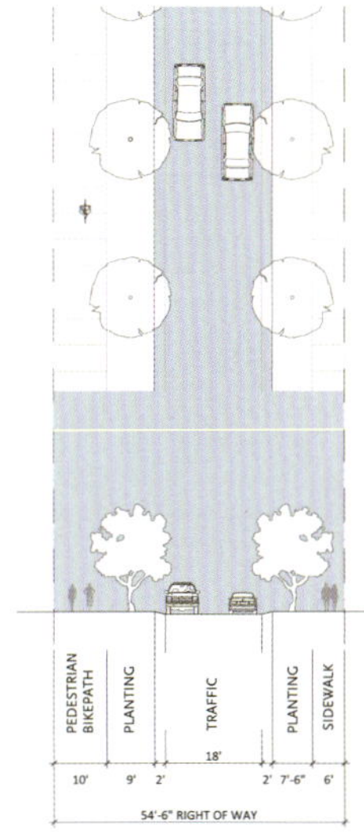

Neighborhood Street 1

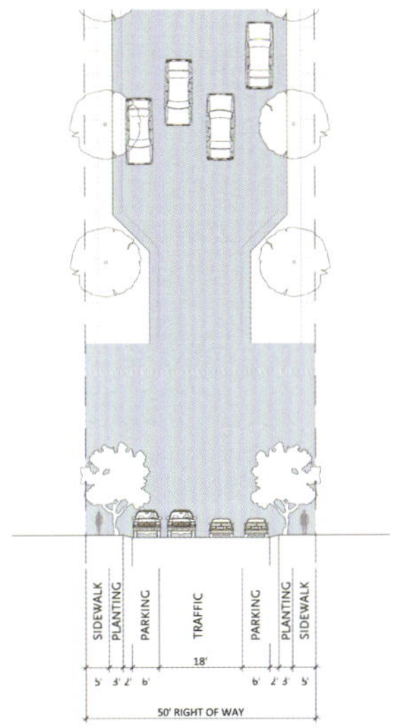

Neighborhood Street 2

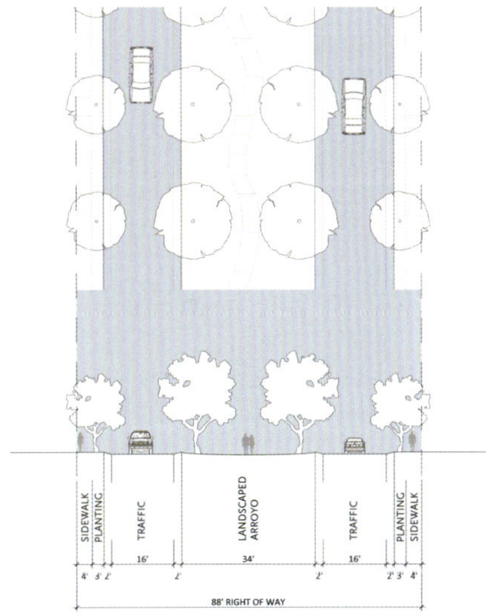

Neighborhood Street 3

Lane

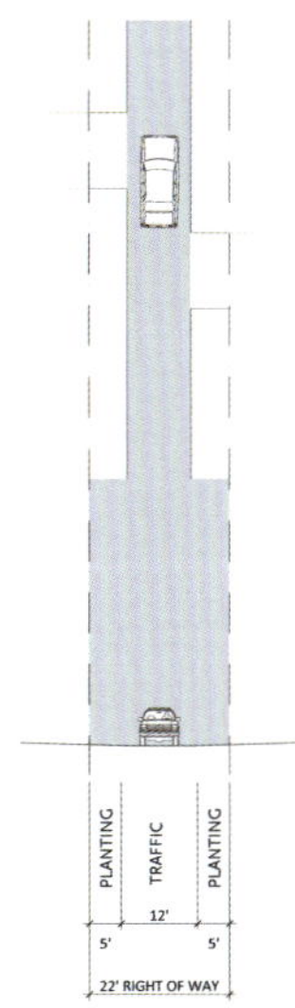

Rear Alley

Street Classification Diagram

- Houghton Road
- Neighborhood Access Street
- Neighborhood Street 1
- Neighborhood Street 2
- Neighborhood Street 3
- Lane
- Rear Alley

Drawings adapted from the Thoroughfare Standards, p.25
Neighborhood One Specific Plan, City of Tucson SP 6a, adopted on October 20, 1997.
Prepared in 2020.

Street Sections

Drawings adapted from the Thoroughfare Standards, p.27
Neighborhood One Specific Plan, City of Tucson SP 6a, adopted on October 20, 1997.
Drawing prepared in 2020.

Drawings courtesy of Moule & Polyzoides.

Views of the process of harvesting the desert flora and storing it in the Civano Nursery.

was no landscape architect present to advise on horticulture or landscape design. A momentous decision by the development team a few months later saved the show in this respect. Over 6,000 plants and trees were salvaged from the Civano site prior to grading. This idea was initially advocated by Wayne Moody and was executed by Les Shipley. The harvested desert flora was moved and stored in Shipley's new local enterprise, the Civano Nursery, located at the entrance to the project.

The Civano Nursery pioneered methods to ensure salvaged plant survival, achieving a mid-90% rate. Reusing salvaged plants from the site helped ensure their health once replanted because they were being replanted in the same soil with the same microbial and mineral makeup from which they had been taken. The massive number of salvaged trees, cacti, and other plants were used for the streetscape of the new grid of thoroughfares, the landscape of the greenways and the private yards. The nursery has since become a thriving business and a transformative force in the ecological evolution of southeast Tucson, and the entire region. (See above.)

THE PUBLIC REALM: STREETSCAPE & LANDSCAPE

The streetscape was designed by MMLA, a Tucson civil engineering firm, and McGann & Associates, a landscape architecture firm. Tom Lodge and John Alexander were the project leads from MMLA, and Tom McGann was the lead from McGann & Associates. It is important to give high credit to these firms on the design of the streetscape, not only because they dared to use the recycled desert trees and plants in lined urban configurations, a first for Tucson at this scale, but also because they promoted xeriscape principles and were engaged in notable civil engineering design for water management.

Views of the greenways and parks defined and populated by the harvested trees and other plants original to the Civano site.

The decision of the developers to harvest the desert flora was as smart as it was unprecedented. Reusing Palo Verde and Mesquite trees for lining streets with formal allées and planting medians in native plant species would provide visual substance to the environment-friendly rhetoric of the project. The richly planted greenways and lanes also proved to be a powerful visual and environmental presence. They encouraged the outdoor life of individual families in a desert environment, particularly during the harsh heat of the summer; attracted the desert fauna; and provided places for community interaction in buildings, fields, pools, and pavilions. All this allowed people to move effortlessly from home to home, and to all kinds of neighborhood destinations. All of this was achieved with thoughtful design and relatively inexpensive and mature plant material. The strategy of spending heavily on the greening and the shading of the public realm would also set a compelling planting example for individual homeowners to follow on their own properties. It proved right on both counts and has provided remarkable place and value dividends. (See above.)

Augmented by ample recycled water irrigation, the streetscape and landscape are a dominant presence today. Their form, color, and shade virtually erase the various shortcomings of Civano's thoroughfare and public realm design, and endow the project with an unmistakable Southwestern character. The planting of private desert gardens also proved to be hugely successful. So much so, that one of the special markers of Civano in the Tucson real estate market is now the richness of the landscape of the front and back yards of houses, planted and maintained by individual homeowners. (See page 159.)

Altogether, the physical impression of greenness in Neighborhood One is so intense that it almost defies the common understandings of what a desert environment should look like. It is a proud dimension of Civano's community identity.

A greenway travels through the Desert Country Homes area. It is both a method for collecting rainwater runoff and a wildlife corridor through the community. The water capture and control strategies used in the section are typical of those used wherever possible throughout Civano. The goal is to capture water and let it be absorbed into the land, nourishing plant life and creating a cooler land footprint during the summer.

1 A collecting drain takes what remaining runoff water there may be and channels it through pipes to the adjacent arroyo.

2 A bridge connects the pedestrian paths on either side, while allowing water and wildlife to pass underneath.

3 Gabions—basically porous dams—are placed along the greenway to slow water and prevent erosion. Slowing the water allows for more absorption to nurture plant life.

The desert walkways onto which the houses face are designed, like the greenway, to slow and capture rainwater. This nurtures the trees planted along them, and they in turn create a shaded and pleasant walking network connected to the pathways that run along either side of the central greenway.

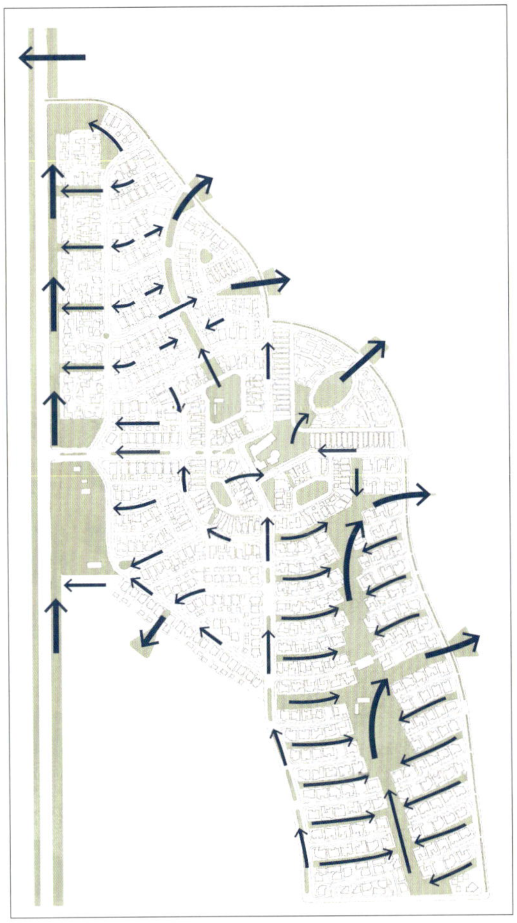

Drainage Diagram
Drawings adapted from the Thoroughfare Standards, p.14
Neighborhood One Specific Plan, City of Tucson SP 6a, adopted on October 20, 1997.
Prepared in 2020.

At right, illustrations of civil engineering techniques for slowing and collecting stormwater at the site and building scale.

(top) Boulevard median treatment: inverted curbs allow rain runoff to flow into a planted median.

(center) After a storm: gabions slow water in swale, allowing plants and the ground to absorb it.

(bottom) Two examples residential-scale water harvesting installations.

Drawings courtesy of Moule & Polyzoides.

(this page) Views of Neighborhood One Civano streetscapes planted with trees harvested from the site.

View of Civano front yards of houses located in various areas of Neighborhood One, planted in a desert xeriscape, with plants recovered from the original site.

Master Planning the Entire Site

In the spring of 2002, Fannie Mae dismissed the last members of the management team that were still abiding by the original ideals of the Civano Initiative. Just a few weeks before, Moule & Polyzoides was asked by CDC to provide a detailed sketch that explored the extension and completion of the project over the remaining site, something that should have been done six years earlier, in 1996. This brief design exploration was initiated in the interest of understanding the project's middle and long-term economic prospects. It was generally based on the experiences drawn from the design, marketing, and sales of Neighborhood One. More specifically, it probed the design and cost of the road and utility infrastructure, the land yield in terms of lots for different house and housing types, and the phasing sequence necessary to lead the project to successful completion.

The scope of work included a three-neighborhood Civano, with an option for a fourth neighborhood across Houghton Road. Moule & Polyzoides were directed to stay true to both the social and environmental dimensions of the Civano Protocols. The drawings produced were very promising. First and foremost, they delivered a commanding overall geometric configuration for the entire project land area, a marvelous image of an integrated and continuous urbanism of streets and blocks superimposed over a network of desert greenways. This potent figure of an urban fabric integrated into nature through a complex field of open space may well be the most important urban design idea to have been contributed by the Civano Initiative.

The details of the completed Master Plan sketch are also notable. The open space field is made up of the interconnected figures of existing arroyos crisscrossing the site. This move enables the conservation of the drainage courses and landscape, which is also the habitat for the wildlife living there. It remains accessible by pedestrian paths to all neighborhoods. The proposed thoroughfare network is hierarchical and connects all the neighborhoods. Diverse, integrated, and multimodal, it allows direct movement in and out of the entire project, while it also accommodates vehicular access to every part of its neighborhoods at appropriate speeds.

The proposed block structure enables house and housing of various types and densities to be assembled under the typology menu implemented in Neighborhood One. The Desert Country homes, located in some of the most remote land peninsulas, generate a greenway-based urbanism, and all the rest of the types, a street-based one. Neighborhood Center buildings are also strategically located within Neighborhoods Two and Three, as shown on the map on the following page. (A Neighborhood Center was also planned for the possible Neighborhood Four. See conceptual map on page 55.) It is notable that this final scheme anticipates the accomplishment of the one performance measure of the Civano project not previously addressed: the development of a mixed-use district. The scheme fronts it on Houghton Road and centers it on Drexel Avenue, at center left on the sketch.

However promising, this last drawing was never implemented. The events of June 2002 were decisive. Fannie Mae abandoned the Civano vision, liquidated the development team, and handed the project to development and national building interests that would betray the entire trajectory of Civano's extraordinary history. At this point, disillusionment, fragility, and exhaustion became the order of the day. The project's ideals were forgotten because there was no one left in a position of authority to either forcefully advocate for them or implement them. In a well-documented process, Fannie Mae handed the development of the remainder of the project over to Pulte to complete it. Pulte was then a national builder with a long history of antipathy for New Urbanism and New Urbanists. In a classic divide-and-rule move, Fannie Mae and Pulte together managed to persuade the community and the City of Tucson that it was possible to complete Civano by separating its social ideals from its environmental ones.

In practical terms, this was translated into a hybrid development pattern for the design and production of Neighborhoods Two and Three. The houses that were constructed met the Civano environmental protocol but abandoned the principle of organizing them along the lines of a traditional neighborhood. The new project assumed the name of Sierra Morado. Its subdivision design was a return to the hard-core practices of conventional suburban development:

- A high-speed access boulevard bisecting it, with houses turning their backs to it;
- No street hierarchy, lots of cul-de-sac streets, and no alleys;
- An anemic range of house types delivered in typical, neutral, could-be-anywhere box styles;
- A stifling repetition of models with front-loaded garages and no interest in defining a sense of street identity;
- Residual versus purposed, planned, and designed public space throughout;
- No mix of uses and little walkability; and
- Just another subdivision with houses routine in design, with no community or Civano-level environmental performance ambitions.

The original ideal of Civano that the pioneers of the passive solar movement had dreamed up, and the developers of Neighborhood One had realized in their own way, was now officially dead. Concurrent with the early stages of Sierra Morado's buildout, Diamond Interests built the Mesquite Ranch subdivision south of Bilby Road, the southern boundary of Sierra Morado. It was not bound by either the New Urbanist or environmental dimensions of the Civano Protocols. This was one more instance of the idea of Civano, both its origins in the Tucson Solar Village and in its final implementation in Neighborhood One, being pushed aside in favor of business interests and institutions that had grown wealthy embracing and perpetuating the production sprawl model, and who were not interested in exploring any alternative to it—not then, not now, and not in the future.

But life evolves in strange ways. The current climate crisis, resource depletion, social trends favoring urban living, smaller houses, and limited commuting by car have conspired to again bring the issue of containing urban sprawl to the forefront of the discussion on design, planning, and development. Fifteen years after its completion, the market success of Civano, its durability, resilience, and place value, are making it an example to study on our way to rethinking our urban growth and development priorities.

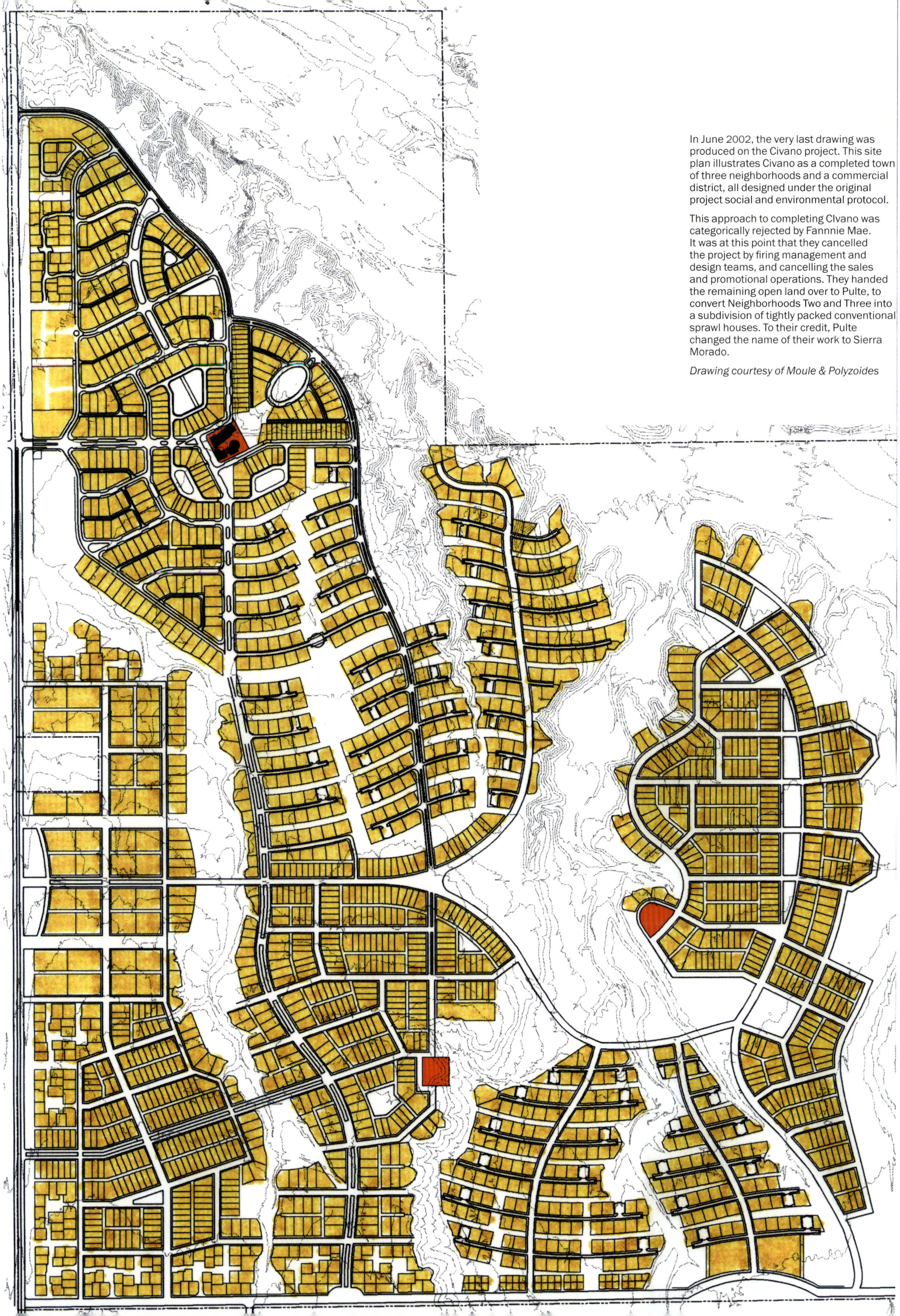

In June 2002, the very last drawing was produced on the Civano project. This site plan illustrates Civano as a completed town of three neighborhoods and a commercial district, all designed under the original project social and environmental protocol.

This approach to completing Clvano was categorically rejected by Fannnie Mae. It was at this point that they cancelled the project by firing management and design teams, and cancelling the sales and promotional operations. They handed the remaining open land over to Pulte, to convert Neighborhoods Two and Three into a subdivision of tightly packed conventional sprawl houses. To their credit, Pulte changed the name of their work to Sierra Morado.

Drawing courtesy of Moule & Polyzoides

Civano and Sierra Morado are portrayed here deployed on the Sonoran Desert, facing each other, like armies ready to do battle, their streets, blocks, buildings, public realm, landscape, and overall urban and environmental design form as ideologically and pragmatically different as can be.

The battle is to guarantee the continuation of human life on earth in the context of the city and nature. That is, the physical survival, the emotional stability, and the spiritual growth of all of us, including our offspring and theirs, forever and ever.

Life begins to lose its meaning when our built surroundings are debased, when nature is polluted and its flora and fauna are in retreat, when social life is undermined and economic prosperity becomes unreachable for the many. Over the last eighty years, the sprawl development pattern has been a prime contributor to the decline of the quality of life in our nation and the world. It is for that reason that the battle for sustainability must and will go on.

Here is the irony: While the Civano experiment is over, the battle against sprawl and the forces and interests that cause it has never been more fierce.

CIVANO VS. SIERRA MORADO

Comparing Civano, Neighborhood One and Sierra Morado (aka Neighborhoods Two and Three)

Date of Information:	**December 2019**			
	Civano Neighborhood One		**Sierra Morado**	
General Information				
Size (acres)	394		424	
Number of Homes	645	1	565	2
Land Set Aside	30%		28%	
Housing Density in Non-set-aside Land	**2.34/acre**		**1.90/acre**	
Commercial Space (Other than HOA Office)	Yes		No	
Retail Space	Yes		No	
Neighborhood Center	Yes		No	
Community Garden	Yes		No	
Grade School (Charter)	Yes		No	
Middle School (Charter)	Yes		No	
Compliance with IMPACT Standards				
Energy use reduced by 50%. Actual achieved:	**49%**	4	**40%**	4
Beneficial Use of Solar				
Passive DHW	**Every house**		**About 1/2 of houses**	
PV Installations (see Note #2): % of homes	**15%**		**21%**	
Reduced VMT	**See comments p. 165**		**See comments p. 165**	
Potable water reduction of 60%. Actual achieved:	**59%**	4	**38%**	4
Employment				
(300 sf of non-residential for every 2 homes built)				
Square Footage Required by Standard	96,750		84,750	
Square Footage Achieved: Stand-alone buildings (see **Note #1**)	64,000	3	11,400	3
Square Footage Achieved: In-Home Businesses (as recognized by City of Tucson)	13,000	3	0	3
Total as % of calculated requirement	**80%**		**13%**	
Affordability	**See comments p. 165**		**See comments p. 165**	
Waste Reduction (not tracked)				
Holding Value				
Impact of 2008 Housing Crisis: % lost market value (For Resales only)	**8.5% to 25%**	5	**consistently @ 33%**	5
Avg. PSF Price of Homes at the time of this book	**\$158/sf** @25% higher	6	**\$126/sf**	6

Information Sources:

1. Civano Neighborhood One HOA **2**. Sierra Morado HOA **3**. Final IMPACT Standards Report, 2011
4. Inside Civano, Nichols 2007 **5**. Tucson Multiple Listing Service **6.** Trulia website and Tucson MLS.

NOTE #1

In calculating the commercial/retail space built in Civano Neighborhood One, only the **built structures** of Civano Nursery were included. If the outdoor areas were included, an additional 133,000 sf of non-residential use would be added.

NOTE #2

Virtually all of the PV in Civano Neighborhood One was installed by private homeowners; usually ranging between 2.0 to 3 kwh systems. In Sierra Morado, virtually all PV was installed by the builder, ***instead of*** installing a passive hot water heater. The PV systems there averaged about 1.1kw, enough to cover a small portion of an average home's needs.

Chart comparing key metrics of Civano and Sierra Morado, which would have been Neighborhoods Two and Three of Civano before being separated. The chart shows the latest available data.

A Comparison Twenty Years On

There is no simple, linear way of telling the story of Civano. We are conditioned to think about human enterprises as eventually resulting either in success or failure. This is definitely true in the case of urbanism and development. Yet it is common that projects that are initially judged as failures can eventually be recognized as trending on the right side of history.

As is the case of all great visions, the ideas of Civano were born during trying times, times of social and political friction, environmental uncertainty, economic instability, and professional flux. It seems prudent then, that under such circumstances, projects such as Civano be judged not by their distance from their initial goals, but by their degree of approximating them. In that case, what matters the most is not what the project and place may have been, but what they are now, what we have learned from how they came to be, and what we are learning daily from being there.

The tragedy—we will call it that—of the truncated Civano experiment does have a useful silver lining. The forced bifurcation of the originally envisioned three-neighborhood community into two separate communities offers a rich venue for comparison. As we have noted previously, the last two neighborhoods, renamed Sierra Morado, were developed with standard production sprawl protocols in a marked and deliberate contrast to the New Urbanist protocols of Civano Neighborhood One.

There were other marked differences, most notable being the approach to landscape design, house design, and site engineering. There was no attempt to salvage the native plant life that so marked the development of Neighborhood One. Grading and hydrology protocols in Sierra Morado were much better versions of standard sprawl development, but were notable regressions in comparison to the approaches taken in Neighborhood One. House designs were standard Pulte national models with a few touches to suggest nothing more than a vague reference to Western production models—lots of tile roofs and a few kind-of-Southwest details applied to the front elevations. Gone was the rich hierarchy of streets and alleys that so visually organized Neighborhood One, an organization which gave its residents a mental map that helped encourage walking. Sierra Morado had a major spine full of speeding cars and a much more haphazard network of streets, streets onto which the garages of virtually all the homes faced.

There was one critical constant: the IMPACT Standards. Though they had been made more aspirational, they still needed to be pursued and measured as they were in Neighborhood One. The City required a periodic third-party review report from the developer. A number of outside studies of compliance were done, notably by Al Nichols, who had a long history with Civano and its predecessors. In addition, a number of academic studies were done at Arizona State and elsewhere. They have created an unusual body of data which can be used to consider the impact of walking away from the success of Neighborhood One. The comparison chart to the left summarizes comparative data for the two communities on a number of topics. It is revealing on several points. First is overall density. Despite all of Fannie Mae's rationales about needing to abandon the Neighborhood One planning protocols to achieve more home lots, it's Neighborhood One that comes out ahead. And that includes all the land taken up by the amenities Neighborhood One has, but that are missing in Sierra Morado.

The comparison of how close each community came to meeting the IMPACT Standards shows some significant differences. Just a few notes on each standard:

- Energy use reduction: All of Sierra Morado's models were certified to meet the 50% reduction goal. Where we believe the certification crumbled was in the field. It is one thing to certify a perfect example on paper, quite another to measure the built results. There was no counterpart of the IBACOS/Build America training in Sierra Morado, and the results show it.
- Note #2 of the chart explains the different approach to implementing the beneficial use of solar in each community. Since domestic hot water is one of the most intensive energy uses in a home, perhaps the decision by Pulte to eliminate passive DHW systems in about the last third of the houses in Sierra Morado and replace them with token PV systems contributed to the difference in energy reduction.
- Reduced VMT: This one is a hard one to measure. There is, however, a study done by Ellen Schwaller from Arizona State University that measured metrics of social life in the two communities. The study found a more vital social life in Civano Neighborhood One, as measured by more community clubs and with more meetings. The study also indicated that there was more walking in Neighborhood One, not surprising given that there are things to walk to, including a Neighborhood Center with a number of service businesses. All this suggests that cars are used less frequently in Neighborhood One. The streetscapes in Neighborhood One, without all the driveway cuts and with virtually all houses having front porches, are simply more inviting.
- The commitment to use reclaimed water for landscape irrigation, both in public areas and in private yards, makes a huge difference in overall potable water use.
- The employment standard is perhaps the one most directly connected to the use of New Urbanist protocols in Neighborhood One. Many of the home models were designed to easily accommodate ancillary units that could be used as offices. Critically, the Specific Plan for Neighborhood One ensured that the special zoning made in-home businesses doable. And, of course, Neighborhood One was promoted and planned as a mixed-use community. None of these features were duplicated in Neighborhoods Two and Three.
- Affordability is a very complex topic. Neighborhood One's lowest price models were, unfortunately, the RGC models. RGC's failure and how the market itself bid up prices in Neighborhood One made adhering to the initial affordability intentions all but impossible. In Sierra Morado, Fannie Mae and Pulte made a deal with the City to contribute $100,000 to several local housing nonprofits and called it a day.
- Arizona was one of the epicenters of the 2007/2008 housing collapse. The difference in how much resale prices dropped in the two neighborhoods speaks to two things. Neighborhood One's amenities, overall design, and better energy performance made a difference. All that contributed to a sense of tangible value that would last. It is a subjective thing, but the buying public, not these authors, made a statement in one of the most harrowing of times for housing. That sense of value remains to this day, as reflected in a 25% premium for houses in Neighborhood One versus those in Neighborhoods Two and Three.

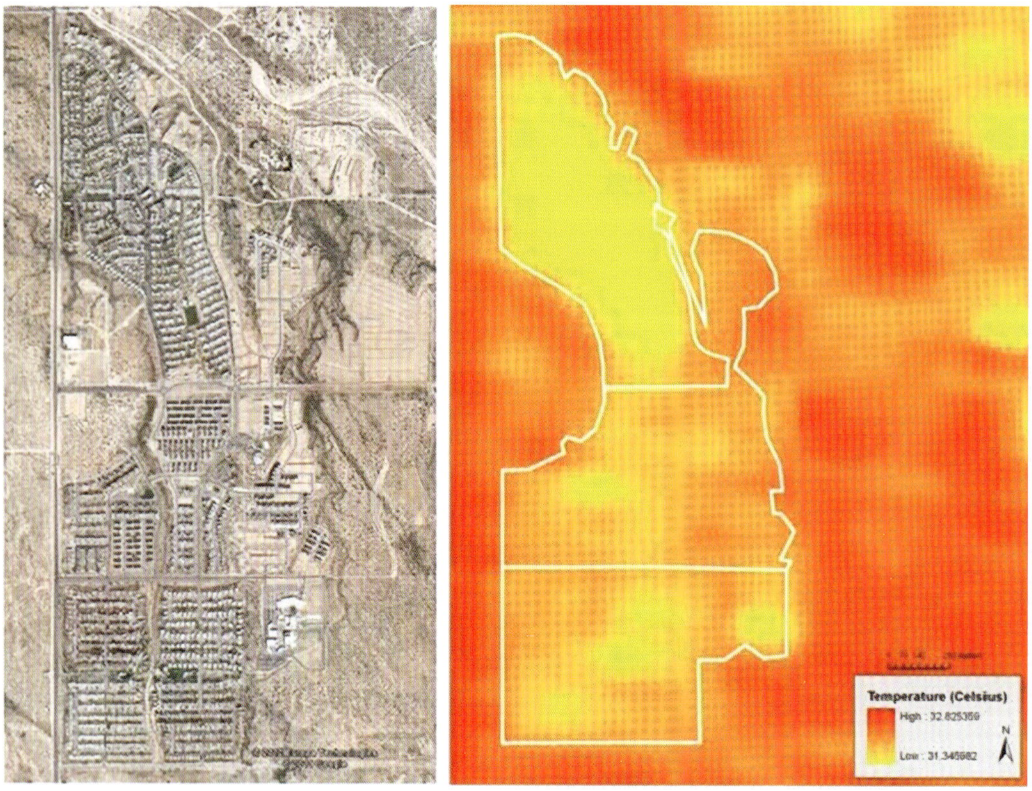

Land surface temperature estimate derived from Landsat of Civano and adjacent communities. Civano Neighborhood One is the upper left quadrant in the image. Sierra Morado (the old Neighborhoods Two and Three of Civano), the middle-outlined community at the lower left. Mesquite Ranch, a Diamond Ventures community, is the bottom left outlined community. Image taken in June 2010. The heat differential measured is 1.5 degrees Celsius, with yellow denoting the lower end of the scale.

EXCEPTIONAL COST

No doubt, Fannie Mae would look at all the above and dismiss some of it on the basis that you can achieve anything if you just spend enough money, even foolishly. This was the core of their message, that the only way to ensure some portion of the Civano goals being incorporated in a middle-market housing project was to get back to basics, the tried and true production sprawl development model. Again, this argument rests on the idea that the first phase of the Civano experiment, Neighborhood One, was financially irresponsible. When one rejects this forced, limited viewpoint and chooses to look at how Neighborhood One evolved from mid-2001 on, a different possibility is seen. Once operational expenditures had stabilized, and sales were strong and consistent, a more accurate assessment of costs could be made.

That assessment would show that creating a community like Civano would cost more, but with critical caveats. We know from the Civano Neighborhood One builders that getting a house built to the IMPACT and Civano standards cost them about 12–15% more than their standard production homes (circa 2000). This "Civano premium" was of concern as sales started in 1999. However, the builders soon found that once a buyer understood that the energy savings of a Civano house would quickly offset that premium, it ceased to be an issue. The overall development probably costs about 20% more than a standard middle-income production community. Amenities like a Neighborhood Center do cost something, as did subsidies to keep cafés and service businesses going while the community built out toward a population sufficient to support them. But these features add tangible value to the community, and the market takes note. In Civano, the energy savings potential and the community amenities created a compelling marketing story, as well as helping meet the environmental and social goals of the project. The comparison of home values during the housing collapse of 2007–2008 and post collapse noted on the chart on page 164 between Neighborhood One and Neighborhoods Two and Three tell a story about creating value, and value that is lasting. Had the development team for Civano been more stable, participated more in the building and sale of homes, and modulated the sale of lot options to builders more carefully, the profitability of Civano would have been a story of note.

A LARGER PERSPECTIVE

What was the Civano experiment, at its core, about? It was a response to the growing realization of the impact of a particular kind of growth accommodation, sprawl, on a particular environment, the Sonoran Desert. That particularity, though, was a part of a more general understanding that carbon-fueled growth was having an increasingly measurable impact on the global environment. Civano was an imperfect attempt to implement a model for growth accommodation that recognized that challenge and tried to do something about it.

In 2014, Kelly Turner and Christopher Galletti published *Climate Regulation, Primary Productivity, and Provisioning of Water Resources in Sustainable Planned Development: A Case Study of Civano in Tucson, Arizona* as part of their academic work at Arizona State University. This was a detailed study investigating whether planning protocols have an impact on critical resource use. Civano Neighborhood One and Sierra Morado Neighborhoods Two and Three were perfect candidates for their study, precisely because of the post-Pulte bifurcation of the project. As with the studies done by Al Nichols, their findings showed some differences between the two communities in terms of individual home energy and water use, but not significant ones, as would be expected given the City-mandated constant of the IMPACT Standards.

On the other hand, thermal satellite images taken as part of the study revealed striking differences between the two communities. (See above.)

What this image shows is heat being reflected into the atmosphere from the ground mass below. It is a direct measure of the heat island effect, heat being retained in built-up areas. These give an indirect approximation of levels of CO2 generation. Areas that have higher heat island footprints tend to be

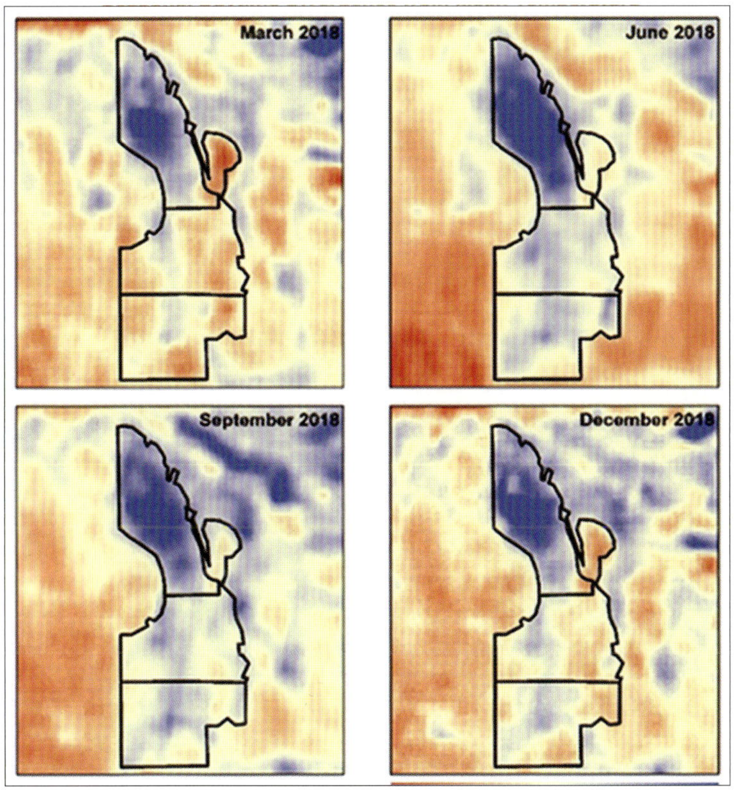

Seasonal Landsat surface temperature estimate images of Civano Neighborhood One, Sierra Morado Neighborhoods Two and Three, and Mesquite Ranch. In these images, blue represents a cooler heat signature, with red at the other end of the heat spectrum.

higher CO2 generators. The heat range goes from the yellow lows to the higher reds. On the upper left image, the range delta is about 1.8 degrees Celsius.

There are two things that are striking in this image. Civano Neighborhood One is an almost solid full yellow, nearly up to the edges of its boundaries. Neighborhoods Two and Three, on the other hand, are a mottled mix of colors, and thus heat reflection values. Curiously, it is not much better than the outlined neighborhood at the very bottom. This is Mesquite Ranch, a Diamond Ventures community developed without any special environmental requirements.

This was a snapshot in time, true. Continued investigation by Kelly at UCLA showed that the temperature delta in this image was not an isolated event. Throughout the year, Civano Neighborhood One is shown to have a consistently lower heat signature. Importantly, the cooler temperature is almost completely within its boundaries. Neighborhoods Two and Three are more mottled, with far smaller cooler areas. (See above.)

So what can we make of this? The City-mandated IMPACT Standards for energy and water use did not significantly change when Fannie Mae and Pulte became the developers of Sierra Morado. The model homes in Neighborhoods Two and Three were certified to meet virtually the same energy code standards as Neighborhood One. Pulte is probably the best production builder and quality control is a major company focus; their homes were built to meet the standards required.

While the plant life in Civano is more mature, Sierra Morado is more heavily landscaped than a typical production housing subdivision. It would be fair to assume that some percentage of the heat difference can be attributed to a more mature plant cover in Neighborhood One, but it is not enough to explain the dramatic difference.

So what is left? The land-planning and home-design protocols used in Civano and the New Urbanist nature of that community.

The homes in Civano are not constructed of magic materials; they are simply more thoughtfully and mindfully designed, with the place in which they were built always in mind. Many of the Civano home designs took into deep consideration the lessons offered by the vernacular traditions of the desert Southwest. Great emphasis was paid to the flow of enclosed interior space to moderated exterior spaces. A great gift of the Sonoran Desert is that for seven months out of the year, the exterior climate is wonderfully supportive. The home designs in Civano encourage living beyond the “thermos bottle” of the sealed home.

More than all that, these homes were also seen as components of a larger system of systems: the community in which they were built. Planning that thoughtfully created human-scaled relationships among buildings, the interrelation of public and private space, the variety of home types, the presence of accessible public amenities, the focus on open space, the use of salvaged plant life to create a rich and mature landscape—these are just some of the components of the urban and natural systems in balance that Civano so brilliantly features.

The combination of better building practices, taking lessons from the adaptive vernacular tradition, and the New Urbanist plan of Civano all combined to create a notably different heat and energy use footprint. The commitment in Civano Neighborhood One to use New Urbanist planning and design protocols was a critical foundation for those infrared images. The studies and data noted in this chapter suggest, if not outright demonstrate, that the abandonment of that commitment in Sierra Morado lead mightily to its significantly poorer performance.

In a time of increasingly obvious environmental challenges, having at hand a model for community building that can address the core underlying causes of these challenges with success seems a critical legacy, and even a hopeful one.

LEARNING FROM SUCCESS & PARTICULARLY FROM FAILURE

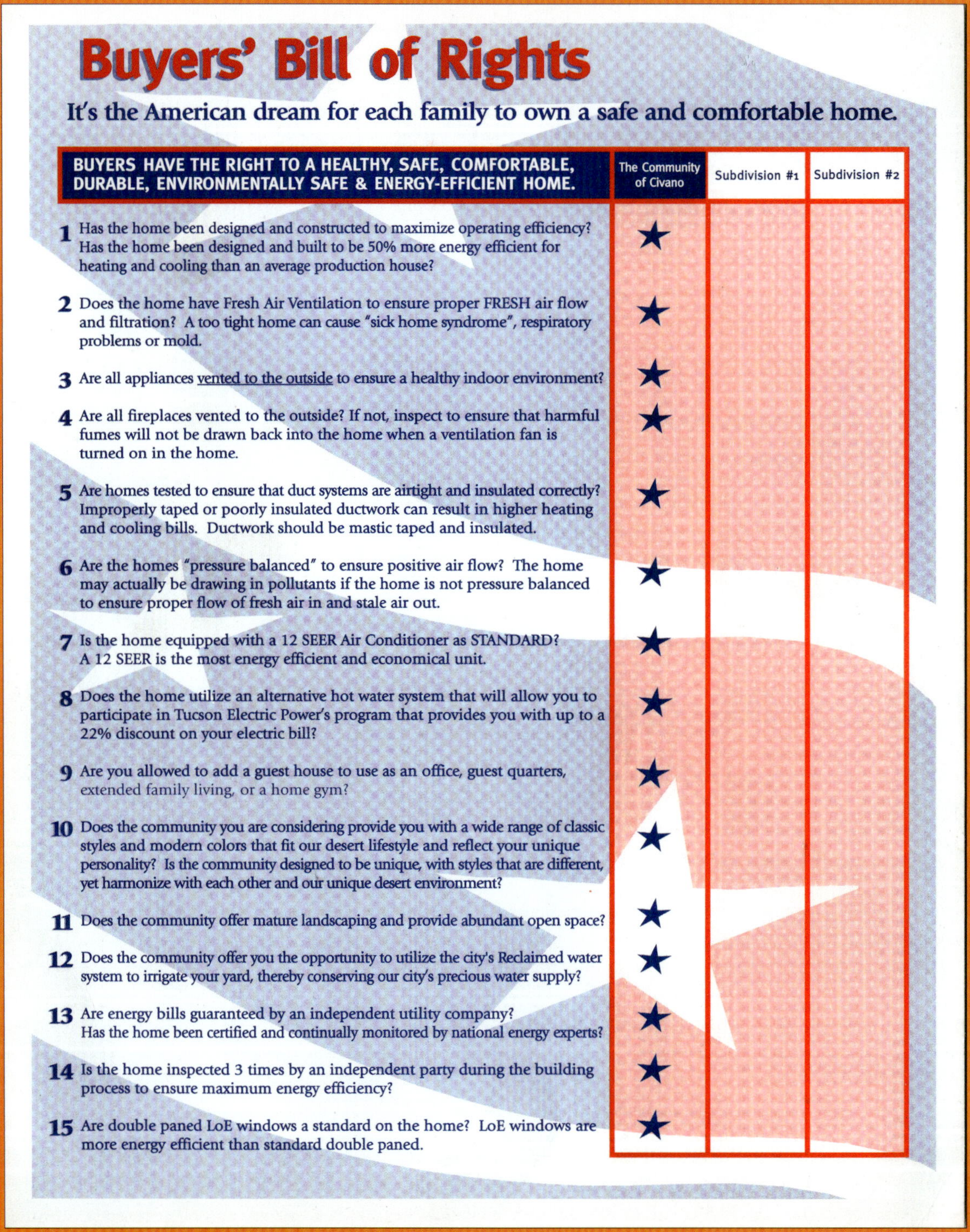

Buyers' Bill of Rights

It's the American dream for each family to own a safe and comfortable home.

BUYERS HAVE THE RIGHT TO A HEALTHY, SAFE, COMFORTABLE, DURABLE, ENVIRONMENTALLY SAFE & ENERGY-EFFICIENT HOME.	The Community of Civano	Subdivision #1	Subdivision #2
1 Has the home been designed and constructed to maximize operating efficiency? Has the home been designed and built to be 50% more energy efficient for heating and cooling than an average production house?	★		
2 Does the home have Fresh Air Ventilation to ensure proper FRESH air flow and filtration? A too tight home can cause "sick home syndrome", respiratory problems or mold.	★		
3 Are all appliances vented to the outside to ensure a healthy indoor environment?	★		
4 Are all fireplaces vented to the outside? If not, inspect to ensure that harmful fumes will not be drawn back into the home when a ventilation fan is turned on in the home.	★		
5 Are homes tested to ensure that duct systems are airtight and insulated correctly? Improperly taped or poorly insulated ductwork can result in higher heating and cooling bills. Ductwork should be mastic taped and insulated.	★		
6 Are the homes "pressure balanced" to ensure positive air flow? The home may actually be drawing in pollutants if the home is not pressure balanced to ensure proper flow of fresh air in and stale air out.	★		
7 Is the home equipped with a 12 SEER Air Conditioner as STANDARD? A 12 SEER is the most energy efficient and economical unit.	★		
8 Does the home utilize an alternative hot water system that will allow you to participate in Tucson Electric Power's program that provides you with up to a 22% discount on your electric bill?	★		
9 Are you allowed to add a guest house to use as an office, guest quarters, extended family living, or a home gym?	★		
10 Does the community you are considering provide you with a wide range of classic styles and modern colors that fit our desert lifestyle and reflect your unique personality? Is the community designed to be unique, with styles that are different, yet harmonize with each other and our unique desert environment?	★		
11 Does the community offer mature landscaping and provide abundant open space?	★		
12 Does the community offer you the opportunity to utilize the city's Reclaimed water system to irrigate your yard, thereby conserving our city's precious water supply?	★		
13 Are energy bills guaranteed by an independent utility company? Has the home been certified and continually monitored by national energy experts?	★		
14 Is the home inspected 3 times by an independent party during the building process to ensure maximum energy efficiency?	★		
15 Are double paned LoE windows a standard on the home? LoE windows are more energy efficient than standard double paned.	★		

Sales piece developed to encourage visitors to Civano's Welcome Center to compare features standard in all Civano homes to competing typical subdivision homes. The chart was distributed with a clipboard with the Civano logo on it. It was a remarkably successful sales and marketing tool, developed by CDC's J. Tober.

Lessons Learned from an Imperfect Civano

"There is no such thing as a failed experiment, just unexpected data to be understood."
—Buckminster Fuller to Lee Rayburn after a lecture, University of Pennsylvania, 1974

There can be no denying that the original, and even the evolved, vision of Civano never reached its full and complete realization. However, much was learned from building this imperfect Civano, both from its many successes, but particularly through its compromises and occasional failures. While less pure than its initial advocates hoped for, it has yielded many lessons that can only be seen as good and valuable.

From the beginnings of the Tucson Solar Village to the handoff to the private sector of a revamped and expanded Civano, the focus of its stakeholders was on establishing the performance goals of the project. Little thought was given to the operational protocols by which these goals would be realized. It was assumed that the private-sector developer chosen to execute the project would bring these along, and so they did. As previous chapters have demonstrated, the intended and unintended consequences of their development strategies and organizational decisions are a large part of the Civano story.

We explore below a list of operational issues that serve as a real estate and development primer, considered through the lens of the experience of developing Civano. We offer it for consideration for any future, innovative real estate project. By innovative, we mean the kind of project that is developed through a combination of social and environmental protocols and aims to mitigate the ravages of sprawl and address the rising challenges of climate change. Our purpose is to move beyond bemoaning what intentions were lost or modified during the process of building Civano and focus on the lessons learned.

SECURING THE LAND

The Right Location

The land designated by state and city agencies for the location of Civano presented, at the project's initiation, a major challenge. The site was far from established urban centers and there was no public transportation connecting it to any other urban center, much less the central business district of Tucson. There was virtually no retail to speak of within eight miles. This made the IMPACT goals of job creation and reducing Vehicle Miles Traveled tough to start with, much less to achieve. There were general expectations among the early home buyers that retail would be built in the first phase, and that public transportation would arrive shortly thereafter. Neither of these was realistic and did not happen as expected, despite efforts by the development team. They were simply beyond the development team's power to create on their own, or they were not economically feasible at that time. Had Civano been located on land more connected to existing urban centers, those two IMPACT Standards would have been much easier to achieve.

It is also reasonable to speculate that a more connected location could have resulted in earlier and more accelerated home sales. This could have decreased the financial strain in the first years of development and perhaps avoided the need for a partnership with Fannie Mae at all. Once about fifty homes were built, and the physical character of the community could be seen and felt, its "out on the edge of town" location became a less important factor. By 2009, significant retail and commercial activity had moved closer to Civano, albeit in a suburban strip center format, and public transportation arrived in 2010.

The takeaway lesson here is to be sure that the stated goals of an innovative project are supported by the regional location of the land on which it is to be built. Seems simple enough, but the availability of inexpensive or, in some manner, subsidized land can cloud a developer's vision.

Incremental Takedown

There was an option not considered by the City or State that could have countered the impact of the land's relatively remote location: have the developer take down the land in a series of defined increments. It was always assumed that Civano would be built out in three neighborhoods of about the same size, and that these would be developed sequentially. The state land auction requirement to purchase all the land at once meant that precious capital was burned away during the early years of the project on the financial carrying costs for land that could not be developed until much later stages of development.

Had the original purchase of the 818 acres of Civano land been set up as a rolling option with a new neighborhood parcel being taken down as each previous neighborhood neared completion, the history of Civano would have been dramatically different. It would have diminished the financial strain on the initial development team, an innovative but thinly capitalized company. It would also have made it easier to create a more flexible builders' lot option program, one that could have more effectively captured for the developer the rising value of the project once the marketplace had discovered it.

Every project is different, along with the land dynamics running through it. The more universal statement of this lesson is to embrace incremental land purchases with payments for land spread out over time, contingent on the successful completion of previous phases of a project. Whether a land development like Civano or some other innovative project, breaking its implementation into smaller increments is often wise. This is especially true when challenging established institutions and practice paradigms are involved. Smaller increments help define and control risk and make implementation adjustments easier to achieve.

Easy Access

Any new development project depends on a network of established arterial roads for its visibility and the easy access of its residents to services. As Civano was located in the outer reaches of the Tucson basin, it was assumed from the beginning that it was going to be a motor vehicle-oriented development. Houghton Road, a major thoroughfare on Tucson's east side, was its accessibility lifeline. Even with the later arrival of transit in the form of public buses, an extensive sidewalk, bike and walking path system, and the poetic presence of horse trails leading into the open desert countryside, car trips have remained the basic form of mobility in Civano.

Understanding the evolving implications of digital commuting, social networking, and e-commerce will take time, but their growing impact on how communities are planned, accessed, and lived in is already here. Civano is notable for the number of in-home and auxiliary-unit businesses. These save thousands of vehicle trips every year. If Civano were being started today, the attention paid to wireless infrastructure would be much greater. Even more effort would be directed to creating flexible live-work home designs.

A multimodal revolution is also happening in transportation. That revolution varies dramatically by metropolitan location, settlement type, and densivy. In a growing number of cases, though, we are witnessing roadways being designed to share car traffic with all other mobility modes, including walking, biking, delivery and service vehicles, and transit. As we venture further into the post-petro- and carbon-centric world, the importance of multimodality will grow.

There are other new trends that are emerging that may change what we think of as public transportation. The emerging market prominence of electric cars will have impacts on transportation planning that are still not clear. Their superior environmental performance may actually encourage private car use and continued high expenditures of public funds for expanded road systems. The use of shared cars, scooters, and bike services is also expanding throughout urban centers. These new means of mobility reduce the need for private transportation in the form of motor vehicles, which often sit idle for much of the day, while the annual cost to their owners is ongoing and significant. Data are also emerging that indicate shared vehicular use is decreasing ridership on public transportation.

Topography and Ecological Character: The Nature of the Land

It is quite typical that in the process of preparing for the development of subdivisions and strip commercial centers, land is most commonly leveled by mass grading. This is ostensibly done for the sake of efficiency and economy, but the results are most often devastating.

When the natural topography of the land is erased, the native flora and fauna are displaced or treated as nuisances, if not waste products to be disposed of. Water courses are modified, their natural flows and rates of absorption into the ground disrupted. The heat island impact is almost always magnified, and overwhelming investments in oversized engineered infrastructure and road systems become necessary. The physical, visible presence of the natural landscape recedes, and the deadening presence of an impermanent and residual hardscape becomes magnified and dominant.

Civano sought to reverse this conventional site engineering strategy entirely. The land was not scraped flat; rather, as much of its natural topography was retained as possible, lending a visible, low-sloping ground form to the project. The existing flora was harvested and replanted in the public and private realm. Wildlife corridors were preserved, and the native fauna is often present. Rainwater was treated as a resource to be reused, not a waste product to be contained and treated. Rainwater runoff was channeled into natural areas to aid in their rejuvenation and recharge the aquifer. All these measures helped lessen the heavy costs of mitigation and the construction of expensive infrastructure. Overall, the physical character of the Sonoran Desert was maintained and celebrated.

The elements of an extensive public realm—streets, parks, pools, various community facilities, and the open desert—all flow seamlessly into each other. Together, they provide a unique and engaging sense of place, successfully blending the ecology of the desert with a built neighborhood, the two together enabling life to flourish in what can normally be an inhospitable environment.

This is ultimately the lesson of Civano: that in its final form, a development project should reflect and enhance the physiognomy and ecological character of the setting where it is located for the sake of identity, livability, and the creation of a balance between the natural and the built dimensions of the human habitat—a balance which is currently in crisis, but we know can be sustained over time.

FINANCIAL STRATEGY

Friendly and Patient Capital

Money rules. The availability of a steady cash flow at key times in the development process is an absolute necessity. Securing it is a high priority and the most important factor in a project's success or failure. Every project wants access to "patient money," and that goes so much more so for innovative ones. It takes time to figure out and implement innovation. Patient money almost always means money sources that are sympathetic to a project team's goals.

During Civano's difficult first years after the land auction, the development team depended on financial support from private investors with strong personal connections to them, who believed in the rhetoric and promoted outcomes of the project. Their patience was tested early on by delays and lack of progress. By the fall of 1997, the ability to depend on this kind of financial support was fading fast. Fannie Mae then joined the project. As it turned out, its support was equivocal, financially conditional, and increasingly unsympathetic. Significant financial support continued, but at the cost of the loss of control by the development team. Along with this came a decreasing commitment to Civano's focus on innovation, which was the purpose of the project.

In 1992, Will Orr had recognized and emphasized the critical role patient money would play in the unfolding of Civano's implementation. He advocated the use of some public funding, his version of patient money. John Laswick's financial analysis in 1995 carried that recognition further and lead to a series of public-sector measures of support, the potential subsidies included in the Development Agreement. The falling away of some of those public-sector contributions, largely because of schedule delays, had a serious negative impact on the project. It is reasonable to speculate that if Civano had been scaled something like discussed above, more patient, private financial resources than Fannie Mae could have been found, ones which would have embraced Civano's key goals. In retrospect, we can now recognize that Civano never attracted the scale of truly patient capital from investors to support its business plan or the cultural impact the project sought to achieve.

To be clear, we are not advocating that patient capital be permissive of failure. The tragedy of Civano was that when success was finally emerging, there was no financial partner who was willing to capitalize on it, least of all Fannie Mae, which ignored that budding success and abandoned the project for institutional, financial, and political reasons. Any innovative project must heed the need to seek and nurture a patient and committed investor, be it a public or private source of money.

Stability

In the long history of the journey from a Solar Village to Civano, much emphasis was placed on the environmental and social goals of the project, but a financial implementation strategy and the resultant long-term financial stability were never as seriously explored and established. It was assumed that the project's early financial uncertainties were temporary inconveniences that would somehow work themselves out. Sufficient patient money can enable the financial situation of a difficult development project to remain manageable, if not stable. That was never true at Civano. An understandable reliance on the most optimistic of projections and schedules ruled the day, until that optimism faded as delays and unforeseen constraints began to pile up. With that, a self-propelling, chaotic process of management began, focused all too often, out of necessity, on short-term viability.

So, what should the basis be for establishing a project's financial stability? In the case of Civano, the easy answer would have been awarding the project to an experienced developer after a deep vetting of their financial resources by the City and State. However, that does not quite get at what happened during the first years of the project's implementation. Although relatively untested at the scale of the proposed project, David Butterfield was transparent in committing his personal resources for the very first stages and in stating that they were limited. He made clear that he was depending on his assumption that past institutional investors would step forward to also support this new project, even though it was more innovative and much larger than anything he had ever done before. Early optimistic sales projections and pledges of public-sector support both strengthened that assumption. On a more standard project, all of this would have more than likely been a safe bet. Civano was far from a standard project, though. For its time, it was a cutting-edge undertaking, with its core social, environmental, and economic propositions untested. No one at the time understood how averse financial institutions would be to this little known and untried new model of development.

Of course, the conundrum in the Civano case was that it was unlikely that anyone but a highly motivated and smaller scale developer looking for innovation in development would have ventured to take it on. That only one party bid at the Civano land auction speaks volumes about the then-prevailing state of the art in community development. Civano would never have been built without the action of its imperfectly vetted, underfunded developer and his soon-to-be partners, Case Enterprises.

What should have been done to address this conundrum? First and foremost, all the stakeholders, private and public, should have realized that a pioneering project cannot be supported, entitled, planned, financed, promoted, and sold by strictly conventional means. Each of these dimensions of the project—administrative, economic, and technical—needed new, innovative financial instruments to enable its development, instruments that were as audacious as the project vision itself.

As noted elsewhere, the land takedown could have been phased. The City of Tucson and State of Arizona could have fulfilled all their pledges to the project, even in the face of delays. All levels of government, including federal, could have created development bonds and acted as the bank for this project and others like it, a method that is not unheard of. At the end of the day, perhaps the lesson to be taken away here is that all the stakeholders in the project bear some responsibility for failing it. No one's failure was intentional, of course, but came about by not insisting on finding the right balance among its social and environmental goals, public and private responsibilities for its administration, ease of entitlement, infrastructure construction support, and allocation of financial resources.

It is a sign of our society's unwillingness to challenge the sprawl cartel that in the end, financial stability was gained at the cost of abandoning the foundational purposes of Civano. Business as usual prevailed, and twenty years later still prevails.

Financial Models and Schedules

When Fannie Mae became the 100% owner of Civano, it took nearly a month to convert the project's very complex financial model—by then more than four years old and populated with many patches—into a simple, usable, and easily modified predictor and tracker of costs and cash flow. This new version was able to reflect real-time realities and became an important tool and guide for the project to first break even and then make a profit. But how did the initial modeling process at Civano get to be so burdensome? How did it interfere with the smooth, reality-based evolution of financial strategy?

Electronic and interactive spreadsheets and schedules, especially the former, are an essential part of the development process. They allow predictive projections. The ability to change an entire financial model by adjusting one or just a few factors is powerful, allowing for essential "what if" thinking. They can also be used as diagnostic tools when crises and challenges arise. Because these programs can handle infinite variables and their interrelationships, it is tempting to think that one can come close to creating a perfect forecasting model, with every variable considered and accounted for.

However, when financial models start to contain hundreds or even thousands of cells, many interconnected by formulas, their usefulness can rapidly diminish. They can become, without it being realized, dangerous impediments to timely and intelligent decision-making. As complicated financial models are so labor intensive to create and change, the more complex the spreadsheets and formulas, the more resistant they become to consistent and timely updating. One overlooked error can flow through a pro forma with shocking results. All too often, rather than the frequent and thorough rechecking of every aspect of a model, workarounds and patches are created to respond to an immediate concern. These patches can multiply and begin to pile up, worsening the possibility of errors and overlooked connections that can magnify to the point that a model becomes as much a burden as a useful tool.

Overly complex modeling can also subtly encourage decision makers to favor the most optimistic of scenarios. In a perfect world, projects would be framed into three similarly structured but differently loaded models: a most optimistic one; a worst-case scenario one; and in between, an operational one. As the name implies, it is the operational one that should be the guide to ongoing development decisions and action. Obviously, all three would have the same components with the clearly identified trigger points differentiating them updated concurrently and consistently. It is generally the case that human nature leads us to gravitate toward heeding the most optimistic modeling outcomes. If these models are overly complex, that gravitation can likely become a permanent focus, obscuring potential problems and increasing the chances of development process failure.

The same considerations can be applied to interactive project schedules. If they are made too complex and too detailed in tracking the resources and deadlines of a project, they can become difficult to adjust and so more unrealiable to use on a real-time basis. This can become an acute problem, as schedules are often seen and used as punitive mechanisms to highlight failure and assign blame. A more focused, simpler, and frequently adjusted schedule can become an early warning system allowing timely and anticipatory action on emerging issues by all parties.

Roles: Builder and Land Developer

The original Civano development team wanted very much to be not only in the land development business, but also, at some scale, in the innovative home-building business. They thought they could build better and more sustainable homes, and in the process, lead the Tucson builders to do the same.

Their limited financial capacity prevented this from happening in any significant way. The development team had to cover all the costs associated with entitlements, design, planning, site improvements, and most of the marketing. Income to the developer to offset these costs came from selling blocks—called options — of finished lots to builders. Because of financial pressure at the onset of the project and the initial difficulty of getting builders to sign on to build in Civano, the option lots were in larger blocks at prices that often did not contain much profit for the developer. This made it more difficult to increase lot prices to the builders as the project gained recognition in the marketplace, and home prices increased accordingly. The opportunity of engaging in home building by the developer was exhausted.

Scale again comes into play here. If the Civano land had been taken down in smaller increments, thus decreasing the financial carrying load for the land, it might have been possible for the developer to have played a more extensive role as a home builder. Had the developer team been one of the initial home builders, they would have more directly benefited from the market-driven increase in home and land prices that happened from 2000 on.

The takeaway lesson here is to understand early on the various cash flows a project can create and the ways in which the project's implementation can incrementally increase in all kinds of value, then find a way to participate in as many of them as possible. Simple advice, but often difficult to implement.

Recouping the Cost of Innovation: Public/Private Partnerships

The greatest financial challenge faced by the Civano development team was the twin burden of covering both the normal set of upfront infrastructure costs and the cost of all the innovation and special consideration components required of the project. Among the latter were a Neighborhood Center; sizing all water and sewer infrastructure for anticipated future growth south of the project; creating an employment center and regional recreation center; and, of course, the cost of meeting the IMPACT Standards. Varying kinds of public-sector commitments of support were created to help offset that challenge. The Neighborhood Center cost was supposed to be partially offset by a grant from the State of Arizona to install innovative technology in it, and by the City of Tucson promising a long-term lease of space in the Center. The City did agree to pay $2 million for the oversized utilities. The City and developer committed to paying and floating a $5 million bond to cover the cost of the recreational facilities. We have discussed elsewhere how each of these was compromised or fell away.

Delays and policy intent that exceeded the realities of the moment played a part, but there were more subtle forces at work. John Laswick had promoted the idea that City support for the Civano project would be returned over the years—several times over—in increased tax base valuation, avoided costs, and business activity. His assumptions were well thought out and supported by detailed data. However, we believe several weaknesses lay buried in his analysis. First, the analysis was holistic; it did not break down the projected return by city departments and agencies in terms of their annual budget figures; and that is how institutions and agencies track cost and benefit. The benefits the research noted may simply have been invisible from a common operational point of view. Thus, there was no compelling reason to commit to a set of project supports. Secondly, and building on the first, his analysis results had not ever been committed to as being policy goals. Thus, there was no strong sense of ownership in the outcomes by these departments and agencies. Given that, and lastly, there was no sense of risk at the loss or diminution of those supports to Civano. Neighborhood Center space leasing never came through, thus depriving the developer of a critical cash flow? No one in the City suffered any consequences. The $5 million recreation facility bond that never made it onto a ballot in a timely manner, forcing the developer to come up with the cash to pay for it? Again, no one in the public sector suffered because of this.

This is not a criticism of Laswick's work. To the contrary, it formed a critical early framework for promoting Civano. The point is that the relationship between public-sector support, both in cash and in kind, and the return on that investment is often murky, or conjectural. This can lead to a fickleness of commitment. Public sector support is, at the end of the day, always political in nature and subject to the vicissitudes of shifting political realities. It works best for all parties when the means and mechanisms for measuring a project's support and results are clearly set out at the beginning, and then subject to constant revisiting and recommitment over time.

Covering and Recouping the Cost of Amenities

This is a simple item, often overlooked and not adequately reckoned with during the development process. It is critical to front-end the cost of community amenities that are part of the lifestyle/value presentation of a project. From the beginning of sales, Civano promised a Neighborhood Center building that would include a café and small businesses. It was in fact a requirement of the Development Agreement with the City of Tucson. Within a year of the Neighborhood Center being finished, it featured a café, a small art gallery, and several small businesses, including a bike shop. A café brings life to a community, but even the smallest café could not be self-supporting at first. While construction and interior fit-out money had been budgeted, virtually no operational funding had been allocated to assist the building tenants with staying in business during the construction of Neighborhood One.

Suffice it to say, none of those initial businesses survived. There was just not enough foot and vehicle traffic to support them. Things would eventually change, but it took six years for businesses to become viable in the Neighborhood Center building. Eventually, Fannie Mae sold the building at a deeply discounted price, thinking its concept as a commercial center was unworkable. This dramatically lowered the operating costs to the new owner. When Neighborhood One was finally fully built out, along with nearby residential communities, significant foot and vehicle traffic did consistently appear. The Neighborhood Center's placement at the heart of a unique and beautiful community also became recognized as a desirable office location. Significant neighborhood-serving commercial uses became viable and remain so. Other important community amenities—parks, swimming pools, recreational facilities, walking paths—were all more conventional and did not need the same kind of ongoing operational subsidies. HOA fees covered their cost. The great lesson here is to be ruthlessly honest about how much funding will be needed not only to build out unconventional amenities, but to support them until they become consistently economically viable.

There were other unique additional costs associated with the buildout of Civano Neighborhood One versus standard subdivision developments. This is an indisputable fact. The plant-salvaging effort and reuse was a great environmental story that echoed the core concepts of the project. It came at a cost, though. The general landscaping budget in Civano was about four times that of an average subdivision of similar size. When considered just as an operating cost, it was an issue of some controversy. When seen and promoted as a community amenity, that high cost would be considered in a different light. Not only did the mature trees provide deep shade and encouraged walking, they helped create the sense of an established neighborhood from the earliest days of sales. The community form, with so much mature plant life, was so visually different that it attracted significant numbers of curious potential buyers. The high cost of the landscape ultimately was seen as a marketing advantage, and a highly effective one. Once seen in this light, its cost became easier to accept.

Figuring out how, and if, some of these amenity costs could be passed on to builders in lot option prices, and from builders to home buyers in home sales, became a challenge. Civano could not directly compete in the Tucson market with standard production homes that focused so much on low first costs and defined that as affordability. But when potential buyers were informed of the lifestyle, community, quality, and lasting value advantages of a Civano home purchase, they became more open to the idea of spending marginally more for buying their homes there. The ongoing energy savings, which could be very substantial compared to a standard production home, brought continuing value to Civano homes well on into the future. When these homes, including their high energy performance, were compared in price with what buyers would need to pay for upgrades in a lower first-cost home for the same features, the price differential largely disappeared.

One of the first things that Joan Tober did when she joined the Civano marketing and sales team in 2001 was to capitalize on this idea. She prepared a "Buyers Bill of Rights" handout, a copy of which is illustrated on page 168. This was given to each visitor to the Civano sales center. They were invited to take it to competing communities to see what amenities and other advantages they really got in a lowest first-cost production home, compared to what was standard at Civano. It was an imaginative and remarkably successful sales tool.

PLANNING, DESIGN, AND ENTITLEMENT

Learning from the Lessons of the Past

Civano stands out in Tucson and its regional market because of its distinctive look and feel. In the public's eye, Neighborhood One clearly reads as a project that appears to belong to the Sonoran Desert. More than that, that it possesses the architectural character that all such developments of its kind should aspire to, in this and similar desert contexts.

The boom in petroleum-dependent post-World War II sprawl subdivisions was supported by a host of industrial-scaled production-inspired approaches and techniques: heavy and expensive utility infrastructure; dimensionally excessive and discontinuous road networks; nature-erasing site development; and standardized and repetitive home design and construction. In this economic environment, the tried and true methods used for centuries to moderate the impacts of living in a desert climate were first underutilized and then largely abandoned. These were the ingredients of a genuine traditional and durable Southwestern architecture. At the neighborhood, street, and single-site scale, they centered on a light imprint on the land, respecting the existing topography, using a native landscaping plant palette, taking advantage of passive solar access, and keeping the surface flow of water relatively undisturbed. At the individual building scale, they were characterized by construction in adobe and the use of passively daylit and cross-ventilated house types that were centered on a patio or courtyard, whose massing favored passive solar access in winter and generated shade in the summer. Designs based on these practices fell away, as national recipes for constructing production houses uniformly, cheaply, and speedily became the norm.

The combination of expanding climate change impacts and changing energy sources and prices will almost certainly bring some of these time-tested methods back into focus. If they're married with new energy technologies and smart energy use control technologies, all the better. The Civano project showed that the marketplace takes notice of the benefits of combining traditional and innovative design and construction methods and puts lasting value on communities that accomplish that re-incorporation.

The idea of learning from the past while embracing the future is a great challenge for our society and economy to respond to. Meeting this challenge suggests paying attention to the extraordinary building lessons offered by pre-industrial cultures in every region and every biome of the U.S., while toning down the short-term-focused business model of the building industry in our country, along with its capital-intensive, energy-overconsuming, and machinery-dependent ways.

The Charrette and Its Documentation

Ambitious and successful development projects should be designed through an open, participatory charrette process, and not by just involving small groups of people representing limited and often self-serving interests. Charrettes are essential to the development process. They provide an open, cooperative, public forum for introducing and sharing the merit of proposed designs and innovative ideas. They afford designers an opportunity to present initial development alternatives, while empowering clients, stakeholders, and the broader community to provide feedback in real time. This demystifies the creative process, engages diverse social, environmental, and economic perspectives and interests, and can help accelerate the entitlement process. Charrette-designed projects are generally more place-specific, innovative, and broadly supported than projects produced by conventional design means.

A charrette team should be staffed by a capable leader and team that has a complete knowledge of the process of integrating urban, environmental, and architectural design. It should include a consultant team from a wide variety of professions that shares a project's vision and understands that challenging accepted norms is essential to bringing innovative goals to the point of implementation. When planning for Civano was started, finding such designers and engineers could be a challenge. Twenty years on, it is far easier to seek professional support in all disciplines with expertise in New Urbanist and environmentally sensitive planning and design. More to the point of this study, the general knowledge about the ideas and practices of an integrated and sustainable urbanism is today widespread and growing. We see this as a response to the ever more evident failings of the sprawl system of development.

If the full set of the New Urbanist design, documentation, and implementation tools needed to build out a project are not produced, then the most probable development outcome is a New Urbanism Lite. Instead of a fully realized, sound urban and environmental final product, the outcome is more often than not a compromised and hybrid pattern of development, one that almost inevitably lands far from original intentions and expectations.

The Battle of Entitlement

Every developer, architect, and land planner knows that in order to become a reality, a proposed project must be vetted through an entitlement process. This is the process of getting all its applicable standards, including zoning, approved. Related and overlapping is the process of securing permits for infrastructure construction, home models, and all other proposed buildings. It is fair to say that most municipal agencies and departments charged with such reviews approach their tasks on a by-the-book basis. Review staff members are often not up to speed with the latest practices in their professional fields. This is not very surprising, as the typical approach to the approval of entitlements or building designs is based on what is already known and has been experienced before. What is most trusted by them is not novel approaches to planning design and construction, but what has worked before: the precedented, the predictable, the quantifiable.

The development team at Civano was not always successful in getting approval for the various innovative, or just plain different, urban, landscape, utility, or architectural features of the project. The entitlement process was arduous, but involved many more successes than failures. We learned that there was a definite engagement pattern that proved helpful. For openers, communicating to reviewers that the tried and true methods that had seemed to work in the past had in practice resulted in a set of negative consequences, many of them unrecognized and unaccounted for. This effectively framed the innovative ingredients of Civano in the context of being solutions to failures in conventional practices. Probably the most important technique to justify the imperative to innovate was to sincerely listen to the reviewers' responses and concerns, recognizing that they may be legitimate, but then demonstrating how these concerns were in fact addressed differently and more effectively in the innovative approach that was advocated through the project. A simple example from Civano was showing that doing away with retention ponds for holding rainwater runoff also eliminated mosquito breeding grounds. Rather than having water stand for days in these ponds, it was more effectively dealt with by directing it to open areas and slowing its flow with mechanisms like gabions that encouraged its quick absorption into the ground.

Person-to-person communication strategies and manners were also very important. Having a project's site engineers, rather than the developer, take the lead in discussions with reviewers was an effective tactic used during Civano's entitlement efforts. They speak the same language as the reviewers and are not seen as being as driven by a developer's focus on profit. Above all, communications must be kept open, consistent, and remain a two-way street. It is always a mistake to only show up during a crisis and demand action. It guarantees the most rigid reaction from a public-sector reviewer. Under such circumstances, they find it far easier to slip back into a safe "no" than to start thinking and move toward a new way to address old challenges. Tactical compromises should be expected, but only if they are a small part of a larger agenda. They can prove decisive in securing the whole strategic set of innovations desired by a project.

Standards, Regulations, and CC&Rs

In the early days of Civano's planning, so much attention was rightly focused on getting the Neighborhood One Specific Plan drafted and approved that the Covenants, Conditions, and Restrictions (CC&Rs) for Civano were rushed through without enough oversight. They were seen, at a time of enormous pressure on the development team, as being of secondary importance. They were developed by a very capable law firm specializing in CC&Rs, but for standard developments. They had no familiarity with the New Urbanist features Civano would implement, and no one spent enough time educating them. Even though the Specific Plan and all the marketing for Civano promoted mixed use, the CC&Rs hardly recognized its existence. The project team, and later the community HOA, ended up battling the inconsistencies between the CC&Rs and the project's design and planning goals through build-out and to this day. Workarounds for this critical inconsistency had to be developed to help foster Civano Neighborhood One's rich in-home business community and its vibrant mixed-use Neighborhood Center.

Once adopted, changing CC&Rs is an arduous task, one made more important by understanding that they are linked to a project's design and zoning documents. Getting them right at the beginning is critical. The fact is, they will outlive them both, and in the long run, they will be enforced by lay people. The clearer the CC&Rs' link to other documents, the fewer the opportunities for later deviations from original intent, long after the original design and development professionals are gone from the scene.

CONSTRUCTION

The Building Process

The ways and means of home building in the United States are highly standardized, as are common materials, their distribution and use. If all other aspects of a project are in balance, chances are that its construction process will be smooth and predictable, aside from the occasional negative impact of the weather. The scale and pace of production home building emphasizes and depends upon this standardization and is a driving force that must be taken seriously into account in greenfield development. Stepping away from standard building products or practices can have ripple effects. This is not necessarily a flaw, fatal or otherwise. Changes from the typical path of home construction just need to be recognized and dealt with proactively.

The predictability and robustness of the chain of supply of a given material is critical. Materials must always be chosen that are available and in sufficient quantities. This proved to be a major challenge when considering "alternative" building materials for use in Civano. For instance, the straw used for straw bale home construction was of a special variety and only available in substantial quantities during certain times of the year. There was only one dependable regional supplier of RASTRA block, and they had limited production capacity. In both cases, the projects where they were used experienced construction delays. Understanding the peculiarities of any regional and local building environment is critical. Ignoring this reality will only lead to eventual problems. A Civano example discussed earlier was the design of RGC homes that depended on crawl spaces when the local soil is filled with stone and caliche layers that make crawl space excavation prohibitively expensive. A second example was the attempt to avoid asphalted streets in the construction of the compounds. Road Oyl, a stabilizer composed of a mixture of local soil and binding polymers, did not work in Civano due to the specific type of lime found in its soil.

Similarly, understanding the common practices of the local building trades can be a critical factor affecting a construction schedule. If new building technologies (like SIPS panels) are brought into a building project, local trades may not be easily convinced to learn about them and to adopt them. This goes doubly when the market is strong and labor is in demand; no one wants to take the time to be schooled in new and different ways of building, whatever the advantages in efficiency and design.

Especially in large-scale market-sensitive housing projects, understanding the rhythm of home building relative to the expectation of their buyers is critical. Buyers, and their lending institutions, typically assume a four- to five-month timeline for a typical production house, from purchase contract to move-in. Variation from standard construction practices may have an impact on this timing and should be made clear to buyers. For builders, it is important to understand that too much home model variation slows down construction. It is easy for multiple option choices to easily cross over from being a marketing advantage to becoming a production bottleneck. Finally, one cannot stress enough the importance of the dependable post-construction performance of each house and its systems. Well-managed construction and known systems translate into fewer remedial "call backs," the bane of all builders and a significant profit drain. Known construction systems can also be more readily covered by warranties, which offer insurance against failures and protect both the builder and the buyer. New, "alternative," and innovative systems may not be as dependable. Builders need to address them with more closely monitored building practices and guarantees based on a better quality of construction.

A Town Architect and a Builder Guild

A Town Architect is an independent professional hired by a development team whose dedicated job is to be an advocate for a project's construction according to its original design intent. Such architects are tasked with ensuring that buildings, open space, landscape, roads, parking, and infrastructure are delivered in a form consistent with their construction documents. It is a role that requires both professional knowledge and political skill. Too loose of an oversight of the construction process often results in the reduction of the quality of building. A too rigid application of the rules, and the necessary flexibility in the face of changing market realities or other constraints can be stifled. The effectiveness of a Town Architect is linked to having a complete set of appropriate design and construction documents to follow. Their principal role is charting and following a middle course between the intentions and realities of design and construction and the inevitable messiness of the construction process.

At first glance, most developers and builders would balk at taking on what might be seen as the added cost of a position that could possibly be covered by someone on their own staff. The experience at Civano provides a cautionary response in this respect. At Civano, no one served as a dedicated Town Architect. Instead, the role was filled by a qualified member of the development team who had a variety of other project-related responsibilities. While a vigilant advocate for the New Urbanist form of the project,

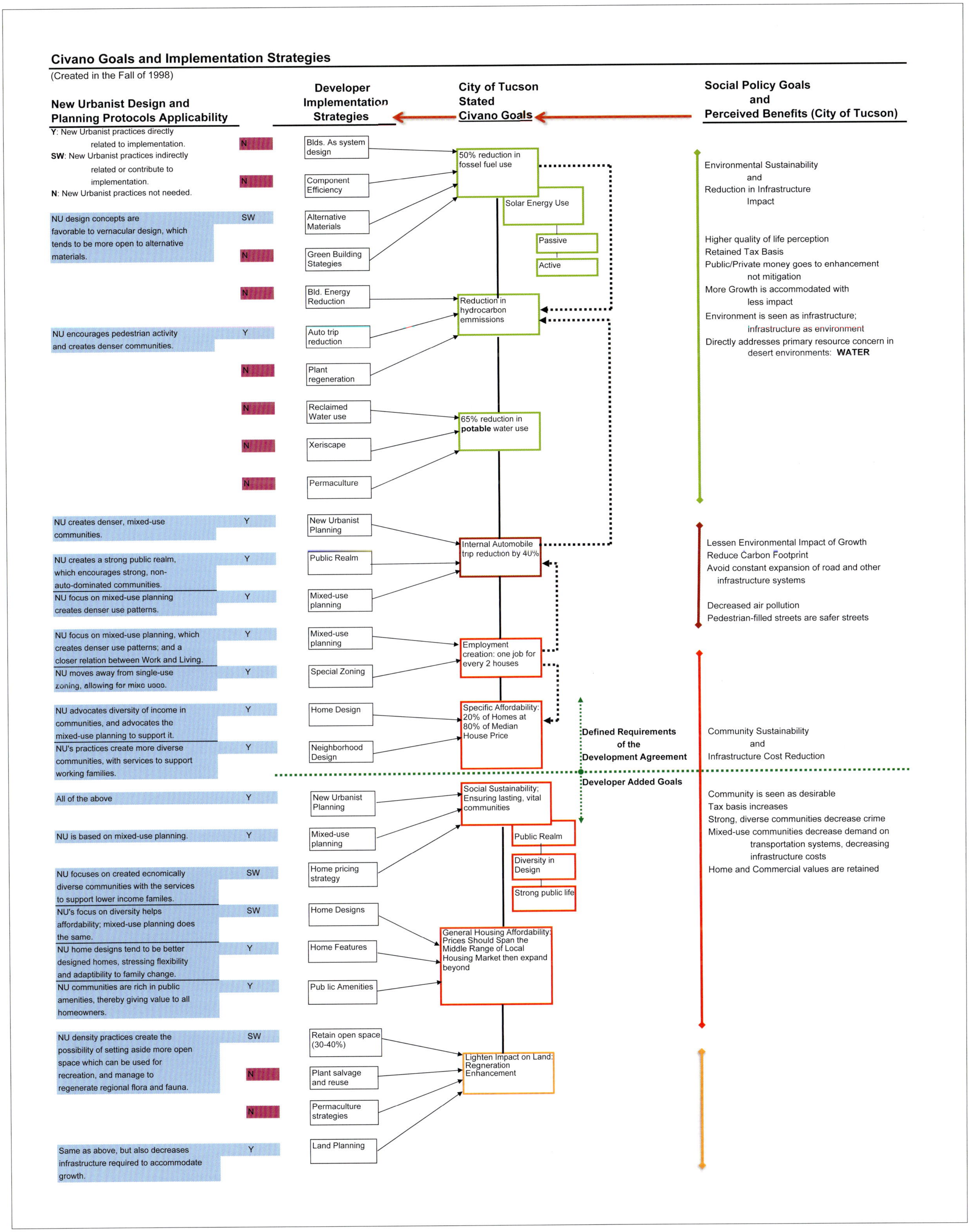

Organization chart showing the inter-relationships among Civano's mandated environmental goals and social goals, and how New Urban design and planning protocols supported and framed them in the physical planning of the community. Developed by Lee Rayburn when he first joined the project in late summer 1997.

he was often placed in situations where financial and schedule pressures compromised his enforcement of the project's design standards during construction. We have discussed elsewhere how tactical development decisions made under administrative or financial pressure, however well-meaning, can result in a slow drift away from core project design goals, often without being realized by a project's development leadership. Hiring a Town Architect can be a critical factor in maintaining a balance between managing and building a project well.

A Town Architect can certainly play a central role in managing a Builders Guild for a project. Finding builders willing to fully partake in the Civano model of development demanded training and committing them to the project's business, aesthetic, and ethical objectives. This was not an easy task to carry out. The builders needed to produce and build designs reflective of Southern Arizona's vernacular traditions and the project's environmental protocol, including its energy reduction standards. The builders that eventually participated in home production at Civano came from a variety of backgrounds, and their companies brought both professional strengths as well as experience-based shortcomings to their work. There was never a formal way set up to provide this kind of education to them. There was no Builder Guild established at Civano, although a quasi-guild effort developed around the Building America training that was offered to builders, and in the on-site builder rep training reinstated in late 2000 through June 2002.

A well-managed guild can help participating builders understand a project's design goals and provide assistance and direction on how to achieve them. It can also create a sense of both cooperation and supportive competition among builders that makes compliance with project standards more a team effort and less of an enforcement challenge. Guilds that generate a shared process of house building can produce exceptional results. Individual buildings that are well-designed and executed through attention to detail and understanding the importance of traditional vernacular crafts and building technologies can generate a profound sense of place. There is a cost to forming a Builders Guild, but it is minor compared to the huge dividends that are reaped throughout a project's buildout.

Meeting the Environmental Goals: Partnering

The core of Civano's innovation challenge lay in trying to achieve the IMPACT Standards while still staying within the affordable middle of the Tucson housing market. There were other smaller housing developments that had implemented aggressive, for their time, environmental goals. However, they tended to be small outliers in the overall housing development world, and they had no intention of meeting the special demands of market-rate production housing. The Civano development team certainly did not have the expertise to figure out how to accomplish all the IMPACT requirements. Finding outside experts to bring into the design and development process became a critical task.

Immediately after the land auction, the development team reached out to a number of local energy and building experts, many associated with the University of Arizona, to help model realistic expectations of potential energy savings and their likely added construction cost per house. Building America, a federally financed program for training builders to build more efficient houses, brought IBACOS to Civano. As noted elsewhere, IBACOS provided critical hands-on training for the builders. The Department of Energy provided additional expertise and some funding for post-building monitoring to ensure the energy-saving design intent was realized. Tucson Electric Power provided, at no cost to the project, testing during construction and after to ensure Civano's energy goals were being met.

Beyond expanding the project's knowledge base, outside experts brought other important benefits. As third parties, they lent a sense of legitimacy to the developer's claims of meeting goals. While associated with the development team, they were perceived as being separated from the pragmatic and economic pressures that drive development.

Partnering may make a project team aware of new opportunities. At Civano, IBACOS brought in the American Lung Association. This led to working with them to build one of their model "healthy homes." No one on the development team had made the connection that building a more energy-efficient house created a healthier house. About one-third of American families have a member of their household living with respiratory issues. The healthier nature of a Civano house became a marketing point. It was another added measure of value that a standard production home did not offer.

Third-party experts can also bring funding to a project. They often have access to grant money to help defray the cost of research, training, implementation, and monitoring. For Neighborhood One, the various partnerships that the development team fostered with academic institutions, nonprofits, and government agencies brought in about 9% of Neighborhood One's design budget. Finally, the participation of the Department of Energy, the Building America program, and National Renewable Energy Laboratory funding also helped offset some of the public-sector commitments to the project that just did not come to fruition.

More likely than not, projects marked by innovation of any kind can find experts willing to participate in achieving project goals. It is an avenue well worth exploring.

MANAGEMENT

Continuity Rules

As the history of Civano amply illustrates, the negative consequences of management discontinuity are many. Time is lost in reorganizing. Outside perception of unwarranted change is most commonly one of concern and worry. This latter point is especially troublesome in a neighborhood-scale project, where change creates uncertainty and buyers hold off until that uncertainty disappears.

There are two other consequences that can be subtler and may not be apparent, except in retrospect. The first is a loss or corruption of project memory: the accumulated lessons, big and small, that have been gained over the life of a project. Too often, the lessons from the immediate past are invisible to new personnel. Also, they may be seen as part of the goals and methods of the regime that had just been replaced, and therefore suspect. Loss of project memory diminishes the ability to perceive trends within a project. Too often, a change comes about because of some crisis, and adjusting to new management is seen as settling a problem, when in fact settling may be masking growing trends in the wrong direction.

The best antidote to the loss of project memory is the accurate and complete documentation of a project's goals, strengths, and weaknesses, one that is consulted constantly. This is especially true of projects that implement New Urbanist planning and design protocols. The failure to do this completely and constantly during the first phases of Civano was the source of confusion and lack of clarity that led to hectic and faulty decision-making in later phases.

A Necessary Road Map

The importance of articulating and understanding project goals and being clear about how they are related to each other, and how they will eventually be measured and verified, cannot be overstated. All too often, the history of innovative projects revolves around the struggles to overcome one political or technical challenge after another. In the process, the focus on immediate crises can obscure, in subtle but accumulating ways, the original organizing vision and implementation strategies of a project. That certainly happened in Civano. The development team consistently overcame one challenge after the other. With some new tactical victories, the core focus on the project was thrown just a little off track, sometimes temporarily, but eventually with growing long-term impacts.

Assembling a Process & Action Map that lists the essential components of a project and tracks their interrelationships can be a very helpful tool. On page 175 is an example for Civano created by one of the authors as he was coming into the project. It was set up to help a newcomer to New Urbanism understand how its planning and design protocols informed the project, and to understand Civano's initial vision and particularly its core environmental goals.

This kind of mapping can be not only a guide to daily development decisions, but a warning system. It helps illustrate how tactical actions involving one component affect others. It can be a guide to spotting, early on, how those actions can impact a project's eventual physical and financial outcomes. It maintains a focus on overall strategy without obscuring the importance or influence of its detailed ingredients.

Embracing Change and Using It to Your Advantage

The Civano development team lost a critical opportunity to make clear to stakeholders that a new direction was being taken after a private-sector developer was chosen to implement the project. If a more inclusive charrette had been held, advocates for the old Solar Village model would have had a chance to understand the necessary private-sector imprint on the project and have had their say. The development team would have had an opportunity to state, point by point, why a new direction was needed and what final form the project would eventually resolve itself into. Some community participants may have left this kind of exchange unhappy, but at least they would have been fully informed. Without an inclusive public charrette, the development team endured a constant undercurrent of criticism for its abandonment of the old, and it must be said, unimplementable model of the Tucson Solar Village.

The lesson here is to recognize, embrace, and exploit inevitable moments of change in order to update project goals and communicate the need for such changes to the public. If the developer's response is articulated in a timely fashion to the appropriate community stakeholders, it is more than likely that those changes will be accepted, even if grudgingly. When they just happen without explanation, they can seem like a betrayal of original causes and principles or just plain ineptitude.

Managing Expectations

The development team at Civano was often guilty of over-promising and underperforming, out of commitment, out of desire, out of passion, and out of determination—all good and necessary things. Problems arose when intent far outstripped the resources needed to explain or to achieve that intent. Especially on this innovative and challenging project, that key missing resource sometimes was simply understanding how to read current challenges and produce effective solutions without sacrificing future outcomes. Civano had two special classes of expectation management to address: those of the homeowners and those that arose out of a complex public/private-sector partnership.

As a project begins and grows, engaging homeowners is imperative. It can help unearth overlooked issues, and nothing beats the testament of homeowners about what is good and right about their community. The exact method of this engagement is a different matter. Creating a community-based entity that thinks they are co-equal with the development team can spell trouble for a project. Community review and input can come to be seen from the residents' viewpoint as the community's right to approve. Developers should be rigorous in ensuring that the documented history of communications and meetings with homeowners is theirs and theirs alone, and that these get published regularly. It should never be doubted that the financial considerations of a project are also strictly the developers' business. At the same time, information that benefits the buyers and homeowners should be shared, and often.

Private/public-sector partnerships are never simple or easy. The people who gravitate to each sector may speak the same language, but the words they each use often have subtle and importantly different nuances, if not outright meanings. Each sector has a different rhythm of decision-making. The public sector usually favors review, consideration, and consensus building over action. The private sector focuses on action—hopefully action after reasonable review and consideration, but action nonetheless. Each sector sees and experiences risk differently. The private sector experiences it as demanding deep assessment and constant care. The public sector sees it as something to be avoided, which too often dictates inaction. These are somewhat simplistic distinctions in principles and style, but there is enough truth in them to bear consideration.

What can be done to bridge what are essentially two different world views? The private-sector side should emphasize opening lines of constant communication. With this continuing dialogue established, the requests for immediate action in times of crisis, real or perceived, can be seen in the context of an ongoing relationship. This approach was critical in addressing various Civano challenges. It was critical in the City staff's rejection of the proposed Diamond Ventures takeover. It manifested itself when the same reviewers who had approached the entitlements for Neighborhood One from an adversarial position become advocates for extending the New Urbanism planning and design protocols of Neighborhood One into Neighborhoods Two and Three.

MARKETING

Centralized Sales

Effective marketing is about presenting the buying public with a compelling and consistent story, one that matches up well with the reality of what is being sold. It took a bit of time to figure out how to properly market a project as different as Civano. It is clear from sales records that when the marketing effort focused on telling the story of a new, beautiful, diverse, environmentally sensitive, and value-laden community, the rate of sales increased, and buyers began to pay a premium for their homes. A good part of this eventual sales success was the result of promoting Civano through both an actual and virtual centralized sales process.

This sales approach focused on materials that presented the whole project first, supplemented to showcase each builder's homes and their unique features. It was carried out by staff that had received mandatory sales training from the developer. This ensured that a common set of messages prevailed in all sales-related contact with the public. Varying, confusing, or partial sales explanations of key concepts of the project were avoided. It helped significantly to emphasize to all buyers Civano's "lifestyle and lasting value" proposition rather than just the merits of individual homes.

At Civano, the sales presentation was housed in a centrally located welcoming facility. This arrival facility's purpose was to present an overview of the entire project, focusing on its goals and special features. Interactive displays helped visitors understand Civano's energy and resource conservation features. That understanding helped many potential buyers to start putting a monetary value on these items and make those savings a positive reason to purchase a home. After this central orienting experience, potential buyers were directed to the models of individual builders.

The centralized sales strategy helped reverse the "Civano premium" into the "Civano advantage" and was an important factor in turning around the financial performance of the project. The overall effort was financed by charging the builders a small fee on each sale. It was not an easy thing to get a builder to do, until they saw how much more effective this sales approach was turning out to be.

The primary print advertisement for Civano, dating from mid-2000. This campaign, with its emphasis on community, unique home designs, and "life in balance" was an important component of the recovery from the trials of 1999, and the beginning of consistent and strong sales at Civano. Everyone pictured in the ad was a homeowner, and the focus on diversity was purposeful.

Marketing by Third-Party Endorsement

Having outside third parties highlight a project almost always carries greater impact than when a developer does. Articles about a project, events at which it was promoted, community celebrations, publication of certification by others of goals accomplished—these are all examples of third-party endorsement. A nimble marketing effort will be sure to use these events to promote an authentic and objective endorsement of a project.

The more innovative or esoteric aspects of a project should be wrapped within a larger marketing message. When idea- or concept-driven presentations take center stage, the market often fails to understand the practical advantages being offered to the buyer of a home. Surveys showed that most buyers in Civano bought a house there because they were attracted to the design of its neighborhood, the appeal of its streets, and the Southwestern form and features of its houses—the look and feel of the neighborhood and its homes. A second generally appealing factor was that the homes could be more easily customized than was the norm in most national builder subdivisions. While the environmental and energy savings aspects of Civano were critical features for a sizable minority of buyers, most found those factors important but ranked behind the physical appearance of the homes.

Assumed vs. Actual Ownership

The horizons of the evolution that carried Civano forward as new ideas and new players came into the project were often seen by the previous set of players as a diminution of the project's original idea. The original players increasingly saw themselves as the owners of the true vision, while in fact, the current ones were actually in control of—and responsible for—building the project and were the owners of its evolving story.

Moving from an aspirational concept, to a community advocacy initiative, to an implementable policy and project almost always involves qualifying and clarifying original intent. Implementation needs measurable goals and definitions, and these are a double-edged sword. They give clear form to an evolving process, but they can also obscure or replace subtle and even important aspects of the original aspirational assumptions.

The literature to date about Civano, with few exceptions, is filled with claims by many individuals and groups that may have had some involvement with the project somewhere along the way. Too often, their imagined ownership claims are based on holding onto some idea of perfection, rather than acknowledging the good that was created by a very imperfect process that evolved past them.

The pragmatic demands of the real world must be addressed, even when you are trying to change the reality of that world. This is a central paradox of successful innovative action. Until this work, there has been little said by those who were tasked with making it a reality. We trust this book will bring a more objective balance to understanding Civano.

(Left) The Webber's energy-efficient masonry SolarBuilt home. (Below) Samantha, Keli and pup Sydney. Joe and Jacque Figueroa's KE&G home combines modern technology with convenience. Civano style—right down to the garden gate.

CIVANO®

Be a Part of It

When you make the community of Civano your home, you'll become part of something truly unique. You'll find a commitment to the idea of sustainable living, crafted into uniquely designed homes that conserve energy and invite activity. You'll find a sense of community with neighbors, friends…people like you…who care about the land and the lives around them. Who value the balance of work, play and life…and find it all here. More than a vision of what might be, Civano is a reality. Be a part of it.

(Top) Meet the Sharifs—Esther, Sidney and Salahuddin. Esther is a member of Civano's welcoming committee. (Above) The Calhouns visit Civano's nursery and garden center. (Right) Civano is designed to promote community interaction and dialogue—Kimberley Clifford and Mary Webber catch up on the latest neighborhood events.

COMMUNITY OF CIVANO
Open Daily 10 a.m. – 5 p.m.
10501 E. Seven Generations Way
Tucson, AZ 85747
(520) 885-6930
Toll-free **888-2-CIVANO**

www.civano.com

KE&G HOMES	SolarBuilt LLC	Bednar Homes	ContraWest	Doucette Homes, Inc
From the mid $100s Wood & Stucco Steel Frame (520) 546-2984	From the low $200s Masonry (520) 546-0999	From the low $100s RASTRA/Wood & Stucco (520) 722-1254	Coming Soon (520) 751-1486	Coming Soon (520) 622-7373

Experience the unique style and spirit of Civano today.
Models open daily, Houghton south of Golf Links.

CIVANO AS A MODEL TO COUNTER SPRAWL

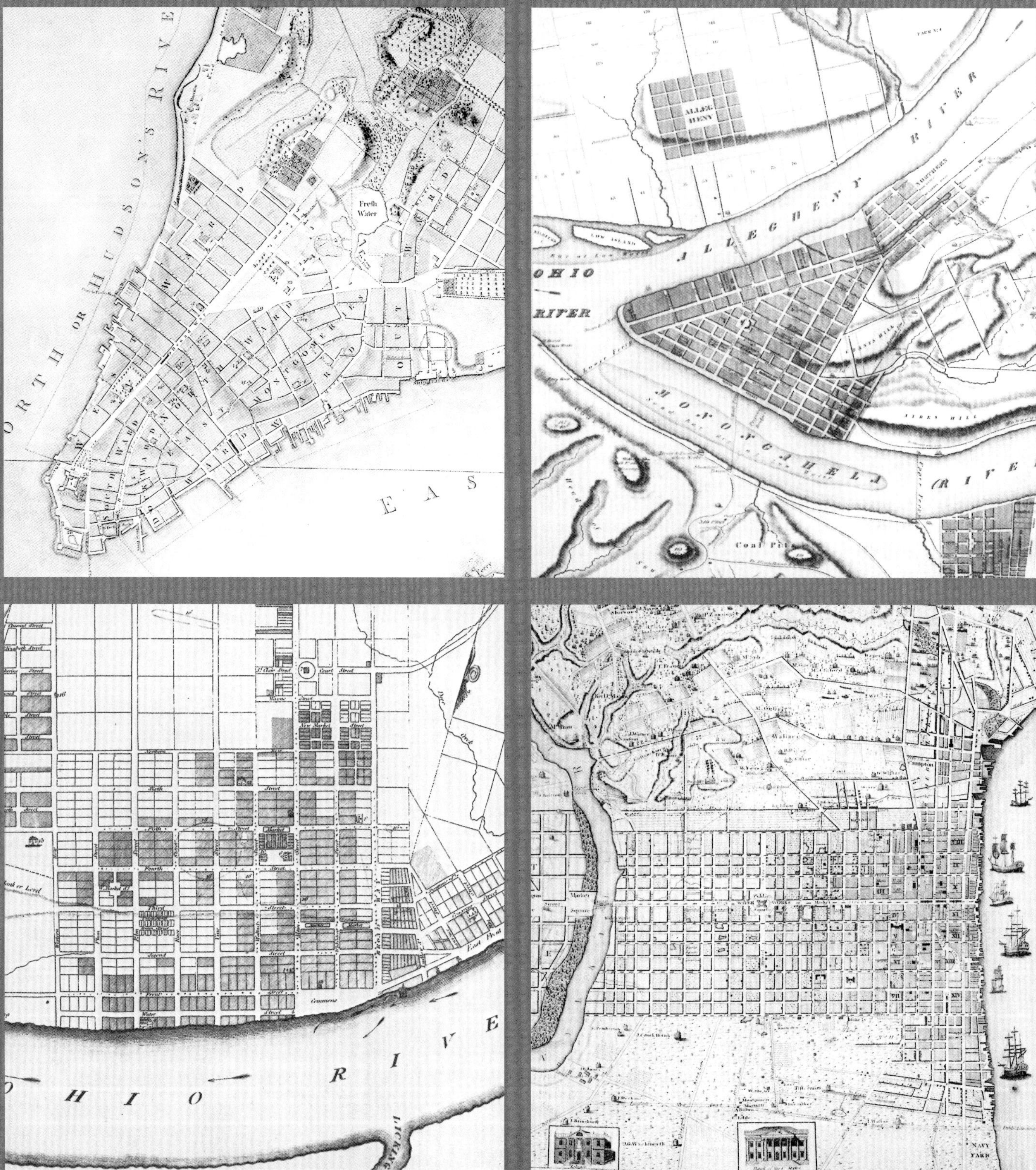

(clockwise, from top left)

New York City, 1767
Pittsburgh, 1815
Philadelphia, 1802
Cincinnatti, 1815

Civano was born as a radical 'green field' project, to take on the sprawl-industrial complex to better serve the emerging social and environmental needs of the people of the Tucson region. The courageous environmentalist pioneers that imagined and promoted it believed that a life well-lived in an economy that builds value for all could only be sustained in a climate, place, and culture-responsive habitat: towns and neighborhoods that would enable social diversity and cooperation among residents, community resilience, physical permanence, and a mindful connection to nature. Today we would expand their vision to include its applicability on a development intensity range from hamlets to metropolitan centers and serving the needs and dreams of people of every culture and biome in the world.

This thirty-year-old Civano ideal stands in stark contrast to current urban growth practices, fueled by impermanent subdivision projects aimed at short economic gain. Forgotten or overwhelmed in the ascendancy of this dominant sprawl model is the knowledge that, it, too, began as a social, political, and financial experiment in the years after WWII. Yet, over the last generation, and as the outcomes of its eventual dominance have been widely studied and found desperately wanting, it has lost its luster. Adherence to an uncontrolled and impermanent model of urban development, characterized by random infill, uncoordinated expansion, and nature contraction, threatens the long-term prosperity and stability of our communities, cities, states and by extension, our entire country. The following have emerged as its principal shortcomings:

Environmental Degradation: The growing and expanding impacts of climate change are here for all to see. The building of endless, horizontal, land consuming, car-centric, single-use, low-quality subdivisions has been a key contributor to the current ecological crisis. It has caused resource depletion; land, water, and air pollution; petroleum dependence; and the continuing erosion of the human habitat in cities and nature. The connection between these impacts and the continuing worldwide adherence to a model of fragmented development is now undeniable. The cost of these practices on the environment is catastrophic and must be urgently addressed.

Social Fragmentation: The direct and significant impacts of business-as-usual, disjointed urban growth on our social lives have also been dire. The creation of new subdivisions lacking in economic and cultural diversity has created a state of segregation by race and income that has disrupted our common interest in building a shared, civil society.

Single-use zoning practices have been a major factor in eroding the social cohesion of the places where most of us live. The disconnection of the daily activities that make up a healthy family living environment is now ever present. The cost in time, money, and resources to reconnect these activities through single-occupancy vehicle trips is exorbitant. The resulting physical and spiritual tension within families and communities that many in this country feel is exhausting, and almost impossible to bear or address.

Finally, the recent delayed reckoning with institutional racism in our country has also revealed the real cost of a pattern of development that promotes class exclusiveness and apartness. Breaking down the interlocking components of this system—financial inequity, political manipulation, social tribalism, and disregard for the environment—must be a part of addressing racial and economic justice going forward. Our social cohesion as a nation is at stake.

Economic Inequity and Fragility: The complex economic interests behind the production of sprawl subdivisions have contributed to the growth of economic inequities that have reached crisis proportions. The fact of the matter is that their business model is dependent on massive public subsidies. Some are obvious and others hidden in obfuscation: tax abatements, income tax credits, tax increment financing, public funds for the construction of freeways, etc. Sprawl development in its dependence on and continuing exponential need for public funding support is impossible to sustain. It may be simplistic to call it a Ponzi scheme, but in that simplicity there is much truth. Further, the subsidies afforded to production builders represent institutional biases and policy choices that are key to compounding the inequities that have plagued our society for decades. Continued adherence to the sprawl model will only perpetuate and deepen this reality. We must acknowledge that these policy biases are inextricably linked to a financial and political system that is increasingly dysfunctional. Its short-term benefits accrue to the few and its long-term externalities accrue to the poor and to people of color, thus leaving the broader society burdened by the need to provide for all those left behind.

Throughout this work, we have focused on how Civano evolved as an intentional vision and policy-driven project to challenge standard sprawl development practices, and we have certainly examined its imperfect implementation. It is not uncommon for people to imagine that the failure of an experiment marks the collapse of the principles and ideas it was meant to validate. Nothing could be further from the truth in the case of Civano. Twenty years after the official opening of Neighborhood One, its urban and architectural form and the process of community advocacy that generated it remain critical examples to emulate.

Considering the urgency of a reconstructive approach to community building in the present, the detailed lessons learned from building an imperfect Civano must be understood as the foundation for changing course in the ways our country approaches the challenges of urban development and nature conservation. By carefully examining these lessons, we have come to define a three-part model. It is a set of new public policies and financial practices which, along with a framework of urban design and environmental protocols, can facilitate our nation's future urban growth, but with a diversity of form and social and economic outcomes that meet the different needs, interests, and aspirations of our diverse society in the very places where we all live.

The first part of the model, On Innovative Development, is the most critical and most currently in need. It proposes a new and intentional development process that may produce durable, resilient settlements and lasting economic benefits. The second part, On Polycentric Urban Form, describes how well-coordinated future urban and architectural forms of development can be developed across every regional transect. The third part, On Environmental Resilience, focuses on defining a path toward high-level environmental performance for all future development projects:

ON INNOVATIVE DEVELOPMENT

Public/Private Planning

The sprawl system of development is dependent on the kind of thinking that ignores the building of long term asset value. Its development methods are organized to serve the short term interests of a small number of landowners, developers, and financial institutions, but not to produce long-term benefits to society as a whole, especially for residents/buyers and small investors.

This state of affairs needs to be reversed in a deep political and administrative restructuring that places responsibility for land planning and infrastructure coordination on the public sector, with the rights and responsibilities for project execution remaining in the hands of landowners and/or developers. With freedom from the demands of short-term returns, a longer-term investment perspective can be incorporated into the master plans and development guidelines created by this new process. This will assure that the newly established pattern of streets, blocks, and public spaces, and the regulatory codes that control their urban form over time will generate privately developed buildings and places that will remain useful and resilient for many decades, if not centuries, to come. Over time, the housing being produced in this context will continue to evolve in density and form, and remain market-relevant, desirable, and ever more valuable.

This was the dominant model of planning and development before the post-WWII dawn of the age of sprawl. It can be adopted again and refined to become the most appropriate way of accommodating urban growth now and into the far future. As all development is local, it may be more effectively adopted as a process and as a project by the action of states, in their capacity as the approving authority for comprehensive, general and specific plans submitted by municipalities and especially counties. It is in the case of counties, that this level of federal, state, and local cooperation may be the most needed and most productive.

- The public sector plans and the private sector builds. Regional, inter-governmental coordination of public investments in transportation, housing, and environmental regeneration can allow private developers to both save and re-allocate financial resources dedicated to the typically contentious, unpredictable, and often extremely expensive process of entitlement planning. These same resources can then be redirected from entitlement fights to the direct task of designing and building, more rapidly, efficiently, and affordably.
- A cooperative public/private process produces less community conflict; faster public expedited reviews; and more permanent, beautiful, and environmentally sustainable projects. It is this community-centered design process that establishes a project's intended urban and architectural long-term form, along with the codes that guide its private development over time. Landowners and developers can then execute freely within the framework of these new public master plans and codes, following the conventional tools of market-attentive development: programming, marketing, design, construction, and management.
- Public/private cooperation decreases the risk created by having private developers first acquire raw land and then having to cover the early costs of its entitlement and infrastructure development. As a result, private money can be redirected to producing more environmentally advanced buildings and landscapes and, therefore, more durable communities. Public support for financing, which can take a variety of forms (see below) is not the same as direct public financing. It can, however, help stabilize private projects at their inception and early phases in return for reaping economic benefits for the public during later ones; particularly when following practices that are focused on creating long term value.
- The re-balancing of public and private interests and responsibilities has the best chance of delivering the key goals of urbanization: environmental conservation and regeneration, natural resource allocation, connectivity of the road network, distribution of densities and uses, initial and eventual building form, integrating open space and landscape form, etc. Regional urban growth in polycentric form can only be delivered by this kind of coordinated process of planning and development.

A More Resilient Finance System

"Innovation cannot happen based on debt."

—Robert Davis, Developer of Seaside Florida

The strengthening of a more equitable and resilient society is directly related to the appropriate and equitable allocation of its public funding. That must start with an accurate and transparent measuring of any development's impact on tax bases and infrastructure demands as measured against how its communities will benefit as a whole.

The systems of financing community development must be made more flexible, stable, transparent, and responsive to developer needs, while encouraging more innovation. Finding methods of recognizing lasting future value in a way that supports current borrowing capacity is a fundamental aspect of the development process, one that is often thrown out of balance by the dysfunctionality of other components of the process. Creating a more transparent and community responsive financial system will go a long way toward rectifying the forces that create those imbalances.

A special focus should be placed on infrastructure costs, which are substantial and come up early in the development process. All too often, this expenditure becomes excessive and increases the cost of each project, and ultimately the housing it contains. In all cases, these costs burden the development process by demanding that some of its most taxing expenditures are front-loaded. The result is the a priori throttling of innovation, and the eventual coarsening of infrastructural construction that often produces routine and impermanent road and utility systems. The resulting dilution of project —vquality, with infrastructure, buildings, public space, and landscape that barely survive the life of thirty-year mortgage—is currently more common than not.

- Incremental development allows site preparation, build-out, and pricing to remain more attuned to evolving market realities. The struggle to match the financial resources necessary to execute the scope and ambitions of this kind of a project is often papered over with leveraged debt, a hallmark of modern capitalism. This trend can be reversed by generating new sources of financing. In turn, and through a record of intermittent and successful project completions, it can encourage developers to dare to pursue more ambitious and innovative projects.
- It is crucial that our national banking system be reformed to better manage investment risk and support developers that are engaged in unconventional projects. Patient and committed financing is essential to the success of any development. We need to return to a three-part financing system that includes small, more community-oriented retail banks; larger commercial banks; and finally, and isolated from the other two, investment banks. Smaller banks disassociated from the pressure of immediate returns typical of investment banking and highly leveraged activity can take a longer view of their returns and thereby engage in more socially and environmentally constructive projects.
- Government at the federal and state level can come to support the broad interests of society by also providing financial incentives that benefit developments that deliver sustainable settlements and buildings. This support can take a variety of forms. Public sector entities can create development bond funding sources. Tax deferment districts have been used extensively in urban re-development and should be explored for ex-urban community development. Public banks, that is, banks owned by citizens through their state government, were once fairly common. Today, they are rare. Reviving this concept, in conjunction with broader banking reform, could create a more community-oriented financing source for executing smaller and more innovative developments, especially for affordable housing.
- A more transparent and accurate accounting of who benefits from infrastructure development and who eventually carries its cost is a critical necessity. All too often, low density sprawl components are subsidized by providing public funds for infrastructure, so that unknowingly or untraceably, it is taxpayers that bear the immediate and long-term cost of its construction. Ending hidden subsidy practices will ensure a more equitable return on the taxpayers' contributions to the process of community building. As part of a more extensive reform of lending practices, private financing may be rewarded with tax credits for energy savings and other positive and quantifiable urban and environmental features designed into residential and non-residential sites and buildings.

A Different Development Process

Rearview mirror, business-as-usual programming, planning, financing, design, and construction are pervasive current conventional practices. They frustrate innovation and result in the relentless imposition of stereotypical past understandings, experiences, and concrete solutions on current social needs and future visions of well-being. The sprawl economic model needs to be first contained and then abandoned and replaced with a development process that combines economic gain with a combination of deeper market insight and social responsibility.

Going forward, the supply side of housing needs to be constantly refreshed. This can be abetted by the supportive actions of financial institutions, as they finally begin to realize and determine that future real estate value should be matched to the evolving reality of how people really wish to live. This could be accomplished through relatively simple policy changes, such as, supporting development in places where for-rent properties predominate and also on projects whose programs include a mixture of building types, particularly missing middle-density ones.

- The process of producing urban development projects based on ambitious social and environmental protocols can only be led by a new breed of developers that see their role as seeking profit while doing pervasive good in the world. Enacting the reforms we have noted will enable and accelerate this new approach and encourage developer innovators to take the risk of rethinking the process of urban growth to greater business advantage.
- A sober, transparent, and current reading of economic realities and the study of generational preference changes as they relate to the housing market is a much more reliable method of establishing future demand. Operating based exclusively on past trends will only serve to perpetuate past imbalances, with the unmet real needs and social inequities that follow.
- Continuity of intent and implementation is ensured by creating a team of knowledgeable consultants who share a project's goals. This team will embrace the idea of collaborating with the reviewing agency personnel with whom they must work will eventually come to assist the development team in accomplishing its project goals.
- With the reforms we are advocating, meaningful and effective responses to the critical challenges of our time—above all, climate change and social inequity—can become more effective. Stability of financing and working with established goals mandated through public sector input enables developers to understand these challenges more as business opportunities rather than threats to financial success.

A Cooperative Public Outreach

The standard sprawl development process is often extremely hostile and antagonistic. While attracting people to live near open land, a continuing process of subdivision development leads to a pitting of communities against each other. Those who find themselves already living in suburban subdivisions often fear that the arrival of adjacent new subdivision projects will have a corrosive impact on the open landscape around them and will negatively affect the quality of their daily lives. This fear is amplified by the closed nature of the private sector development process which does not require an extensive revelation of intent. The epic term NIMBY—not in my back yard—is still a war cry in towns, cities, and metropolises of all political persuasions.

The needed alternative is a cooperative and deeply beneficial process of outreach and design, one directed to gaining community trust and support from the beginning. It is based on the inclusion of all stakeholders without exception in the community at large, in a process of communication that begins at the inception of a project and lasts through to its eventual completion. All too often, public participation is limited and exclusionary. There is a new awareness that equitable and resilient outcomes are highly dependent on the inclusion of stakeholders of all races and economic groups.

Inclusion and ongoing communication with the broadest possible set of individuals and groups does not mean deferring to their opinions and/or demands. The process of outreach is a two-way exchange. The developer informs communities about the latest planning and development practices, as well as their specific intentions. At the same time, listening to public expectations and preferences allows the developer to eventually give their projects the expected and verifiable physical form that they deserve. If the end result of development is to create a more lasting and equitable vision for growth, this is the best way to obtain it.

- A discovery process involving stakeholders is a trusted way of learning about the opportunities and constraints surrounding a proposed project. A timely response on the issues of interest to stakeholders maintains their attention and often cements their confidence and support.
- Engaging community members before any project proposals are made public builds trust and confidence that community ideals, ideas, and concerns, are being fully heard by a development team. Simultaneously, early outreach to the political body that is granting entitlements ensures that public goals relative to development will be incorporated as a project evolves.
- A charrette is the most transparent, effective, and productive design process when it comes to engaging community opinion on the form of a proposed project. It provides a forum for constant, iterative dialogue. It is based on presenting concrete proposals and receiving direct community responses. Learning from community members while in return teaching best planning practices helps create a sense of shared purpose.
- There is no better way to keep the public's trust than to be in touch with community activists every step of the way from the beginning until the conclusion of a project. Citizens are becoming increasingly knowledgeable about innovative community design. Many can now be of assistance to a project, if they see it built and performing per the commitments made by the development team throughout the process of design and construction.

ON POLYCENTRIC URBAN FORM

An Integrated Regional Pattern of Growth

Polycentric planning is best accomplished when practiced on a regional scale. Land is a precious and irreplaceable resource and should not be consumed sloppily for short-term gain.

Metropolitan growth is best accommodated in a pattern that distributes new development into towns composed of neighborhoods, districts, and corridors. These towns enable a vibrant community life without the burden of long commutes. Such towns exhibit some crucial common physical characteristics:

- Neighborhoods, districts and corridors of diverse uses, densities, and forms that, in juxtaposition with their natural setting, produce a unique place character;
- Commercial, employment, and community facilities that enable jobs/housing balance, and accommodate the basic living needs of families within a 5-minute walk, a 10-minute bicycle trip and a 15-minute transit ride;
- Highly interconnected and integrated roads and transit systems linked to regional networks that ease the grip of unnecessary car traffic congestion; and
- Greenways that separate clusters of neighborhoods and allow closeup access and the direct experience of nature.

A Constellation of Neighborhoods, Districts and Corridors

The deadening uniformity of sprawl subdivisions does not reflect the identities and values of the people of our diverse and proud nation. We believe in the uniqueness of the individual, an all-encompassing embrace of the family, and the need to live in the supportive presence of a community of different kinds of people and interests. These beliefs suggest that framing a new approach to urbanism in balance with nature, should be an urgent national priority. There is a traditional built environment that, over the centuries, has been able to nurture our society's needs and character and live up to the challenges posed by our varied and diverse social structure: the neighborhood; its commercial equivalent the district; and the corridor, the linear boundary separating neighborhoods from each other and neighborhoods from districts. It is on the proper design, construction, and management of these urban precincts that the future of our country depends.

- Neighborhoods can support a variety of uses and many densities. They can be configured in an architectural and urban form that is appropriate to the entire transect of development intensity, from rural to urban.
- Neighborhoods are composed of streets, blocks, and lots. Streets are configured in an interconnected network of many types. Blocks accommodate the private realm of buildings and through them define the public realm of streets and parks. Through their number, types, and character of buildings, lots determine the rhythm of the urban fabric, its massing, scale, and proportions.
- Design, through local architectural precedents and emphasis on traditional design and natural construction techniques, guarantees the utility and permanence of buildings and is the main ingredient of a sustainable environment.
- The qualities of a neighborhood depend on the integration of the form of its roadways, environmental and utility infrastructure, its buildings and public realm, its streetscape and its landscape. The physical expression of this integration accrues to the value of individual and generates places of a superior visual and environmental quality.

Programmatic Diversity

Segregating people into uniform subdivisions of different incomes and amenity levels breeds inequality, lack of opportunity, and social and economic fragility. Diversity—both economic and racial—is a hallmark of communities that are vibrant and desirable places to live, produce lasting economic value for their residents, and are resilient in adapting to all manner of challenges and change.

- Historically, communities that include residents of a broad demographic range have generated more social cohesion and deeper shared values over time.
- Housing of a variety of types, sizes, and amenities allows people to live in one place through the various phases of their family's evolution, enabling social mobility and reaping the benefits of rising property values. Focusing on and providing property types appropriate to the true demands of society will open wealth building to a far more diverse citizenry.
- The availability of various tiers of both for-rent and for-sale housing allows families of many kinds and various income levels to live in closer proximity to each other, improving social understanding and cooperation.
- Locating commercial, recreational, and civic uses within close proximity to homes generates pockets of unique local architectural character, identity, and economic opportunity for residents.

Multimodal Transportation

An inescapable fact of the sprawl-dominated world is that the car is the mobility mode that is closest to being a radical monopoly. Those without access to one are severely limited in their reach to work and service destinations. Those who can afford one (or more) are often saddled with high debt.

A state of living quality and environmental balance demands accommodating multiple modes of mobility on city streets. Making these available to residents creates more diverse, equitable, and resilient communities. Multimodality refers to the use of the right-of-way of streets to accommodate

A montage showing community members and community activities in Civano through the years. Everything from 4th of July parades to farmers markets to community anniversary celebrations.

people walking, biking, driving, riding in transit vehicles or cabs, or providing delivery and ride-sharing services. The current fragmented and hyper-extended development patterns foster the absolute dominance of private automobiles in determining mobility patterns, and by extension, urban form.

- Of all the modes, walkability is the most important in the context of the city. It improves the convenience, pleasure, safety, and health of people using streets as it positively affects the economy of districts and the living quality of neighborhoods.
- Neighborhood and district densities determine the type and range of transportation modes that they can be serviced by. The more intense their density, the higher the efficacy of their being serviced by fixed-rail and/or bus transit.
- New transportation modes—shared cars, scooters, self-driving cars, etc.—are now an active presence on our streets. They will become successful and viable only if they are integrated into street design, support both neighborhood and district life, and are compatible with public transit.
- The ultimate test of multimodality is to go far beyond providing for efficient transportation alone. It is to transform streets into a high-quality public realm. The visible presence of a complex multimodal environment can create a robust streetscape and a rich sidewalk life. Rich and community-supporting streetscapes are enhanced by appropriately scaled and sensitively integrated civil engineering elements.

ON ENVIRONMENTAL RESILIENCE

Ecosystem-Specific Design

Sustainability is not a style. It is an ethic that uses architectural, urban, and particularly environmental design on every project to respond to given urban and ecological challenges. Every development site in this vast country and in every other country around the world possesses a particular natural endowment. Place-sensitive design is based on learning from past, pre-industrial, cultural practices, while embracing and integrating new technologies to address a particular and constant end: safeguarding the health of nature and its resources—its flora and fauna, its beauty and its vitality—through every development project; and by doing so, guaranteeing the livability and prosperity of towns and cities for the greatest number of people.

- Understanding the extent and characteristics of each biome is key to defining what an environmentally balanced settlement is. Each ecosystem and its unique climate present particular design challenges and opportunities. Responded to by design, these can effectively guide the form of buildings, neighborhoods, and towns, while safeguarding and regenerating nature within and beyond given project boundaries.
- A rich source of precedent and inspiration for this approach is the study of regional building traditions, especially how they have historically evolved through their society's accommodation with the abundance and regenerative force of the natural environment that they are a part of. Much contemporary building and landscape design disregards the proven wisdom of the ages at its peril.
- Not every project in every society can be executed to a high-tech building standard. A variety of building technologies, from high to low, can be deployed on projects depending on the resources available to carry them out. Urgent regulatory reform can provide the necessary flexibility to meet housing needs across a very wide socio-economic spectrum.
- Ecosystem-specific design can only be effectively carried out by professionals who can think and act outside of their individual silos and beyond the mainstream of their professions. Counter-conventional design can only succeed through the hiring of such professionals into teams, where every cooperating specialist acts as an urbanist first.

Respect for the Land

Nature conservation is enabled when development is strictly limited to land parcels of minor ecological importance. Even within such designated development areas, up to 50% of the landscape can be conserved by increasing the density of a proposed project and dedicating the rest to permanent natural status. Protecting existing land formations and the native landscape whenever possible is the fastest way of diminishing the uniformity of cookie-cutter development.

- Large-scale grading is a knee-jerk approach to preparing a site for construction. It erases the natural form of the land and, with it, the biological systems that have taken millennia to form and prosper. Grading for necessity, not for convenience, reduces the scope and cost of soil disturbance, while also retaining natural hydrology patterns, the beauty of landforms and the local flora.
- An overall formal development plan responding to specific locations can help retain existing landscape features and landforms. This applies to both the design of the infrastructure and to individual blocks, lots, and buildings.
- Where extensive grading is unavoidable, the impacted plant life can be salvaged and reused, preferably on-site.
- Roads and environmental infrastructure can be designed to have a light impact on the land. Carefully laid out to conform to site conditions, they can contribute to the unique character of the places that they service.

A Reduced Environmental Footprint

At the core of the current ecological crisis is the unnecessary consumption of irreplaceable natural resources. On the surface, the sprawl system of development is dependent on the myth of an endless and inexpensive supply of such resources. At a deeper and more subtle level, it transfers the consequences of increasing resource scarcity to the end-user, in the form of ever more expensive first and on-going maintenance costs. The process of mitigating the damage wrought by heavy-handed land planning and careless site engineering is also very costly. All too often it treats valuable assets—the natural landscape and water runoff—as waste products. The practice of mitigation makes living within our means and in abundance and comfort with nature very difficult.

- An exclusive tech-centered approach to energy efficiency is to be avoided. Building energy efficiency should first take advantage of passive environmental control techniques and systems, before utilizing active ones. Buildings can become even more efficient by being subject to an intelligent set of site design strategies, such as proper orientation, lot placement relative to neighboring buildings, and dimensional compatibility with streets.
- Landscape design can also be deployed to contribute to energy and resource conservation. It can minimize heat gain or heat loss by providing shade through garden design and a robust streetscape. Site engineering can be understood as part of the landscape, as it contributes to the proper channeling of storm water on the land, and its eventual absorption into the soil.
- Establishing air pollution reduction standards by limiting VMT (Vehicle Miles Traveled), both within a neighborhood or town and traveling from there to other urban places, is a critical way of reducing environmental impact. By providing a superior public realm, complete neighborhoods and districts encourage walking as the dominant mobility mode. Their mix of uses absorbs auto trips and reduces traffic volumes and needed parking. Their density allows the possibility of introducing public transit as an alternative to single-occupant vehicular trips.
- Setting local incremental energy, potable water, and solid waste reduction standards, and a method for assessing their performance over time, is a key measure for first tracking and then reducing resource consumption.

Design in Balance with Human Needs

The design of buildings and infrastructure should reflect and respond to both the immediate and long-term needs of a community. It should focus on incrementation, adaptability, expandability, and resilience, finding a balance between the initial and future cost of construction, maintenance, or replacement. Failing to find this balance too often leads to dramatic over-engineering and extravagant initial development costs. Ultimately, these are borne by the very communities the infrastructure is meant to serve.

- All too often, road and especially utility infrastructure engineering depends solely on established, nature-disruptive concepts and is directed at accommodating worst-case scenarios. All engineering should be integrated to accommodate the maximum use of natural systems to address infrastructure needs and mitigate design and construction challenges.
- Rather than visually and physically dominating the form of a development, road and utility infrastructure can be frugally designed to be integrated into the landscape. Whenever possible, infrastructure systems can be designed to serve more than one purpose. Drainageways can also be trails, parks, or wildlife corridors, for example.
- All buildings, but especially commercial and civic ones, can be built of durable materials and in a form that allows their adaptive reuse over time. Buildings should not be designed and built to gold-plated standards or under protocols that stress short term returns and a limited lifespan.
- Designing buildings, parking, parks, and all other neighborhood and district ingredients to average, not maximum, use loads guarantees that their initial cost of construction and the costs of their long-term maintenance accommodate as high a degree of performance as necessary, but not more than that.

THE PROMISE

Under our current operative economic model, conspicuous consumption is the engine of our prosperity and a key descriptor of our American identity. Ironically, it is also one of the basic causes of the social fragility of our society. The unsustainable wealth gap between the rich and the poor in our country, as well as the deeply embedded racial disparity, is due in part to the federal incentives that have been historically available, and are currently still in place, to encourage the dominance of national corporate players and practices in producing the supply of housing. Since 1945, subdivision-based sprawl is a prominent part of this economic strategy; one that generally favors the interests and rights of producers over consumers.

Inducing ever-changing fashion is the means of feeding our propensity to consume. Whether it is in the process of designing and delivering to the market clothing, automobiles, or home subdivisions; the methods and scale of industrial production are abetted by incessant advertising promoting the sale of products of want, as symbols of both social status and well-being. For developers and builders, this has meant concentrating on the volume production of standard house models and advertising their appeal based on their ostensible construction newness and incorporation of superficial gadgetry. Since 1945, and increasingly so in more recent years, subdivision housing has been reduced to a mere commodity and has become a part of our national cycle of perpetual consumption.

The weakness of this system is exacerbated by a characteristic dimension of corporate thinking: a focus on short term profit and first-time sales, often independent of the consequences wrought on first-time and future buyers. In the case of subdivision development, this has often meant taking the short view, which is of necessity a race to the lowest common denominator of site planning, design, and construction, and exhibits a preference for routine design, low-cost-driven construction, excessive repetition, poor siting, resource waste, nature erasure, and low environmental performance.

After eighty years of prominence and financial success, sprawl practices are now under critical reconsideration. Because exurban subdivisions are generally so poorly planned with houses so lacking in durability, they rapidly lose utility and appeal for their residents. Not surprisingly, subdivision houses have not lived up to their economic billing, and they are frustrating the upward mobility ambitions of the American middle class. As a form of place-making, they disappoint, if not deceive, those buying production houses with long term value in mind. As they become burdensome assets to their owners, the promises of the production housing industry to solve our society's housing needs sound increasingly more and more hollow. Even if sometimes attained, that promise still remains unattainable for a great and growing number of people. These practices and their false promises are in fact complicit in supporting and accelerating the social, racial, and economic inequity plaguing us.

We now find ourselves at a remarkable point of inflection. Sprawl suburbs are losing their appeal, both as places to live and to invest in. The lack of financial return for those that bought there is creating an underclass by default. Yet, there is no obvious alternative, no counter public policy, business model, or political and administrative vision that provides an alternative path to addressing the multitude of challenges that an unchecked adherence to sprawl practices has created: such as, addressing the growing impact of climate change; creating more diverse, livable, resilient and permanent towns and cities; regenerating a receding nature; and providing access to health, education, security, and many other essential services as a civic obligation to all citizens in the very neighborhoods that they currently inhabit. It is now time to pursue such a new vision of urban growth, and the Civano reconstructive development model proposes one.

If the Civano model, its objectives, and its practices were to become the new normal, we would experience the gradual curbing and eventual ending of the senseless consumption of land and the destruction of nature on the periphery of our growing cities. This would change a lot for the better in our country. Delivering the opportunity for the middle and working class to buy into permanent, resilient, useful, and beautiful mixed-income neighborhoods and towns would provide a tangible catalyst for national renewal. It would steer people toward greater economic security and the country toward increased social cohesion. It may even generate the politics of cooperation.

We would cease to see, or see far less frequently, the boom-and-bust cycles which are virtually an accepted norm under the current finance, building, and land development system. These are cycles encouraged in part by the nature of industrial-scale sprawl development which is so dependent on lowest first cost, leveraged financing, and the avoidance of diversity and complexity.

Under the Civano model, we would witness a shift to a more entrepreneurial and locally connected process of wealth generation that rewards smallness: smaller, more community-based regional finance and development firms; smaller builders; smaller professional design firms. In short, a smallness that encourages a flexibility of approaches to development, thrives on local knowledge, and keeps profits close to the point of production. It is a smallness that rewards practical skills, labor intensity, full employment, and commitment to people and place. It is attuned to operating in a way that accommodates nature conservation, inclusion practices, and acknowledges climate-specific design and regional cultural practices.

We would also note a more incremental and diverse approach to focused community building. A development process that is responsive to and integrated into its locale is by necessity more in line with the real needs of people, different as they may be from place to place. This would be a process that is more resilient, creating value not only at the point of first sale, but also maintaining value in place and even growing it into the future.

The cultural changes that would be unleashed by the prevalence of the Civano model would also be significant. Development under a counter-sprawl model would usher in an era that returns us to the emulating the wisdom of pre-sprawl settlement patterns and building techniques. With standards of comfort, beauty, and economy based on two essential design ingredients: an architecture grounded in vernacular precedents and with less dependence on expensive high technology; and a traditional urbanism recast under the principles of fine place-making and an emphasis on high environmental performance.

Over the centuries, intelligent design and skillful labor have combined to produce the kinds of places and buildings that generate high livability and equity for their owners, and through them pride of ownership and place, community stability and identity. It was like this before the advent of the modernist project. There is no reason to believe that it could not be like this again. As this design ethic becomes the new common practice, today's crushing production house homogeneity would wane. Architectural form variety, specific to regional precedent, would flourish. Construction practices that promote manual labor and the crafts would become common.

Being better able to accommodate the evolution of social and economic needs, the Civano model can become a great source of social resilience. It proposes a development process that is ideal for regenerating the ailing parts of America, which for decades have been excluded from the vertiginous levels of wealth creation on the coasts. Achieved through massive corporate capital investment at the national and international scale, this wealth has been hostile to the idea of meeting the commonsense interests of all Americans.

Existing planning models, zoning and building codes, entitlement processes, and development financing are all tied into a set of rules that currently produce sprawl by design. The process of safeguarding these rules is controlled by an entrenched administrative and political elite. Every community should recognize this and lobby effectively to ensure that the rules affecting development are changed to more accurately reflect its diverse needs, while creating a framework for future urban and environmental design that produces local character, durability, and resilience. Now is the time to lift the regulatory burdens on development in every locality and to pursue a new cooperative and innovative process of planning and development; one locally calibrated to deliver and sustain every community's best version of itself.

Today, Civano is a beautiful, unique, and still relatively affordable neighborhood of some 700 homes. Its community members live there happily, value the place deeply, and daily ensure that it remains vibrant and evolving. The marketplace, as reflected in home sales, continues to put a higher premium on living there, as compared to adjacent Tucson communities. This is a reflection of its special urban, architectural, and environmental character, and its enduring social and economic value.

Our shared goal should be to advance the idea of a responsible and sustainable model for community building that delivers quality of place and high environmental performance throughout our country. And with that, commit to serving the needs of residents, not the least of which is their right to a happy family life and the significant and enduring accumulation of wealth in their homes. This will be a challenge to bring to reality, for sure; but it will also be a true test of an American exceptionalism based on social equity and economic opportunity for all.

The Civano experience is not the answer to all the challenges we face today in devising a national policy for accommodating urban growth. But when considered completely and objectively, it can be seen as a point of departure for moving forward beyond sprawl. Harking back to Al Gore's letter on Civano's grand opening, we do believe that embracing it as a model of future action, can indeed help us "... clearly see the future ... [so that] we as a nation can build stronger communities whose development does not conflict with the environment, but ... can support and enhance a sustainable society."

AFTERWORD

Writing any book is an adventure, one where events shift and modify an author's focus, attention, and perspective as they find their way to its conclusion. In our case, the external forces that pushed and pulled at our ongoing work were dramatic.

In early March 2020, we were finalizing the manuscript for this book. We met in Pasadena for what we hoped would be a final coordination meeting as the news of "a new severe flu" then causing epidemic breakouts around the world was beginning to cause growing concern on these shores. Little did we know.

In the United States, the pandemic that came illuminated many unpleasant realities. It laid bare the frailties of our public health and medical service system. It brought into stark focus the vast and growing economic disparity running through our society. In the midst of that enormous economic dislocation, the killing of George Floyd became the catalyst that unleashed a reckoning of the long history of racial inequity in our country, and the deep work that still lies before us to right it. This, in turn, served to stoke political and cultural divisions, and political acrimony became ever more strident not only in our homeland, but in an increasing number of places globally. These interlocking streams became the context in which we were completing our work and examining its relevance for today.

Deciphering the effects of the confluence of all these epic forces is beyond the scope of this work. There is, however, a theme that runs through them all—a disconnection between the way we aspire to live and the habitats we create. They are separated from nature, are marked by a sense of alienation within our built surroundings and create a sense of apartness between citizens and among communities. In contrast, at the heart of the Civano experience is the deep desire for bottom-up constructive engagement and civic interaction.

The Civano story is best understood as one of a challenge to the forces and institutions that have taken a post-World War II experiment in growth accommodation and elevated that experiment to an almost exclusionary reality—despite the growing evidence of its many deficiencies. Civano's adoption by the City of Tucson as a policy initiative was a critical part of its history. It is so important to remember that this adoption and the components of that policy arose from a long and open public process of discussion and input. Over sixty public meetings gave a venue for the citizenry of Tucson to state what they wanted in "community"— not what "the market," as interpreted by others, told them they were looking for or were entitled to, but what they actually wanted. The IMPACT Standards can be seen as a codification of what citizens in Tucson were looking for. This small but critical part of Civano's long history is a call to action.

We believe that a focus on demanding more livable and connected communities can lead to finding common ground, one based on creating built environments that invite diversity, durability, sustainability and the right and responsibility to live in community however things may evolve. This common ground is not tied to left/right; blue/red; but is measured by whether it supports community or not: your community, the community you want to bequeath your children. This book is a call to action: demand transparency, accountability, timely discussion, and periodic review: not just of individuals but of the institutions in which they are embedded. Get involved. Ask "Why Not?" when told what you want is not "practical" or achievable. What is labeled that way, may in fact, be impossible; but an open exploration of why almost always leads to unexpected possibilities for all stakeholders in the discussion.

Through this search for common ground, we can all embrace the diversity and togetherness that has always been our strength and a driver of true American exceptionalism. Harkening back to that sermon on the Mayflower:

"...we must be knit together in this work as one man [sic], we must entertain each other in brotherly Affection, we must be willing to abridge ourselves of our superfluities, for the supply of others necessities, we must uphold a familiar Commerce together in all meekness, gentleness, patience and liberality, we must delight in each other, make others Conditions our own; rejoice together; mourn together; labor, and suffer together."

Thinking of all that happened in 2020, how many times would this sermon have been a fitting and deeply appropriate thing to have heard? And the same can be said as we look to the present and future.

What we are proposing will not solve all that we have been exposed to in 2020, but it can be a part of looking forward to a process of renewal and a mending of our national fabric, one based on creating built environments that invite the ability to live in community however things may evolve.

We just need to keep talking.

APPENDIX

CANONS OF SUSTAINABLE ARCHITECTURE *and* URBANISM

A Companion to the Charter of the New Urbanism

ELIZABETH MOULE • STEFANOS POLYZOIDES • HANK DITTMAR

GLOBAL CLIMATE CHANGE and habitat destruction, accelerated by unrestrained settlement patterns and sprawl, pose significant challenges requiring a worldwide response. The scale and extent of these problems have come into sharp focus in the decade since the execution of the Charter of the New Urbanism. Timely action is essential, presenting an unprecedented opportunity.

THESE ENVIRONMENTAL CHALLENGES complicate equitable development the world over. Holistic solutions must address poverty, health and underdevelopment, as well ecology and the environment.

THE TRANSPORTATION AND BUILDING SECTORS together account for the majority of energy and non-renewable resource usage, making the design and planning of the totality of the built environment essential in addressing these problems.

SMART GROWTH, GREEN BUILDING & NEW URBANISM each have produced advances in resource conservation and energy efficiency, yet they alone are insufficient and sometimes even at odds with one another in tackling these challenges. It is time for each of their specific strategies to be integrated.

THE CHARTER OF THE NEW URBANISM provides a powerful and enduring set of principles for creating more sustainable neighborhoods, buildings and regions. They have provided guidance to policy makers, planners, urban designers and citizens seeking to address the impact that our towns and cities have on the natural and human environment. Meaningful change has been achieved by simultaneously engaging urbanism, infrastructure, architecture, construction practice and conservation in the creation of humane and engaging places, providing models for future development.

YET THE PROFOUND NATURE of the environmental crisis calls for an amplification and a more detailed enrichment of the Charter. It is imperative that a unified design, building and conservation culture advance the goals of true sustainability.

A SET OF OPERATING PRINCIPLES, as a supplement to the Charter of the New Urbanism, is required to provide action-oriented tools for addressing the urgent need for change in the planning, design and building of communities. These practical principles shall be global in scope and in information sharing. In their application, actions must respond to local conditions and must be continuously developed and refined over time.

WE PROPOSE THESE CANONS as time-honored operating principles for addressing the stewardship of all land and the full range of human settlement: water, food, shelter and energy. They simultaneously engage urbanism, infrastructure, architecture, landscape design, construction practice and resource conservation at all scales.

General:

1. Human interventions in the built environment tend to be long lived and have long-term impacts. Design and financing must therefore recognize long life and permanence rather than transience. City fabric and infrastructure must enable reuse, accommodating growth and change on the one hand and long-term use on the other.
2. Economic benefits shall be realized by investing in human settlements that both reduce future economic impacts of climate change and increase affordability. Patient investors should be rewarded by fiscal mechanisms that produce greater returns over the long term.
3. Truly sustainable design must be rooted in and evolve from adaptations to local climate, light, flora, fauna, materials and human culture as manifested in indigenous urban, architectural and landscape patterns.

4. Design must preserve the proximate relationships between urbanized areas and agricultural and natural lands in order to provide for local food sources, maintain local watersheds, ensure a clean and ready water supply, preserve clean air, allow access to local natural resources, conserve natural habitat and guard regional biodiversity.
5. Human settlements must be seen globally, as part of the earth's ecosystem.
6. The rural-to-urban transect shall provide the essential framework for the organization of the natural, agricultural and urban realms.
7. Buildings, neighborhoods, towns and regions shall serve to maximize social interaction, economic and cultural activity, spiritual development, energy, creativity and time, thus leading to a high quality of life and sustainability.

The Building and Infrastructure

1. The primary objective of the design of new buildings and the adaptive reuse of older ones shall be the creation of a culture of permanence with well-crafted, sound, inspired and beloved structures of enduring quality. Places shall promote longevity and the stewardship of both our natural and man-made environments.
2. Architecture and landscape design shall derive from local climate, flora, fauna, topography, history, cultures, materials and building practice.
3. Architectural design shall derive from local, time-honored building typologies. Building shells must be designed to be enduring parts of the public realm, yet internal building configurations must be designed to be flexible and easily adaptable over the years.
4. The preservation and renewal of historic buildings, districts and landscapes should be encouraged, which will both save embodied energy as well as contribute to cultural continuity.
5. Individual buildings and complexes shall both conserve and produce renewable energy wherever possible in order to promote economies of scale and reduce reliance on costly fossil fuels and inefficient distribution systems.
6. Building design, configuration and sizes shall reduce energy usage and promote easy internal vertical and horizontal walkability. Approaches to energy design should include low technology, passive solutions that are in harmony with local climate to minimize unwanted heat loss and gain.

7. Renewable energy sources such as non-food source biomass, solar, geothermal, wind, hydrogen fuel cells and other non-toxic, non-harmful sources shall be used to reduce carbon and the production of greenhouse gases.

8. Water captured as precipitate, such as rainwater, and that internally harvested in and around individual buildings, shall be cleaned, stored and reused on site and allowed to percolate into local aquifers.

9. Water usage shall be minimized within structures and conserved through landscape strategies that mimic native climate, soil and hydrology.

10. Building materials shall be locally obtained, rapidly renewable, salvaged, recycled, recyclable and have low embodied energy. If this is not possible, materials shall be chosen for their durability, exceptional longevity and sound construction, taking advantage of thermal mass properties to reduce energy usage.

11. Building materials shall be non-toxic and non-carcinogenic with no known negative health impacts.

12. Food production of all kinds shall be encouraged in individual buildings and on their lots, consistent with their setting in order to promote decentralization, self-sufficiency and reduced transportation impacts on the environment.

The Street, Block, and Network

1. The design of streets and the entire right-of-way shall be directed at the positive shaping of the public realm in order to encourage shared pedestrian, bicycle and vehicular use.

2. The pattern of blocks and streets shall be compact and designed in a well-connected network for easy, safe and secure walkability, reducing overall vehicular usage by decreasing travel time and trip length. Design shall strive to minimize material and utility infrastructure.

3. The positive shaping of the public realm shall focus on creating thermally comfortable spaces through passive techniques such as low albedo and shading with landscape and buildings. The techniques shall be consistent with local climate.

4. The design of streets, blocks, platting, landscape and building typologies shall be configured for both reduced overall energy usage and an enhanced quality of life in the public realm.

5. Roadway materials shall be non-toxic and provide for water reuse through percolation, detention and retention. Green streets shall integrate sustainable drainage with the role of the street as defined public space. Their design shall maintain the importance of the building frontage and access to the sidewalk and roadway, balancing the desirability of surface drainage with the need for street connectivity and hierarchy.
6. A wide range of parking strategies (such as park-once districts, shared parking, parking structures, reduced parking requirements, minimized surface parking areas and vehicle sharing) shall be used to constrict the supply of parking in order to induce less driving and to create more human-scaled, amenable public space.

The Neighborhood, Town and City

1. The balance of jobs, shopping, schools, recreation, civic institutions, housing, areas of food production and natural places shall occur at the neighborhood scale and shall be within easy walking distances or reached easily by public transit.
2. Wherever possible, new development shall be sited on underutilized, poorly designed or already developed land. Sites shall be either urban infill or urban-adjacent unless the building is rural in its program, size, scale and character.
3. Prime and unique farmland shall be protected and conserved. In locations with little or declining growth, additional agriculture, parklands and habitat restoration shall be promoted on already urbanized or underutilized land.
4. Neighborhoods, towns and cities shall be as compact as possible, with a range of densities that are compatible with existing places and cultures that hew tightly to projected growth rates and urban growth boundaries while promoting lively mixed urban places.
5. Renewable energy shall be produced at the scale of neighborhood and town as well as at the scale of the individual building in order to decentralize and reduce energy infrastructure.
6. Brownfields shall be redeveloped, utilizing cleanup methods that reduce or eliminate site contaminants and toxicity.

7. Wetlands, other bodies of water and their natural watersheds shall be protected. The natural systems that promote the recharge of aquifers and prevent flooding shall be restored wherever possible, consistent with the urban-to-rural transect and with the desirability of urban waterfronts as public spaces of extraordinary impact and character.
8. Natural places of all kinds shall be within easy walking distance or easily accessible by transit. Public parklands and reserves shall be protected and the creation of new ones promoted.
9. Within neighborhoods, a broad range of housing types, sizes and price levels for a population of diverse ages, cultures and incomes shall be encouraged, providing for self-sufficiency and social sustainability, while promoting compact cities and regions.
10. A steady source of water and the production of a wide range of locally raised foods within an easily accessed distance shall establish the self-sufficiency and overall size of neighborhoods and/or small towns. Nearby rural agricultural settlements shall be promoted to preserve local traditional foods and food culture.
11. Projects shall be designed to reduce light pollution while maintaining safe pedestrian environments. Noise pollution shall also be minimized.
12. The design of neighborhoods and towns shall use natural topography and shall balance cut and fill in order to minimize site disturbance and avoid the import and export of fill.

The Region

1. The finite boundaries of the region shall be determined by geographic and bioregional factors such as geology, topography, watersheds, coastlines, farmlands, habitat corridors, regional parks and river basins.
2. Regions shall strive to be self-sustaining for food, goods and services, employment, renewable energy and water supplies.
3. The physical organization of the region shall promote transit, pedestrian and bicycle systems to maximize access and mobility while reducing dependence on automobiles and trucks.

4. The spatial balance of jobs and housing shall be enabled at the regional scale by extensive transit systems. Development shall be organized primarily around transit lines and hubs.

5. The siting of new development shall prefer already urbanized land. If undeveloped land is used, then the burden for exceptional design, demonstrable longevity and environmental sensitivity shall be more stringent and connections to such regions will be essential.

6. Sensitive or virgin forests, native habitats and prime farmlands shall be conserved and protected. Imperiled species and ecological communities shall be protected. Projects to regenerate and recreate additional agricultural areas and natural habitat shall be promoted.

7. Wetlands, other bodies of water and their natural watersheds and their habitats shall be protected.

8. Development shall be avoided in locations that disrupt natural weather systems and induce heat islands, flooding, fires or hurricanes.

ACKNOWLEDGMENTS

On the opposite page is a personal memo of appreciation written by one of the authors of this book and distributed to a number of people who had been instrumental in getting Civano's Specific Plan and first final plat approved the night before October 20, 1997, in a City Council meeting. That vote was a make-or-break moment in the history of Civano and was the gateway for actual construction to begin. It seems a good place to start giving acknowledgments. On the following pages is a list of people, some mentioned in that document, but many more who are not, and who were essential in making Civano become a reality. No doubt we have overlooked some; put that down to the passage of time and memories grown tired. Distant thunder dimly heard is thunder, nonetheless.

So the Mayor and City Council have passed the Final Plat, the Specific Plan, and all the assorted things that go with them. Somewhere back in the middle of August, when the word had come down from more than one city agency that we just would not be able to get all this approved until some time in late November; Roger Schneider of the Planning Department sat down with John Jones, Wayne and me and gave us the brutal truth.

The best we could hope for every if everything went right, if everything fell into place, if every deadline was met, if every agency cooperated, if every disagreement was resolved-the best we could hope for was maybe getting things to the City Council by October 27th, and he thought that was being wildly optimistic.

It happened.

Some personal appreciations, it's far from being a complete list, but these are people that stood out in my mind last night:

To Wayne Moody

for being the keeper of first principles on this project

for all those one on one meetings with City officials, when I mostly just sat back and looked authoritative and he did the talking

To Lynn Slosberg

for minding the details, over and over

for never accepting "no" for an answer

for being the person who I could always get to explain to me the difference between Master Block Plats, Tentative Plats, Final Plats, Resubs,etc. etc. especially when I first got here and could not tell the difference between a plat, a plot a block, or a sub-whether it was re'ed or not

for sitting through those unbearable City "Coordination" Meetings

To Lisa Picard

for the numbers and giving them form

for always questioning whether the numbers are still real, and then making them so

for knowing the numbers are not the project

for sitting through those unbearable City "Coordination" Meetings

To Bruce Timpkin

for doing the lawyerly things, its a rough job-and someone did it

for grinding out the assurances

To John Jones

for being our "inside guy"

To John Alexander and MMLA

for meeting every request from the city, even the ones he had to grind his teeth to do

To Cathy Signieri, Fred Felix, and Peter Gavin

for being what one would hope every government employee would be

To Roger Schneider

for telling us the brutal truth and then having the decency to stick by it

To Kevin and David

for no fear

for knowing when to put the pressure on and when to hold off

for assembling this group of people that made it happen

and

To Larry, Leea, Peggy, Angie, Teresa

for paying the bills, Larry; and keeping the doors open while on the madness goes on

Memo of thanks sent by Lee Rayburn to key people who helped get the Specific Plan and other critical documents approved by the City Council on October 20, 1997.

Some of those deserving of the deepest acknowledgment have already been mentioned in this book and their roles in the Civano story noted. They include:

John Wesley Miller: So critical in the founding of the precursor to Civano, the Tucson Solar Village. Without his action in those early days, this story would never have unfolded.

Wayne Moody: The memo on the prior page cited him for being the "keeper of first principles" for Civano. The project moved on from his formative contributions, but it never left him, nor he, it.

William Orr: If Wayne was the "keeper" of first principles, Will Orr was the organizer of those principles. His vision of the project proved to be prescient time and time again.

John Laswick: Without his work creating financial modeling for an untried idea, support for Civano at the City of Tucson would have been more reticent. He was instrumental in giving shape and form to the IMPACT Standards, the summation of Civano's goals.

John Jones: A master at working within the interagency world of city government. The number of times Civano could have come to a dead end without his intercession cannot be counted.

David Butterfield: The catalyst for bringing the project to private-sector implementation. The source for bringing New Urbanism into the project.

David Case: His desire to create a lasting legacy was matched by his willingness to risk what he had to make it a reality.

Kevin Kelly: He gave operational form and substance at the beginning of the private-sector implementation of Civano, and worked tirelessly through the early years to overcome every challenge that stood in the way.

Raul Castro and Bruce Babbitt: Two governors whose foresight lead to funding and state support in the earliest days of Civano's history. Without their actions, this story would never have happened.

City of Tucson officials who were critical to Civano becoming a reality:

Michael Brown: The city manager who created the office of Special Projects that gave the project new life, funding, and personnel as it became a city policy initiative.

Luis Gutierrez: The city manager through 2000, he was a protective ally to the project through some of its most challenging times.

Roger Schneider: The head of the City Planning Department, he was instrumental in helping get the first phases of Neighborhood One through entitlements, and the Specific Plan approved.

Janet Marcus: One of the earliest and strongest supporters of Civano on the City Council. It was her pushing to get Civano moving again as a city initiative that changed everything.

Shirley Scott: A constant and active advocate for and defender of Civano on the City Council.

At Moule & Polyzoides, Architects and Urbanists: These are the members of the MP staff who worked on the Civano project. Their individual commitment to New Urbanism and its application to Civano was inspiring; their commitment as a team was formidable and a source of constant renewal.

Vinayak Bharne
Michael Bohn
Bill Dennis
Xiaojian He
Richard Hoffmeister
Tim Kohut
Elizabeth Moule
Paul Mortensen
Stefanos Polyzoides

Duany Plater-Zyberk: Their participation in the 1996 charrette was a critical factor in creating the physical reality of Civano.

Andres Duany, Principal
Galina Tachieva, Project Manager
Iskandar Shafie, Designer
Maciej Mycielski, Designer

MMLA: Tom Lodge and John Alexander of MMLA took their deep experience in civil engineering and their relationships within the City of Tucson to advocate for everything the development team attempted at Civano. Not every battle was won, but Tom and John were instrumental in those that were. Other members of the MMLA team whose work on Civano was constant and critical:

Geoff Harris
Robert Tucker
Regina Beam

McGann & Associates: Don McGann and his staff worked along with Civano Nursery to implement a new approach to large-scale landscape design, one that honored the richness of the Sonoran Desert. They were critical allies in getting the innovative xeriscape features of Civano through approval.

Al Nichols: Al was a critical bridge to the past of Civano, and a reliable resource to call on to understand the nuances of energy savings. Even as the project took new directions, he continued to be a valued supporter.

Paul Weiner: Paul and his firm, Design Build Collaborative, were a vital bridge between the development team and the community of alternative builders and energy advocates in Tucson. His firm designed some of the most successful home models for the project.

Staff members of the various iterations of the development team:

Mike Baruch: Hired to help organize and manage the development team's efforts to achieve the IMPACT Standards, he was instrumental in demonstrating the complexity of the public/private partnership that would be needed to achieve them.

Mary L'Esperance: The first director of sales and marketing for Civano. She was instrumental in organizing the centralized sales effort and training the first set of salespeople. She helped formulate how to translate Civano's special features into successful marketing messages.

Joan Tober: One of the original L'Esperance-hired salespeople, Tober took on the task of outreach to the larger Tucson realtor community. During the period she headed sales, Civano had its best market results. She helped all the on-site agents be more knowledgeable and effective.

Rick Ashley: The on-site superintendent for all the development entities. It is a testament to his skill that so many worthy projects were built well.

Les Shipley and Family: Though not formally a part of the development team, their cooperation was so essential and integral to the development efforts, they might as well have been. The robust and thriving landscape of Civano owes so much to their environmental commitments and stands as a lasting testament to them.

The Original Civano Builders: These were the local and regional builders who had the courage to accept the challenge of building under a new paradigm and taking a chance on something never tried before.

Karol George: He came to the project because he was attracted to its emphasis on building community. As one of the largest independent home builders in Tucson, his company's presence helped, in the early days, to give Civano market appeal and legitimacy.

Ted Bednar: He came to the project because he liked the emphasis on creating housing designs that were authentic to the region, and as an opportunity to grow his company.

RGC: Headed by Jim Murrar, RGC was an award-winning California-based home builder specializing in housing innovation, both in design and in construction methodologies.

Gale Marsland: An established builder of solar-powered homes, she brought valuable advocacy for pushing the solar agenda in Civano. Her homes offered a product to buyers wanting to emphasize solar above all else.

Tom Doucette: One of Tucson's most respected mainline home builders, Doucette was attracted to the project because of its commitment to innovation and energy savings, and because of the presence of community-enhancing amenities.

Their individual reasons for coming to the project, when seen as a whole, reflected the environmental and social goals of Civano. Together they created a living community that brought those goals to life.

Others:

The Many People Who Attended the Sixty Workshops in 1990–'92. It was their interest in finding an alternative to the standard sprawl growth accommodation, and their input about what a new model should be like, that set the foundation for the IMPACT Standards.

Richard Dreyfus and the Department of Energy: A determined advocate for innovation in housing, he was instrumental in bringing resources, both monetary and in kind, to Civano, especially to ensure that the home built would meet the energy goals. It was through his efforts that the following became involved:

The Building America Program and IBACOS, who provided essential training to the builders.

The National Renewable Energy Laboratory (NREL), who provided proof of concept post-building monitoring to document that the energy savings goals were being met.

Dr. Nadar Chalfoun of the University of Arizona: He, along with others, demonstrated and quantified what the energy savings goals of the project could mean to homeowners in terms of cost savings, and to everyone the potential reduction in greenhouse gas emissions that could be achieved.

TEP and Betsy Boling: Tucson Electric Power, at the urging of Betsy Boling, became an important partner in ensuring that all homes in Civano met the energy goals. They provided testing throughout construction, and tracked energy use after move-in. This was critical data demonstrating proof of concept.

Finally... Fannie Mae and the American Community Fund

Throughout this book we have focused more on institutions and institutional forces as they impacted the evolution of Civano, and less on individuals. This is especially true when discussing Fannie Mae and the American Communities Fund. There were people associated with Fannie Mae and especially the American Communities Fund that truly supported Civano and what it was trying to be, at least as far as their institutional perspective would allow. John McIlwain certainly is in this category. There were others who tried to find an appropriate balance between being good custodians of an asset that Fannie Mae came to own outright, and keeping the project going as we wanted while bending it into a shape more in line with the corporate core of Fannie Mae. Though we may have differed with their intent, we never questioned their integrity and decency. Bruce Read stands out in this category. There were others in Fannie Mae whose intent and purpose was simple and direct: shut down the Civano experiment, declare some kind of victory, and move on. We recognize that they were instruments of an institutional culture and force. Whatever the consequences of their actions, we grant them that.

In the end it must be said that Civano would have died in 1999, and maybe earlier, without Fannie Mae's financial support. The Community of Civano is a living testament to another way of accommodation growth and building diverse and resilient communities. The paradox is that Fannie Mae both enabled it to become that reality and abandoned that reality. Both sides of that paradox need to be recognized and understood.

BIBLIOGRAPHY
PHOTO & IMAGE CREDITS
INDEX

Bibliography

ORIGINAL SOURCE MATERIALS

Memorandum of Meeting; Arizona Solar Energy Commission; Helen Kessler, John Wesley Miller, attending; August 1982

Tucson Solar Village: Project Management A Project in Sustainable Community Development; William Orr, Project Manager, Gwyn Sanders, Project Manager; Report Presented to Energy Task Force of the Urban Consortium; Public Technologies, Incorporated; November 1991

Civano: Tucson Solar Village Final Development Plan; Wayne Moody, Community Design Associates; P&D Technologies; Report to Tucson-Pima County Metropolitan Energy Commission and Tucson City Council; December 1991

Memorandum on IMPACT Standards; John Laswick, City of Tucson Special Projects, City of Tucson; October 1995

Civano: A Study to Determine the Keys of Success for Developing the Community of Civano; Petersen, Jacuzzi & Green Market; April 1997

Report on Surveys About Civano Using American Lives Market Segmentation; Dr. Paul H. Ray; American Lives; April 1997

INTERVIEWS WITH AND/OR NOTES FROM

TITLES NOTED ARE THOSE HELD DURING THE TIME OF CIVANO'S DEVELOPMENT

John Jones, Office of Special Projects, City of Tucson
John Laswick, Office of Special Projects, City of Tucson
John Wesley Miller, Builder and Chairman of the Arizona Solar Energy Commission
Wayne Moody Archives
Kevin Kelly, Partner in Case Enterprises, and later Principal of Civano Development
Archives of Moule & Polyzoides, Architects and Urbanists
Archives of Lee R. Rayburn, Director of Design and Planning and Later Managing Partner of CDC Partners
Archives of the *Tucson Citizen*
Archives of the *Arizona Daily Star*

BOOKS, ARTICLES, AND ACADEMIC STUDIES

"Tucson's Holy War: A Brief History of the City's Crusade for More Turf," Dave Devine and Molly McKasson, *Tucson Weekly,* July 1997

Sustainable Design: A Planbook for Sonoran Desert Dwellings, Eileen Alduenda, Editor; Tucson Institute for Sustainable Communities, 1999

Exploring Environmental Values and Policy in the United States: Case Studies in Arizona and Louisiana, Diane Austin and Thomas McGuire, Editors; University of Arizona, 2001

Forging Environmentalism: Justice, Livelihood and Contested Environments, Joanne Bauer, Editor; Carnegie Council on Ethics and International Affairs, 2006

Inside the Civano Project, C. Alan Nichols and Jason A. Laros; McGraw Hill, 2010

Institutional Barriers to Sustainable Development: A Case Study of Civano in Tucson, Arizona, Kelly Turner; CATE (Cities and the Environment), 2014

Addressing Climate Change through Design: A Land Systems Approach to Assessing Microclimate Regulation in New Urbanist Developments, Kelly Turner and Christopher Galletti; Public Square, 2017

Effects of Neighborhood Design on Residential Habits and Sense of Community, Testing the Claims of the New Urbanism, Ellen Schwaller, Thesis for Master of Urban and Environmental Planning; Arizona State University, 2012

BOOKS FOR FURTHER STUDY ON TOPICS ADDRESSED IN THIS BOOK

Cadillac Desert: The American West and Its Disappearing Water, Marc Reisner; Viking Press, 1986

The End of Nature, Bill McKibben; Random House, 1989

The Plazas of New Mexico, Chris Wilson and Stefanos Polyzoides, Editors; Trinity University Press in Association with the Foundation for Landscape Studies, 2012

Reckless Endangerment: How Outsized Ambition, Greed and Corruption Led to Economic Armageddon, Gretchen Morgenson and Joshua Rosner; Times Books/Henry Holt and Company, 2011

Charter of the New Urbanism, Second Edition, Emily Talen, Editor; Congress of the New Urbanism; McGraw Hill, 2013

Sustainable Urbanism: Urban Design with Nature, Douglas Farr; John Wiley & Sons, 2008

Urbanism in the Age of Climate Change, Peter Calthorpe; Island Press, 2011

Truth to Power; An Inconvenient Sequel, Al Gore; Penquin Books Random House, 2017

Drawdown: The Most Comprehensive Plan Ever Proposed to Reverse Global Warming, Paul Hawken, Editor; Penquin Books, 2017

Sustainable Nation: Urban Design Patterns for the Future, Douglas Farr; John Wiley & Sons, 2018

RELIABLE, SCIENCE-BASED SOURCES ON CLIMATE CHANGE AND ITS IMPACTS

Truth in Ten Slide Show, with links to other data presentations www.climaterealtyproject.org/truth; Al Gore; updated constantly

Union of Concerned Scientists Climate Change Website www.ucsusa.org/climate; updated constantly

NASA Climate Change Website, www.climate.nasa.gov; updated constantly

Photo & Image Credits

Cover: James Nicholas Polyzoides

Back cover: Moule & Polyzoides, Architects and Urbanists

Page 2: L. Rayburn project archives

Page 4: Library of Congress, Print#97684108

Page 6.1: N.C. Wyeth, 1945; from the cover of Women's Day, November, 1945

Page 6.2: *Better Homes and Gardens,* March, 1947

Page 7.1: National Homes Corporation, Advertisement, May 1953

Page 7.2: Levittown House, Getty Images # 50324702

Page 7.3: Alamy Stock Photograph

Page 7.4: Hulton Archive, Getty Images

Page 8: Environmental Protection Agency, 2016

Page 9: Adam Auel, from The New Urbanism, Peter Katz

Page 10–11: James Nicholas Polyzoides

Page 12: Sonoran Desert Museum

Page 14.1: University of Arizona, Water in Tucson Area

Page 14.1: University of Arizona, Water in Tucson Area

Page 15.1: Rendering by Michael Hampshire, Archeology Southwest Center

Page 15: Photographs by Authors

Page 16: Photographs by Authors

Page 17.1: United States Census Bureau data

Page 17.2: MAP, Making Action Possible for Southern Arizona, 2017

Page 18.1: University of Arizona, Water in Tucson Area

P18.2: Pima Association of Governments

Page 19.1: University of Arizona, Water in Tucson Area

Page 19.2: www.azhomebuyerinfo.com

P19.3: University of Arizona, Water in Tucson Area

Page 20: Wayne Moody Archive, 1991–1992 Design Guidelines

Page 22.1: John Wesley Miller

Page 22.2 : *Tucson Daily Citizen,* November 6, 1974

Page 22.3: *Washington Post,* date unknown

Page 23.1: John Wesley Miller

Page 23.2: Google Earth Image

Page 23.3: John Wesley Miller

Page 23.4: John Wesley Miller

Page 23.5: www.theconstructor.org

Page 24: Google Earth image

Page 26: Wayne Moody Archive, 1991–1992 Tucson Solar Village study plans

Page 27: Wayne Moody Archive, 1991–1992 Tucson Solar Village study plans

Page 31.1: John Laswick

Page 31.2: John Jones

Page 35.1: Darren Stone for the *Vancouver Times Colorist*

Page 35.2: Darren Stone for the *Vancouver Times Colorist*

Page 37: John Laswick

Page 38.1: Brochure, Case Enterprises

Page 38.2: Case Enterprises

Page 38.3: Case Enterprises

Page 43.1–2: Photograph by Authors

Page 43.3: Case Enterprises

Page 44: Photograph by Authors

Page 45: Photograph by Authors

Page 47.1–5: Case Enterprises

Page 49.1–2: Case Enterprises

Page 51.1: University of Arizona

Page 51.2: Photograph by Authors

Page 55.1: Moule & Polyzoides, Architects and Urbanists

Page 55.2–3: Photographs by Authors

Page 58.1: Moule & Polyzoides, Architects and Urbanists

Page 58.2: Google Earth

Page 59.1–2: Photographs by Authors

Page 60: Photographs by Authors

Page 62: Moule & Polyzoides, Architects and Urbanists

Page 64 : Wayne Moody Archive, 1991–1992 Design Guidelines

Page 65.1–5: Wayne Moody Archive, 1991–1992 Design Guidelines

Page 66.1: Duany Plater-Zyberk

Page 66.2: Google Earth

Page 67: Duany Plater-Zyberk

Page 69.1: Moule & Polyzoides, Architects and Urbanists

Page 69.2: Google Earth Image

Page 70–75: Stefanos Polyzoides

Page 76: Photographs by Authors

Page 77: Photographs by Authors

Page 79.1–4: Duany Plater-Zyberk, Architects / Moule & Polyzoides, Architects and Urbanists, Community Design Associates

Page 80: John Laswick

Page 81.1 : John Laswick

Page 81.2: Duany Plater-Zyberk

Page 82–97: Moule & Polyzoides, Architects and Urbanists

Page 98–99: James Nicholas Polyzoides

Page 100: Wayne Moody Archives

Page 101.1–3: Moule & Polyzoides, Architects and Urbanists

Page 103–107: Moule & Polyzoides, Architects and Urbanists

Page 108.1: James Nicholas Polyzoides

Page 108–109: Photographs by Authors

Page 110–111: James Nicholas Polyzoides

Page 113–114.1: Moule & Polyzoides, Architects and Urbanists

Page 114.2: Photographs by Authors

Page 115.1–5: Photographs by Authors

Page 115.6: Simmons Buttin

Page 116–117: James Nicholas Polyzoides

Page 119–122: Moule & Polyzoides, Architects and Urbanists

Page 123: Photographs by Authors

Page 124–125: James Nicholas Polyzoides

Page 126–129: Moule & Polyzoides, Architects and Urbanists

Page 130: James Nicholas Polyzoides

Page 131: Photographs by Authors

Page 132–133: Moule & Polyzoides, Architects and Urbanists

Page 134: James Nicholas Polyzoides

Page 135.1 : James Nicholas Polyzoides

Page 135.2–5: Design Build Collaborative, Paul Wiener

Page 136: Photographs by Authors

Page 137: James Nicholas Polyzoides

Page 138–141: Moule & Polyzoides, Architects and Urbanists

Page 142–145: Moule & Polyzoides, Architects and Urbanists

Page 146–147: James Nicholas Polyzoides

Page 148: Photographs by Authors

Page 149.1–2: Photographs by Authors

Page 149.3 : Photograph by Simmons Buntin

Page 149.4–6: Photographs by Authors

Page 150–151: Case Enterprises, Civano Development Company

Page 153: Moule & Polyzoides, Architects and Urbanists

Page 154–155: Photographs by Authors

Page 156.1: Google Earth

Page 156.2–4: Photographs by Authors

Page 157.1: Moule & Polyzoides, Architects and Urbanists

Page 157.2–5: Photographs by Authors

Page 158–159: Photographs by Authors

Page 161: Moule & Polyzoides, Architects and Urbanists

Page 162–163: James Nicholas Polyzoides

Page 142: Lee R. Rayburn

Page 166: University of Arizona, Victoria Turner

Page 167: University of California, Los Angeles, Victoria Turner

Page 168: CDC Partners, Joan Tober

Page 175: Lee R. Rayburn

Page 179: Gordley and Associates

Page 180: All images from *The Making of Urban America, A History of City Planning in the United States,* John W. Reps

Page 184.1–4: Photographs by Simmons Buttin

Page 185.1–4: Photographs by Simmons Buttin

Page 185.7: CDC Partners

Page 189.1–4: Moule & Polyzoides, Architects and Urbanists

Index

Numbers in bold indicate photos, illustrations, or maps.